TEAC

SIDE *by* SIDE

THIRD EDITION

BOOK 1

Steven J. Molinsky
Bill Bliss

Contributing Authors

Sarah Lynn
Mary Ann Perry

with

Elizabeth Handley, Christine Harvey, John Kopec

Longman

Side by Side, 3rd edition
Teacher's Guide

Pearson Education, 10 Bank Street, White Plains, NY 10606

Vice president, director of publishing: *Allen Ascher*
Editorial manager: *Pam Fishman*
Vice president, director of design and production: *Rhea Banker*
Associate director of electronic production: *Aliza Greenblatt*
Production manager: *Ray Keating*
Director of manufacturing: *Patrice Fraccio*
Digital layout specialists: *Kelly Tavares, Paula Williams, Wendy Wolf*
Interior design: *Wendy Wolf*
Interior art: *Judy A. Wolf*
Cover design: *Elizabeth Carlson*
Cover art: *Richard E. Hill*

The authors gratefully acknowledge the contribution
of Tina Carver in the development of the original
Side by Side program.

ISBN 0-13-026753-8

3 4 5 6 7 8 9 10 – CRK – 05 04 03 02

CONTENTS

INTRODUCTION

Side by Side is an English language program for young-adult and adult learners from beginning to high-intermediate levels. The program consists of Student Books 1 through 4 and accompanying Activity Workbooks, Teacher's Guides, Communication Games Books, an Audio Program, a Video Program, a Picture Program, and a Testing Program.

Side by Side offers learners of English a dynamic, communicative approach to learning the language. Through the methodology of guided conversations, *Side by Side* engages students in meaningful conversational exchanges within carefully structured grammatical frameworks, and then encourages students to break away from the textbook and use these frameworks to create conversations on their own. All the language practice that is generated through the texts results in active communication between students . . . practicing speaking together "side by side."

The Guided Conversation lessons serve as the "anchor" for the presentation of the grammatical and functional language core of the program. These lessons are followed by a variety of reading, writing, listening, pronunciation, role-playing, and discussion activities that reinforce and expand upon this conversational core.

A special feature of this third edition are the "*Side by Side* Gazette" pages that appear periodically throughout the texts. These magazine-style pages contain feature articles, fact files, vocabulary expansion, cross-cultural topics, authentic listening activities, e-mail exchanges, and cartoon springboards for interactive role-playing activities.

The goal of *Side by Side* is to engage students in active, meaningful communicative practice with the language. The aim of the *Side by Side* Teacher's Guides is to offer guidelines and strategies to help achieve that goal.

Student Text Overview

CHAPTER OPENING PAGES

The opening page of each chapter provides an overview of the grammatical structures and topics that are treated in the chapter. A Vocabulary Preview depicts some of the key vocabulary words that students will encounter within the chapter. Some teachers may wish to present and practice these words before beginning the chapter. Other teachers may prefer to wait until the words occur in the particular lesson in which they are introduced.

GUIDED CONVERSATION LESSONS

Grammatical Paradigms

A new grammatical structure appears first in the form of a grammatical paradigm, or "grammar box"—a simple schema of the structure. (Grammar boxes are in a light blue tint.) These paradigms are meant to be a

reference point for students as they proceed through a lesson's conversational activities. While these paradigms highlight the structures being taught, they are not intended to be goals in themselves. Students are not expected to memorize or parrot back these rules. Rather, we want students to take part in conversations that show they can *use* these rules correctly.

Model Guided Conversations

Model conversations serve as the vehicles for introducing new grammatical structures and many communicative uses of English. Because the model becomes the basis for all the exercises that follow, it is essential that students be given sufficient practice with it before proceeding with the lesson.

Side by Side Exercises

In the numbered exercises that follow the model, students pair up and work "side by side," placing new content into the given conversational framework. These exercises form the core learning activity of each conversation lesson.

FOLLOW-UP EXERCISES AND ACTIVITIES

- **Reading** selections offer enjoyable reading practice that simultaneously reinforces the grammatical and thematic focus of each chapter.

- **Reading Check-Up** exercises provide focused practice in reading comprehension.

- **Listening** exercises enable students to develop their aural comprehension skills through a variety of listening activities.

- **Pronunciation** exercises provide models of authentic pronunciation and opportunities for student listening and speaking practice.

- **How to Say It!** activities expose students to key communication strategies.

- **Talk About It!** and **Think About It!** activities offer additional opportunities for conversational practice.

- **In Your Own Words** activities provide topics and themes for student compositions and classroom discussions in which students write about their friends, families, homes, schools, and themselves.

- *Side by Side* **Journal** activities provide the opportunity for students to write about things that are meaningful to them.

- **Role Play**, **Interactions**, and **Interview** activities provide opportunities for dynamic classroom interaction.

- **On Your Own** and **How About You?** activities give students valuable opportunities to apply lesson content to their own lives and experiences and to share opinions in class. Through these activities, students bring to the classroom new content based on their interests, their backgrounds, and their imaginations.

SIDE BY SIDE GAZETTE

- **Feature Articles** provide interesting and stimulating content.

- **Fact Files** present facts about the world for class discussion.

- **Build Your Vocabulary!** sections provide enrichment in key vocabulary areas.

- **Around the World** sections offer rich opportunities for cross-cultural comparison.

- **Global Exchange** activities give students experience with online communication.

- **Listening** sections offer students authentic listening opportunities.

- **What Are They Saying?** cartoons serve as springboards for interactive role-playing activities.

SUPPORT AND REFERENCE SECTIONS

- The **Chapter Summary** at the end of each chapter provides charts of the grammar structures presented in the chapter along with a listing of key vocabulary words. This summary is useful as a review and study guide after students have completed the chapter.

- An **Appendix** contains Listening Scripts, a Thematic Vocabulary Glossary, and a list of Cardinal Numbers and Past Tense Irregular Verbs.

- An **Index** provides a convenient reference for locating grammatical structures in the text.

Ancillary Materials

ACTIVITY WORKBOOKS

The Activity Workbooks offer a variety of exercises for reinforcement, fully coordinated with the student texts. A special feature of the Activity Workbooks is the inclusion of GrammarRaps for practice with rhythm, stress, and intonation and GrammarSongs from the *Side by Side TV* videos. Periodic check-up tests are also included in the workbooks.

AUDIO PROGRAM

The Student Text audios are especially designed to serve as a student's speaking partner, making conversation practice possible even when the student is studying alone. In addition to the guided conversation models and exercises, the audios contain the vocabulary preview words at the beginning of each chapter, the listening and pronunciation exercises, the reading selections, and the *Side by Side* Gazettes.

The Activity Workbook audios contain the listening and pronunciation exercises, along with the GrammarRaps and GrammarSongs.

VIDEO PROGRAM

The *Side by Side TV* videos and accompanying Video Workbooks are designed to serve as a video accompaniment to the series. These innovative videos offer original comedy sketches, on-location interviews, rap numbers, music videos, and other popular TV formats. The *Side by Side TV* videos are fully coordinated with the *Side by Side* student texts.

COMMUNICATION GAMES BOOKS

This innovative teacher resource provides a wealth of interactive language games designed to serve as enjoyable and motivating reinforcement of key grammatical structures presented in the student texts. All of the games are accompanied by reproducible activity masters for ease of classroom use.

PICTURE PROGRAM

Side by Side Picture Cards illustrate key concepts and vocabulary items. They can be used for introduction of new material, for review, for enrichment, and for role-playing activities. Suggestions for their use are included in the Teacher's Guide. Also, the Appendix to the Teacher's Guide contains a triple listing of the Picture Cards: numerically, alphabetically, and by category.

TESTING PROGRAM

The *Side by Side* Testing Program consists of a placement test and individual chapter tests, mid-book tests, and final tests for each level of the program.

Format of the Teacher's Guide

CHAPTER OVERVIEW

The Chapter Overview provides the following:

- Functional and grammatical highlights of the chapter

- A listing of new vocabulary and expressions

CHAPTER OPENING PAGE

The Teacher's Guide offers suggestions for presenting and practicing the words depicted in the Vocabulary Preview.

STEP-BY-STEP LESSON GUIDE

Conversation Lessons

Included for each conversation lesson are the following:

- **FOCUS:** the grammatical and topical focus of the lesson
- **CLOSE UP:** short grammar explanations accompanied by examples from the lesson
- **GETTING READY:** suggestions for introducing the new concepts in the lesson
- **INTRODUCING THE MODEL:** steps for introducing model conversations
- **SIDE BY SIDE EXERCISES:** suggestions for practicing the exercises, as well as a listing of new vocabulary
- **LANGUAGE NOTES, CULTURE NOTES,** and **PRONUNCIATION NOTES**
- **WORKBOOK:** page references for exercises in the Activity Workbook that correspond to the particular lesson
- **EXPANSION ACTIVITIES:** optional activities for review and reinforcement of the content of the lesson

Reading Lessons

Included for each reading lesson are the following:

- **FOCUS** of the reading
- **NEW VOCABULARY** contained in the reading
- **READING THE STORY:** an optional preliminary preview stage before students begin to read the selection, along with suggestions for presenting the story and questions to check students' comprehension
- **READING CHECK-UP:** answer keys for the reading comprehension exercises
- **READING EXTENSION:** additional questions and activities that provide additional skill reinforcement of the reading selection

Other Follow-Up Lessons

Included for other follow-up lessons are the following:

- **LISTENING** scripts and answer keys for the listening exercises
- Strategies for presenting and practicing the *How to Say It!, How About You?, On Your Own, In Your Own Words, Role Play, Interactions, Interview, Talk About It!, Think About It!, Pronunciation*, and *Side by Side Journal* activities

Chapter Summary

Included for each Chapter Summary are the following:

- **GRAMMAR SUMMARY** tasks
- **KEY VOCABULARY** reinforcement and expansion activities
- **END-OF-CHAPTER EXPANSION ACTIVITIES** that review and reinforce the grammar structures and vocabulary presented in the chapter

Side by Side Gazette

Included for the *Side by Side* Gazette pages are the following:

- Strategies for introducing, practicing, and expanding upon the *Feature Articles, Fact Files, Build Your Vocabulary!, Around the World, Global Exchange, Listening,* and *What Are They Saying?* sections of the Gazette

WORKBOOK ANSWER KEYS AND LISTENING SCRIPTS

Answers and listening scripts for all exercises contained in the Activity Workbooks are provided at the end of each chapter of the Teacher's Guide.

General Teaching Strategies

VOCABULARY PREVIEW

You may wish to introduce the words in the Vocabulary Preview before beginning the chapter, or you may choose to wait until they first occur in a specific lesson. If you choose to introduce them at this point, the Teacher's Guide offers these suggestions:

1. Have students look at the illustrations and identify the words they already know.

2. Present the vocabulary. Say each word and have the class repeat it chorally and individually. Check students' understanding and pronunciation of the words.

3. Practice the vocabulary as a class, in pairs, or in small groups. Have students cover the word list and look at the pictures. Practice the words by saying a word and having students tell the number of the illustration and/or giving the number of the illustration and having students say the word.

GUIDED CONVERSATION LESSONS

Introducing Model Conversations

Given the importance of the model conversation, it is essential that students practice it several times in a variety of ways before going on to the exercises.

This Teacher's Guide offers the following comprehensive 8-step approach to introducing the model:

1. Have students look at the model illustration. This helps establish the context of the conversation.

2. Set the scene.

3. *Present the model.* With books closed, have students listen as you present the model or play the audio one or more times. To make the presentation of the model as realistic as possible, you might draw two stick figures on the board to represent the speakers in the dialog. You can also show that two people are speaking by changing your position or by shifting your weight from one foot to the other as you say each speaker's lines.

4. *Full-Class Repetition.* Model each line and have the whole class repeat in unison.

5. Have students open their books and look at the dialog. Ask if there are any questions, and check understanding of new vocabulary.

6. *Group Choral Repetition.* Divide the class in half. Model line A and have Group 1 repeat. Model line B and have Group 2 repeat. Continue with all the lines of the model.

7. *Choral Conversation.* Have both groups practice the dialog twice, without a teacher model. First Group 1 is Speaker A and Group 2 is Speaker B; then reverse.

8. Call on one or two pairs of students to present the dialog.

In steps 6, 7, and 8, encourage students to look up from their books and *say* the lines rather than read them. (Students can of course refer to their books when necessary.)

The goal is not memorization or complete mastery of the model. Rather, students should become familiar with the model and feel comfortable saying it.

At this point, if you feel that additional practice is necessary before going on to the exercises, you can do Choral Conversation in small groups or by rows.

Alternative Approaches to Introducing Model Conversations

Depending upon the abilities of your students and the particular lesson you're teaching, you might wish to try the following approaches to vary the way in which you introduce model conversations.

- **Pair Introduction**

  Have a pair of students present the model. Then practice it with the class.

- **Trio Introduction**

  Call on *three* students to introduce the model. Have two of them present it while the third acts as the *director*, offering suggestions for how to say the lines better. Then practice the dialog with the class.

- **Cloze Introduction**

  Write a cloze version of the model conversation on the board for student reference as you introduce the model. For lessons that provide a skeletal framework of the model (for example, Book 1 pp. 41, 70, 71, 111, 135), you can use that as the cloze version. For other lessons, you can decide which words to delete from the dialog.

- **Scrambled Dialog Introduction**

  Write each line of the dialog on a separate card. Distribute the cards to students and have them practice saying their lines, then talk with each other to figure out what the correct order of the lines should be. Have them present the dialog to the class, each student in turn reading his or her line. Have the class decide if it's in the correct order. Then practice the dialog with the class.

  Warning: Do a scrambled dialog introduction *only* for conversations in which there is only one possible sentence order!

- **Disappearing Dialog Introduction**

  Write the dialog on the board and have students practice saying it. Erase a few of the words and practice again. Continue practicing the dialog several times, each time having erased more of the words, until the dialog has completely *disappeared* and students can say the lines without looking at them.

- **Eliciting the Model**

  Have students cover up the lines of the model and look only at the illustration. Ask questions based on the illustration and the situation. For example: *Who are these people? Where are they? What are they saying to each other?* As a class, in groups, or in pairs, have students suggest a possible dialog. Have students present their ideas and then compare them with the model conversation in the book. Then practice the dialog with the class.

Side by Side Exercises

The numbered exercises that follow the model form the core learning activity in each conversation lesson. Here students use the illustrations and word cues to create conversations based on the structure of the model. Since all language practice in these lessons is conversational, you will always call on a pair of students to do each exercise. Your primary role is to serve as a resource to the class — to help students with new structures, new vocabulary, intonation, and pronunciation.

The Teacher's Guide recommends the following three steps for practicing the exercises. (Students should be given thorough practice with the first two exercises before going on.)

1. **Exercise 1:** Introduce any new vocabulary in the exercise. Call on two students to present the dialog. Then do Choral Repetition and Choral Conversation practice.

2. **Exercise 2:** Same as for Exercise 1.

3. For the remaining exercises, there are two options: either Full-Class Practice or Pair Practice.

   Full-Class Practice: Call on a pair of students to do each exercise. Introduce new vocabulary one exercise at a time. (For more practice, you can call on other pairs of students or do Choral Repetition or Choral Conversation.)

   Pair Practice: Introduce new vocabulary for all the exercises. Next have students practice all the exercises in pairs. Then have pairs present the exercises to the class. (For more practice, you can do Choral Repetition or Choral Conversation.)

The choice of Full-Class Practice or Pair Practice should be determined by the content of the particular lesson, the size and composition of the class, and your own teaching style. You might also wish to vary your approach from lesson to lesson.

- **Suggestions for Pairing Up Students**

  Whether you use Full-Class Practice or Pair Practice, you can select students for pairing in various ways.

  - You might want to pair students by ability, since students of similar ability might work together more efficiently than students of dissimilar ability.

  - On the other hand, you might wish to pair a weaker student with a stronger one. The slower student benefits from this pairing, while the more advanced student strengthens his or her abilities by helping a partner.

You should also encourage students to look at each other when speaking. This makes the conversational nature of the language practice more realistic. One way of ensuring this is *not* to call on two students who are sitting next to each other. Rather, call on students in different parts of the room and encourage them to look at each other when saying their lines.

- **Presenting New Vocabulary**

  Many new words are introduced in each conversation lesson. The illustration usually helps to convey the meaning, and the new words are written for students to see and use in these conversations. In addition, you might:

  - write the new word on the board or on a word card.
  - say the new word several times and ask students to repeat chorally and individually.
  - help clarify the meaning with visuals.

  Students might also find it useful to keep a notebook in which they write each new word, its meaning, and a sentence using that word.

- **Open-Ended Exercises**

  In many lessons, the final exercise is an open-ended one. This is indicated in the text by a *blank box*. Here students are expected to create conversations based on the structure of the model, but with vocabulary that they select themselves. This provides students with an opportunity for creativity, while still focusing on the particular structure being practiced. These open-ended exercises can be done orally in class and/or assigned as homework for presentation in class the following day. Encourage students to use dictionaries to find new words they want to use.

General Guiding Principles for Working with Guided Conversations

- *Speak*, not *Read* the Conversations

  When doing the exercises, students should practice *speaking* to each other, rather than *reading* to each other. Even though students will need to refer to the text to be able to practice the conversations, they should not read the lines word by word. Rather, they should scan a full line and then look up from the book and *speak* the line to the other person.

- **Intonation and Gesture**

  Throughout, you should use the book to teach proper intonation and gesture. (Capitalized words are used to indicate spoken emphasis.) Students should be encouraged to truly *act out* the dialogs in a strong and confident voice.

- **Student-Centered Practice**

  Use of the texts should be as student-centered as possible. Modeling by the teacher should be efficient and economical, but students should have every opportunity to model for each other when they are capable of doing so.

- **Vocabulary in Context**

  Vocabulary can and should be effectively taught in the context of the conversation being practiced. Very often it will be possible to grasp the meaning from the conversation or its accompanying illustration. You should spend time drilling vocabulary in isolation only if you feel it is absolutely essential.

- **No "Grammar Talk"**

  Students need not study formally or be able to produce grammatical rules. The purpose of the texts is to engage students in active communication that gets them to *use* the language according to these rules.

Relating Lesson Content to Students' Lives and Experiences

- **Personalize the Exercises**

  While doing the guided conversation exercises, whenever you think it is appropriate, ask students questions that relate the situations in the exercises to their own lives and personal experiences. This will help make the leap from practicing language in the textbook to using the language for actual communication.

- **Interview the Characters**

  Where appropriate, as students are presenting the exercises to the class, as a way of making the situations come alive and making students feel as though they really *are* the characters in those situations, ask questions that students can respond to based on their imaginations.

READINGS

If you wish, preview the story by having students talk about the story title and/or illustrations. You may choose to introduce new vocabulary beforehand, or have students encounter the new vocabulary within the context of the reading.

Have students read silently, or follow along silently as the story is read aloud by you, by one or more students, or on the audio program. Ask students if they have any questions and check understanding of new vocabulary. Then do the Reading Check-Up exercises.

How to Say It!

How to Say It! activities are designed to expose students to important communication strategies. Present the conversations the same way you introduce model guided conversations: set the scene, present the model, do full-class and choral repetition, and have pairs of students present the dialog. Then divide the class into pairs and have students practice other conversations based on the *How to Say It!* model and then present them to the class.

How About You?

How About You? activities are intended to provide students with additional opportunities to tell about themselves. Have students do these activities in pairs or as a class.

 ## ON YOUR OWN

On Your Own activities offer students the opportunity to contribute content of their own within the grammatical framework of the lesson. You should introduce these activities in class and assign them as homework for presentation in class the next day. In this way, students will automatically review the previous day's

grammar while contributing new and inventive content of their own.

These activities are meant for simultaneous grammar reinforcement and vocabulary building. Students should be encouraged to use a dictionary when completing the *On Your Own* activities. In this way, they will use not only the words they know but also the words they would *like* to know in order to really bring their interests, backgrounds, and imaginations into the classroom.

As a result, students will teach each other new vocabulary as they share a bit of their lives with others in the class.

 ## IN YOUR OWN WORDS

Have students do the activity as written homework, using a dictionary for any new words they wish to use. Then have students present and discuss what they have written, in pairs or as a class.

 ## ROLE PLAY

Have pairs of students practice role-playing the activity and then present their role plays to the class.

 ## INTERACTIONS

Divide the class into pairs and have students practice conversations based on the skeletal models. Then call on students to present their conversations to the class.

 ## INTERVIEW

Have students circulate around the room to conduct their interviews and then report back to the class.

TALK ABOUT IT!

Call on a few different pairs of students to present the model dialogs. Then divide the class into pairs and have students take turns using the models to ask and answer questions about the characters and situations depicted on the page. Then call on pairs to present conversations to the class.

 THINK ABOUT IT!

Divide the class into pairs or small groups. Have students discuss the questions and then share their thoughts with the class.

th PRONUNCIATION

Pronunciation exercises provide students with models of natural English pronunciation. The goal of these exercises is to enable learners to improve their own pronunciation and to understand the pronunciation of native speakers using English in natural conversational contexts.

Have students first focus on listening to the sentences. Say each sentence in the left column or play the audio one or more times and have students listen carefully and repeat. Next, focus on pronunciation. Have students say each sentence in the right column and then listen carefully as you say it or play the audio. If you wish, you can have students continue practicing the sentences to improve their pronunciation.

 JOURNAL

The purpose of the *Side by Side Journal* activity is to show students how writing can become a vehicle for communicating thoughts and feelings. Have students begin a journal in a composition notebook. In these journals, students have the opportunity to write about things that are meaningful to them.

Have students write their journal entries at home or in class. Encourage students to use a dictionary to look up words they would like to use. They can share their written work with other students if appropriate. Then as a class, in pairs, or in small groups, have students discuss what they have written.

If time permits, you may want to write a response in each student's journal, sharing your own opinions and experiences as well as reacting to what the student has written. If you are keeping portfolios of students' work, these compositions serve as excellent examples of students' progress in learning English.

 CHAPTER SUMMARY

- **Grammar**

  Divide the class into pairs or small groups, and have students take turns forming sentences from the words in the grammar boxes. Student A says a sentence, and Student B points to the words from each column that are in the sentence. Then have students switch: Student B says a sentence, and Student A points to the words.

- **Key Vocabulary**

  Have students ask you any questions about the meaning or pronunciation of the vocabulary. If students ask for the pronunciation, repeat after the student until the student is satisfied with his or her own pronunciation.

- **Key Vocabulary Check**

  When completing a chapter, as a way of checking students' retention of the key vocabulary depicted on the opening page of the chapter, have students open their books to the first page of the chapter and cover the list of vocabulary words. Either call out a number and have students tell you the word, or say a word and have students tell you the number.

 SIDE by SIDE **Gazette**

 FEATURE ARTICLE

Have students read silently, or follow along silently as the article is read aloud by you, by one or more students, or on the audio program. You may choose to introduce new vocabulary beforehand, or have students encounter it within the context of the article. Ask students if they have any questions, and check understanding of vocabulary.

 FACT FILE

Present the information and have the class discuss it.

 BUILD YOUR VOCABULARY!

Have students look at the illustrations and identify any words they already know. Then say each word and have the class repeat it chorally and individually. Check students' understanding and pronunciation of the words.

 AROUND THE WORLD

Divide the class into pairs or small groups and have students react to the photographs and answer the questions. Then have students report back to the class.

 GLOBAL EXCHANGE

Have students read silently or follow along silently as the message is read aloud by you, by one or more students, or on the audio program.

For additional practice, you can have students write back to the person and then share their writing with the class. You may also wish to have students correspond with a keypal on the Internet and then share their experience with the class.

 WHAT ARE THEY SAYING?

Have students talk about the people and the situation in the cartoon, and then create role plays based on the scene. Students may refer back to previous lessons as a resource, but they should not simply reuse specific conversations. You may want to assign this exercise as written homework, having students prepare their role plays, practice them the next day with other students, and then present them to the class.

EXPANSION ACTIVITIES

This Teacher's Guide offers a rich variety of optional Expansion Activities for review and reinforcement. Feel free to pick and choose or vary the activities to fit the particular needs and learning styles of students in your class. These ideas are meant to serve as a springboard for developing your own learning activities.

We encourage you to try some of the teaching approaches offered in this Teacher's Guide. In keeping with the spirit of *Side by Side*, these suggestions are intended to provide students with a language learning experience that is dynamic . . . interactive . . . and fun!

Steven J. Molinsky
Bill Bliss

GRAMMAR

To Be

am	I am from Mexico City. (I am)
is	What's your name? (What is) My name is Maria.
are	Where are you from?

FUNCTIONS

ASKING FOR AND REPORTING INFORMATION

What's your name?
   My name is *Maria*.
What's your first name?
   Sarah.
What's your last name?
   Kelly.
How do you spell that?
   K-E-L-L-Y.
What's your address?
   My address is *235 Main Street*.
What's your phone number?
   My phone number is *741-8906*.
Where are you from?
   I'm from *Mexico City*.

I'm American.

My license number is *921DCG*.
My apartment number is *4-B*.
My social security number is
   044-35-9862.
My e-mail address is
   TeacherJoe@worldnet.com.

MEETING PEOPLE

Hello.
Hi.

My name is _____.
I'm _____.

Nice to meet you.
   Nice to meet you, too.

NEW VOCABULARY

People

actor
actress
American
athlete
Mr.
Mrs.
Ms.
president
prime minister

Places

Brooklyn
Florida
Mexico City
New York
San Francisco

country

Personal Information

address
apartment
apartment number
e-mail address
fax number
first name
last name
license number
name
number
phone number
social security number
street
telephone number

Cardinal Numbers

0	oh (zero)
1	one
2	two
3	three
4	four
5	five
6	six
7	seven
8	eight
9	nine
10	ten

Articles

a
the

Possessive Adjectives

my
your

Prepositions

from
of

Question Words

What
Where

Subject Pronouns

I
you

Verbs

are
is
am ('m)

EXPRESSIONS

Hello.
Hi.
Nice to meet you.
Nice to meet you, too.

Text Page 1: Chapter Opening Page

VOCABULARY PREVIEW

1. The Alphabet

You may want to introduce the alphabet at this point, or you may choose to wait until the *Interview* activity on text page 5. If you wish to present the alphabet now, here are some suggestions:

a. Use flash cards or write the letter *A* on the board. Have students repeat: "A."

b. Next to *A*, use the flash card *B* or write the letter *B*. Have students repeat: "A, B."

c. Continue with the letters *C*, *D*, and *E*.

d. Next, point to these letters at random. Have students say the letters.

e. Continue the above steps with groups of five or six letters at a time until you have completed the alphabet.

f. Have the class repeat the alphabet.

2. Numbers 0–10

You may want to introduce the numbers 0–10 at this point, or you may choose to wait until the lesson on text page 2. If you wish to present the numbers now, here are some suggestions:

a. Write 0 on the board. Have students repeat: "Zero."

b. Write 1 on the board. Have students repeat: "One."

c. Next to 1, write 2. Have students repeat: "Zero, one, two."

d. Continue with the numbers 3, 4, and 5.

e. Point to these numbers at random and have the class say them.

f. Continue the above steps with the numbers 6–10.

3. Vocabulary Words 3–5

You may want to introduce these words before beginning the chapter, or you may choose to wait until they first occur in a specific lesson. If you choose to introduce them at this point, here are some suggestions:

a. Have students look at the illustrations on text page 1 and identify the words they already know.

b. Present the vocabulary. Say each word and have the class repeat it chorally and individually. Check students' understanding and pronunciation of the words.

c. Practice the vocabulary as a class, in pairs, or in small groups. Have students cover the word list and look at the pictures. Practice the words in the following ways:

- Say a word and have students tell the number of the illustration.

- Give the number of an illustration and have students say the word.

Text Page 2: What's Your Name?

FOCUS

- To Be: Introduction

CLOSE UP

RULE:	The verb *to be* in the present tense is commonly contracted with subject pronouns and the question word *what*.
EXAMPLES:	**I am** ⟶ **I'm** from Mexico.
	What is ⟶ **What's** your name?

GETTING READY

1. Teach the first question and answer in the conversation before students open their books. (*What's your name? My name is _____.*)

   a. Begin by saying *your* name: "My name is _____."

   b. Then ask individual students: "What's your name?" Students answer: "My name is _____."

   c. Next, have individual students ask each other.

2. If you haven't already introduced the numbers 0–10, refer to the teaching steps on page 4 of this Teacher's Guide. (Be sure to tell students that in telephone numbers, people usually say "oh" rather than "zero." Have students repeat "Oh.")

3. Practice the numbers.

   a. Write the numbers 0–10 on the board or use flash cards. Point to numbers at random and have the class say them.

   b. Continue with individual students.

INTRODUCING THE MODEL

1. Have students look at the model illustration.

2. Set the scene: "A teacher and student are talking."

3. With books closed, have students listen as you present the model or play the audio one or more times.

4. **Full-Class Repetition:** Model each question and answer in the dialog and have students repeat.

5. Have students open their books and look at the dialog. Ask students if they have any questions. Check understanding of vocabulary.

6. **Group Choral Repetition:** Divide the class in half. Model the 1st question of the dialog and have Group 1 repeat; model the answer and have Group 2 repeat. Continue this way with the other questions and answers in the dialog.

7. **Choral Conversation:** Groups 1 and 2 practice the dialog twice, without teacher model. First, Group 1 asks the questions and Group 2 gives the answers; then reverse.

8. Call on one or two pairs of students to present the dialog.

   (For additional practice, do Choral Conversation in small groups or by rows.)

Pronunciation Note

The pronunciation focus of Chapter 1 is **Linked Sounds** (text page 6). You may wish to model this pronunciation at this point and encourage students to incorporate it into their language practice.

My name is . . .

My address is . . .

My phone number is . . .

ANSWER THESE QUESTIONS

Students use the questions of the model to give their own names, addresses, and phone numbers, and tell where they are from.

1. Call on a few pairs of students to ask and answer the questions, using information about themselves in the answers.

2. Divide the class into pairs, and have the pairs ask and answer the questions. Then call on pairs of students to present their dialogs to the class.

Note that the numbers in students' addresses may be higher than the ones they have learned. For this exercise you can have students read each digit in their addresses. For example, 232 might be read as *two, three, two* rather than *two thirty-two*. (Higher numbers will be taught in Chapter 5.)

WORKBOOK

Pages 2–4, Exercises A–D

EXPANSION ACTIVITIES

1. Disappearing Dialog

   a. Write the model conversation on the board.

   b. Ask for two student volunteers to read the conversation.

   c. Erase a few of the words from the dialog. Have two different students read the conversation.

   d. Erase more words and call on two more students to read the conversation.

   e. Continue erasing words and calling on pairs of students until everyone has had a turn.

2. Name Game

   a. Ask each student in the room: "What's your name?" Have each student respond.

   b. Call on volunteers to name as many of the students in the class as they can.

3. Number Clapping

   a. Clap your hands or tap on the desk. Have students respond by saying the number of claps.

   b. Have a student clap out or tap out a number. Have the class say the number.

4. Telephone

   a. Have students sit in a circle.

   b. Whisper a name, address, or telephone number to the first student. For example: 489-7213.

   c. The first student whispers the message to the second student, and so forth around the room.

   d. When the message gets to the last student, that person says it aloud. Is it the same message you started with?

   e. Give each student in the class a chance to start his or her own message.

   Variation: This activity can also be done in small groups.

5. Match the Sentences

a. Make several sets of split sentence cards, such as the following, with different names, addresses, phone numbers, and places. For example:

My name is	Tom.
My address is	10 Main Street.
My phone number is	289-5387.
I'm from	New York.

b. Distribute a card to each student.

c. Have students look at their cards, then walk around the room trying to find their corresponding match.

d. Then have pairs of students say their completed sentences aloud to the class.

6. English Name Game

a. Divide the class into teams.

b. Draw a male and female face on the board. For example:

c. Call out common English names, such as:

Peter	David
Susan	Sarah
Mary	William
Joe	Julie

d. Have team members decide if the names are male or female. A team wins one point for each name correctly identified. The team with the most points wins the *English Name Game.*

ROLE PLAY *A Famous Person*

This is a role-play exercise that reviews the questions on text page 2. Students pretend to be famous celebrities who are being interviewed on television. One student is the interviewer and asks the questions. Another pretends to be the famous person. Talk shows are popular in the United States and usually feature a well-known host talking with famous people.

1. Have students think of famous people in the categories suggested on text page 3. If they have difficulty, make some suggestions. You can use magazine and newspaper photographs as cues. The students can assume the role of the celebrity in the photograph.

2. Have pairs of students practice and then role-play their interviews in front of the class, making up addresses and phone numbers for the famous people.

How to Say It!

Meeting People: In the United States, it is common to initiate a conversation with self-introduction (*Hello. My name is . . . , Hi. I'm . . .*). "Hello" and "Hi" are equally common ways to greet people. "Hi" is more informal than "Hello."

---

1. Have students look at the illustration.

2. Set the scene: "Two people are meeting each other."

3. With books closed, have students listen as you present the conversation or play the audio one or more times.

4. **Full-Class Repetition:** Model each line and have students repeat.

5. Have students open their books and look at the dialog. Ask students if they have any questions. Check understanding of new vocabulary: *Hello; Hi; Nice to meet you; Nice to meet you, too.*

6. **Group Choral Repetition:** Divide the class in half. Model line A and have Group 1 repeat; model line B and have Group 2 repeat.

7. **Choral Conversation:** Groups 1 and 2 practice the dialog twice, without teacher model. First Group 1 is Speaker A and Group 2 is Speaker B; then reverse.

8. Call on one or two pairs of students to present the dialog.

9. Have students walk around the classroom, introducing themselves to each other.

10. Call on several pairs of students to present their conversations to the class.

READING *What's Your Name?*

FOCUS

- To Be: Introduction

NEW VOCABULARY

American	Ms.
apartment number	Mrs.
Brooklyn	nationality
e-mail address	New York
fax number	San Francisco
Florida	social security
license number	number
Mr.	telephone number

READING THE STORY

Optional: *Preview the story by having students talk about the story title and/or illustrations. You may choose to introduce new vocabulary beforehand, or have students encounter the new vocabulary within the context of the reading.*

1. Have students read silently, or follow along silently as the story is read aloud by you, by one or more students, or on the audio program.

2. Ask students if they have any questions. Check understanding of vocabulary.

Culture Note

Social security number: Anyone who earns money in the United States must report his or her earnings to the federal government. Individuals are given social security numbers. Social security taxes are used to support a national program of life insurance and old-age pensions.

Language Note

E-mail addresses are said in a specific way. The first portion of the address is said as one word, even when it includes two or three words. Sometimes people will clarify this when giving the address. The symbol @ is pronounced *at*, and the period (.) is pronounced *dot*. Thus, the e-mail address *TeacherJoe@worldnet.com* is pronounced *TeacherJoe* (one word) *at worldnet-dot-com*.

✔ READING *CHECK-UP*

This exercise is based on the reading on text page 4.

MATCH

1. d	**4.** b
2. e	**5.** f
3. a	**6.** c

READING EXTENSION

What's the Answer?

Ask students the following questions and have them scan the reading on text page 4 for the information.

Your name is Mrs. Grant.
What's your telephone number?

Your name is Peter Black.
What's your address?

Your name is David Carter.
Where are you from?

Your name is William Chen.
What's your social security number?

Your name is Ms. Martinez.
What's your fax number?

Your name is Susan Miller.
What's your apartment number?

Your name is Mr. Santini.
What's your e-mail address?

LISTENING

Listen and choose the correct answer.

1. A. What's your name?
   B. Mary Black.

2. A. What's your address?
   B. Two sixty-five Main Street.

3. A. What's your apartment number?
   B. Five C.

4. A. What's your telephone number?
   B. Two five nine–four oh eight seven.

5. A. What's your social security number?
   B. Oh three two–eight nine–six one seven nine.

6. A. What's your e-mail address?
   B. maryb-at-worldnet-dot-com.

Answers

1.	a	4.	b
2.	b	5.	b
3.	a	6.	a

INTERVIEW *Spelling Names*

GETTING READY

If you haven't already introduced the alphabet, refer to the teaching steps on page 4 of this Teacher's Guide.

INTRODUCE THE CONVERSATION

1. Have students look at the illustration.

2. Set the scene: "A person is interviewing someone."

3. With books closed, have students listen as you present the conversation or play the audio one or more times.

4. **Full-Class Repetition:** Model each line and have students repeat.

5. Have students open their books and look at the dialog. Ask students if they have any questions. Check understanding of new vocabulary: *last name, first name, How do you spell that?*

6. **Group Choral Repetition:** Divide the class in half. Model line A and have Group 1 repeat; model line B and have Group 2 repeat.

7. **Choral Conversation:** Groups 1 and 2 practice the dialog twice, without teacher model. First Group 1 is Speaker A and Group 2 is Speaker B; then reverse.

8. Call on one or two pairs of students to present the dialog.

9. Have students walk around the classroom and interview five other students, asking and answering the questions in the model conversation as they complete the chart.

10. Follow up by asking students to read aloud the names of the students they interviewed.

WORKBOOK

Pages 4–5 Exercises E–H

EXPANSION ACTIVITY

Stand in Order!

1. Have students write their last names in large print on a piece of paper.

2. Have students stand up, hold their name in front of them so everyone can see, and arrange themselves in alphabetical order.

3. When everyone is in order, have students spell out their last names and then say their names. For example:

   Student 1: A-L-V-A-R-E-Z—Alvarez
   Student 2: C-H-A-N-G—Chang
   Student 3: L-E-E—Lee
   Student 4: S-I-M-O-N—Simon

th PRONUNCIATION

> **Linked Sounds:** Final consonants are
> often linked to beginning vowel sounds
> in the word that follows

Focus on Listening

Practice the sentences in the left column. Say
each sentence or play the audio one or more
times. Have students listen carefully and
repeat.

Focus on Pronunciation

Practice the sentences in the right column. Have
students say each sentence and then listen
carefully as you say it or play the audio.

If you wish, have students continue practicing
the sentences to improve their pronunciation.

JOURNAL

Have students write their journal entries at
home or in class. They can share their written
work with other students if appropriate. As a
class, in pairs, or in small groups, have students
discuss what they have written.

Have students keep a journal of their written
work. If time permits, you may want to write a
response in each student's journal, sharing your
own opinions and experiences as well as
reacting to what the student has written. If you
are keeping portfolios of students' work, these
compositions serve as excellent examples of
students' progress in learning English.

✓ CHAPTER SUMMARY

GRAMMAR

1. Divide the class into pairs or small groups.

2. Have students take turns reading the
   sentences in the grammar boxes.

KEY VOCABULARY

Have students ask you any questions about the
meaning or pronunciation of the vocabulary. If
students ask for the pronunciation, repeat after
the student until the student is satisfied with
his or her pronunciation.

EXPANSION ACTIVITIES

1. *Vocabulary Review*

   Check students' retention of the vocabulary
   depicted on the opening page of Chapter 1 by
   doing the following activity:

   a. Have students open their books to page 1.

   b. Write letters of the alphabet on the board in
      random order and have students say the
      name of the letter.

   c. Write the numbers from 0–10 on the board in
      random order and have students tell you the
      number.

   d. Tell students to cover words 3–5 at the
      bottom of the page. Either call out a number
      and have students tell you the word, or say a
      word and have students tell you the number.

   Variation: You can also do this activity as a
   game with competing teams.

   (continued)

EXPANSION ACTIVITIES (Continued)

2. Student-Led Dictation

a. Tell each student to choose a word or phrase from the Key Vocabulary list on text page 6 and look at it very carefully.

b. Have students take turns dictating their words to the class. Everybody writes down that student's word.

c. When the dictation is completed, call on different students to write each word on the board to check the spelling.

END-OF-CHAPTER ACTIVITY

Scrambled Sentences

1. Divide the class into two teams.

2. One sentence at a time, write individual sentences and questions out of order on the board. For example:

```
first    My    is    Maria    name

apartment    is    My    4C    number

from    you    are    Where

is    address    Street    My    Main    7
```

3. The first person to raise his or her hand, come to the board, and write the sentence in the correct order earns a point for that team.

4. The team with the most points wins the scrambled sentence game.

Variation: Write the words to several sentences on separate cards. Divide the class into small groups, and have students work together to put the sentences into the correct order.

WORKBOOK ANSWER KEY AND LISTENING SCRIPTS

WORKBOOK PAGE 2

A. WHAT ARE THEY SAYING?

1. What's, name
2. address, My, is
3. your, phone number
4. your, name
5. What's, address
6. phone, My, number
7. Where are, I'm from

WORKBOOK PAGE 3

B. NAME/ADDRESS/PHONE NUMBER

(Answers will vary.)

C. LISTENING

Listen and circle the number you hear.

1. My address is five Main Street.
2. My address is seven Main Street.
3. My address is two Main Street.
4. My address is six Main Street.
5. My address is one Main Street.
6. My address is three Main Street.
7. My address is four Main Street.
8. My address is eight Main Street.
9. My address is ten Main Street.
10. My address is nine Main Street.

Answers

1.	5	6.	3
2.	7	7.	4
3.	2	8.	8
4.	6	9.	10
5.	1	10.	9

WORKBOOK PAGE 4

D. NUMBERS

4	six
7	two
1	seven
8	three
10	one
2	eight
9	ten
6	four
5	nine
3	five

E. LISTENING

Listen and write the missing numbers.

1. A. What's your phone number?
   B. My phone number is 389-7932.

2. A. What's your telephone number?
   B. My telephone number is 837-2953.

3. A. What's your apartment number?
   B. My apartment number is 6-B.

4. A. What's your address?
   B. My address is 10 Main Street.

5. A. What's your fax number?
   B. My fax number is 654-7315.

6. A. What's your license number?
   B. My license number is 2613498.

Answers

1.	2	2.	5
3.	6	4.	10
5.	7, 3	6.	1, 4, 8

WORKBOOK PAGE 5

F. LISTENING

Listen and write the missing letters.

1. A. What's your last name?
   B. Carter.
   A. How do you spell that?
   B. C-A-R-T-E-R.

2. A. What's your last name?
   B. Johnson.
   A. How do you spell that?
   B. J-O-H-N-S-O-N.

3. A. What's your first name?
   B. Gerald.
   A. How do you spell that?
   B. G-E-R-A-L-D.

4. A. What's your last name?
   B. Anderson.
   A. How do you spell that?
   B. A-N-D-E-R-S-O-N.

5. A. What's your first name?
   B. Phillip.
   A. How do you spell that?
   B. P-H-I-L-L-I-P.

6. A. What's your last name?
   B. Martinez.
   A. How do you spell that?
   B. M-A-R-T-I-N-E-Z.

Answers

1. R, E
2. H, S, N
3. G, A, D
4. R, O
5. P, L
6. M, T, Z

G. WHAT ARE THEY SAYING?

1. name
2. Hi
3. meet
4. Nice
5. you
6. My
7. is
8. Hello
9. I'm
10. to
11. you

Teacher's Notes

GRAMMAR

SUBJECT PRONOUNS
TO BE + LOCATION

	am	I?
Where	is	he? she? it?
	are	we? you? they?

(I am)	I'm	
(He is) (She is) (It is)	He's She's It's	in the kitchen.
(We are) (You are) (They are)	We're You're They're	

FUNCTIONS

ASKING FOR AND REPORTING INFORMATION

Henry is *Chinese*.
He's from *Shanghai*.

INQUIRING ABOUT LOCATION

Where are *you*?
Where's the *pen*?

GIVING LOCATION

I'm in the *kitchen*.
It's on the *desk*.

GREETING PEOPLE

Hi. How are you?
   Fine. And you?
Fine, thanks.

NEW VOCABULARY

Classroom

board
book
bookshelf
bulletin board
chair
class
clock
computer
desk
dictionary
English class
globe
map
notebook
pen
pencil
ruler
table
wall

Home

attic
basement
bathroom
bedroom
dining room
garage
kitchen
living room
yard

Places Around Town

bank
hospital
library
movie theater
office
park
post office
restaurant
social security office
supermarket
zoo

People

dentist
everybody
friend
friends
students
teacher

Animals

monkey

Objects

bed
car
cell phone
newspaper
telephone book

Nationalities

Chinese
Greek
Italian
Japanese
Korean
Mexican
Puerto Rican

Places Around the World

Athens
Mexico City
Rome
San Juan
Seoul
Shanghai
Tokyo

countries

Adjectives

absent
all
different
interesting
many

Possessive Adjectives

our

Adverbs

even
today
very
yes

Prepositions

at
except
in
on

Conjunctions

and

Subject Pronouns

he
she
it
we
they

Object Pronouns

me

Verbs

am ('m)
are ('re)
is ('s)

Question Words

Which

EXPRESSIONS

in bed
What a shame!

Text Page 7: Chapter Opening Page

VOCABULARY PREVIEW

You may want to introduce these words before beginning the chapter, or you may choose to wait until they first occur in a specific lesson. If you choose to introduce them at this point, here are some suggestions:

1. Have students look at the illustrations on text page 7 and identify the words they already know.

2. Present the vocabulary. Say each word and have the class repeat it chorally and individually. Check students' understanding and pronunciation of the words.

3. Practice the vocabulary as a class, in pairs, or in small groups. Have students cover the word list and look at the pictures. Practice the words in the following ways:

   • Say a word and have students tell the number of the illustration.

   • Give the number of an illustration and have students say the word.

Text Pages 8-9: In the Classroom/Where Is It?

FOCUS

- Objects in the Classroom
- To Be
- To Be + Location
- Subject Pronoun: *it*

The focus of the lesson on text page 9 is on the third person singular of *to be* with the subject pronoun *it*.

CLOSE UP

RULE:	The word order in a question with the verb *to be* is: Question word + verb + subject.
EXAMPLE:	**Where + is + the pen?**
RULE:	The question word *where* asks about location.
EXAMPLE:	**Where** is the pen? It is **on the desk**.
RULE:	The verb *to be* is used to indicate location.
EXAMPLE:	Where **is** the board? It **is** on the wall.
RULE:	The subject pronoun *it* refers to inanimate objects.
EXAMPLE:	Where is the globe? **It** *(the globe)* is on the table.
RULE:	In spoken and informal written English, the third person singular form of the verb *to be* contracts with the question word *where* and the subject pronoun *it*.
EXAMPLES:	**Where is** the pen? ⟶ **Where's** the pen? **It is** on the desk. ⟶ **It's** on the desk.

GETTING READY

1. Teach the vocabulary on text page 8.

   a. Have students look at the classroom scene on text page 8 and identify the words they already know.

   b. Present the vocabulary, using the illustration on text page 8 or *Side by Side* Picture Cards 1–17. Say each word and have the class repeat it chorally and individually. Check students' understanding and pronunciation of the words.

   c. Practice the vocabulary as a class, in pairs, or in small groups. Have students cover the word list on text page 8 and look at the illustration, and practice the words in the following ways:

      • Say a word and have students tell the number in the illustration.

      • Give the number in the illustration and have students say the word.

2. Introduce the preposition *on*.

   a. Write on the board:

   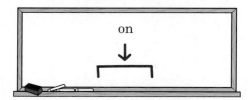

   b. Place a book on a desk, point to it, and say:

      A. Where's the book?
      B. It's on the desk.

   c. Ask the class: "Where's the book?" Have the class repeat: "It's on the desk."

   d. Place a pen on the book and say:

      A. Where's the pen?
      B. It's on the book.

   e. Ask the class: "Where's the pen?" Have the class repeat: "It's on the book."

INTRODUCING THE MODELS

There are three model conversations on text page 9. Introduce and practice each model before going on to the next. For each model:

1. Have students look at the model illustration.

2. Set the scene: "Students are talking in a classroom."

3. With books closed, have students listen as you present the model or play the audio one or more times.

4. **Full-Class Repetition:** Model each line and have students repeat.

5. Have students open their books and look at the dialog. Ask students if they have any questions. Check understanding of new vocabulary: *where's, it's, on, the*.

6. **Group Choral Repetition:** Divide the class in half. Model line A and have Group 1 repeat; model line B and have Group 2 repeat.

7. **Choral Conversation:** Groups 1 and 2 practice the dialog twice, without teacher model. First, Group 1 is Speaker A and Group 2 is Speaker B; then reverse.

8. Call on one or two pairs of students to present the dialog.

   (For additional practice, do Choral Conversation in small groups or by rows.)

SIDE BY SIDE EXERCISES

Examples

1. A. Where's the pen?
   B. It's on the desk.

2. A. Where's the board?
   B. It's on the wall.

1. **Exercise 1:** Call on two students to present the dialog. Then do Choral Repetition and Choral Conversation practice.

2. **Exercise 2:** Same as above.

3. Exercises 3–9: Either

Full-Class Practice: Call on a pair of students to do each exercise. (For more practice, call on other pairs of students, or do Choral Repetition or Choral Conversation.)

    or

Pair Practice: Have students in pairs practice all the exercises. Then have pairs present the exercises to the class. (For more practice, do Choral Repetition or Choral Conversation.)

EXPANSION ACTIVITIES

1. What's the Object?

Hold up a visual (*Side by Side* Picture Cards 1–17), or point to a real classroom object and have students identify it.

2. Clap in Rhythm

Object: Once a clapping rhythm is established, the students must continue naming different classroom objects.

a. Have students sit in a circle.

b. Establish a steady even beat—one-two-three-four, one-two-three-four—by having students clap their hands to their laps twice and then clap their hands together twice. Repeat throughout the game, maintaining the same rhythm.

c. The object is for each student in turn to name a classroom word *each time the hands are clapped together twice*. Nothing is said when students clap their hands on their laps.

Note: The beat never stops! If a student misses a beat, he or she can either wait for the next beat or else pass to the next student.

3. Letter Game

a. Divide the class into teams.

b. Say: "I'm thinking of a classroom object that starts with *r*."

c. The first person to raise his or her hand and guess correctly [*ruler*] wins a point for his or her team.

d. Continue with other letters of the alphabet and other classroom items.

The team that gets the most correct answers wins the game.

4. Remember the Words!

a. Tell students to spend one minute looking very carefully at text page 8.

b. Have students close their books and write down as many words from the page as they can remember.

c. Have students read their lists as a class, in pairs, or in small groups.

d. Call on students to come to the board and write their list of words. Have the class check the spelling of the words.

5. Drawing Game

a. Write the names of classroom objects on two sets of separate cards.

b. Place the two piles of cards on a table or desk in the front of the room. Also have a pad of paper and pencil next to each team's set of cards.

(continued)

c. Divide the class into two teams. Have each team sit together in a different part of the room.

d. When you say "Go!," a person from each team comes to the front of his or her team, picks a card from the pile, and draws the object. The rest of the team then guesses what the object is.

e. When a team correctly guesses an object, another team member picks a card and draws the object written on that card.

f. Continue until each team has guessed all the objects in their pile.

The team that guesses the objects in the shortest time wins the game.

6. True or False?

a. Have students open their books to text page 8.

b. Make statements about the location of classroom objects on text page 8 and have students tell you "True" or "False." If the statement is false, have students correct it. For example:

Teacher: The pen is on the desk.
Student: True.

Teacher: The ruler is on the chair.
Student: False. The ruler is on the desk.

Variation: You can call on students to make true or false statements about the illustration and have other students respond.

 Make a List!

1. Divide the class into pairs.

2. Tell students to make a list of all the objects they can identify in the classroom. Have pairs of students read their lists aloud. Who wrote the best list?

FOCUS

- Rooms of the House
- To Be (non-3rd person singular)
- Subject Pronouns: *I, you, we, they*

All the forms of *to be* are presented in the grammar box at the top of text page 11.

- The focus of the lesson on text page 11 is the verb *to be* in the non-3rd person singular forms *(Where are you? I'm in the kitchen./We're in the living room., Where are they? They're in the yard.)*

- The focus of the lesson on text page 12 is the verb *to be* in the 3rd person singular.

CLOSE UP

RULE:	In spoken and informal written English, the verb *to be* contracts with the subject pronouns *I, we, you, they.*
EXAMPLES:	**I am** in the kitchen. ⟶ **I'm** in the kitchen.
	We are in the living room. ⟶ **We're** in the living room.
	You are in the dining room. ⟶ **You're** in the dining room.
	They are in the yard. ⟶ **They're** in the yard.

GETTING READY

Teach the vocabulary on text page 10.

1. Have students look at the illustration on text page 10 and identify the words they already know.

2. Present the vocabulary, using the illustration on text page 10 or *Side by Side* Picture Cards 18–26. Say each word and have the class repeat it chorally and individually. Check students' understanding and pronunciation of the words.

3. Practice the vocabulary as a class, in pairs, or in small groups. Have students cover the word list on text page 10 and look at the illustration. Practice the words in the following ways:

- Say a word and have students tell the number in the illustration.

- Give the number in the illustration and have students say the word.

INTRODUCING THE MODELS

There are three model conversations. Introduce and practice each model before going on to the next. For each model:

1. Have students look at the model illustration.

2. Set the scene: "People are talking at home."

3. With books closed, have students listen as you present the model or play the audio one or more times.

4. **Full-Class Repetition:** Model each line and have students repeat.

5. Have students open their books and look at the dialog. Ask students if they have any questions. Check understanding of new vocabulary:

    1st model: *I'm,*
    2nd model: *we're*
    3rd model: *Mr., and, Mrs., they're*

Culture Notes

Yard: Many U.S. families relax, plant gardens, and play sports in this grassy area around the house.

Forms of address:

Mr.   refers to both married and single men.
Mrs. refers to married women.
Miss refers to single women.
Ms.   refers to all women, whether they are married or single.

6. Group Choral Repetition: Divide the class in half. Model line A and have Group 1 repeat; model line B and have Group 2 repeat.

7. Choral Conversation: Groups 1 and 2 practice the dialog twice, without teacher model. First, Group 1 is Speaker A and Group 2 is Speaker B; then reverse.

8. Call on one or two pairs of students to present the dialog.

(For additional practice, do Choral Conversation in small groups or by rows.)

9. Expand each model with further practice.

a. After students practice the model *(Where are you? I'm in the kitchen)*, cue other conversations orally or by using *Side by Side* Picture Cards 18–26. For example:

    Teacher cue: bedroom
      Teacher: Where are you?
      Student: I'm in the bedroom.

    Teacher cue: living room
      Teacher: Where are you?
      Student: I'm in the living room.

This practice can be done chorally, or you can call on individual students.

b. When practicing *we're*, you can make this more realistic by asking about two of your students.

For example:

    Teacher cue: dining room
      Teacher: Where are you and *(Carlos)*?
      Student: We're in the dining room.

c. When practicing *they're*, use names of students in your class. For example:

    Teacher cue: yard
      Teacher: Where are *(David)* and *(Maria)*?
      Student: They're in the yard.

SIDE BY SIDE EXERCISES

Examples

1. A. Where are you?
   B. I'm in the bedroom.

2. A. Where are you?
   B. We're in the kitchen.

3. A. Where are Jim and Pam?
   B. They're in the living room.

1. Exercise 1: Call on two students to present the dialog. Then do Choral Repetition and Choral Conversation practice.

2. Exercise 2: Same as above.

3. Exercises 3–9:

Culture Note

Basement (Exercise 8): Basements are common in buildings located in colder climates. The heating system is often located in the basement.

Either

Full-Class Practice: Call on a pair of students to do each exercise. (For more practice, call on other pairs of students, or do Choral Repetition or Choral Conversation.)

or

Pair Practice: Have students in pairs practice all of the exercises. Then have pairs present the exercises to the class. (For more practice, do Choral Repetition or Choral Conversation.)

Pronunciation Note

The pronunciation focus of Chapter 2 is **Reduced *and*** (text page 16). You may wish to model this pronunciation at this point and encourage students to incorporate it into their language practice.

Mr. and Mrs. Jones

Jim and Pam

Mr. and Mrs. Park

Mr. and Mrs. Hernandez

WORKBOOK

Page 7

EXPANSION ACTIVITIES

1. Where Is Everybody?

Use your own visuals, word cards, or *Side by Side Picture Cards 18–26* to review the structures on text page 11. Have students pretend to be in various places, and ask and answer questions.

a. To practice *I'm*, give a visual of the living room to Student A and ask: "Where are you?" Student A answers: "I'm in the living room."

b. Practice *I'm* this way with other students, using other locations.

c. Call on pairs of students to practice both the question and answer with *I'm* as you give a visual to one student.

d. To practice *we're*, give a visual to Student B and ask Student A: "Where are you and Student B?" Student A answers: "We're in the _____."

e. Practice *we're* with other students, using other locations. Then call on pairs of students to practice both the question and the answer.

f. To practice *they're*, give a visual to Student A and Student B and ask Student C: "Where are Students A and B?" Student C answers: "They're in the _____." Continue with other students and locations.

2. What's the Contraction?

a. Say the full forms of *to be* and have students say the contracted forms. For example:

Teacher	Students
I am	I'm
He is	He's
We are	We're
She is	She's

b. Next say the contracted forms and have students say the full forms. For example:

Teacher	Students
They're	They are
She's	She is
He's	He is
You're	You are

3. Can You Hear the Difference?

a. Write on the board:

①	②
I am in the kitchen.	I'm in the kitchen.
You are in the yard.	You're in the yard.
We are in the attic.	We're in the attic.
They are in the basement.	They're in the basement.

b. Choose a sentence randomly from one of the two columns and say it to the class. Have the class listen and identify the column by saying "One" or "Two." For example:

Teacher	Students
We are in the attic.	One
They're in the basement.	Two
I'm in the kitchen.	Two
You are in the yard.	One

c. Have students continue the activity in pairs. One student pronounces a sentence, and the other identifies the column. Then have them reverse roles.

d. Write similar sentences on the board and continue the practice.

Text Page 12: Where's Bob?

FOCUS

- To Be (3rd person singular)
- Subject Pronouns: *he, she, it*

CLOSE UP

RULE:	The subject pronoun *he* refers to a male. The subject pronoun *she* refers to a female.
EXAMPLES:	Where's Bob? ⟶ Where's Mary? **He**'s in the living room. ⟶ **She**'s in the bedroom.

RULE:	In spoken and informal written English, the verb *to be* contracts with the subject pronouns *he* and *she*.
EXAMPLES:	**He is** in the bedroom. ⟶ **He's** in the bedroom. **She is** in the yard. ⟶ **She's** in the yard. **It is** in the kitchen. ⟶ **It's** in the kitchen.

GETTING READY

Review the vocabulary on text page 10. Use *Side by Side* Picture Cards 18–26 or the illustration in the text to practice these words. Point to a place and have students say the name. Have students respond chorally, then individually. Practice each word several times.

INTRODUCING THE MODELS

There are three model conversations. Introduce and practice each model before going on to the next. For each model:

1. Have students look at the model illustration.

2. Set the scene: "People are talking at home."

3. With books closed, have students listen as you present the model or play the audio one or more times.

4. **Full-Class Repetition:** Model each line and have students repeat.

5. Have students open their books and look at the dialog. Ask students if they have any questions. Check understanding of new vocabulary:

    1st model: *he's*
    2nd model: *she's*
    3rd model: *car*

6. **Group Choral Repetition:** Divide the class in half. Model line A and have Group 1 repeat; model line B and have Group 2 repeat.

7. **Choral Conversation:** Groups 1 and 2 practice the dialog twice, without teacher model. First, Group 1 is Speaker A and Group 2 is Speaker B; then reverse.

8. Call on one or two pairs of students to present the dialog.

26   CHAPTER 2

(For additional practice, do Choral Conversation in small groups or by rows.)

9. Expand the first two models with further practice.

a. After students practice the first model *(Where's Bob? He's in the living room)*, cue other similar conversations, using names of male students in the class. For example:

    Teacher cue: kitchen
         Teacher: Where's *(Tom)*?
         Student: He's in the kitchen.

    Teacher cue: basement
         Teacher: Where's *(John)*?
         Student: He's in the basement.

b. Similarly, after presenting the second model, cue other similar conversations, using names of female students in the class. For example:

    Teacher cue: dining room
    Teacher: Where's *(Jane)*?
    Student: She's in the dining room.

SIDE BY SIDE EXERCISES

Examples

1. A. Where's Tim?
   B. He's in the bedroom.

2. A. Where's Rosa?
   B. She's in the yard.

3. A. Where's the newspaper?
   B. It's in the kitchen.

1. **Exercise 1:** Call on two students to present the dialog. Then do Choral Repetition and Choral Conversation practice.

2. **Exercise 2:** Same as above.

3. **Exercises 3–9:**

> **New Vocabulary**
>
> 3. newspaper
> 5. telephone book
> 9. cell phone

Either

Full-Class Practice: Call on a pair of students to do each exercise. Introduce the new vocabulary as you do exercises 3, 5, 9. (For more practice, call on other pairs of students, or do Choral Repetition or Choral Conversation.)

    or

Pair Practice: Introduce all the new vocabulary. Next, have students in pairs practice all the exercises. Then have pairs present the exercises to the class. (For more practice, do Choral Repetition or Choral Conversation.)

WORKBOOK

Pages 8–9

EXPANSION ACTIVITIES

1. Where Is Everybody?

You can review the structures on text page 12 by using your own visuals or *Side by Side* Picture Cards 18–26. Use the same method you used on text page 11. Again, use visuals to show the location of students in a house.

a. Ask questions about students in your class. For example:

> Teacher: Where's (Ramon)?
> Student: He's in the _____.

> Teacher: Where's (Barbara)?
> Student: She's in the _____.

b. Next, have students ask each other questions about the person holding a visual for location.

c. For practicing *it*, you can use objects in the classroom along with the visuals.

2. Who Is It?/What Is It?

a. Have students open their books to text page 12.

b. Make statements such as the following and have students identify who or what you're talking about. For example:

Teacher	Students
He's in the garage.	Kevin
She's in the yard.	Rosa
It's in the kitchen.	the cell phone
She's in the living room.	Peggy
He's in the bathroom.	Harry
She's in the dining room.	Ellen
He's in the bedroom.	Tim
It's in the bedroom.	the telephone book

3. What's the Subject?

a. Put the following on the board:

b. Make a statement using a pronoun and have students tell you the number that corresponds to the pronoun they hear. For example:

Teacher	Students
She's in the living room.	Two
He's in the kitchen.	One
They're in the yard.	Four
We're in the attic.	Four
It's in the dining room.	Three
He's in the bathroom.	One
She's in the basement.	Two
They're in the garage.	Four
It's in the kitchen.	Three

READING *The Students in My English Class*

FOCUS

- To Be + Location
- Subject Pronouns

NEW VOCABULARY

Athens	Korean
Chinese	many
class	Mexican
countries	Puerto Rican
different	Rome
English class	San Juan
friend	Seoul
friends	Shanghai
Greek	students
interesting	Tokyo
Italian	very
Japanese	yes

READING THE STORY

Optional: *Preview the story by having students talk about the story title and/or illustration. You may choose to introduce new vocabulary beforehand, or have students encounter the new vocabulary within the context of the reading.*

1. Have students read silently, or follow along silently as the story is read aloud by you, by one or more students, or on the audio program.

2. Ask students if they have any questions. Check understanding of vocabulary.

3. Check students' comprehension, using some or all of the following questions:

What nationality is Henry?
Where is he from?

What nationality is Linda?
Where is she from?

What nationality are Mr. and Mrs. Kim?
Where are they from?

What nationality is George?
Where is he from?

What nationality is Carla?
Where is she from?

What nationality are Mr. and Mrs. Sato?
Where are they from?

What nationality are Maria and I?
Where are we from?

✔ READING *CHECK-UP*

TRUE OR FALSE?

1. False   4. True

2. True   5. False

3. False   6. True

READING EXTENSION

Finish the Sentence!

a. Write the following list on the board:

Chinese	Athens
Greek	Mexico City
Japanese	San Juan
Korean	Seoul
Mexican	Shanghai
Puerto Rican	Tokyo

b. Begin statements such as the following and have students scan the reading on text page 13 to complete them. For example:

Teacher	Students
Henry is . . .	Chinese.
He's from . . .	Shanghai.
Carla is . . .	Italian.
She's from . . .	Rome.
George is from . . .	Athens.
He's . . .	Greek.
Mr. and Mrs. Kim are . . .	Korean.
They're from . . .	Seoul.
Maria is from . . .	Mexico City.
She's . . .	Mexican.
Mr. and Mrs. Sato are . . .	Japanese.
They're from . . .	Tokyo.

How About You?

If possible, bring a map of the world to class.

1. Have students introduce themselves to the class and indicate on the map which country they're from.

2. As a memory exercise, have pairs of students work together to list the names of their classmates and their countries of origin.

3. Have pairs of students read their lists aloud as the class listens and makes any corrections.

EXPANSION ACTIVITIES

1. Nationalities

   a. Divide the class into two teams.

   b. Put a map on the wall and point to various countries. Have the teams take turns identifying the countries and their nationalities.

2. Concentration

   a. Write 12 sentences based on the characters in the reading on text page 13. For example:

Henry is from Shanghai.	He's Chinese.
Linda is from San Juan.	She's Puerto Rican.

Mr. and Mrs. Kim are from Seoul.	They're Korean.
Mr. and Mrs. Sato are from Tokyo.	They're Japanese.
George is from Athens.	He's Greek.
Carla is from Rome.	She's Italian.

b. Shuffle the cards and place them face down in three rows of 4 each.

c. Divide the class into two teams. The object of the game is for students to find the matching cards. Both teams should be able to see all the cards, since *concentrating* on their location is an important part of playing the game.

d. A student from Team 1 turns over two cards. If they match, the student picks up the cards, that team gets a point, and the student takes another turn. If the cards don't match, the student turns them face down, and a member of Team 2 takes a turn.

e. The game continues until all the cards have been matched. The team with the most correct matches wins the game.

Variation: This game can also be played in groups or pairs.

How to Say It!

Greeting People: "How are you?" "Fine. And you?" is a common way of greeting people. In this context, "How are you?" is not really a request for information, but rather a way of extending a greeting. The response is usually so automatic that a person may answer "Fine" even when he or she isn't feeling well.

1. Have students look at the illustration.

2. Set the scene: "Two people are greeting each other."

3. With books closed, have students listen as you present the conversation or play the audio one or more times.

4. **Full-Class Repetition:** Model each line and have students repeat.

5. Have students open their books and look at the dialog. Ask students if they have any questions. Check understanding of new vocabulary: *How are you? Fine. And you? Fine, thanks.*

6. **Group Choral Repetition:** Divide the class in half. Model line A and have Group 1 repeat; model line B and have Group 2 repeat.

7. **Choral Conversation:** Groups 1 and 2 practice the dialog twice, without teacher model. First Group 1 is Speaker A and Group 2 is Speaker B; then reverse.

8. Call on one or two pairs of students to present the dialog.

9. Have students walk around the classroom, introducing themselves to each other.

10. Call on several pairs of students to present their conversations to the class.

Text Page 14: Where Are They?

FOCUS

- Review of *Where's? / Where are?*
- Introduction of *Where am I?*
- Places Around Town

GETTING READY

Practice the following places around town: *restaurant, bank, supermarket, library, park, movie theater, post office, zoo, hospital.* Use *Side by Side* Picture Cards 27–35, your own visuals or word cards, or the illustrations on text page 7 for *bank, supermarket, post office, restaurant,* and *library.* Point to one visual or word card at a time, say the word, and have students repeat.

SIDE BY SIDE EXERCISES

Examples

> 1. A. Where's Albert?
>   B. He's in the restaurant.
>
> 2. A. Where's Carmen?
>   B. She's in the bank.

1. **Exercise 1:** Check understanding of the word *restaurant.* Call on two students to present the dialog. Then do Choral Repetition and Choral Conversation practice.

2. **Exercise 2:** Check understanding of the word *bank.* Same as above.

3. **Exercises 3–9:**

New Vocabulary	
3. supermarket	7. post office
4. library	8. monkey
5. park	zoo
6. movie theater	9. hospital

Either

Full-Class Practice: Call on a pair of students to do each exercise. Introduce new vocabulary one exercise at a time. (For more practice, call on other pairs of students, or do Choral Repetition or Choral Conversation.)

or

Pair Practice: Introduce new vocabulary for all the exercises. Next have students practice all these exercises in pairs. Then have pairs present the exercises to the class. (For more practice, do Choral Repetition or Choral Conversation.)

4. **Exercises 10–12:**

In these exercises, students practice questions and answers using the patterns:

> *Where's _____? Where are _____?*
> *Where am I?*

Students can use any names and any places they wish. The object is to get students to practice the structures with vocabulary of their choice in order to talk about real-life places and people. Although only three exercises are indicated in the book, you may want your students to do more. Encourage students to use dictionaries to find new words they want to use.

This exercise can be done orally in class or for written homework. If you assign it for homework, do one example in class to make sure students understand what's expected. Have students present their questions and answers in class the next day.

WORKBOOK

Pages 10–11

EXPANSION ACTIVITIES

1. Where Is Everybody?

Use *Side by Side* Picture Cards 27–35, or your own visuals or word cards for the vocabulary on text page 14. Practice asking and answering questions about these locations as you did for places in the home, using all the forms of the verb *to be*. Pay special attention to the use of contractions and the pronunciation of the final *s* in *she's*, *he's*, and *it's*.

2. True or False?

a. Have students open their books to text page 14.

b. Make statements about the location of the characters on text page 14 and have students tell you "True" or "False." If the statement is false, have students correct it. For example:

> Teacher: Mary is in the supermarket.
> Student: True.
>
> Teacher: Albert is in the bank.
> Student: False. He's in the restaurant.

Variation: You can call on students to make true or false statements about the illustrations and have other students respond.

3. Remember the Words!

a. Tell students to spend one minute looking very carefully at text page 14.

b. Have students close their books and write down as many places around town from the page as they can remember.

c. Have students read their lists as a class, in pairs, or in small groups.

d. Call on students to come to the board and write their list of words. Have the class check the spelling of the words.

4. Drawing Game

a. Write the names of places around town on two sets of separate cards.

b. Place the two piles of cards on a table or desk in the front of the room. Also have a pad of paper and pencil next to each team's set of cards.

c. Divide the class into two teams. Have each team sit together in a different part of the room.

d. When you say "Go!," a person from each team comes to the front of his or her team, picks a card from the pile, and draws the place. The rest of the team then guesses what the place is.

e. When a team correctly guesses a place, another team member picks a card and draws the place written on that card.

f. Continue until each team has guessed all the places in their pile.

The team that guesses the places in the shortest time wins the game.

READING *All the Students in My English Class Are Absent Today*

FOCUS

- To Be + Location
- Subject Pronouns

NEW VOCABULARY

absent	even	our
all	everybody	social security office
at	except	teacher
bed	in bed	today
dentist	me	What a shame!

READING THE STORY

Optional: *Preview the story by having students talk about the story title and/or illustration. You may choose to introduce new vocabulary beforehand, or have students encounter the new vocabulary within the context of the reading.*

1. Have students read silently, or follow along silently as the story is read aloud by you, by one or more students, or on the audio program.

2. Ask students if they have any questions. Check understanding of vocabulary.

✓ READING *CHECK-UP*

WHAT'S THE ANSWER?

1. He's in the hospital.
2. She's at the dentist.
3. They're at the social security office.
4. He's home in bed.

READING EXTENSION

1. Write on the board:

> George
> Maria
> Mr. and Mrs. Sato
> the English teacher

2. Make a statement and have students tell you who is talking. For example:

Teacher	Students
I'm at the dentist.	Maria
I'm home in bed.	the English teacher
I'm in the hospital.	George
We're at the social security office.	Mr. and Mrs. Sato

How About You?

Have students answer the questions in pairs or as a class.

 LISTENING

WHAT'S THE WORD?

Listen and choose the correct answer.

1. Mr. and Mrs. Lee are in the park.
2. Jim is in the hospital.
3. She's in the living room.
4. He's in the kitchen.
5. They're in the basement.
6. We're in the yard.

Answers

1. b		4. a	
2. a		5. b	
3. b		6. a	

WHERE ARE THEY?

Listen and choose the correct place.

1. A. Where's David?
   B. He's in the living room.

2. A. Where's Patty?
   B. She's in the bedroom.

3. A. Where are Mr. and Mrs. Kim?
   B. They're in the yard.

4. A. Where are you?
   B. I'm in the bathroom.

5. A. Where's the telephone book?
   B. It's in the kitchen.

6. A. Where are you and John?
   B. We're in the basement.

Answers

1. a   4. a
2. b   5. a
3. b   6. b

PRONUNCIATION

 CHAPTER SUMMARY

> **Reduced *and*:** The word *and* is usually reduced to the sound /n/.

Focus on Listening

Practice the sentences in the left column. Say each sentence or play the audio one or more times. Have students listen carefully and repeat.

Focus on Pronunciation

Practice the sentences in the right column. Have students say each sentence and then listen carefully as you say it or play the audio.

If you wish, have students continue practicing the sentences to improve their pronunciation.

 JOURNAL

Have students draw a picture in their journals of their apartment or house, labeling the rooms. If you wish, you can then have pairs or small groups of students show each other their drawings and talk about them.

 Project

Have students work in pairs to draw a picture of the classroom and label all the objects they can identify. Encourage students also to draw other students in their pictures and to include their names.

WORKBOOK

Page 12

GRAMMAR

1. Divide the class into pairs or small groups.
2. Have students take turns forming sentences from the grammar boxes. Student A says a sentence, and Student B points to the words from each column that are in the sentence. Then have students switch: Student B says a sentence, and Student A points to the words.

KEY VOCABULARY

Have students ask you any questions about the meaning or pronunciation of the vocabulary. If students ask for the pronunciation, repeat after the student until the student is satisfied with his or her pronunciation.

EXPANSION ACTIVITIES

1. **Do You Remember the Words?**

   Check the students' retention of the vocabulary depicted on the opening page of Chapter 2 by doing the following activity:

   a. Have students open their books to page 7 and cover the list of vocabulary words.

   b. Either call out a number and have students tell you the word, or say a word and have students tell you the number.

   Variation: You can also do this activity as a game with competing teams.

2. **Student-Led Dictation**

   a. Tell each student to choose a word from the Key Vocabulary list on text page 16 and look at it very carefully.

   b. Have students take turns dictating their words to the class. Everybody writes down that student's word.

c. When the dictation is completed, call on different students to write each word on the board to check the spelling.

3. Beanbag Toss

a. Call out a topic from the chapter—for example: *Places Around Town.*

b. Have students toss a beanbag back and forth. The student to whom the beanbag is tossed must name a word in that category. For example:

   Student 1: bank
   Student 2: post office
   Student 3: restaurant

c. Continue until all the words in the category have been named.

END-OF-CHAPTER ACTIVITIES

1. Question the Answers!

a. Dictate answers such as the following to the class:

   She's in the kitchen.
   They're from Mexico City.
   It's on the desk.
   We're in English class.
   He's from Tokyo.

b. Have students write questions for which these answers would be possible. For example:

Answers	Questions
She's in the kitchen.	Where is she?
They're from Mexico City.	Where are they from?
It's on the desk.	Where's the book?

c. Have students compare their questions with each other.

Variation: Write the answer cards. Divide the class into groups and give each group a set of cards.

2. True or False Classroom Memory Game

a. Tell students to spend three minutes looking very carefully at the classroom on text page 8, then close their books.

b. Make statements about the location of classroom objects on text page 8 and have students tell you "True" or "False." If the statement is false, have students correct it. For example:

   Teacher: The map is on the wall.
   Student: True.

   Teacher: The pen is on the chair.
   Student: False. The pen is on the desk.

Variation: This can be done as a dictation with a *True* column and a *False* column. Tell students to write each statement in the appropriate column. At the end of the dictation, have students check the picture to see if they were correct.

WORKBOOK PAGE 6

A. PUZZLE

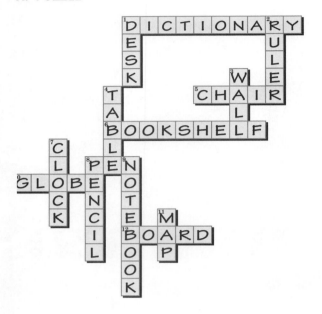

B. LISTENING

Listen and put a check under the correct picture.

1. A. Where's the book?
   B. It's on the desk.

2. A. Where's the dictionary?
   B. It's on the chair.

3. A. Where's the ruler?
   B. It's on the desk.

4. A. Where's the map?
   B. It's on the bulletin board.

5. A. Where's the globe?
   B. It's on the bookshelf.

6. A. Where's the computer?
   B. It's on the table.

Answers

1. ✔ ___   2. ___ ✔   3. ✔ ___

4. ✔ ___   5. ___ ✔   6. ✔ ___

WORKBOOK PAGE 7

C. WHAT ARE THEY SAYING?

1. Where, I'm, bedroom
2. are, They're, yard
3. are, We're, kitchen
4. Where, I'm, dining room
5. Where are, They're, basement
6. are, We're, attic
7. Where are, They're, living room
8. Where are, I'm, bathroom

WORKBOOK PAGE 8

D. WHAT ARE THEY SAYING?

1. Where's, He's, garage
2. Where's, She's, living room
3. Where's, It's, classroom

E. WHERE ARE THEY?

1. They   6. It
2. She   7. He
3. He   8. She
4. They   9. It
5. We

F. WHERE ARE THEY?

1. He's   5. It's
2. They're   6. She's
3. We're   7. You're
4. I'm   8. Where's

WORKBOOK PAGE 9

G. THE BAKER FAMILY

1. in the living room
2. in the bathroom
3. in the yard
4. in the kitchen
5. in the bedroom
6. in the garage

H. WHERE ARE THEY?

1. She's in the living room.
2. He's in the bathroom.
3. They're in the yard.
4. He's in the kitchen.
5. She's in the bedroom.
6. It's in the garage.

WORKBOOK PAGE 10

I. WHAT'S THE SIGN?

1. PARK, in the park
2. POST OFFICE, in the post office
3. RESTAURANT, in the restaurant
4. SUPERMARKET, in the supermarket
5. MOVIE THEATER, in the movie theater

6. HOSPITAL, in the hospital
7. ZOO, in the zoo
8. LIBRARY, in the library

WORKBOOK PAGE 11

J. LISTENING

Listen and write the number under the correct picture.

1. Our English teacher is in the hospital.
2. Mr. and Mrs. Sanchez are in the restaurant.
3. Mary is at the dentist.
4. Billy and Jimmy are in the park.
5. Mr. and Mrs. Lee are at the social security office.
6. James is home in bed.

Answers

5	1	3
2	4	6

K. LISTENING

Listen and circle the word you hear.

1. Where are you?
2. Ms. Jones is in the bank.
3. We're friends.
4. Hi. How are you?
5. Where's the newspaper?
6. He's from Korea.
7. The computer is on the table.
8. It's in the bathroom.

Answers

1. you
2. Ms.
3. We're
4. How
5. Where's
6. He's
7. on
8. It's

L. MATCHING

1. c
2. e
3. a
4. g
5. b
6. d
7. f

CHAPTER 3 OVERVIEW: Text Pages 17–24

3

GRAMMAR

PRESENT CONTINUOUS TENSE

	am	I	
What	is	he she it	doing?
	are	we you they	

(I am)	I'm	
(He is) (She is) (It is)	He's She's It's	eating.
(We are) (You are) (They are)	We're You're They're	

FUNCTIONS

ASKING FOR AND REPORTING INFORMATION

What are you doing?
 I'm *reading.*

What's *Mr. Jones* doing?
 He's reading the newspaper.

INQUIRING ABOUT LOCATION

Where's *Walter?*

GIVING LOCATION

He's in the *kitchen.*

CHECKING UNDERSTANDING

In the kitchen?

NEW VOCABULARY

Everyday Activities

cooking
drinking
eating
listening
planting
playing
reading
singing
sleeping
studying
swimming
teaching
watching

School

book
cafeteria
classroom
mathematics

People

family
Miss

Entertainment

music
radio
TV

Meals

breakfast
lunch
dinner

Beverages

lemonade
milk

Sports

baseball

Animals

birds
dog

Games

cards

Instruments

guitar
piano

Adjectives

beautiful
happy

Prepositions

with

Articles

a

Additional Words

beach
day
flowers
shining
sun

Text Page 17: Chapter Opening Page

VOCABULARY PREVIEW

You may want to introduce these words before beginning the chapter, or you may choose to wait until they first occur in a specific lesson. If you choose to introduce them at this point, here are some suggestions:

1. Have students look at the illustrations on text page 17 and identify the words they already know.

2. Present the vocabulary. Say each word and have the class repeat it chorally and individually. Check students' understanding and pronunciation of the words.

3. Practice the vocabulary as a class, in pairs, or in small groups. Have students cover the word list and look at the pictures. Practice the words in the following ways:

   • Say a word and have students tell the number of the illustration.

   • Give the number of an illustration and have students say the word.

FOCUS

- Present Continuous Tense
- Everyday Activities

CLOSE UP

RULE:	The present continuous tense describes an action in progress at the moment of speaking.
EXAMPLE:	What are you doing? *[right now]* I'm reading.
RULE:	The present continuous tense is formed with the present tense of *to be* plus the *-ing* form of the verb.
EXAMPLES:	I**'m** read**ing**. He**'s** cook**ing**. She**'s** watch**ing** TV. It**'s** sleep**ing**. We**'re** eat**ing**. They**'re** study**ing**.
RULE:	The word order of a question in the present continuous is: Question word + *to be* + subject + verb + *-ing*.
EXAMPLES:	**What + are + you + doing?** **What + is + Tom + doing?**

GETTING READY

Review contractions of the verb *to be*. Say the full forms and have students tell you the contracted forms.

Teacher	Students
I am	I'm
he is	he's
she is	she's
it is	it's
we are	we're
you are	you're
they are	they're

INTRODUCING THE MODELS

There are six model conversations. Introduce and practice each model before going on to the next. For each model:

1. Have students look at the model illustration.
2. Set the scene: "Neighbors are talking."
3. With books closed, have students listen as you present the model or play the audio one or more times.

4. **Full-Class Repetition:** Model each line and have students repeat.

5. Have students open their books and look at the dialog. Ask students if they have any questions. Check understanding of new vocabulary:

    1st model: *doing, reading*
    2nd model: *cooking*
    3rd model: *studying*
    4th model: *eating*
    5th model: *watching TV*
    6th model: *sleeping*

6. **Group Choral Repetition:** Divide the class in half. Model line A and have Group 1 repeat; model line B and have Group 2 repeat.

7. **Choral Conversation:** Groups 1 and 2 practice the dialog twice, without teacher model. First, Group 1 is Speaker A and Group 2 is Speaker B; then reverse.

8. Call on one or two pairs of students to present the dialog.

    (For additional practice, do Choral Conversation in small groups or by rows.)

9. After all of the models have been introduced, go back to the first and practice it again by cuing other verbs. For example:

    Teacher cue: cooking
    Teacher: What are you doing?
    Student: I'm cooking.

    Teacher cue: eating
    Teacher: What are you doing?
    Student: I'm eating.

Continue this with the next four models to practice *we're, they're, he's, she's.*

Pronunciation Note

A pronunciation focus of Chapter 3 is **Reduced *What are*** (text page 24). You may wish to model this pronunciation at this point and encourage students to incorporate it into their language practice.

What are you doing?

What are Mary and Fred doing?

SIDE BY SIDE EXERCISES

Examples

> 1. A. What are you doing?
>   B. I'm reading the newspaper.
> 2. A. What are Mr. and Mrs. Lane doing?
>   B. They're cooking dinner.

1. **Exercise 1:** Call on two students to present the dialog. Then do Choral Repetition and Choral Conversation practice.

2. **Exercise 2:** Introduce the new word *dinner*. Same as above.

3. **Exercises 3–7:**

    > **New Vocabulary**
    > 7. playing the piano

    ### *Culture Note*

    Breakfast, lunch, and dinner: In general, people in the United States eat three meals a day: *breakfast* (before work or school), *lunch* (around noon), and *dinner* (in the early evening).

    Either

    Full-Class Practice: Call on a pair of students to do each exercise. Check understanding of *playing the piano* before doing exercise 7. (For more practice, call on other pairs of students, or do Choral Repetition or Choral Conversation.)

    or

    Pair Practice: Check understanding of vocabulary. Next have students practice all of the exercises in pairs. Then have pairs present the exercises to the class. (For more practice, do Choral Repetition or Choral Conversation.)

4. **Exercise 8:** In this exercise, the window is *blank*. Ask students to imagine they are living in the building, and have them answer using any vocabulary they wish. Call on several pairs of students to practice this exercise.

EXPANSION ACTIVITIES

1. Beanbag Toss

Have students toss a beanbag back and forth. The student to whom the beanbag is tossed says an activity with *I'm*. For example:

Student 1: I'm reading.
Student 2: I'm cooking.
Student 3: I'm playing the piano.

2. Practice with Realia

Use real objects to represent ongoing activities that students can talk about. Some suggested objects are:

- a pot and spoon for *cooking*
- a newspaper for *reading*
- a textbook for *studying*
- an eating utensil (such as a fork or chopsticks) for *eating*

Use one object at a time to practice *What _____ doing?*, using all the pronouns. For example:

a. Hold a pot and spoon and say: "I'm cooking." Have students repeat.

b. Give the objects to Student A and ask: "What are you doing?" Student A answers: "I'm cooking."

c. Ask another student: "What's (*Student A*) doing?" ("He's/She's cooking.") Ask several other students. Give the objects to different students in order to practice *he's* and *she's*.

d. Practice *we're*. Give objects to two students. Ask each one: "What are you and _____ doing?" ("We're cooking.") Practice *we're* with several pairs of students.

e. Practice *they're*. Give the objects to two students. Ask another student: "What are they doing?" Give the visual to several pairs of students. Call on other pairs of students to ask and answer "What are they doing?"

f. Practice *you're*. Hold an object and ask: "What am I doing?"

Practice this way with other objects. Be sure to have students practice asking as well as answering.

3. Practice with Visuals

Use your own visuals, word cards, or *Side by Side Picture Cards 36–42* to practice the present continuous tense. Use the same method as in Activity 2 above, but use visuals in place of objects.

4. Can You Hear the Difference?

a. Write on the board

①	②
He's cooking.	She's cooking.
We're sleeping.	They're sleeping.
We're studying.	You're studying.
I'm reading.	I'm eating.

(continued)

b. Choose a sentence randomly from one of the two columns and say it to the class. Have the class listen and identify the column by saying "One" or "Two." For example:

Teacher	Students
He's cooking.	One
She's cooking.	Two
They're sleeping.	Two
We're sleeping.	One

c. Have students continue the activity in pairs. One student says a sentence, and the other identifies the column. Then have them reverse roles.

d. Write similar sentences on the board and continue the practice.

5. Remember the Actions!

a. Tell students to spend a few minutes looking very carefully at the illustrations on text pages 18 and 19.

b. Have students close their books and write down as many actions depicted in the illustrations as they can remember—for example: *reading, eating, cooking, watching TV.*

c. Have students read their lists as a class, in pairs, or in small groups.

d. Call on students to come to the board and write their list of words. Have the class check the spelling of the words.

Text Pages 20–21: What's Everybody Doing?

FOCUS

- Review and Contrast of *Where _____?* and *What _____ doing?*
- Everyday Activities

GETTING READY

Review vocabulary for places in the home and community. Use *Side by Side* Picture Cards 18–35, your own visuals, or the illustrations on text pages 10 and 14. Indicate a place and have students say the name.

INTRODUCING THE MODEL

1. Have students look at the model illustration.
2. Set the scene: "Two people are talking about Walter."
3. Present the model.
4. Full-Class Repetition.
5. Ask students if they have any questions. Check understanding of new vocabulary: *breakfast.*
6. Group Choral Repetition.
7. Choral Conversation.
8. Call on one or two pairs of students to present the dialog.

   (For additional practice, do Choral Conversation in small groups or by rows.)

Pronunciation Note

The pronunciation focus of Chapter 3 is **Reduced *What are* and *Where are*** (text page 24). You may wish to model this pronunciation at this point and encourage students to incorporate it into their language practice.

What are you doing?

Where are Mr. and Mrs. Clark?

Where are Gary and Jane?

SIDE BY SIDE EXERCISES

Examples

1. A. Where's Karen?
   B. She's in the park.
   A. What's she doing?
   B. She's eating lunch.
2. A. Where are Mr. and Mrs. Clark?
   B. They're in the dining room.
   A. What are they doing?
   B. They're eating dinner.

1. **Exercise 1:** Introduce the new word *lunch.* Call on two students to present the dialog. Then do Choral Repetition and Choral Conversation practice.

2. **Exercise 2:** Same as above.

3. **Exercises 3–11:**

New Vocabulary	
3. guitar	8. Ms.
4. cards	classroom
5. baseball	teaching
6. Miss	mathematics
cafeteria	9. singing
drinking	11. listening to
milk	music

Culture Note

Baseball (Exercise 5): Along with football, baseball is a very popular spectator sport in the United States.

Either

Full-Class Practice: Call on a pair of students to do each exercise. Introduce the new vocabulary one exercise at a time. (For more practice, call on other pairs of students, or do Choral Repetition or Choral Conversation.)

   or

Pair Practice: Introduce all the new vocabulary. Next have students practice all of the exercises in pairs. Then have pairs present the exercises to the class. (For more practice, do Choral Repetition or Choral Conversation.)

4. **Exercise 12:** Have students use the model as a guide to create their own conversations, using vocabulary of their choice. (They can use any names, places, and activities they wish.) Encourage students to use dictionaries to find new words they want to use. This exercise can be done orally in class or for written homework. If you assign it for homework, do one example in class to make sure students understand what's expected. Have students present their conversations in class the next day.

WORKBOOK

Pages 14–17

EXPANSION ACTIVITIES

1. Practice with Visuals or Realia

   Review *Where _____ ?* and *What _____ doing?* by using a combination of visuals and realia as cues for oral practice. Use two cues at a time: one represents a location, such as *park, kitchen,* or *library.* The other represents an ongoing activity, such as *eating* or *studying English.*

   - For locations, use your own visuals, word cards, or *Side by Side* Picture Cards 18–35.

   - For activities, use your own visuals, word cards, or *Side by Side* Picture Cards 36–49, or objects such as:
     - a few cards—for *playing cards*
     - an eating implement, such as a knife or chopsticks—for *eating lunch*
     - a cup—for *drinking milk*
     - a book—for *studying English*
     - a ball—for *playing baseball*

   a. Hold up a cue for *park* and *eating*; say: "I'm in the park. I'm eating lunch." Give these cues to a student and ask: "Where are you?" "What are you doing?"

   b. Use these two cues (either visuals or a combination of visuals and objects) to practice all the other pronouns:

   Where am I? What am I doing?
   Where is _____ ? What is he/she doing?
   Where are _____ and _____ ?
       What are they doing?
   Where are you and _____ ? What are you doing?

   c. As you practice each pronoun, call on pairs of students to ask and answer whenever possible.

2. Picture Card Game

   Use *Side by Side* Picture Cards for locations and ongoing activities.

   a. Place the cards in two separate piles, face down.

   b. Have two students come to the front of the room. Student A takes the top card from each pile. Student B asks: "Where are you?" Student A answers based on the *location* card he or she has taken. Student B then asks: "What are you doing?" Student A answers based on his or her *activity* card.

   c. Continue the activity by calling on additional pairs of students.

3. Guess Who!

Have students open their books to text pages 20–21. For listening practice, make statements about the people in the exercises. Have students respond by telling you who you're talking about. For example:

Teacher	Students
I'm in the hospital.	Martha
I'm in the classroom.	Ms. Johnson
We're playing baseball.	Gary and Jane
I'm singing.	Marvin
We're eating dinner.	Mr. and Mrs. Clark
I'm in the park.	Karen
I'm drinking milk.	Miss Baker

4. Associations

a. Divide the class into pairs or small groups.

b. Call out a location and tell students to write down all the words they associate with that location. For example:

kitchen:	cooking, eating, breakfast, lunch, dinner
park:	listening to music, baseball, friends
living room:	listening to music, playing cards, watching TV

c. Have a student from each pair or group come to the board and write their words.

Variation: Do the activity as a game with competing teams. The team with the most number of associations is the winner.

5. Question the Answers!

a. Dictate answers such as the following to the class:

I'm in the kitchen.
He's singing.
They're eating dinner.
We're in the park.
I'm cooking.
She's in the hospital.
They're studying.
He's playing the guitar.

b. Have students write questions for which these answers would be correct. For example:

Answers	Questions
I'm in the kitchen.	Where are you?
He's singing.	What's he doing?
They're eating dinner.	What are they doing?

c. Have students compare their questions with each other.

Variation: Write the answers on cards. Divide the class into groups and give each group a set of cards.

6. Match the Sentences

a. Make a set of split sentence cards such as the following:

She's drinking	milk.
He's cooking	dinner.
They're playing	cards.
I'm playing the	guitar.
She's listening to	music.
We're watching	TV.
They're studying	English.

b. Distribute a card to each student.

c. Have students memorize the sentence portion on their cards, then walk around the room, trying to find their corresponding match.

(continued)

d. Then have pairs of students say their completed sentences aloud to the class.

7. **Match the Sentences**

a. Make the following set of matching cards:

I'm reading in the living room.	I'm reading in the living room.
I'm reading in the dining room.	I'm reading in the dining room.
I'm reading in the yard.	I'm reading in the yard.
I'm eating in the kitchen.	I'm eating in the kitchen.
I'm eating in the dining room.	I'm eating in the dining room.
I'm studying in the library.	I'm studying in the library.

I'm studying in the kitchen.	I'm studying in the kitchen.
I'm studying in the living room.	I'm studying in the living room.
I'm watching TV in the kitchen.	I'm watching TV in the kitchen.
I'm watching TV in the bedroom.	I'm watching TV in the bedroom.
I'm watching TV in the living room.	I'm watching TV in the living room.

b. Distribute a card to each student.

c. Have students memorize the sentence on their cards, and then have students walk around the room, saying their sentence until they find their match.

d. Then have pairs of students say their matched sentences aloud to the class.

How to Say It!

Checking Understanding: One way to check your understanding of what the other person said is to repeat the information with a question intonation. For example: *In the kitchen? Eating breakfast?*

1. Set the scene: "Someone is looking for Walter."

2. With books closed, have students listen as you present the conversation or play the audio one or more times.

3. Full-Class Repetition.

4. Have students open their books and look at the dialog. Ask students if they have any questions.

5. Group Choral Repetition.

6. Choral Conversation.

7. Call on one or two pairs of students to present the dialog.

8. Have students ask you questions about the characters on text pages 20 and 21 and then check for understanding. For example:

   Student: Where's Karen?
   Teacher: She's in the park.
   Student: In the park?
   Teacher: Yes.

9. Have students ask and answer similar questions about the characters on text pages 20 and 21.

10. Call on several pairs of students to present their conversations to the class.

Action Game!

1. Write down on cards the activities from text pages 18–21 or use *Side by Side* Picture Cards 36–49.

2. Have students take turns picking a card from the pile and pantomiming the action on the card.

3. The class must guess what the person is doing.

Variation: This can be done as a game with competing teams.

READING *In the Park /
At Home in the Yard*

FOCUS

- Present Continuous Tense
- Everyday Activities

NEW VOCABULARY

Story 1		Story 2
a	family	book
beautiful	happy	flowers
birds	radio	lemonade
day	shining	planting
dog	sun	with

READING THE STORIES

*Optional: Preview the stories by having
students talk about the story titles and/or
illustrations. You may choose to introduce new
vocabulary beforehand, or have students
encounter the new vocabulary within the context
of the reading.*

1. Have students read the story silently, or
   follow along silently as the story is read
   aloud by you, by one or more students, or on
   the audio program.

2. Ask students if they have any questions.
   Check understanding of vocabulary.

3. Check students' comprehension, using some
   or all of the following questions:

   Story 1
   Where's the Jones family today?
   What's Mr. Jones doing?
   What's Mrs. Jones doing?
   What are Sally and Patty Jones doing?
   What's Tommy Jones doing?

Story 2
Where's the Chen family today?
What's Mr. Chen doing?
What's Mrs. Chen doing?
What are Emily and Jason Chen doing?
What's Jennifer Chen doing?

✔READING *CHECK-UP*

TRUE OR FALSE?

1. False   4. False
2. True   5. False
3. True   6. True

Q & A

1. Call on a pair of students to present the
   model.

2. Have students work in pairs to create new
   dialogs.

3. Call on pairs to present their new dialogs to
   the class.

READING EXTENSION

Who's Talking?

Make statements such as the following, and
have students scan the stories and tell who is
talking.

Teacher	Students
I'm reading the newspaper.	Mr. Jones
I'm drinking lemonade and reading a book.	Mrs. Chen
We're studying.	Sally and Patty Jones
I'm planting flowers.	Mr. Chen
I'm playing the guitar.	Tommy Jones
We're playing with the dog.	Emily and Jason Chen
I'm listening to the radio.	Mrs. Jones
I'm sleeping.	Jennifer Chen
We're singing.	the birds

LISTENING

Listen and choose the correct answer.

1. What are you doing?
2. What's Mr. Carter doing?
3. What's Ms. Miller doing?
4. What are Jim and Jane doing?
5. What are you and Peter doing?
6. What am I doing?

Answers

1.	b	**4.**	b
2.	a	**5.**	a
3.	b	**6.**	a

IN YOUR OWN WORDS

1. Make sure students understand the instructions.

2. Have students do the activity as written homework, using a dictionary for any new words they wish to use.

3. Have students present and discuss what they have written, in pairs or as a class.

PRONUNCIATION

Reduced *What are* & *Where are*: In spoken English, the question words *what* and *where* are contracted with the *are* form of the verb *to be*. These contracted pronunciations do not occur in writing.

Focus on Listening

Practice the sentences in the left column. Say each sentence or play the audio one or more times. Have students listen carefully and repeat.

Focus on Pronunciation

Practice the sentences in the right column. Have students say each sentence and then listen carefully as you say it or play the audio.

If you wish, have students continue practicing the sentences to improve their pronunciation.

 JOURNAL

Have students write their journal entries at home or in class. Encourage students to use dictionaries to help them express their thoughts. Students can share their written work with each other if appropriate. Have students discuss what they have written as a class, in pairs, or in small groups.

WORKBOOK

Pages 18–19

Check-Up Test: Page 20

 CHAPTER SUMMARY

GRAMMAR

1. Divide the class into pairs or small groups.
2. Have students take turns forming sentences from the grammar boxes. Student A says a sentence, and Student B points to the words from each column that are in the sentence. Then have students switch: Student B says a sentence, and Student A points to the words.

KEY VOCABULARY

Have students ask you any questions about the meaning or pronunciation of the vocabulary. If students ask for the pronunciation, repeat after the student until the student is satisfied with his or her pronunciation.

EXPANSION ACTIVITIES

1. **Vocabulary Check**

   Check the students' retention of the vocabulary depicted on the opening page of Chapter 3 by doing the following activity:

   a. Have students open their books to page 17 and cover the list of vocabulary words.

   b. Either call out a number and have students tell you the word, or say a word and have students tell you the number.

   Variation: You can also do this activity as a game with competing teams.

2. **Student-Led Dictation**

   a. Tell each student to choose a word or phrase from the Key Vocabulary list on text page 24 and look at it very carefully.

   b. Have students take turns dictating their words to the class. Everybody writes down that student's word.

c. When the dictation is completed, call on different students to write each word on the board to check the spelling.

3. Beanbag Toss

a. Have students toss a beanbag back and forth. The student to whom the beanbag is tossed must name an everyday activity. For example:

    Student 1: cooking dinner
    Student 2: studying English
    Student 3: watching TV

b. Continue until all the words have been named.

END-OF-CHAPTER ACTIVITIES

1. True or False Memory Game

a. Tell students to spend three minutes looking very carefully at the illustration on text page 23. Then have students close their books.

b. Make statements about the characters in the illustration on text page 23 and have students tell you "True" or "False." If the statement is false, have students correct it. For example:

    Teacher: Mr. Martinez is cooking.
    Student: True.

    Teacher: Jimmy Martinez is reading.
    Student: False. He's listening to music.

Variation: This can be done as a dictation with a *True* column and a *False* column. Tell students to write each statement in the appropriate column. At the end of the dictation, have students check the picture to see if they were correct.

2. Scrambled Sentences

a. Divide the class into teams.

b. One sentence at a time, write individual sentences or questions out of order on the board. For example:

| Mary | Fred | are | What | and |
| doing |
dinner	They're	in	eating	dining
the	room
guitar	playing	the	living	the
room	She's	in

c. The first person to raise his or her hand, come to the board, and write the sentence in the correct order earns a point for that team.

d. The team with the most points wins the *scrambled sentence* game.

Variation: Write the words to several sentences on separate cards. Divide the class into small groups, and have students work together to put the sentences into correct order.

3. Change the Sentence!

a. Write a sentence on the board, underlining and numbering portions of the sentence. For example:

(continued)

1	2	3
I'm	playing	cards.

b. Explain that when you say a number, the first student makes a change in that part of the sentence. Write the change on the board. For example:

Teacher: Three.
Student 1: I'm playing baseball. [*Teacher erases "cards" and writes in "baseball".*]

c. The second student keeps the first student's sentence, but changes it based on the next number you say. For example:

Teacher: Two.
Student 2: I'm watching baseball.

d. Continue this way with other students in the class. For example:

Teacher: One.
Student 3: She's watching baseball.

Teacher: Three
Student 4: She's watching TV.

4. Information Gap: Full House

a. Tell students that your house is full of friends. Make up a map of your house with the names of friends placed in each room, but divide the information between two different maps. For example:

House Map A:

Living room Mr. and Mrs. Clark	Kitchen	Bedroom Irene
Yard		Dining room Rita
Library Judy and Walter	Basement	Bathroom

Questions to Ask
Where's Fred?
Where are Carol and Ken?
Where are Gary and Jane?
Where's Marvin?

House Map B:

Living room	Kitchen Fred	Bedroom
Yard Carol and Ken		Dining room
Library	Basement Gary and Jane	Bathroom Marvin

Questions to Ask
Where are Mr. and Mrs. Clark?
Where's Irene?
Where are Judy and Walter?
Where's Rita?

b. Divide the class into pairs. Give each member of the pair a different map. Have students ask each other their questions and fill in their house maps with the correct names. Encourage them to check for understanding. For example:

Student A: Where's Fred?
Student B: He's in the kitchen.
Student A: In the kitchen?
Student B: Yes.

[*Student A writes the information in House Map A*]

c. The pairs continue until each has a filled map.

d. Have students look at their partners' maps to make sure that they have written the information correctly.

WORKBOOK ANSWER KEY AND LISTENING SCRIPTS

WORKBOOK PAGE 13

A. WHAT ARE THEY SAYING?

1. What, studying
2. doing, She's eating
3. What's, He's sleeping
4. What are, They're reading
5. What are, We're watching
6. What are, doing, I'm playing
7. What's, He's cooking

WORKBOOK PAGE 14

B. WHAT ARE THEY DOING?

1. eating	2. drinking
3. studying	4. reading
5. sleeping	6. teaching
7. listening	8. watching
9. cooking	10. singing
11. playing	

WORKBOOK PAGE 15

C. LISTENING

Listen and put a check under the correct picture.

1. He's eating lunch.
2. We're drinking milk.
3. I'm playing the guitar.
4. She's playing the piano.
5. We're cooking breakfast.
6. It's in the classroom.
7. I'm reading.
8. He's watching TV.
9. She's studying mathematics.
10. They're playing baseball in the yard.

Answers

1. ✔ __	2. __ ✔
3. __ ✔	4. __ ✔
5. __ ✔	6. ✔ __
7. ✔ __	8. ✔ __
9. __ ✔	10. __ ✔

WORKBOOK PAGE 17

E. WHAT'S THE QUESTION?

1. Where are you?
2. What's he doing?
3. Where are they?
4. What are you doing?
5. Where is he?

6. What's she doing?
7. Where is she?
8. Where are you?
9. What's he doing?
10. Where is it?
11. What are they doing?
12. Where are you?

WORKBOOK PAGE 20

CHECK-UP TEST: Chapters 1–3

A. *(Answers will vary.)*

B.

1. lunch	4. mathematics
2. What's	5. meet
3. singing	6. pencil

C.

1. in	6. Where's
2. reading	7. doing
3. He's	8. It's
4. watching	9. What
5. We're	10. and

D.

Listen and write the letter or number you hear.

Ex. A. What's your first name?
   B. Mark.
   A. How do you spell that?
   B. M-A-R-K.

1. A. What's your last name?
   B. Carter.
   A. How do you spell that?
   B. C-A-R-T-E-R.

2. A. What's your telephone number?
   B. My telephone number is 354-9812.

3. A. What's your fax number?
   B. My fax number is 890-7462.

4. A. What's your first name?
   B. Julie.
   A. How do you spell that?
   B. J-U-L-I-E.

5. A. What's your telephone number?
   B. My telephone number is 672-3059.

6. A. What's your license number?
   B. My license number is 5170349.

Answers

1. T	4. J
2. 8	5. 7
3. 6	6. 0

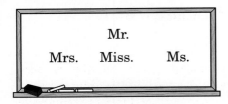

FACT FILE

TITLES

1. Write on the board:

Mr.

Mrs.   Miss.   Ms.

2. Explain the following:

    Mr. is for a man.
    Mrs. is for a married woman.
    Miss is for a single woman.
    Ms. is for a single woman or a married woman.

3. Have students look in Chapter 2 and Chapter 3 for examples of these titles.

NICKNAMES

1. Explain that nicknames are often used among friends and family members.

2. Ask students if they have nicknames. Have them tell their nicknames to the class.

3. For additional practice, divide the class into pairs or small groups and do either or both of the following:

    • Give full names and have students guess what the nicknames are.

    • Give nicknames and have students guess what the full names are.

 ## GLOBAL EXCHANGE

1. Set the scene: "Two people, Sung Hee and Daniel, are writing to each other on the Internet. They're each looking for a keypal."

2. Have students read silently or follow along silently as the messages are read aloud by you, by one or more students, or on the audio program.

3. Ask students if they have any questions. Check understanding of vocabulary.

also	right now
keypal	tell me
looking for	

Culture Note

Many people use the Internet to communicate with each other in "chat rooms" or "exchange" sites.

4. Suggestions for additional practice:

    • Divide the class into pairs. Have one member of the pair be *Sung Hee*, and the other *Daniel*. Have them continue the correspondence: Sung Hee writes to Daniel, and he responds to her.

    • Have students correspond with a keypal on the Internet and then share their experience with the class.

 ## BUILD YOUR VOCABULARY!
Playing Instruments, Sports, and Games

violin	basketball
clarinet	chess
trumpet	checkers
soccer	tic tac toe
tennis	

1. Have students look at the illustrations and identify any words they already know.

2. Present the vocabulary. Say each word and have the class repeat it chorally and individually. Check students' understanding and pronunciation of the words.

EXPANSION ACTIVITIES

1. Category Dictation

a. Have students make three columns on a piece of paper:

Instruments   Sports   Games

b. Dictate words and have students write them under the appropriate column. For example:

Instruments   Sports   Games
                soccer

2. Word Search

a. Have students make three columns on a piece of paper:

Instruments   Sports   Games

b. Have students look in Chapter 3 for expressions with *playing*, and tell them to write each expression under the appropriate column. For example:

Instruments   Sports   Games
playing the piano

c. Have students compare their lists.

3. Miming

a. Write each *playing* expression on a separate card.

b. Have students take turns picking a card from the pile and pantomiming the expression on the card.

c. The class then guesses what the student is doing. For example:

You're playing the violin.
You're playing soccer.
You're playing tic tac toe.

AROUND THE WORLD
Greetings

1. Have students read silently or follow along silently as the text is read aloud by you, by one or more students, or on the audio program. Check understanding of vocabulary:

all around	hugging
bowing	kissing
greeting	shaking hands

2. Have students first work in pairs or small groups, reacting to the photographs and responding to the question. Then have students tell the class what they talked about.

EXPANSION ACTIVITY

Cultural Differences

1. Have students present introductions to the class in their own language. If possible, have students present introductions between men and men, women and women, and men and women.

2. As the class observes the introductions, have them note the following:

Are they smiling?
Are they shaking hands or bowing?
Are they hugging?
Are they kissing?
Are they happy?

3. Have the class discuss their observations.

LISTENING *You Have Seven Messages!*

Before students listen to the audio, introduce the new vocabulary.

1. Write on the board:

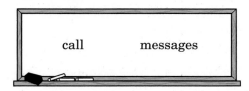

call   messages

2. Introduce *call* by miming the action. Introduce *message* by pointing to the illustration of the answering machine. Have students practice saying the words.

Language Note

In English there are several informal ways to address one's mother and father. *Mom* and *Dad* are the most common forms in the United States.

LISTENING SCRIPT

Listen to the messages on Bob's machine. Match the messages.

You have seven messages.

Message Number One: "Hello. I'm calling for Robert White. This is Henry Drake. Mr. White, please call me at 427-9168. That's 427-9168. Thank you." [*beep*]

Message Number Two: "Hi, Bob! It's Patty. How are you? Call me!" [*beep*]

Message Number Three: "Bob? Hi. This is Kevin Carter from your guitar class. My phone number is 298-4577." [*beep*]

Message Number Four: "Mr. White? This is Linda Lee, from the social security office. Please call me. My telephone number is 969-0159." [*beep*]

Message Number Five: "Hello, Bob? This is Jim. I'm in the park. We're playing baseball. Call me, okay? My cell phone number is 682-4630." [*beep*]

Message Number Six: "Hello. Mr. White? This is Mrs. Lane on River Street. Your dog is in my yard. Call me at 731-0248." [*beep*]

Message Number Seven: "Hello, Bob. This is Dad. I'm at home. I'm reading the newspaper. Mom is planting flowers in the yard. It's a beautiful day. Where are you? What are you doing? Call us." [*beep*]

Answers

1.	c	**5.**	f
2.	e	**6.**	a
3.	g	**7.**	d
4.	b		

 WHAT ARE THEY SAYING?

Have students talk about the people and the situation, and then create role plays based on the scene. Students may refer back to previous lessons as a resource, but they should not simply reuse specific conversations.

Note: You may want to assign this exercise as written homework, having students prepare their role plays, practice them the next day with other students, and then present them to the class.

Teacher's Notes

GRAMMAR

TO BE: SHORT ANSWERS

Yes,	I	am.
	he she it	is.
	we you they	are.

POSSESSIVE ADJECTIVES

I'm He's She's It's We're You're They're	cleaning	my his her its our your their	room.

FUNCTIONS

GREETING PEOPLE

Hi!

ASKING FOR AND REPORTING INFORMATION

What are you doing?
   I'm *fixing my sink*.

Are you busy?
   Yes, I am. I'm *washing my hair*.

INQUIRING ABOUT LOCATION

Where's *Mr. Molina*?

GIVING LOCATION

He's in the *park*.

ATTRACTING ATTENTION

Jane?

NEW VOCABULARY

Everyday Activities

brushing *my* teeth
cleaning
doing *my* exercises
doing *my* homework
feeding
fixing
painting
washing

School

homework

Home

apartment
room
sink
windows

Around Town

health club
laundromat
parking lot

The Body

hair
teeth

People

children
neighbors

Animals

cat

Adjectives

busy

Adverbs

too

Possessive Adjectives

my
his
her
its
our
your
their

Additional Nouns

bicycle
clothes

EXPRESSIONS

of course

Text Page 27: Chapter Opening Page

Vocabulary Preview

You may want to introduce these words before beginning the chapter, or you may choose to wait until they first occur in a specific lesson. If you choose to introduce them at this point, here are some suggestions:

1. Have students look at the illustrations on text page 27 and identify the words they already know.

2. Present the vocabulary. Say each word and have the class repeat it chorally and individually. Check students' understanding and pronunciation of the words.

3. Practice the vocabulary as a class, in pairs, or in small groups. Have students cover the word list and look at the pictures. Practice the words in the following ways:

   • Say a word and have students tell the number of the illustration.

   • Give the number of an illustration and have students say the word.

Text Page 28: I'm Fixing My Sink

FOCUS

- Possessive Adjectives
- Present Continuous Tense
- Everyday Activities

CLOSE UP

RULE:	Possessive adjectives indicate possession. They are always used with nouns.
EXAMPLES:	**my** sink **our** apartment **his** car **their** homework **her** room

RULE:	Possessive adjectives reflect the possessor and not the noun possessed.
EXAMPLES:	She's calling **her** friend. He's calling **his** friend.

GETTING READY

1. Read the forms in the grammar box at the top of the page. Have students repeat after you.

2. Demonstrate the idea of possession.

   a. Point to your book and say: "my book." Point to a male student's book and say: "his book." Point to a female student's book and say: "her book." Continue with *your*, *our*, and *their*.

   b. Call on individual students to make statements about other objects, such as a pen, a pencil, or a notebook, using different possessive adjectives.

INTRODUCING THE MODELS

There are five model conversations. Introduce and practice each model before going on to the next. For each model:

1. Have students look at the model illustration.

2. Set the scene: "People are talking on the telephone."

3. Present the model.

4. Full-Class Repetition.

5. Ask students if they have any questions. Check understanding of new vocabulary:

   1st model: *Hi!, fixing, my, sink*
   2nd model: *his*
   3rd model: *cleaning, her, room*
   4th model: *our, apartment*
   5th model: *children, doing, their, homework*

6. Group Choral Repetition.

7. Choral Conversation.

8. Call on one or two pairs of students to present the dialog.

   (For additional practice, do Choral Conversation in small groups or by rows.)

Language Notes

Some students will have difficulty distinguishing *his* from *he's*.

The homonyms *they're* and *their* are often confused in writing.

Pronunciation Note

The pronunciation focus of Chapter 4 is **Deleted *h*** (text page 34). You may wish to model this pronunciation at this point and encourage students to incorporate it into their language practice.

He's fixing his car.

She's cleaning her room.

WORKBOOK

Page 21

EXPANSION ACTIVITIES

1. Clap and Listen

Present the conversations again. This time clap your hands instead of saying the possessive adjectives, and have students fill in the missing words. For example:

Teacher	Students
What are you doing?	
I'm fixing [clap] sink.	my
What's Bob doing?	
He's fixing [clap] car.	his

Continue with the remaining conversations.

2. Practice with Students' Names

Have pairs of students practice the model conversations again. This time have them pretend to call other students on the telephone, using names of people in the class in place of those in the book.

3. Practice with Visuals

Use your own visuals or *Side by Side* Picture Cards 53–55 to practice *What _____ doing?* and answers with possessive adjectives.

a. Hold up a visual and say: "I'm fixing my (*sink/car/TV*)." Give the visual to a student and ask: "What are you doing?"

b. Ask a neighboring student: "What's *(he/she)* doing?"

c. Hand another visual to a pair of students and ask: "What are you doing?"

d. Ask a neighboring student: "What are they doing?"

e. Continue until all the students have had a chance to respond.

4. Practice with Students' Belongings

a. Collect personal items from students (such as a pen, a pencil, a book, a notebook, homework). If necessary, teach new vocabulary. Hold up the item for the class to see and have students identify their particular belongings.

Teacher: (holding up student's pen)
Student: *my* pen

Teacher: (holding up student's book)
Student: *my* book

b. Have students identify the items again, this time using *his, her, our, their*.

Teacher: (holding up Student A's pen)
Student B: *(his/her)* pen

Teacher: (holding up Student A's book)
Student B: *(his/her)* book

Teacher: (holding up several books)
Student: *(their/our)* books

5. Student-Led Dictation

a. Tell each student to choose a sentence from text page 28 and look at it very carefully.

b. Have students take turns dictating their sentences to the class. Everybody writes down that student's sentence.

c. When the dictation is completed, call on different students to write each sentence on the board to check the spelling.

6. Can You Hear the Difference?

a. Write on the board:

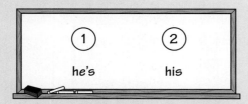

b. Choose one of the words and say it to the class. Have the class listen and identify the column.

c. Have students continue the activity in pairs. One student pronounces one of the words, and the other identifies the column. Then have students reverse roles.

7. Sentences Alive!

a. Make up several sentences based on this lesson. For example:

> She's fixing her sink.
> I'm cleaning my bedroom.
> They're cleaning their apartment.
> We're doing our homework in the dining room.
> He's fixing his car in the garage.

b. Write the words to each of these sentences on separate cards.

c. One sentence at a time, distribute the cards randomly to students in the class.

d. Have students decide on the correct word order of the sentence and then come to the front of the room. Have students make the sentence *come alive* by standing in order while holding up their cards and saying the sentence aloud one word at a time.

FOCUS

- Yes/No Questions
- Short Answers
- Present Continuous Tense
- Possessive Adjectives

CLOSE UP

RULE: The word order in a Yes/No question with the verb *to be* is: *To be* + subject + complement.

EXAMPLES: **Are + you + busy?**
Is + Frank + busy?
Are + Jim and Lisa + busy?

RULE: It is common to respond to Yes/No questions with a short answer. A short answer includes the subject and the auxiliary verb (often called the *helping verb*).

EXAMPLES: Are you busy?   Is Richard busy?
Yes, I am.   **Yes, he is.**

RULE: *Am, is,* and *are* do not contract with subject pronouns in short answers.

EXAMPLES: Are you busy?   Is Rita busy?
Yes, **I am**.   Yes, **she is**.
I'm washing my hair.   **She's** feeding her cat.

GETTING READY

1. Have students listen and repeat as you read the short answers in the grammar box at the top of the page.
2. Review contractions with the verb *to be*. Say the full form and have students give the contracted form.

INTRODUCING THE MODEL

1. Have students look at the model illustration.
2. Set the scene: "Two friends are talking on the telephone."
3. Present the model.
4. Full-Class Repetition.

5. Ask students if they have any questions. Check understanding of new vocabulary: *busy, washing, hair*.

6. Group Choral Repetition.

7. Choral Conversation.

8. Call on one or two pairs of students to present the dialog.

   (For additional practice, do Choral Conversation in small groups or by rows.)

SIDE BY SIDE EXERCISES

Examples

1. A. Is Frank busy?
   B. Yes, he is.
      He's cleaning his apartment.

2. A. Is Helen busy?
   B. Yes, she is.
      She's feeding her cat.

3. A. Are you busy?
   B. Yes, we are.
      We're fixing our TV.

4. A Are Jim and Lisa busy?
   B. Yes, they are.
      They're painting their bedroom.

1. **Exercise 1:** Call on two students to present the dialog. Then do Choral Repetition and Choral Conversation practice.

2. **Exercise 2:** Check understanding of new vocabulary: *feeding, cat.* Same as above.

3. **Exercises 3–15:** Either Full-Class Practice or Pair Practice.

New Vocabulary

4. painting	10. bicycle
6. washing clothes	13. brushing teeth
9. exercises	14. windows

WORKBOOK

Pages 22–25

EXPANSION ACTIVITIES

1. Beanbag Toss

a. Have students sit in a circle.

b. Have students toss a beanbag back and forth. The student to whom the beanbag is tossed says an activity. For example:

   Student 1: I'm washing my hair.
   Student 2: I'm cleaning my yard.
   Student 3: I'm doing my exercises.

c. Continue until all the students have named an activity.

2. Associations

a. Divide the class into pairs or small groups.

b. Call out a verb and tell students to write down all the words they associate with that verb. For example:

   fix: car, sink, desk, chair, TV
   clean: apartment, room, kitchen, bathroom, yard
   wash: clothes, car, windows, hair
   do: exercises, homework

c. Have a student from each pair or group come to the board and write their words.

(continued)

Variation: Do the activity as a game with competing teams. The team with the most number of associations is the winner.

3. Finish the Sentence!

Begin a sentence, and have students repeat what you said and add an appropriate ending. For example:

Teacher	Students
I'm washing . . .	I'm washing my car.
	I'm washing my windows.
	I'm washing my clothes.
He's feeding . . .	He's feeding his dog.
	He's feeding his cat.
We're cleaning . . .	We're cleaning our yard.
	We're cleaning our apartment.
	We're cleaning our garage.
She's doing . . .	She's doing her homework.
	She's doing her exercises.
They're painting . . .	They're painting their kitchen.
	They're painting their bedroom.
	They're painting their bathroom.

Variation: This activity may be done as a class, in pairs or small groups, or as a game with competing teams.

4. Finish the Conversation!

a. Make word cards for the following and put them in a pile face down on a desk or table in front of the room.

car	dog	yard
apartment	bicycle	clothes
homework	exercises	teeth
windows	cat	TV
garage	hair	e-mail

b. Write the following conversational model on the board:

> A. Are you busy?
> B. Yes, I am.
> A. What are you doing?
> B. I'm _____.

c. Have pairs of students come to the front of the room. One student (Speaker B) picks a card and the other (Speaker A) initiates a conversation based on the model on the board. Speaker B must answer using an appropriate verb (such as *cleaning* or *fixing*) and the object on the card. For example, for the card *bicycle*, the student can answer: "I'm washing my bicycle" or "I'm fixing my bicycle."

5. Pick-a-Sentence!

a. Write words from the lesson on separate word cards, mix up the cards, and put them in a pile on a desk or table in front of the room.

b. Have students take turns picking up one card at a time. (Students should keep all the cards they've picked.)

c. The object of the activity is to see how many sentences the class can *pick*. When someone has collected a group of cards that form a sentence, that student should read it to the class to see if others agree that it's a correct sentence. If it's a sentence, have that student write it on the board.

d. The activity continues until all the cards have been picked.

Variation: Do the activity as a game with competing teams. The team with the most sentences is the winner.

How to Say It!

Attracting Someone's Attention: One way to attract someone's attention is to say the person's name with a questioning intonation. For example: *Jane? Richard?* The most common response is *Yes?*, spoken with a rising intonation.

1. Set the scene: "Jane's mother wants to speak to her."

2. Present the model.

3. Full-Class Repetition. (Pay special attention to the rising intonation in lines one and two.)

4. Ask students if they have any questions.

5. Group Choral Repetition.

6. Choral Conversation.

7. Call on one or two pairs of students to present the dialog.

8. Have pairs of students create similar conversations and then present them to the class.

EXPANSION ACTIVITY

Role Play: What Are You Doing?

1. Place Side by Side Picture Cards 36–67 face down in pile in the front of the room.

2. Have pairs of students come to the front of the class. One student (Student B) picks a card from the pile and pantomimes the action on the card. The other student (Student A) interrupts and says line one of the dialog. For example:

   Student B: (picks up card and begins to mime *playing the piano*)
   Student A: *Juan?*
   Student B: *Yes?*
   Student A: *What are you doing?*
   Student B: *I'm playing the piano.*

3. Continue until all the students have had a chance to perform one role play.

Text Page 31

💬 **TALK ABOUT IT!** *Where Are They, and What Are They Doing?*

FOCUS

- Review of the Present Continuous Tense
- Review of Possessive Adjectives

The illustration for this exercise shows people involved in different activities in various places around town. Students use the conversational models at the bottom of the page to talk about the scene.

INTRODUCING THE MODELS

1. Have students look at the illustration.

2. Introduce the new words: *parking lot, laundromat, health club.*

3. Present the two conversational models.

4. Full-Class Repetition.

5. Ask students if they have any questions. Check understanding of new vocabulary.

   ### Culture Note

   Laundromat: In the United States many people take their laundry to a laundromat—a place where they pay to use machines to wash and dry their clothes.

6. Group Choral Repetition.

7. Choral Conversation.

8. Call on one or two pairs of students to present the dialogs.

CONVERSATION PRACTICE

Examples

A. Where's Ms. Roberts?
B. She's in the park.
A. What's she doing?
B. She's reading the newspaper.

A. Where's Charlie Harris?
B. He's in the health club.
A. What's he doing?
B. He's doing his exercises.

Call on pairs of students to ask and answer questions about the people depicted in the scene. This can be done as either Full-Class Practice or Pair Practice. You can also assign it as written homework.

For the ? location next to the health club, students can choose any vocabulary to answer the question. This can be done as either Full-Class Practice or Pair Practice. If you decide to do it as Pair Practice, call on several pairs to present their conversations to the class.

WORKBOOK

Page 26

EXPANSION ACTIVITIES

1. True or False?

   a. Have students open their books to text page 31.

   b. Make statements about the characters on text page 31 and have students tell you "True" or "False." If the statement is false, have students correct it. For example:

   Teacher: Patty Williams is washing her car.
   Student: True.

   Teacher: Mr. and Mrs. Lopez are cooking.
   Student: False. Mr. and Mrs. Lopez are eating.

72 CHAPTER 4

Variation: You can call on students to make true or false statements about the scene and have other students respond.

2. Guess Who!

a. Have students look at the illustration on text page 31.

b. Describe the location or activity of a character and have students identify the character. For example:

Teacher: He's listening to the radio.
Student: Mr. Molina.

Teacher: They're washing their clothes.
Student: Mr. and Mrs. Sharp.

Teacher: He's in the health club.
Student: Charlie Harris.

3. Remember the Activities!

a. Tell students to spend one minute looking very carefully at the illustration on text page 31.

b. Have students close their books and write down as many activities from the page as they can remember.

c. Have students read their lists as a class, in pairs, or in small groups.

d. Call on students to come to the board and write their list of words. Have the class check the spelling of the words.

READING *A Busy Day*

FOCUS

- Possessive Adjectives
- Present Continuous Tense

NEW VOCABULARY

neighbors   too
of course

READING THE STORY

Optional: *Preview the story by having students talk about the story title and/or illustration. You may choose to introduce new vocabulary beforehand, or have students encounter the new vocabulary within the context of the reading.*

1. Have students read the story silently, or follow along silently as the story is read aloud by you, by one or more students, or on the audio program.

2. Ask students if they have any questions. Check understanding of vocabulary.

   ### *Pronunciation Note*

   Some students may have difficulty distinguishing between *watching* and *washing*. Point out the differences between the [*ch*] sound in *watching* and the [*sh*] sound in *washing*. Give students additional listening and pronunciation practice with these words if you feel it's necessary.

3. Check students' comprehension, using some or all of the following questions:

   What's Mr. Price doing?
   What's Ms. Hunter doing?
   What's Ricky Gomez doing?
   What are Mr. and Mrs. Wong doing?
   What's Mrs. Martin doing?
   What are Judy and Larry Clark doing?
   What am I doing?

✓ READING *CHECK-UP*

TRUE OR FALSE?

1. True   4. True
2. False   5. False
3. False

Q & A

1. Call on a pair of students to present the model.
2. Have students work in pairs to create new dialogs.
3. Call on pairs to present their new dialogs to the class.

READING EXTENSION

Ask students the following questions and have them scan the reading on text page 32 for the answers.

You're Mr. Price. What are you cleaning?
You're Ms. Hunter. What are you painting?
You're Ricky Gomez. Who are you feeding?
You're Mr. and Mrs. Wong. What are you washing?
You're Mrs. Martin. What are you doing?
You're telling the story. What are you washing? Who are you watching?

LISTENING

 IN YOUR OWN WORDS

Listen and choose the correct answer.

1. What are you eating?
2. What is she reading?
3. What is he playing?
4. What are they painting?
5. What are you watching?
6. What is he washing?

Answers

1. b   4. a
2. a   5. a
3. b   6. b

1. Make sure students understand the instructions.
2. Have students do the activity as written homework, using a dictionary for any new words they wish to use.
3. Have students present and discuss what they have written, in pairs or as a class.

Text Page 34

 PRONUNCIATION

> **Deleted *h*:** When the words *her* and *his* occur in the middle of a phrase or sentence, the initial /h/ sound is deleted.

Focus on Listening

Practice the sentences in the left column. Say each sentence or play the audio one or more times. Have students listen carefully and repeat.

Focus on Pronunciation

Practice the sentences in the right column. Have students say each sentence and then listen carefully as you say it or play the audio.

If you wish, have students continue practicing the sentences to improve their pronunciation.

 JOURNAL

Have students go to a place in the community, look at what people are doing, and write about it in their journals. Encourage students to take a dictionary with them so they can look up words they would like to use in their descriptions. Have students discuss what they have written as a class, in pairs, or in small groups.

 CHAPTER SUMMARY

GRAMMAR

1. Divide the class into pairs or small groups.
2. Have students take turns forming sentences from the grammar boxes. Student A says a

sentence, and Student B points to the words from each column that are in the sentence. Then have students switch: Student B says a sentence, and Student A points to the words.

KEY VOCABULARY

Have students ask you any questions about the meaning or pronunciation of the vocabulary. If students ask for the pronunciation, repeat after the student until the student is satisfied with his or her pronunciation.

EXPANSION ACTIVITIES

1. **Vocabulary Check**

   Check the students' retention of the vocabulary depicted on the opening page of Chapter 4 by doing the following activity:

   a. Have students open their books to page 27 and cover the list of vocabulary words.

   b. Either call out a number and have students tell you the word, or say a word and have students tell you the number.

   Variation: You can also do this activity as a game with competing teams.

2. **Student-Led Dictation**

   a. Tell each student to choose a phrase from the Key Vocabulary list on text page 34 and look at it very carefully.

   b. Have students take turns dictating their phrases to the class. Everybody writes down that student's phrase.

   c. When the dictation is completed, call on different students to write each phrase on the board to check the spelling.

END-OF-CHAPTER ACTIVITIES

1. True or False Memory Game

a. Tell students to spend three minutes looking very carefully at the illustration text page 33. Then have students close their books.

b. Make statements about the characters in the illustration on text page 33 and have students tell you "True" or "False." If the statement is false, have students correct it. For example:

    Teacher: Hector Lopez is washing his car.
    Student: True.

    Teacher: Mr. Sharp is feeding his dog.
    Student: False. He's cleaning his kitchen.

Variation: This can be done as a dictation with a *True* column and a *False* column. Tell students to write each statement in the appropriate column. At the end of the dictation, have students check the illustration to see if they were correct.

2. Scrambled Sentences

a. Divide the class into teams.

b. One sentence at a time, write individual sentences out of order on the board. For example:

> their   doing   They're   homework
> painting   She's   kitchen   her
> our   fixing   We're   bicycles

c. The first person to raise his or her hand, come to the board, and write the sentence in the correct order earns a point for that team.

d. The team with the most points wins the *scrambled sentences* game.

Variation: Write the words to several sentences on separate cards. Divide the class into small groups, and have students work together to put the sentences into correct order.

3. Miming

a. Place *Side by Side* Picture Cards 36–67 in a pile in the front of the room.

b. Have students take turns picking a card from the pile and pantomiming the action on the card.

c. The class must guess what the person is doing.

Variation: This can be done as a game with competing teams.

4. Sense or Nonsense?

a. Divide the class into four groups.

b. Make four sets of split sentence cards with beginnings and ends of sentences. For example:

She's feeding	her cat.
He's watching	TV.
They're painting	their living room.
They're playing	baseball.
We're washing	our clothes.
I'm fixing	my bicycle.
I'm doing	my homework.
She's brushing	her hair.
They're planting	flowers.
We're listening to	music.

(continued)

c. Mix up the cards and distribute sets of cards to each group, keeping the beginning and ending cards in different piles.

d. Have students take turns picking up one card from each pile and reading the sentence to the group. For example:

We're painting	her cat.

e. That group decides if the sentence makes sense or is *nonsense*.

f. After all the cards have been picked, have the groups lay out all the cards and put together all the sentence combinations that make sense.

5. What's Wrong?

a. Divide the class into pairs or small groups.

b. Write several sentences, such as the following, on the board or on a handout. Some of the sentences should be correct, and others incorrect. For example:

> Mr. Lee is cleaning his apartment.
> They're brushing their homework.
> I'm feeding my dog.
> We're washing TV.
> She's brushing her teeth.
> We're fixing are bicycles.
> She's painting her dog.
> We're cleaning our yard.
> Their playing soccer.
> What is you doing?
> His painting his bedroom.

c. The object of the activity is for students to identify which sentences are incorrect and then correct them.

d. Have students compare their answers.

Variation: Do the activity as a game with competing teams. The team that successfully completes the task in the shortest time is the winner.

6. Question the Answers!

a. Dictate answers such as the following to the class:

> My clothes.   Their exercises.
> Their apartment.   Her book.
> His kitchen.   My bicycle.
> Her car.

b. Have students write questions for which these answers would be correct. For example:

Answers	Questions
My clothes.	What are you washing?
Their apartment.	What are they cleaning?

c. Have students compare their questions with each other.

Variation: Write the answers on cards. Divide the class into groups and give each group a set of cards.

7. Memory Chain

a. Write on the board:

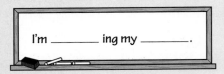

b. Divide the class into groups of five or six students each.

c. Tell each student to think of an activity from the chapter.

d. One group at a time, have Student 1 begin. That student pantomimes an activity and says what he or she is doing. For example:

> I'm fixing my sink.

e. Student 2 repeats what Student 1 said and adds another activity while pantomiming it. For example:

> Maria is fixing her sink, and I'm doing my exercises.

f. Student 3 continues in the same way. For example:

> Maria is fixing her sink. Robert is doing his exercises. And I'm cleaning my apartment.

g. Continue until everyone has had a chance to play the *Memory Chain*.

WORKBOOK ANSWER KEY AND LISTENING SCRIPTS

WORKBOOK PAGE 21

A. WHAT ARE THEY DOING?

1. What's, cleaning his
2. doing, fixing her
3. What, my apartment
4. children, their homework
5. are, our sink

WORKBOOK PAGE 22

B. WHAT'S THE WORD?

1. my
2. our
3. their
4. her
5. its
6. your
7. his

C. LISTENING

Listen and circle the word you hear.

1. We're cleaning our room.
2. He's doing his homework.
3. She's washing her hair.
4. They're fixing their car.
5. You're fixing your TV.
6. I'm feeding my cat.

Answers

1. our
2. his
3. her
4. their
5. your
6. my

D. PUZZLE

WORKBOOK PAGE 23

E. WHAT ARE THEY SAYING?

1. Yes, he is.
2. Yes, we are.
3. Yes, she is.
4. Yes, they are.
5. Yes, he is.
6. Yes, she is.
7. Yes, I am.
8. Yes, you are.

WORKBOOK PAGE 24

G. LISTENING

Listen and circle the word you hear.

1. He's studying.
2. She's doing her homework.
3. I'm feeding my cat.
4. He's cleaning his yard.
5. We're fixing our car.
6. They're washing their clothes.

Answers

1. he's
2. her
3. feeding
4. yard
5. our
6. washing

WORKBOOK PAGE 25

H. WHAT ARE THEY DOING?

1. washing
2. cleaning
3. doing
4. reading
5. painting
6. feeding

I. WHAT'S THE WORD?

1. They're, their
2. Where
3. He's, his
4. Where's
5. our
6. Is
7. are
8. its

J. A BUSY DAY

1. restaurant
2. eating
3. in
4. They're
5. their
6. park
7. reading
8. listening
9. and
10. doing
11. playing
12. laundromat
13. She's
14. her
15. are
16. washing
17. his
18. fixing
19. Where's
20. library
21. What's
22. He's

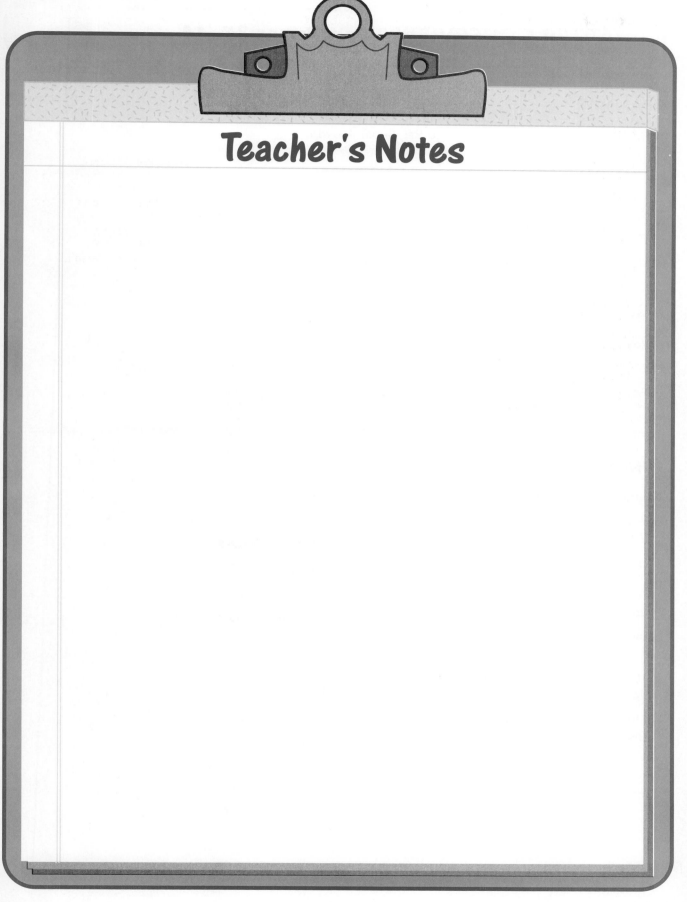

Teacher's Notes

GRAMMAR

To Be: Yes / No Questions

Am	I	
Is	he she it	tall?
Are	we you they	

To Be: Short Answers

Yes,	I	am.
	he she it	is.
	we you they	are.

No,	I'm	not.
	he she it	isn't.
	we you they	aren't.

Possessive Nouns

Robert**'s** house

Peggy**'s** neighbors

George**'s** apartment

FUNCTIONS

Asking for and Reporting Information

Is *Bob tall* or *short*?
  He's tall.

Tell me about *your new car*.

I'm calling from *Miami*.

What are you doing *in Miami*?

How's the weather *in Miami*?
  It's *raining*.

Is it *hot*?
  No, it isn't. It's *cold*.

Is this *Julie*?
  Yes, it is.

Describing

He's *tall*.

Greeting People

Hello.

Hi, *Jack*. This is *Jim*.

Expressing Dissatisfaction

I'm having a terrible time.

Sympathizing

I'm sorry to hear that.

Leave Taking

See you soon.

NEW VOCABULARY

Adjectives

big
bored
cheap
difficult
easy
expensive
fat
good
handsome
heavy
large
little
loud
married
new
noisy
old
poor
pretty
quiet
rich
short
single
small
tall
terrible
thin
ugly
young

Weather

cloudy
cold
cool
hot
raining
snowing
sunny
warm

Places Around the World

Honolulu
Miami
Tahiti

People

boss
repairperson

Family

brother
mother
sister

Everyday Activities

calling
writing (to)

Verbs

be
isn't
aren't

Additional Nouns

chapter
city
clinic
food
hotel
house
question
Santa Claus
stomach
weather

Miscellaneous

a few
about
but
here
how
or
other
out
so
this
together

Time Words

now
soon

EXPRESSIONS

Dear *Mother*,
for a few days
having a *good* time
having problems (with)
I'm sorry to hear that.
in fact
looking out the window
Love, *Ethel*
on vacation
"raining cats and dogs"
See you soon.
tell me about
to tell the truth

VOCABULARY PREVIEW

You may want to introduce these words before beginning the chapter, or you may choose to wait until they first occur in a specific lesson. If you choose to introduce them at this point, here are some suggestions:

1. Have students look at the illustrations on text page 35 and identify the words they already know.

2. Present the vocabulary. Say each word and have the class repeat it chorally and individually. Check students' understanding and pronunciation of the words.

3. Practice the vocabulary as a class, in pairs, or in small groups. Have students cover the word list and look at the pictures. Practice the words in the following ways:

   • Say a word and have students tell the number of the illustration.

   • Give the number of an illustration and have students say the word.

Text Pages 36–37: Tall or Short?

FOCUS

- Yes/No Questions with *To Be*
- Questions with *Or*
- Possessive Nouns: *Robert's, Peggy's, George's*
- Describing People and Things

CLOSE UP

RULE:	Adjectives describe nouns.
EXAMPLES:	Vanessa is **beautiful**. The questions are **easy**.
RULE:	An apostrophe (') and an *-s* are used with nouns to show possession.
EXAMPLES:	Robert**'s house** is large. Peggy**'s neighbors** are quiet. George**'s apartment** is little.
RULE:	*Or* offers a choice.
EXAMPLES:	Is Kate young **or** old? Is Howard heavy **or** thin?

GETTING READY

1. Introduce possessive nouns.

   a. Point to a few students and name some of their possessions. Have students repeat after you. For example:

Jane	Tom
Jane's pencil	Tom's pen

   b. Write the possessive forms on the board. For example:

   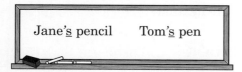

2. Demonstrate the idea of opposites.

   a. Draw and label two stick figures on the board:

   Say: "Bob is *tall*."
   "Bill is *short*."

   Have students repeat.

b. Draw two more stick figures on the board:

Howard   Mike

Say: "Howard is *heavy*."
"Mike is *thin*."

Have students repeat.

INTRODUCING THE MODEL

1. Have students look at the model illustration.

2. Set the scene: "Two people are talking about Bob and Bill."

3. Present the model.

4. Full-Class Repetition.

5. Ask students if they have any questions. Check understanding of new vocabulary: *tall, short, or.*

6. Group Choral Repetition.

7. Choral Conversation.

8. Call on one or two pairs of students to present the dialog.

   (For additional practice, do Choral Conversation in small groups or by rows.)

SIDE BY SIDE EXERCISES

Examples

1. A. Is Kate young or old?
   B. She's young.

2. A. Is Peggy young or old?
   B. She's old.

5. A. Is Howard's car new or old?
   B. It's new.

6. A. Is Mike's car new or old?
   B. It's old.

1. **Exercises 1 and 2:** Check understanding of the new words *young, old.* Call on two students to present each dialog. Then do

Choral Repetition and Choral Conversation practice.

2. **Exercises 3 and 4:** Check understanding of the new words *heavy, fat, thin.* Same as above.

3. **Exercises 5–22:** Either Full-Class Practice or Pair Practice.

New Vocabulary

5–6. new, old
7–8. married, single
9–10. handsome, ugly
11–12. beautiful, ugly, pretty
13–14. house, large, small, big, little
15–16. noisy, quiet, loud
17–18. expensive, cheap
19–20. easy, difficult, questions, chapter
21–22. rich, poor

Language Note

Handsome (Exercises 9 and 10) is commonly used to refer to men; *beautiful* and *pretty* (Exercises 11 and 12) are commonly used for women and things.

Pronunciation Note

The pronunciation focus of Chapter 5 is **Yes/No Questions with *or*** (text page 44). You may wish to model this pronunciation at this point and encourage students to incorporate it into their language practice.

Is Bob tall or short?
Is Kate young or old?

4. Have students use the model as a guide to create their own conversations, using vocabulary of their choice. (They can use any names, adjectives, and objects they wish.) Encourage students to use dictionaries to find new words they want to use. This exercise can be done orally in class or for written homework. If you assign it for homework, do one example in class to make sure students understand what's expected. Have students present their conversations in class the next day.

WORKBOOK

Page 27

1. Practice with Visuals

You can review the structures and vocabulary on text pages 36–37 using visuals of opposite adjectives. Use your own visuals, stick figures on the board, or *Side by Side* Picture Cards 68–79.

a. Point to a visual of *tall* and *short* and ask: "Is he tall or short?" Have students respond.

b. Continue with other adjectives.

Variation: Divide the class into small groups. Distribute visuals or picture cards among the groups. Have students ask and answer questions about the visuals.

2. Describing Newspaper and Magazine Pictures

Bring to class pictures or photographs from newspapers and magazines. Have students make statements about the people and the objects, using adjectives.

3. Miming

a. Write down on cards the adjectives from text pages 36 and 37.

b. Have students take turns picking a card from the pile and pantomiming the adjective on the card.

c. The class must guess what the adjective is.

Variation: This can be done as a game with competing teams.

4. True or False?

a. Have students look at the illustrations on text pages 36 and 37.

b. Make statements about the characters in the illustrations and have students tell you "True" or "False." If the statement is false, have students correct it. For example:

    Teacher: Bob is tall.
    Student: True.

    Teacher: Kate is old.
    Student: False. Kate is young.

Variation: Call on students to make true or false statements about the illustrations and have other students respond.

5. Drawing Game

a. Write down on two sets of cards the following adjectives:

tall	short	heavy	thin
married	handsome	beautiful	ugly
large	small	noisy	expensive
cheap	rich	poor	

b. Place the two piles of cards on a table or desk in the front of the room. Also have a pad of paper and pencil next to each team's set of cards.

c. Divide the class into teams. Have each team sit together in a different part of the room.

d. When you say "Go!," a person from each team comes to the front of his or her team, picks a card from the pile, and draws the adjective. The rest of the team then guesses what the adjective is.

e. When a team correctly guesses an adjective, another team member picks a card and draws the adjective written on that card.

f. Continue until each team has guessed all the adjectives in their pile.

    The team that guesses the adjectives in the shortest time wins the game.

6. Opposites Match Game

a. Write down on separate cards the adjectives from text pages 36 and 37.

(continued)

b. Distribute the cards randomly to students.

c. Have students memorize their adjectives and leave their cards on their desks.

d. Have students circulate around the room, saying their words until they find their matching opposite.

e. When all the pairs have been matched, have students say their adjectives for the whole class.

7. Opposites Concentration

a. Write down on separate cards the adjectives from text pages 36 and 37.

b. Shuffle the cards and place them face down in eight rows of four each.

c. Divide the class into two teams. The object of the game is for students to find the matching opposites. Both teams should be able to see the cards, since *concentrating* on their location is an important part of playing the game.

d. A student from Team 1 turns over two cards. If they match, that team gets a point and the student takes another turn. If they don't match, the student turns them face down and a member of Team 2 takes a turn.

e. The game continues until all the cards have been matched. The team with the most correct *matches* wins the game.

Variation: This game can also be played in small groups and pairs.

8. Tic Tac Vocabulary

a. Have students draw a tic tac grid on their papers and then fill in their grids with the following adjectives:

married	expensive
small	pretty
short	difficult
young	thin
noisy	

b. Tell students that you're going to say the *opposites* of the words in their grids. When they hear a word, they should look for the opposite of that word and cross it out.

c. The first person to cross out three opposites in a straight line—either vertically, horizontally, or diagonally—wins the game.

d. Have the winner call out the words to check the accuracy.

9. Board Game

a. On poster boards or on manila file folders, make up game boards with a pathway consisting of separate spaces. You may use any design you wish. For example:

1 START	2	3	4	5	6	7	8
18 END							9
17	16	15	14	13	12	11	10

b. Divide the class into groups of two to four students. Give each group a game board, a die, and something to be used as a playing piece.

c. Give each group a pile of cards face-down with questions such as the following:

What's the opposite of *young?*
What's the opposite of *heavy?*

d. Each student in turn rolls the die, moves the playing piece along the game path, and after landing on a space, picks a card and answers the question.

Option: You should decide on the rules of the game. You may want each student to take his or her turn only once, or you may want a student who successfully answers a question to take another turn.

e. The first student to reach the end of the pathway is the winner.

Text Pages 38–39: Tell Me About . . .

FOCUS

- Yes/No Questions with *To Be*
- Negative Short Answers
- Describing People and Things

CLOSE UP

RULE: In informal English, the word *not* usually contracts with *is* and *are*.

EXAMPLES: Is it new?
No, it (is not) **isn't**.
Is he young?
No, he (is not) **isn't**.
Are they noisy?
No, they (are not) **aren't**.

GETTING READY

Say the sentences in the grammar boxes at the top of the page and have students repeat after you. (Read from left to right.)

Am I tall?	Yes, I am.	No, I'm not.
Is he tall?	Yes, he is.	No, he isn't.
Is she tall?	Yes, she is.	No, she isn't.
Is it tall?	Yes, it is.	No, it isn't.
Are we tall?	Yes, we are.	No, we aren't.
Are you tall?	Yes, you are.	No, you aren't.
Are they tall?	Yes, they are.	No, they aren't.

INTRODUCING THE MODELS

There are three conversations. Introduce and practice each model before going on to the next. For each model:

1. Have students look at the model illustration.

2. Set the scene: "Two people are talking."

3. Present the model.

4. Full-Class Repetition.

5. Ask students if they have any questions. Check understanding of new vocabulary: *tell me about*.

6. Choral Choral Repetition.

7. Choral Conversation.

8. Call on one or two pairs of students to present the dialog.

   (For additional practice, do Choral Conversations in small groups or by rows.)

SIDE BY SIDE EXERCISES

Examples

1. A. Tell me about your computer.
      Is it new?
   B. No, it isn't. It's old.

2. A. Tell me about your new boss.
      Is he young?
   B. No he isn't. He's old.

1. **Exercise 1:** Call on two students to present the dialog. Then do Choral Repetition and Choral Conversation practice.

2. **Exercise 2:** Introduce the new word *boss*. Same as above.

3. **Exercises 3–10:** Either Full-Class Practice or Pair Practice.

New Vocabulary

5. *brother*   10. *Santa Claus*
6. *sister*

Culture Note

Santa Claus (Exercise 10) is a legendary man who is traditionally associated with Christmas celebrations (December 25th) in the United States. Children believe he lives at the North Pole and brings Christmas gifts to their homes every year.

WORKBOOK

Pages 28–31

EXPANSION ACTIVITIES

1. **Practice with Visuals**

Use visuals of people or things or *Side by Side Picture Cards 68–79* to review opposite adjectives.

a. Point to a person in one of the visuals and say: "Tell me about _____." Have students give several descriptive responses. For example:

Teacher: [*pointing to the character on picture card 69*]: Tell me about Kate.
Student: She's young. She's thin. She's pretty.

Teacher: [*pointing to a car in an advertisement*] Tell me about the car.
Student: It's new. It's expensive. It's small.

b. Continue until all the students have had a chance to respond.

2. **Students Talk about Themselves**

a. Write the following on the board:

A. Tell me about your _____.
   Is/Are _____?

B. Yes, _____.
   or
   No, _____.

---

brother	boss	cat
sister	apartment	dog
neighbors	house	car

young	cheap	quiet	single
new	fat	noisy	married
rich	thin	beautiful	big
old	expensive	handsome	
poor	loud	ugly	

b. Divide the class into pairs.

c. Have the pairs create conversations using the conversational framework and list of words on the board.

d. Call on students to report about their conversations. For example:

Bill's car is new. His house is old. His dog is small.

3. **What's the Opposite?**

a. Write the following on the board and have students repeat after you: "He's tall. He isn't short. They aren't young. They're old."

| He's tall. | They aren't young. |
| He isn't short. | They're old. |

---

b. Say a sentence with an adjective and have students give you a sentence with the opposite adjective. For example:

Teacher	Students
He isn't thin.	He's heavy.
She's married.	She isn't single.
My neighbors are quiet.	They aren't noisy.
My sister is young.	She isn't old.
My car is old.	It isn't new.
She isn't short.	She's tall.
The questions are easy.	They aren't difficult.

4. Question the Answers!

a. Dictate answers such as the following to the class:

No, he isn't. He's young.
No, she isn't. She's married.
No, they aren't. They're noisy.
No, it isn't. It's old.
No, he isn't. He's short.
No, it isn't. It's large.
No, you aren't. You're thin.

b. Tell students to write questions for which these answers would be correct. (There are many possible correct questions.) For example:

Answer: No, he isn't. He's young.
Questions: Is he old?/Is your boss old?/Is your brother old?/Is Bob old?

Answer: No, she isn't. She's married.
Questions: Is she single?/Is your sister single?/Is Patty single?

c. Have students compare their questions with each other.

Variation: Write the answers on cards. Divide the class into groups and give each group a set of cards.

Text Page 40: How's the Weather Today?

FOCUS

* Weather Expressions

INTRODUCING THE WEATHER

There are eight weather expressions. Practice each one before going on to the next. (Note the use of thermometers to indicate *hot, warm, cool,* and *cold*.)

1. Have students listen as you read from the book or play the audio.

2. Have students repeat after you chorally and individually.

3. Practice conversationally by asking students: "How's the weather?" Students answer: "It's sunny" chorally and individually.

4. Call on pairs of students to ask each other.

5. Practice the other weather expressions this way.

6. When students have learned and practiced all the vocabulary, ask: "How's the weather in our city today?"

WORKBOOK

Pages 32–33

EXPANSION ACTIVITIES

1. **Practice with Visuals**

   Use your own visuals or *Side by Side* Picture Cards 80–87 to review weather vocabulary.

   a. Point to visuals one by one and ask: "How's the weather?" Have students answer chorally and/or individually: "It's _____."

   b. Have students point to visuals and ask each other: "How's the weather?"

2. **Mime the Weather!**

   a. Divide the class into two groups.

   b. Write down on cards the weather expressions from text page 40.

   c. Have students take turns picking a card from the pile and pantomiming the weather on the card.

   d. The group must guess what the weather is.

3. **Learn the Numbers!**

   a. Review the numbers 1–10. Then teach the numbers 11–100. (See suggestions for teaching numbers on page 4 of this *Teacher's Guide*.) The numbers are given on page 172 of the student text.

   b. Contrast difficult numbers. Put this list on the board:

A	B
13	30
14	40
15	50
16	60
17	70
18	80
19	90

Listening Practice: Say a number from column A or column B. Have students indicate the correct column by saying or writing A or B.

Pronunciation Practice: Have students say a number from column A or B. Other students indicate which is the correct column.

4. Hot, Warm, Cool, or Cold?

a. Write the following on the board:

Fahrenheit	Centigrade/Celsius
100°	38°
70°	21°
50°	10°
32°	0°
0°	-17°

b. Tell students the names of the two temperature scales: *Fahrenheit* and the scale that's called either *Centigrade* or *Celsius*. Point out the temperature equivalents on the two scales.

c. Write the following on the board:

hot   warm   cool   cold

d. Give temperatures in Fahrenheit and Centigrade and have students tell you whether those temperatures are *hot, warm, cool,* or *cold.*

5. Look It Up!

a. Make several copies of the weather section from the newspaper.

b. Write the following on the board:

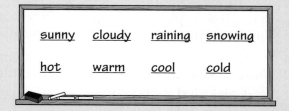

sunny	cloudy	raining	snowing
hot	warm	cool	cold

c. Divide the class into small groups. Give each group a copy of the weather listings. Tell each group to write down the name of one city around the world where it's *sunny, cloudy, raining, snowing, hot, warm, cool,* and *cold.*

d. Have the groups write the names of those cities on the board under the appropriate headings.

How to Say It!

> **Calling Someone You Know on the Telephone:** When you call someone you know, it is common to try to identify the person who answers the phone (*Hello. Is this Julie?*). *This* refers to the voice the caller hears on the phone.

1. Set the scene: "Two friends are talking on the phone."

2. With books closed, have students listen as you present the conversation or play the audio one or more times.

3. Full-Class Repetition.

4. Have students open their books and look at the dialog. Ask students if they have any questions. Check understanding of new vocabulary: *this.*

5. Group Choral Repetition.

6. Choral Conversation.

7. Call on one or two pairs of students to present the dialog.

8. Next have pairs of students practice the model, using their own names and continuing the conversation any way they wish.

9. Call on pairs to present their conversations to the class.

FOCUS

- Review of Weather Expressions
- Review of Yes/No Questions and Short Answers

INTRODUCING THE MODEL

1. Have students look at the model illustration.

2. Set the scene: "Jim is on vacation in Miami, Florida. He's calling his friend Jack on the telephone. Jim is very upset."

3. Present the model.

4. Full-Class Repetition.

5. Ask students if they have any questions. Check understanding of new vocabulary: *calling, Miami, on vacation, having a good time, having a terrible time, here, I'm sorry to hear that.*

6. Group Choral Repetition.

7. Choral Conversation.

8. Call on one or two pairs of students to present the dialog.

9. Have students practice the model in pairs as you walk around the room listening and helping.

SIDE BY SIDE EXERCISES

Have students use the dialog below the model as a guide for the exercises that follow. In these exercises, Student A pretends to be on vacation and is calling Student B. You can add realism to the dialog by bringing a telephone to class or by having each student pretend to hold a telephone receiver to his or her ear.

Example

> A. Hi, (*name*). This is (*name*). I'm calling from British Columbia.
> B. From British Columbia? What are you doing in British Columbia?
> A. I'm on vacation.
> B. How's the weather in British Columbia? Is it cool?
> A. No, it isn't. It's warm.
> B. Is it snowing?
> A. No, it isn't. It's raining.
> B. Are you having a good time?
> A. No, I'm not. I'm having a TERRIBLE time. The weather is TERRIBLE here!
> B. I'm sorry to hear that.

1. Do exercises 1 and 2 in class, either as Full-Class Practice or as Pair Practice. Point out the locations of British Columbia and Tahiti on a world map.

2. Have students use the model as a guide to create their own conversations, using vocabulary of their choice. Encourage students to use dictionaries to find new words they want to use. This exercise can be done orally in class or for written homework. If you assign it for homework, you should do one example in class to make sure students understand what's expected. Have students present their conversations in class the next day.

WORKBOOK

Page 34

EXPANSION ACTIVITIES

1. **Scrambled Dialog**

    a. Divide the class into three groups.

    b. Make three sets of the model conversation from page 41, writing each line on a separate card.

    c. Give each group one set of the cards, and have the group members reorder the conversation.

    d. Have each group read their conversation aloud while the others listen to check for accuracy.

2. **Dictation Game**

    a. Make up a 5- or 6-sentence story about Jack's vacation. Write the story in large print on a piece of paper. For example:

    > Jack is having a terrible vacation.
    > He's at the beach.
    > The sun isn't shining.
    > He isn't swimming.
    > It's cold and it's raining.
    > He isn't happy.

    b. Put the paper on the far side of the room or out in the hallway so that students can't read it from their seats.

    c. Divide the class into pairs. One student from each pair runs to read the directions and then returns to dictate the directions to the partner. The runner may go back and forth as many times as necessary. The first pair to finish writing the story wins.

Text Pages 42–43

 READING: *Dear Mother*

FOCUS

- Adjectives

NEW VOCABULARY

a few	mother
bored	other
but	problems
clinic	raining cats and dogs
Dear _____,	repairperson
food	right now
for a few days	See you soon.
good	sitting
having	so
hotel	stomach
in fact	to be
looking out the	together
window	to tell the truth
Love, _____	writing (to)

READING THE STORY

Optional: *Preview the story by having students talk about the story title and/or illustrations. You may choose to introduce new vocabulary beforehand, or have students encounter the new vocabulary within the context of the reading.*

1. Have students read the story silently, or follow along silently as the story is read aloud by you, by one or more students, or on the audio program.

2. Ask students if they have any questions. Check understanding of vocabulary.

3. Check students' comprehension, using some or all of the following questions:

   Where are Ethel and Ralph?
   How's the weather at Sludge Beach?

Is it raining?
Are the children happy?
What are they doing?
Tell about the restaurants at Sludge Beach.
Where's Ralph?
Why?
Tell about the other hotels at Sludge Beach.
Is Ethel and Ralph's hotel beautiful and new?
Ethel and Ralph are having a few problems on their vacation, but they're happy. Why?

✔ READING *CHECK-UP*

TRUE OR FALSE?

1. False   5. False
2. False   6. True
3. True   7. False
4. False   8. False

READING EXTENSION

Ask students the following questions and have them review the reading on text pages 42–43 for the answers.

What's another title for the reading?
Find an adjective in the reading for each of the following:

the weather
the children
the restaurants
the hotel
their vacation

 LISTENING

WHAT'S THE ANSWER?

Listen and choose the correct answer.

1. Tell me about your apartment.

2. Tell me about your new car.

3. Tell me about your neighbors.

4. How's the weather?

96   CHAPTER 5

5. Tell me about your hotel.

6. How's the food at the restaurant?

Answers

1. a   **4.** b

2. b   **5.** a

3. a   **6.** a

TRUE OR FALSE?

Listen to the conversation. Then answer *True* or *False*.

A. Hello.

B. Hello. Is this Betty?

A. Yes, it is.

B. Hi, Betty. This is Louise. I'm calling from Mud Beach.

A. From Mud Beach?

B. Yes. I'm on vacation in Mud Beach for a few days.

A. How's the weather in Mud Beach?

B. It's terrible! It's cold, and it's cloudy.

A. Cold and cloudy? What a shame! How's the hotel?

B. The hotel is terrible! It's old, it's noisy, and the rooms are very small.

A. I'm sorry to hear that. Tell me about the restaurants.

B. The restaurants in Mud Beach are expensive, and the food isn't very good. In fact, I'm having problems with my stomach.

A. What a shame! So, Louise, what are you doing?

B. I'm sitting in my room, and I'm watching TV. I'm not having a very good time.

A. I'm sorry to hear that.

Answers

1. True   **4.** False

2. False   **5.** True

3. True

PRONUNCIATION *th*

Students can share their written work with each other if appropriate. Have students discuss what they have written as a class, in pairs, or in small groups.

> **Yes/No Questions with *or*:** When asking a question with *or*, the speaker emphasizes the choice between one thing *or* another. The intonation rises on the first and falls on the second. The word *or* is not stressed. For example:
>
> tall or short?   young or old?

Focus on Listening

Practice the sentences in the left column. Say each sentence or play the audio one or more times. Have students listen carefully and repeat.

Focus on Pronunciation

Practice the sentences in the right column. Have students say each sentence and then listen carefully as you say it or play the audio.

If you wish, have students continue practicing the sentences to improve their pronunciation.

 JOURNAL

Have students write their journal entries at home or in class. Encourage students to use a dictionary to look up words they would like to use in their descriptions. Write the following framework on the board for students to use as a guide when writing their letters:

```
                              Date
Dear _____,
_____
_____
_____
                         Sincerely,
                         _____
```

✔ CHAPTER SUMMARY

GRAMMAR

1. Divide the class into pairs or small groups.
2. Have students take turns forming sentences from the grammar boxes. Student A says a sentence, and Student B points to the words from each column that are in the sentence. Then have students switch: Student B says a sentence, and Student A points to the words.

KEY VOCABULARY

Have students ask you any questions about the meaning or pronunciation of the vocabulary. If students ask for the pronunciation, repeat after the student until the student is satisfied with his or her pronunciation.

EXPANSION ACTIVITIES

1. Vocabulary Check

   Check students' retention of the vocabulary depicted on the opening page of Chapter 5 by doing the following activity:

   a. Have students open their books to page 35 and cover the list of vocabulary words.

   b. Either call out a number and have students tell you the word, or say a word and have students tell you the number.

   Variation: You can also do this activity as a game with competing teams.

2. Student-Led Dictation

   a. Tell each student to choose a word or phrase

from the Key Vocabulary list on text page 44 and look at it very carefully.

b. Have students take turns dictating their words to the class. Everybody writes down that student's word.

c. When the dictation is completed, call on different students to write each word on the board to check the spelling.

3. Beanbag Toss

a. Call out a topic from the chapter—for example: *Weather*

b. Have students toss a beanbag back and forth. The student to whom the beanbag is tossed must name a weather expression. For example:

Student 1: It's snowing.
Student 2: It's raining.
Student 3: It's hot.

c. Continue until all the words in the category have been named.

END-OF-CHAPTER ACTIVITIES

1. Scrambled Sentences

a. Divide the class into two teams.

b. One sentence at a time, write individual sentences (or questions) out of order on the board. For example:

the ? weather Honolulu how's in having are good you ? time a restaurants very here good aren't the

c. The first person to raise his or her hand, come to the board, and write the sentence in the correct order earns a point for that team.

d. The team with the most points wins the scrambled sentence game.

Variation: Write the words to several sentences on separate cards. Divide the class into small groups, and have students work together to put the sentences into correct order.

2. What's the Opposite?

a. Divide the class into teams.

b. Call out an adjective, and have the students raise their hands and tell you the opposite adjective.

c. The team with the most correct answers wins.

3. Describe the Pictures

a. Bring in several pictures or ask students to bring in pictures of people on vacation.

b. Write the following on the board:

(continued)

Where are they?
What are they doing?
How's the weather?
Describe the people.

c. Divide the class into pairs, and have each pair choose a picture and describe it by answering the questions on the board.

d. Have students read their descriptions aloud as the class listens and tries to identify the picture.

4. Pantomime Role Play

a. Make up role-play cards such as the following:

You're in your apartment. It's hot. You're painting your apartment. You're having a terrible time.

You're in your apartment. It's very cold. You're studying English. You're having a terrible time.

You're at the beach. It's sunny. You're playing cards. You're having a good time.

You're in a health club. It's hot. You're doing your exercises. You're having a good time.

You're in a movie theater. It's warm. You're watching a movie. You're having a good time.

You're in a restaurant. It's cool in the restaurant. You're eating dinner. You're having a good time.

You're in a park. It's raining. You're playing basketball. You're having a terrible time.

b. Have pairs or groups of students pantomime their role plays. The class watches and answers the following questions:

Where are they?
How's the weather?
What are they doing?
Are they having a good time?

WORKBOOK PAGE 27

A. MATCHING OPPOSITES

1. d	**8.** n
2. a	**9.** l
3. g	**10.** i
4. c	**11.** j
5. f	**12.** h
6. b	**13.** k
7. e	**14.** m

B. WHAT ARE THEY SAYING?

1. tall	**5.** small
2. thin	**6.** noisy
3. young	**7.** expensive
4. married	**8.** ugly

C. LISTENING

Listen and circle the word you hear.

1. Sally's brother is very tall.
2. Their dog is very heavy.
3. The questions in my English book are very easy.
4. My friend George is single.
5. Mary's cat is very ugly!
6. This book is very cheap.

Answers

1. tall
2. heavy
3. easy
4. single
5. ugly
6. cheap

WORKBOOK PAGE 28

D. WHAT'S WRONG?

1. It isn't new. It's old.
2. They aren't quiet. They're noisy.
3. It isn't large. It's small.
4. He isn't single. He's married.
5. She isn't young. She's old.
6. They aren't short. They're tall.

E. SCRAMBLED QUESTIONS

1. Are you busy?
2. Is your dog large?
4. Are they married?
4. Am I beautiful?
5. Is English difficult?
6. Is their car new?
7. Is she tall or short?/Is she short or tall?
8. Is he noisy or quiet?/Is he quiet or noisy?

WORKBOOK PAGE 30

G. WHOSE THINGS?

1. Albert's car
2. Jenny's bicycle
3. George's guitar
4. Fred's dog
5. Kate's computer
6. Mr. Price's house
7. Jane's piano
8. Mike's TV
9. Mrs. Chang's book
10. Alice's cat

WORKBOOK PAGE 31

H. WHAT'S THE WORD?

1. Her
2. Their
3. His
4. Her
5. Its
6. Her
7. His
8. Their

I. MR. AND MRS. GRANT

1. Yes, he is.
2. No, he isn't.
3. No, he isn't.
4. Yes, he is.
5. Yes, she is.
6. No, she isn't.
7. Yes, she is.
8. No, it isn't.
9. Yes, it is.
10. Yes, it is.
11. No, it isn't.
12. No, they aren't.
13. Yes, they are.
14. No, it isn't.

WORKBOOK PAGE 32

J. HOW'S THE WEATHER?

1. It's warm.
2. It's sunny.
3. It's snowing.
4. It's raining.
5. It's cool.
6. It's hot.
7. It's cold.

K. LISTENING

Listen and circle the word you hear.

1. A. How's the weather in Rome today?
   B. It's cool.
2. A. How's the weather in Tokyo today?
   B. It's snowing.
3. A. How's the weather in Seoul today?
   B. It's sunny.
4. A. How's the weather in Shanghai today?
   B. It's hot.
5. A. How's the weather in New York today?
   B. It's raining.
6. A. How's the weather in Miami today?
   B. It's cloudy.

Answers

1. cool
2. snowing
3. sunny
4. hot
5. raining
6. cloudy

WORKBOOK PAGE 33

L. WHAT'S THE NUMBER?

1. 24
2. 31
3. 72
4. 46
5. 97

M. WHAT'S THE WORD?

thirty-eight
eighty-three
fifty-five
ninety-nine
sixty-four

N. NUMBER PUZZLE

WORKBOOK PAGE 34

O. LISTENING

Listen to the temperature in Fahrenheit and Celsius. Write the numbers you hear.

1. In Los Angeles, it's 86° Fahrenheit/ 30° Celsius.
2. In Seoul, it's 32° Fahrenheit/ 0° Celsius.
3. In San Juan, it's 81° Fahrenheit/ 27° Celsius.
4. In Hong Kong, it's 72° Fahrenheit/ 22° Celsius.
5. In Miami, it's 93° Fahrenheit/ 34° Celsius.
6. In London, it's 56° Fahrenheit/ 13° Celsius.
7. In Mexico City, it's 66° Fahrenheit/ 19° Celsius.
8. In Moscow, it's 34° Fahrenheit/ 1° Celsius.

Answers

1. 86° / 30°
2. 32° / 0°
3. 81° / 27°
4. 72° / 22°
5. 93° / 34°
6. 56° / 13°
7. 66° / 19°
8. 34° / 1°

Q. MATCHING

1. e
2. h
3. d
4. a
5. i
6. c
7. f
8. b
9. g

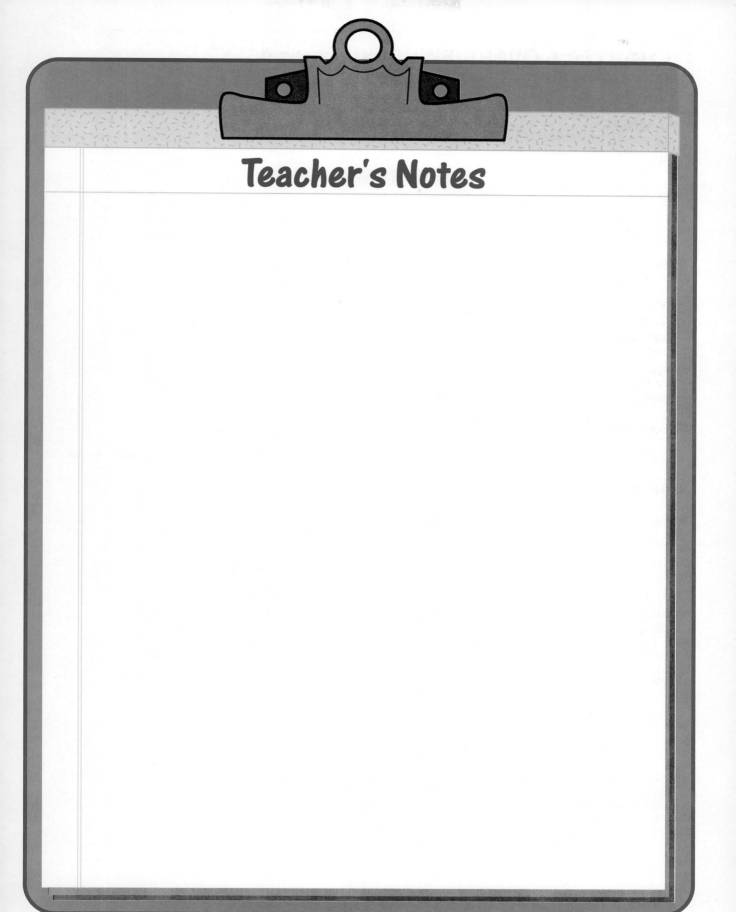

Teacher's Notes

GRAMMAR

PRESENT CONTINUOUS TENSE

What's	he she	doing?
What are	they	doing?

He's She's	sleeping.
They're	swimming.

TO BE

Who is	he? she?
Who are	they?

He's my father. She's my wife.
They're my parents.

PREPOSITIONS OF LOCATION

She's in the park.	He's sitting **on** his bed.
He's **at** the beach.	We're **in front of** our house.

FUNCTIONS

ASKING FOR AND REPORTING INFORMATION

Who is he?
  He's *my father*.
What's his name?
  His name is *Paul*.
What's he doing?
  He's *standing in front of the Eiffel Tower*.

INQUIRING ABOUT LOCATION

Where is *he?*

GIVING LOCATION

He's in *Paris*.

INTRODUCING SOMEONE

I'd like to introduce _____.
  Nice to meet you.
    Nice to meet you, too.

NEW VOCABULARY

Family

aunt
cousin
daughter
father
grandchildren
granddaughter
grandparents
grandson
husband
nephew
niece
parents
son
uncle
wife

People

man
people
teenagers
woman

Everyday Activities

acting
baking
crying
dancing
having *dinner*
laughing
making noise
riding
skateboarding
standing
taking *her* photograph
talking (about)
vacuuming
wearing

Adjectives

angry
favorite
late
sentimental
special
tired
wonderful

Prepositions

in front of

Question Words

Who

Places Around the World

Paris
Washington, D.C.

Famous Sights

Eiffel Tower
White House

Additional Words

a lot
apartment building
argument
band
bench
birthday party
clock
computer game
corner
drums
music
night
photograph

picture
play
popular music
rugs
sofa
wedding cake
wedding day
wedding gown

EXPRESSIONS

getting to know each other
having a big argument
having a wonderful time
"the good old days"
What a *terrible* night!

Text Page 45: Chapter Opening Page

VOCABULARY PREVIEW

You may want to introduce these words before beginning the chapter, or you may choose to wait until they first occur in a specific lesson. If you choose to introduce them at this point, here are some suggestions:

1. Have students look at the illustrations on text page 45 and identify the words they already know.

2. Present the vocabulary. Say each word and have the class repeat it chorally and individually. Check students' understanding and pronunciation of the words.

3. Practice the vocabulary as a class, in pairs, or in small groups. Have students cover the word list and look at the pictures. Practice the words in the following ways:

   • Say a word and have students tell the number of the illustration.

   • Give the number of an illustration and have students say the word.

FOCUS

- Questions with *Who*
- To Be: Review
- Present Continuous Tense: Review
- Prepositions of Location: *in, at, on, in front of*

CLOSE UP

RULE:	The question word *who* asks about people.
EXAMPLES:	**Who** is she? **Who** are they?
	She's my mother. They're my parents.

RULE:	A preposition of location indicates where someone or something is located in relation to another noun.
EXAMPLES:	She's **in** the park.
	He's **at** the beach.
	They're **in front of** the White House.
	He's sitting **on** his bed.

GETTING READY

Introduce or review the vocabulary for family members depicted on text page 45. If you are introducing the vocabulary for the first time, refer to the suggestions for presenting it on the previous page.

INTRODUCING THE MODEL

1. Have students look at the model illustration.
2. Set the scene: "Two co-workers are talking."
3. Present the model.
4. Full-Class Repetition.

5. Ask students if they have any questions. Check understanding of new vocabulary: *who, father, photograph, Paris, standing, in front of, Eiffel Tower.*

   ### Culture Note

   The Eiffel Tower is a well-known landmark in Paris, France.

6. Group Choral Repetition.
7. Choral Conversation.
8. Call on one or two pairs of students to present the dialog.

   (For additional practice, do Choral Conversation in small groups or by rows.)

SIDE BY SIDE EXERCISES

Examples

> 1. A. Who is she?
>   B. She's my mother.
>   A. What's her name?
>   B. Her name is _____.*
>   A. Where is she?
>   B. She's in the park.
>   A. What's she doing?
>   B. She's riding her bicycle.
>
> 2. A. Who are they?
>   B. They're my parents.
>   A. What are their names?
>   B. Their names are _____
>   and _____.*
>   A. Where are they?
>   B. They're in the dining room.
>   A. What are they doing?
>   B. They're having dinner.

* Tell students that they can use any names they wish.

1. **Exercise 1:** Introduce the new words *riding*, *bicycle*. Call on two students to present the dialog. Then do Choral Repetition and Choral Conversation practice.

2. **Exercise 2:** Introduce the new expression *having dinner*. Same as above.

3. **Exercises 3-14:** Either Full-Class Practice or Pair Practice.

New Vocabulary

6. sofa	11. school
7. baking	acting
cake	play
8. wedding	13. game
crying	14. birthday party
9. Washington, D.C.	dancing
the White House	
10. apartment	
building	
skateboarding	

Culture Note

The White House (Exercise 9) is a popular tourist site in Washington D.C., the U.S. capital. It is the official residence of the president of the United States.

Language Note

Exercise 9: The word *aunt* has two accepted pronunciations: [ænt] and [ant].

Pronunciation Note

The pronunciation focus of Chapter 6 is **Stressed and Unstressed Words** (text page 52). You may wish to model this pronunciation at this point and encourage students to incorporate it into their language practice.

She's ríding her bícycle.

He's sléeping on the sófa.

WORKBOOK

Pages 35–39

EXPANSION ACTIVITIES

1. Clap and Listen

a. With students' books closed, read the model conversation.

b. Read it again, this time clapping your hands or tapping on the desk to indicate missing words. For example: "[*clap*] is he?" Have students respond: "Who."

c. Say: "He's [*clap*] father." Have students respond: "my."

d. Continue in the same way with the other lines of the conversation.

2. Scrambled Dialogs

a. Write each line of the three lists of questions from page 46 on a separate card. Scramble the cards.

b. Give the cards to 12 students. Have them unscramble the lines and put together the three sets of questions.

c. Form pairs and have each pair read their set of three questions.

3. Pictures Alive!

Review family members by having students look at the illustrations on text page 45 and make them *come alive*.

a. Write on the board:

Who is he?   He's my _____.
Who is she?   She's my _____.
Who are they?   They're my _____.

[*top left picture*]

b. Have a female and male student come to the front of the room. Point to the male student and ask the female student: "Who is he? " ("He's my husband."). Point to the female student and ask the male student: "Who is she?" ("She's my wife.")

[*top right picture*]

c. Call on another female and another male student to come to the front along side the *husband* and *wife*. Continue by pointing and asking about other family relationships: *mother, father, parents, daughter, son, children, sister, brother.*

d. Continue with the remaining two illustrations.

4. Famous People!

Bring to class newspaper or magazine photographs of famous local, national, and international personalities. Have students use the questions on text page 46 to talk about the people. For example:

[*photograph of national politician*]

A. Who is she?
B. She's the prime minister of our country.
A. What's her name?
B. Her name is _____.
A. Where is she in this photograph?
B. She's _____.
A. What's she doing?
B. She's _____ing.*

* You may need to introduce some new vocabulary, especially for answers to the question "What's he/she doing?"

5. Finish the Sentence!

Begin a sentence about an activity, using the vocabulary from text pages 46–48. Tell students to add any location they wish to complete the sentence. For example:

Teacher: She's washing her car . . .
Students: She's washing her car in front of her apartment building.
           She's washing her car in front of the garage.
Teacher: They're singing and dancing . . .

(continued)

Students: They're singing and dancing at my
            birthday party.
            They're singing and dancing in the
            park.
Teacher: He's sleeping . . .
Students: He's sleeping in the bedroom.
            He's sleeping on the sofa in the
            living room.

Variation: This activity may be done as a class, in
pairs or small groups, or as a game with
competing teams.

6. Question the Answers!

   a. Dictate answers such as the following to the
      class:

      She's my mother.
      His name is Ralph Jones.
      They're playing a game.
      We're washing our car.
      They're at my wedding.
      She's having dinner.
      We're at the beach.
      He's in front of his house.
      They're my cousins.
      She's in the yard.
      He's planting flowers.

   b. Have students write questions for which
      these answers would be correct. For
      example:

Questions	Answers
She's my mother.	Who is she?
His name is Ralph Jones.	What's his name?

   c. Have students compare their questions with
      each other.

Variation: Write the answers on cards. Divide the
class into groups and give each group a set of
cards.

7. Sentences Alive!

   a. Make up several sentences based on this
      lesson. For example:

      My daughter is riding her bicycle in the park.
      My wife is standing in front of our apartment
      building.

My husband is swimming at the beach.
My son is sitting on his bed and playing the
   guitar.
My grandparents are sitting on the sofa and
   watching TV.
My uncle is painting his living room.
My friends are dancing at my birthday party.

   b. Write the words to each of these sentences
      on separate cards.

   c. One sentence at a time, distribute the cards
      randomly to students in the class.

   d. Have students decide on the correct word
      order of the sentence and then come to the
      front of the room, and make the sentence
      come alive by standing in order while holding up
      their cards and saying the sentence aloud one
      word at a time.

8. Change the Sentence!

   a. Write a sentence on the board, underlining
      and numbering different portions of the
      sentence. For example:

   b. Have students sit in a circle.

   c. Tell them that when you say a number, the
      first student in the circle makes a change in
      that part of the sentence. For example:

      Teacher: Two.
      Student 1: My sister <u>is reading</u> in the yard.

   d. The second student keeps the first student's
      sentence, but changes it based on the next
      number you say. For example:

      Teacher: Three.
      Student 2: My sister is reading in <u>the living
                  room</u>.

e. Continue this way with the rest of the students in the circle. For example:

Teacher: One.
Student 3: <u>My grandfather</u> is reading in the living room.

Teacher: Two.
Student 4: My grandfather <u>is playing cards</u> in the living room.

9. Information Gap: Sam's Family

a. Tell students that Sam's family is home today. Make up a map of his house with his family members placed in different rooms and a description of what they are doing. Divide the information between two different maps. For example:

House Map A:

Living room	Kitchen	Bedroom
_____ _____	Sam's mother baking a cake	_____ _____
Yard Sam's grandparents planting flowers		Dining room Sam's cousin Tom doing his homework
Attic _____ _____	Garage Sam's brother fixing his car	Bathroom _____ _____

House Map B:

Living room	Kitchen	Bedroom
Sam's aunt and uncle watching TV	_____	Sam's brother playing the guitar
Yard _____ _____		Dining room _____
Attic Sam's father cleaning	Garage _____ _____	Bathroom Sam's sister brushing her teeth

b. Divide the class into pairs. Give each member of the pair a different map. Have students ask each other questions and fill in their house maps. For example:

Student A: Who's in the living room?
Student B: Sam's aunt and uncle.
Student A: What are they doing?
Student B: They're watching TV.
Student A *[writes the information in House Map A]*

c. The pairs continue until each has a filled-in map.

d. Have students look at their partners' maps to make sure that they have written the information correctly.

Have students bring in photographs from home. Bring several of your own. (Note that large photographs of a limited number of people work best.)

1. Introduce the example in the text. Check students' understanding of the word *bench*. Call on a few students to read about the photograph of Amanda and her sister.

2. Tell about one of your photographs in a similar way.

3. As a class, in pairs, or in small groups, have students tell about photographs they have brought in.

READING *Arthur Is Very Angry*

FOCUS

- **To Be: Review**

NEW VOCABULARY

a lot of	music
angry	night
barking	people
clock	rugs
drums	teenagers
having a big	tired
argument	vacuuming
late	violin
making noise	What a terrible night!
man	woman

READING THE STORY

Optional: Preview the story by having students talk about the story title and / or illustration. You may choose to introduce new vocabulary beforehand, or have students encounter the new vocabulary within the context of the reading.

1. Have students read the story silently, or follow along silently as the story is read aloud by you, by one or more students, or on the audio program.

2. Ask students if they have any questions. Check understanding of vocabulary.

3. Check students' comprehension, using some or all of the following questions:

    What's Arthur doing?
    Is he happy?
    Why not?
    What are the people in Apartment 2 doing?

What's the man in Apartment 3 doing?
What's the woman in Apartment 4 doing?
What are the teenagers in Apartment 5 doing?
What's the dog in Apartment 6 doing?
What are the people in Apartment 7 doing?

✓ READING *CHECK-UP*

Q & A

1. Call on a pair of students to present the model.

2. Have students work in pairs to create new dialogs.

3. Call on pairs to present their new dialogs to the class.

CHOOSE

1. a		**4.** a	
2. b		**5.** b	
3. a		**6.** a	

READING EXTENSION

Ask students the following questions and have them review the text for the answers.

Who is sitting on his bed and looking at his clock?
These people are dancing. What's their apartment number?
These people are having an argument. What's their apartment number?
These people are listening to loud music. What's their apartment number?
This man is vacuuming his rugs. What's his apartment number?
This woman is playing the drums. What's her apartment number?
Who is tired and angry?
What's another title for the reading?

EXPANSION ACTIVITY

Class Discussion

1. Write the following questions on the board:

   > Who are your neighbors?
   > Are they good neighbors?
   > Are they noisy or quiet?

2. Have students discuss their responses in pairs and then share their opinions with the class.

READING *Tom's Wedding Day*

FOCUS

- To Be: Review

NEW VOCABULARY

band	taking her
corner	photograph
favorite	talking (about)
fireplace	"the good old days"
getting to know	wearing
each other	wedding cake
laughing	wedding day
popular music	wedding gown
sentimental	white
special	wonderful

READING THE STORY

Optional: Preview the story by having students talk about the story title and/or illustrations. You may choose to introduce new vocabulary beforehand, or have students encounter the new vocabulary within the context of the reading.

1. Have students read silently, or follow along silently as the story is read aloud by you, by one or more students, or on the audio program.

2. Ask students if they have any questions. Check understanding of new vocabulary.

✓ READING *CHECK-UP*

WHAT'S THE ANSWER?

1. She's standing in front of the fireplace.
2. She's wearing a beautiful white wedding gown.
3. He's taking her photograph.
4. She's crying.
5. She's dancing with Jane's father.
6. They're sitting in the corner and talking about "the good old days."

READING EXTENSION

Ask students the following questions and have them scan the text for the answers.

Who is wearing the wedding gown?
Who is taking her picture?
Who is crying?
Who is playing music?
Who is dancing with Jane's father?
Who is dancing with Jane's mother?
Who is sitting in the corner and talking about the "the good old days"?
What's another title for the reading?

Text Page 51

 LISTENING

QUIET OR NOISY?

Listen to the sentence. Are the people quiet or noisy?

1. He's listening to loud music.
2. She's reading.
3. He's sleeping.
4. The band is playing.
5. Everybody is singing and dancing.
6. He's studying.

Answers

1. b   **3.** a   **5.** b
2. a   **4.** b   **6.** a

WHAT DO YOU HEAR?

Listen to the sound. What do you hear? Choose the correct answer.

1. [sound: singing]
2. [sound: crying]
3. [sound: vacuuming]
4. [sound: laughing]
5. [sound: drums]

Answers

1. b   **3.** a   **5.** b
2. a   **4.** b

 IN YOUR OWN WORDS

1. Make sure students understand the instructions.
2. Have students do the activity as written homework, using a dictionary for any new words they wish to use.

3. Have students present and discuss what they have written, in pairs or as a class.

How to Say It!

Introducing People: This is one of many ways to make an introduction. *I'd* is a contraction of *I would*. *I'd like to* is a polite way of saying *I want to*. In the United States, it is customary to shake hands when being introduced. The handshake is usually firm and brief—usually just two shakes.

1. Set the scene: "Someone is introducing her brother."
2. With books closed, have students listen as you present the conversation or play the audio one or more times.
3. Full-Class Repetition.
4. Have students open their books and look at the dialog. Ask students if they have any questions. Check understanding of new vocabulary: *I'd like to, introduce.*
5. Group Choral Repetition.
6. Choral Conversation.
7. Call on one or two groups of students to present the dialog. You may want them to stand in front of the class to demonstrate the handshake that accompanies an introduction.
8. Group Practice: Have students practice the model in groups of three as you walk around the room listening and helping.
9. Have students practice using their own names in the dialog.
10. Call on several groups of students to present their conversations to the class.

EXPANSION ACTIVITY

Celebrity Introductions

1. Tell students to choose a celebrity personality and pretend to *be* that person. Have them make a name tag with that person's name.

2. Have students circulate around the room introducing each other. Set a time limit of 5 minutes.

3. Have students make a list of all the names of celebrities they just met. Have students share their lists with the class. Who has the longest list?

PRONUNCIATION

Stressed and Unstressed Words

Content words receive more stress in a sentence because they carry more information. They are spoken more clearly and at a higher pitch.

Structure words are the grammatical markers in a sentence. They don't carry as much information and are therefore not as stressed. They are spoken with reductions and at a lower pitch. For example:

He's pláying the guitár.

Focus on Listening

Practice the sentences in the left column. Say each sentence or play the audio one or more times. Have students listen carefully and repeat.

Focus on Pronunciation

Practice the sentences in the right column. Have students say each sentence and then listen carefully as you say it or play the audio.

If you wish, have students continue practicing the sentences to improve their pronunciation.

 JOURNAL

Have students write their journal entries at home or in class. Encourage students to use a dictionary to look up words they would like to use. Students can share their written work with other students if appropriate. Have students discuss what they have written as a class, in pairs, or in small groups.

WORKBOOK

Check-up Test: Page 40

 CHAPTER SUMMARY

GRAMMAR

1. Divide the class into pairs or small groups.
2. Have students take turns forming sentences from the grammar boxes. Student A says a sentence, and Student B points to the words from each column that are in the sentence. Then have students switch: Student B says a sentence, and Student A points to the words.

KEY VOCABULARY

Have students ask you any questions about the meaning or pronunciation of the vocabulary. If students ask for the pronunciation, repeat after the student until the student is satisfied with his or her pronunciation.

EXPANSION ACTIVITIES

1. **Do You Remember the Words?**

   Check students' retention of the vocabulary depicted on the opening page of Chapter 6 by doing the following activity:

   a. Have students open their books to page 45 and cover the list of vocabulary words.

   b. Either call out a number and have students tell you the word, or say a word and have students tell you the number.

   Variation: You can also do this activity as a game with competing teams.

2. Student-Led Dictation

a. Tell each student to choose a word from the Key Vocabulary list on text page 52 and look at it very carefully.

b. Have students take turns dictating their words to the class. Everybody writes down that student's word.

c. When the dictation is completed, call on different students to write each word on the board to check the spelling.

3. Beanbag Toss

a. Call out a topic from the chapter—for example: *Family Members.*

b. Have students toss a beanbag back and forth. The student to whom the beanbag is tossed must name a word in that category. For example:

Student 1: grandmother
Student 2: grandfather
Student 3: grandchild

c. Continue until all the words in the category have been named.

1. Category Dictation

a. Have students draw three columns on a piece of paper. At the top of one column, have students write <u>Male</u>. At the top of the second column, have them write <u>Female</u>. At the top of the third column, have them write <u>Male and Female</u>.

b. Dictate various family member words from the text and have students write them in the appropriate column. For example:

Male	Female	Male and Female
father	mother	parents
son	daughter	children

2. Scrambled Sentences

a. Divide the class into two teams.

b. One sentence at a time, write individual sentences out of order on the board. For example:

> Sam's are parents having dining dinner room the in
>
> sister brother and Sam's kitchen in cake the baking a are
>
> aunt in uncle and Washington are Sam's standing the White House in front of

c. The first person to raise his or her hand, come to the board, and write the sentence in the correct order earns a point for that team.

d. The team with the most points wins the *Scrambled Sentence* game.

Variation: Write the words to several sentences on separate cards. Divide the class into small groups, and have students work together to put the sentences into correct order.

3. Which Picture?

a. Bring in several pictures or ask students to bring in pictures of people at special occasions.

b. Write the following on the board:

> Where are they?
> What are they doing?
> Describe the people.

c. Divide the class into pairs, and have each pair choose a picture and describe it by answering the questions on the board.

d. Have students read their descriptions aloud as the class listens and tries to identify which picture they're describing.

4. Do You Remember?

a. Divide the class into pairs.

b. Tell students to spend three minutes looking carefully at the illustration on text page 51.

c. Have students close their books and write down what they remember about the scene.

d. Have students compare their sentences with their partner and then look at the illustration in the book to see how much they remembered.

Note: This activity can also be done with any picture you bring to class from a newspaper or magazine depicting situations relevant to Chapter 6.

5. Board Game

a. On poster boards or on manila file folders, make up game boards with a pathway consisting of separate spaces. You may use any design you wish. For example:

1 START	2	3	4	5	6	7	8
18 END							9
17	16	15	14	13	12	11	10

b. Divide the class into groups of two to four students and give each group a game board, a die, and something to be used as a playing piece.

c. Give each group a pile of cards face-down with statements such as the following. Students have to tell who the person is.

This person is your mother's sister.	(aunt)
This person is your father's brother.	(uncle)
This person is your father's mother.	(grandmother)
This person is your mother's father.	(grandfather)
This person is your sister's daughter.	(niece)
This person is your brother's son.	(nephew)
This person is your daughter's daughter.	(granddaughter)
This person is your son's son.	(grandson)
These people are your son's children.	(grandchildren)
This person is your aunt's daughter.	(cousin)

d. Each student in turn rolls the die, moves the playing piece along the game path, and after landing on a space, picks a card and answers the question.

Option: You should decide on the rules of the game. You may want each student to take his or her turn only once, or you may want a student who successfully answers a question to take another turn.

e. The first student to reach the end of the pathway is the winner.

6. Dictation Game

a. Make up a story about *Jane's Special Day.* Write the story in large print on a piece of paper. For example:

> Today is a special day for Jane.
> It's her wedding day.
> Everybody is at her wedding.
> Her cousins, her friends, and her parents are here.
> Her mother is crying.
> She's very sentimental.
> Jane isn't crying.
> She laughing and dancing with her new husband.
> It's a wonderful day for Jane.

b. Put the paper on the far side of the room or out in the hallway so that students can't read it from their seats.

c. Divide the class into pairs. One student from each pair runs to read the story and then returns to dictate it to the partner. The runner may go back and forth as many times as necessary. The first pair to finish writing the story wins.

WORKBOOK ANSWER KEY AND LISTENING SCRIPTS

WORKBOOK PAGE 35

A. A FAMILY

1. wife
2. husband
3. children
4. son
5. daughter
6. brother
7. sister
8. father
9. mother
10. grandparents
11. grandfather
12. grandmother
13. grandchildren
14. grandson
15. granddaughter
16. uncle
17. aunt
18. nephew
19. niece
20. cousin

WORKBOOK PAGE 36

B. LISTENING

Listen and put a check under the correct picture.

1. In this photograph, my sister is skateboarding in the park.
2. In this photograph, my son is acting in a play.
3. In this photograph, my friends are dancing at my wedding.
4. In this photograph, my uncle is baking a cake.
5. In this photograph, my cousin is playing a game on her computer.
6. In this photograph, my husband is standing in front of our apartment building.
7. In this photograph, my grandparents are having dinner.
8. In this photograph, my aunt is planting flowers.

Answers

1. ✔ ___ 2. ___ ✔
3. ✔ ___ 4. ___ ✔
5. ✔ ___ 6. ✔ ___
7. ___ ✔ 8. ✔ ___

C. THE WRONG WORD!

1. cheap (The others indicate size.)
2. park (The others are rooms of the house.)
3. baseball (The others are musical instruments.)
4. tall (The others describe people's appearance.)
5. dinner (The others describe the weather.)
6. rugs (The others are family members.)
7. bank (The others are classroom items.)
8. Mr. (The others are titles for women.)
9. poor (The others describe sound.)
10. sister (The others are male.)

WORKBOOK PAGE 37

D. GrammarSong

1. smiling
2. living
3. living
4. looking
5. hanging
6. dancing
7. having
8. crying
9. looking
10. hanging
11. smiling
12. looking

WORKBOOK PAGE 38

E. AN E-MAIL FROM LOS ANGELES

1. It's in Los Angeles.
2. It's warm and sunny.
3. It's 78° Fahrenheit.
4. They're in the park.
5. She's reading a book.
6. He's listening to music.
7. She's Bob's sister.
8. She's riding her bicycle.
9. He's Bob's brother.
10. He's skateboarding.
11. No, they aren't.
12. They're at home.
13. She's baking.
14. He's planting flowers in the yard.
15. No, he isn't.
16. He's in New York.

WORKBOOK PAGE 40

CHECK-UP TEST: Chapters 4-6

A.

1. nephew
2. in
3. beach
4. its
5. on
6. reading
7. fixing
8. brushing

B.

1. Where
2. grandmother
3. niece
4. Who
5. her
6. their
7. his

C.

1. He's thin.
2. They're tall.
3. It's new.

D.

1. Are you married?
2. Are they quiet?
3. Is she young?

E.

Listen and choose the correct response.

Ex. Is he old?

1. Is it large?
2. Is she poor?
3. Is it sunny?
4. Is he quiet?

Answers

1. b
2. a
3. b
4. b

FEATURE ARTICLE
A Family Tree

PREVIEWING THE ARTICLE

Have students look at the diagram of the family tree. Introduce the expression *family tree*. Tell students to refer to the diagram while they read or listen to the article.

READING THE ARTICLE

1. Have students read silently, or follow along silently as the article is read aloud by you, by one or more students, or on the audio program.

2. Ask students if they have any questions. Check understanding of new vocabulary: *diagram*, *members*.

3. Check students' comprehension, using some or all of the following questions:

   Who are the grandparents?
   Who are Betty and Henry's children?
   Who are Betty and Henry's grandchildren?
   Who is Tom's wife?
   Is Linda married?
   Who is Sally's husband?
   Who are Sally and Jack's children?
   Who are Jimmy's cousins?
   Who is Sarah's uncle?
   Who are Sarah's aunts?
   Who are Linda's nieces?
   Who are Linda's nephews?

4. Have students individually draw their own family trees and write an explanation. In pairs, have students share their drawings and writing.

   Variation: Divide the class into pairs, and have Student A tell about his or her family members while Student B draws a family tree based on the relationships that Student A describes.

EXPANSION ACTIVITIES

1. **Family Tree Game**

   a. Divide the class into teams.

   b. Have members of each team take turns answering questions about the family tree depicted on text page 53. You may use one or more of the following question types:

   - Make a statement about a family relationship and have students name the person. For example:

     This person is Tom's wife.   (Patty)
     This person is Sarah's brother.   (Jimmy)

   - Give two names and have students state the relationship. For example:

     Linda: Tom   (*Linda is Tom's sister.*)
     Henry: Betty   (*Henry is Betty's husband.*)

   - Make true/false statements about the family relationships. If the answer is false, have students correct it. For example:

     Kevin is Tom's son.   True.
     Julie is Linda's nephew. False. Julie is her niece.

2. **Family Words**

   As a class, in pairs, or in small groups, have students tell common ways in their language of referring to close family members. For example, in English:

mother:	mom, mommy, mum, mummy, ma
father:	dad, daddy, papa, pa
grandmother:	grandma, grammie, granny, nana
grandfather:	grandpa, gramps, grampie

BUILD YOUR VOCABULARY!
Classroom Activities

reading	closing my book
writing	erasing the board
raising my hand	using a calculator
opening my book	

1. Have students look at the illustrations and identify any words they already know.

2. Present the vocabulary. Say each word and have the class repeat it chorally and individually. Check students' understanding and pronunciation of the words.

EXPANSION ACTIVITIES

1. Miming

a. Write down on cards the classroom activities from text page 53.

b. Have students take turns picking a card from the pile and pantomiming the action on the card.

c. The class must guess what the person is doing.

Variation: This can be done as a game with competing teams.

2. Category Dictation

a. Have students draw three columns on a piece of paper. At the top of the first column, have students write the word <u>write</u>. At the top of the second column, have them write <u>close</u>. At the top of the third column, have them write <u>use</u>.

b. Dictate words students have learned and have students write them in the appropriate column. For example:

<u>write</u>	<u>close</u>	<u>use</u>
your name	the window	a calculator
your address	your notebook	a ruler
a story		a computer

3. Association Game

a. Divide the class into several teams.

b. Call out a classroom activity verb.

c. Have the students in each group work together to see how many words they can associate with that verb. For example:

read:	book, newspaper, story
write:	journal, letter
open:	window, door, book,

The team with the most items wins.

4. TPR, Please!

This game consists of a series of rapid commands which students follow only when the command is preceded by *please*. If a student follows the command when *please* is not spoken, that student must stop playing the game.

a. Say: "Please open your notebook." (Students open their notebooks.)

b. Say: "Please write your name in your notebook." (Students write their names in their notebooks.)

c. Say: "Erase your name." (Any students who erase their names drop out of the game.)

5. Picture Description

a. Find a picture of a classroom in a magazine or a textbook. Duplicate it and hand it out to every other student.

b. Have pairs of students sit back-to-back. Student A describes the picture and Student B writes down what Student A says.

c. Stop the activity after five minutes. See which pair has written the most sentences.

LISTENING *Today's Weather*

AROUND THE WORLD
Extended and Nuclear Families

1. Write on the board:

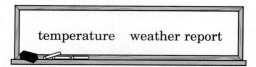

   temperature   weather report

2. Introduce *temperature* by drawing a thermometer on the board and indicating the degrees. Remind students that 100 degrees Fahrenheit is very hot and that 32 degrees Fahrenheit is cold.

LISTENING SCRIPT

Listen to the weather reports. Match the weather and the cities.

This is Robby T. with the weather report from WXBC. It's a hot day in Honolulu today. The temperature here is one hundred degrees, and everybody is swimming at the beach.

This is Annie Lu with the weather report from WCLD in Atlanta. It's snowing here in Atlanta today, and everybody is at home.

This is Herbie Ross with today's weather from WFTG radio. It's warm and sunny here in Los Angeles today. The temperature is seventy degrees. It's a beautiful day.

This is Jimmy G. with your weather on WHME radio. It's cool and sunny here in Toronto today. It's a very nice day.

This is Lisa Lee with your WQRZ weather report. It's cold and cloudy in Chicago today. The temperature here is thirty-two degrees. Yes, it's a cold and cloudy day!

Answers

1. d
2. a
3. e
4. c
5. b

1. Have students read silently or follow along silently as the text is read by you, by one or more students, or on the audio program. Check understanding of new vocabulary:

another	nuclear family
building	only
common	same
extended family	

2. As a class, in pairs, or in small groups, discuss the questions. For each type of family (*nuclear* and *extended*), draw a set of two columns on the board to contrast its advantages and disadvantages.

GLOBAL EXCHANGE

1. Set the scene: "Ken425 is writing to his keypal."

   Language Note

   Ken425 is this person's *screen name*. This is the name he uses when he is on the Internet.

2. Have students read silently or follow along silently as the message is read aloud by you, by one or more students, or on the audio program.

3. Ask students if they have any questions. Check understanding of vocabulary.

4. Suggestions for additional practice:

   • Have students write a response to Ken425 and share their writing in pairs.

   • Have students correspond with a keypal on the Internet and then share their experience with the class.

FACT FILE
Family Relationships

1. Explain that *in-law* indicates a family relationship through marriage.

2. Read the text aloud as students follow along.

3. Ask students if they have anyone in their family who is an *in-law*. Have students name the person and explain the relationship. For example:

   Student 1: Rick is my brother-in-law. He's my sister's husband.

   Student 2: Elena is my daughter-in-law. She's my son's wife.

4. For additional practice, do either or both of the following:

   a. Have students look at the illustration on page 53 and identify all the *in-law* relationships.

   b. Review all family relationships. Divide the class into teams and quiz them with the following clues:

your daughter's husband	*(son-in-law)*
your sister's daughter	*(niece)*
your brother's wife	*(sister-in-law)*
your mother's mother	*(grandmother)*
your brother's son	*(nephew)*
your mother's brother	*(uncle)*
your father's sister	*(aunt)*
your aunt's children	*(cousins)*
your father's father	*(grandfather)*
your sister's husband	*(brother-in-law)*
your son's wife	*(daughter-in-law)*
your husband's mother	*(mother-in-law)*
your wife's father	*(father-in-law)*
your daughter's son	*(grandson)*
your son's children	*(grandchildren)*

WHAT ARE THEY SAYING?

FOCUS

- Talking about Families

Have students talk about the people and the situation, and then create role plays based on the scene. Students may refer back to previous lessons as a resource, but they should not simply reuse specific conversations.

Note: You may want to assign this exercise as written homework, having students prepare their role plays, practice them the next day with the other students, and then present them to the class.

GRAMMAR

THERE IS/THERE ARE

> There's one window in the bedroom.
>
> Is there a laundromat in this neighborhood?
> > Yes, there is.
> > No, there isn't.

> There are two windows in the bedroom.
>
> Are there any children in the building?
> > Yes, there are.
> > No, there aren't.

PREPOSITIONS

> It's next to the bank.
> It's across from the movie theater.
> It's between the library and the park.
> It's around the corner from the hospital.

SINGULAR/PLURAL: INTRODUCTION

> There's one bedroom in the apartment.
> There are two bedrooms in the apartment.

FUNCTIONS

INQUIRING ABOUT LOCATION

Where's the *restaurant*?
Where is it?

GIVING LOCATION

It's next to *the bank*.
It's across from *the movie theater*.
It's between *the library* and *the park*.
It's around the corner from *the hospital*.

There's a *laundromat* on *Main Street*, next to *the supermarket*.

ATTRACTING ATTENTION

Excuse me.

CHECKING UNDERSTANDING

Two bedrooms?
> Yes. That's right.

ASKING FOR AND REPORTING INFORMATION

Is there *a laundromat* in *this neighborhood*?
> Yes. There's a *laundromat* on *Main Street*.

Is there a *stove* in *the kitchen*?
> Yes, there is.
> No, there isn't.
Are there any *mice* in *the basement*?
> Yes, there are.
> No, there aren't.

How many *bedrooms* are there in *the apartment*?
> There are *two bedrooms* in *the apartment*.

Tell me, _____?

EXPRESSING GRATITUDE

Thank you./Thanks.
> You're welcome.

NEW VOCABULARY

Places Around Town

airport
bakery
barber shop
book store
bus station
church
clothing store
department store
drug store
fire station
gas station
hair salon
mall
police station
school
shopping mall
store
supermarket
train station
video store

Housing

air conditioner
bus stop
closet
cockroach
elevator
fire escape
floor
hole
jacuzzi
landlord

mailbox
mice
refrigerator
roof
satellite dish
stove
superintendent
tenant
washing machine

Community

avenue
center
neighborhood
place
sidewalk
town

People

men
women

Adjectives

broken
convenient
nice
open
upset

Time Words

all day
all night
now

Prepositions of Location

across from
around the corner from
between
next to
near
outside

Miscellaneous

almost
any
because
every
however
more than
some
there
there are
there's (there is)

EXPRESSIONS

Excuse me.
in this neighborhood
Oh, good.
Oh, I see.
Tell me, . . .
That's right.

VOCABULARY PREVIEW

You may want to introduce these words before beginning the chapter, or you may choose to wait until they first occur in a specific lesson. If you choose to introduce them at this point, here are some suggestions:

1. Have students look at the illustrations on text page 55 and identify the words they already know.

2. Present the vocabulary. Say each word and have the class repeat it chorally and individually. Check students' understanding and pronunciation of the words.

3. Practice the vocabulary as a class, in pairs, or in small groups. Have students cover the word list and look at the pictures. Practice the words in the following ways:

   • Say a word and have students tell the number of the illustration.

   • Give the number of an illustration and have students say the word.

Text Page 56: Where's the Restaurant?

FOCUS

- Prepositions of Location
- Places Around Town

CLOSE UP

RULE: Prepositions of location indicate where something is located in relation to other nouns.

EXAMPLES: It's **next to** the bank.
It's **across from** the movie theater.
It's **between** the library and the park.
It's **around the corner from** the hospital.

GETTING READY

1. Use your own visuals, *Side by Side* Picture Cards 27–35, 91, or refer to the illustrations on text pages 7, 14, and 31 to practice the following locations in the community.

   Review: *restaurant, bank, post office, supermarket, movie theater, park, library, hospital*

   Introduce: *school*

2. Introduce the prepositions *next to, across from,* and *between.* Use your students' names and locations in the classroom and say:

   (Jim) is next to (Jane).
   (Maria) is across from (Ken).
   (Linda) is between (Carlos) and (Paul).

INTRODUCING THE MODELS

There are four model conversations. Introduce and practice each model before going on to the next. For each model:

1. Have students look at the model illustration.

2. Set the scene: "Two people are talking."

3. Present the model.

4. Full-Class Repetition.

5. Ask students if they have any questions. Check understanding of new vocabulary: *next to, across from, between, around the corner from.*

6. Group Choral Repetition.

7. Choral Conversation.

8. Call on one or two pairs of students to present the dialog.

   (For more practice, do Choral Conversation in small groups or by rows.)

9. Give students extra pronunciation practice with the final [z] sound in *where's.*

   a. Have students repeat: "Where's the restaurant?" Then cue questions, such as:

      park: "Where's the park?"
      church: "Where's the church?"

   b. Practice the final [s] sound in *it's.* Have students repeat: "It's next to the bank." Cue other sentences, such as:

      school: "It's next to the school."
      post office: "It's next to the post office."

SIDE BY SIDE EXERCISES

Use your own visuals, *Side by Side* Picture Cards 92–99, or the illustrations on text page 55 to practice the following locations in the community that are included in the exercises: *hotel, gas station, bus station, clinic, fire station, bakery, video store, barber shop.*

Examples

1. A. Where's the bank?
   B. It's next to the school

2. A. Where's the post office?
   B. It's across from the park.

1. **Exercise 1:** Call on two students to present the dialog. Then do Choral Repetition and Choral Conversation practice.

2. **Exercise 2:** Same as above.

3. **Exercises 3–8:** Either Full-Class Practice or Pair Practice.

WORKBOOK

Page 41

EXPANSION ACTIVITIES

1. **Beanbag Toss**

   Have students toss a beanbag back and forth. The student to whom the beanbag is tossed must name a place around town. For example:

   Student 1: restaurant
   Student 2: bank
   Student 3: hospital

2. **Create a Street Scene with Your Students**

   Give visuals of places in the community to ten students. Use your own visuals, word cards, or *Side by Side* Picture Cards. Have students hold these visuals and stand in front of the class in three lines, to form two intersecting streets. For example:

   Call on pairs of students to ask and answer *where* questions about the locations in this street scene. For example:

   A. Where's the bank?
   B. It's across from the bakery.

3. **Create a Street Scene on the Board**

   On the board, create a simple street map showing two intersecting streets. You can tape visuals of locations to the board or you can write place names. For example:

   Call on pairs of students to ask and answer *where* questions about these locations as in Expansion Activity 2.

4. **What's the Building?**

   Use the illustrations for exercises 1–8 on text page 56. (Students should ignore the questions and just look at the illustrations.) Have students look at these illustrations as you describe the location of different buildings. For example, "It's across from the park." Students then tell which building fits the location you described. Students can compete individually or in teams.

Teacher	Students
It's across from the park.	the post office
It's around the corner from the movie theater.	the hospital
It's between the video store and the barber shop.	the bakery
It's next to the bus station.	the gas station
It's around the corner from the fire station.	the clinic
It's across from the library.	the hotel
It's between the bank and the library.	the restaurant
It's next to the school.	the bank

5. Collaborative Map Game

a. Divide the class into groups of eight students.

b. Make sets of the map information, writing each line of information on a separate card.

> The hospital is between the restaurant and the post office.

> The hotel is across from the hospital.

> The post office is across from the movie theater.

> The movie theater is next to the hotel.

> The bakery is next to the hotel and across from the restaurant.

> The gas station is around the corner from the movie theater.

> The bank is around the corner from the bakery.

> The clinic is between the bank and the gas station.

c. Give each group one set of cards and one copy of the following map:

d. Have students take turns reading their information cards to their group. Have the group members listen and write the location of each place on the map.

e. The first group to finish should draw its map on the board for the rest of the class to check.

FOCUS

- There Is
- Prepositions of Location
- Places Around Town

CLOSE UP

RULE:	*There is* indicates the existence or location of something. The verb *to be* agrees in number with the noun that follows. If a single noun follows, the verb is in its singular form (*is*).
EXAMPLES:	**There's** a laundromat on Main Street. **There's** a department store on Central Avenue.

RULE:	*There is* usually contracts to *There's* in informal English.
EXAMPLE:	(There is) **There's** a post office on Main Street.

RULE:	The word order of a question with *there is* is: *To be* + *there* + noun . . . ?
EXAMPLES:	**Is + there + a post office** in this neighborhood? **Is + there + a movie theater** in this neighborhood?

GETTING READY

1. Use your own visuals, *Side by Side* Picture Cards 100–109, or the illustrations on text page 55 to practice the following locations in the community that are included in this lesson: *laundromat, drug store, church, department store, police station, hair salon, book store, health club, cafeteria, train station.*

2. Teach the following abbreviations:

   St. for Street, as in *Main St.* and *State St.*
   Ave. for Avenue, as in *Central Ave.*

INTRODUCING THE MODEL

1. Have students look at the model illustration.

2. Set the scene: "A man and a woman are talking. The man is in a new neighborhood. He's looking for a laundromat."

3. Present the model.

4. Full-Class Repetition.

5. Ask students if they have any questions. Check understanding of new vocabulary: *Excuse me, there's, in this neighborhood.*

Language Note

Many students have difficulty with the final [z] sound in the contraction *there's*, as in *There's a laundromat on Main Street.*

6. Group Choral Repetition.

7. Choral Conversation.

8. Call on one or two pairs of students to present the dialog.

(For additional practice, do Choral Conversation in small groups or by rows.)

SIDE BY SIDE EXERCISES

Examples

> 1. A. Excuse me. Is there a drug store in this neighborhood?
>   B. Yes. There's a drug store on Main Street, across from the church.
> 2. A. Excuse me. Is there a clinic in this neighborhood?
>   B. Yes. There's a clinic on Main Street, between the bank and the barber shop.

1. **Exercise 1:** Call on two students to present the dialog. Then do Choral Repetition and Choral Conversation practice.

2. **Exercise 2:** Same as above.

3. **Exercises 3–6:** Either Full-Class Practice or Pair Practice.

WORKBOOK

Page 42

EXPANSION ACTIVITIES

1. Clap in Rhythm

a. Have students sit in a circle.

b. Establish a steady, even beat—one-two-three-four, one-two-three-four—by having students clap their hands to their laps twice and then clap their hands together twice. Repeat throughout the game, maintaining the same rhythm.

c. The object is for each student in turn to name a place around town each time the hands are clapped together twice. Nothing is said when students clap their hands on their laps.

Note: The beat never stops! If a student misses a beat, he or she can either wait for the next beat or else pass to the next student.

2. Create a Street Scene

Create a simple street map on the board (as in Expansion Activity 3 for text page 56). Tape visuals or write names on the board to show various locations on two intersecting streets. Have pairs of students role-play the model conversation. Student A pretends to be looking for an unfamiliar location; Student B tells where it is.

3. Building a Town!

a. Create a street map on the board showing two intersecting streets. You can tape visuals of locations to the board or you can write place names. DO NOT write all of the place names. For example:

(continued)

bank			
		park		clinic

b. Give students cards with place names on them, tell students where the place is located on the board, and have students either tape the card on the board or write the place in the appropriate spot. For example:

> The teacher gives a card that says *church* and tells students the directions: "between the park and the clinic."

> The teacher gives a card that says *post office* and tells students the directions: "across from the bank."

> The student places the card or writes the name in the appropriate spot.

4. Picture This!

Describe a city street, and have students draw and label what you describe. For example:

> "This is First Avenue. There's a bank on First Avenue. Next to the bank there's a supermarket. Across from the supermarket there's a cafeteria." (Etc.)

Variation 1: Do the activity in pairs, where students take turns describing city streets.

Variation 2: One student comes to the board, and the rest of the class gives instructions for that student to draw.

5. Drawing Game

a. Write down on two sets of cards as many of the following places around town as you wish:

post office	drug store	bakery
hair salon	book store	video store
clinic	hospital	health club
video store	restaurant	train station
church	laundromat	supermarket
gas station	fire station	barber shop
department store	police station	

b. Divide the class in teams. Have each team sit together in a different part of the room.

c. Place each set of cards on a table or desk in front of the room. Also place a pad of paper and pencil next to each team's set of cards.

d. When you say "Go!," a person from each team comes to the table, picks a card from that team's pile, draws something that gives a clue to that place, and shows the drawing to their team—for example, a letter with a stamp (*post office*), a book (*book store*), a cake (*bakery*). The team then guesses what the place is.

e. When a team correctly guesses a word, another team member picks a card and draws a clue to the place written on that card.

f. Continue until each team has guessed all the words in their pile.

g. The team that guesses the words in the shortest time wins the game.

How to Say It!

> **Expressing Gratitude:** *Thanks* is a more informal way of expressing gratitude than *thank you*. It is common, and polite, to acknowledge the gratitude by saying *You're welcome.*

1. Set the scene: "The same two people from the model conversation above are ending their conversation."

2. With books closed, have students listen as you present the conversation or play the audio one or more times.

3. Full-Class Repetition.

4. Have students open their books and look at the dialog. Ask students if they have any questions. Check understanding of new vocabulary: *Thank you, thanks, you're welcome.*

5. Group Choral Repetition.

6. Choral Conversation.

7. Call on one or two pairs to present the model conversation again, expressing gratitude at the end of the conversation.

8. Divide the class into pairs, and have them practice other conversations on the page, concluding each conversation with gratitude.

9. Call on several pairs to present their conversations to the class.

FOCUS

- Short Answers with *There Is*
- Places Around Town

CLOSE UP

RULE:	It is common to respond to Yes/No questions with a short answer. A short answer includes the subject (*there*) and the auxiliary verb (*is*).
EXAMPLES:	Is there a cafeteria in your neighborhood? **Yes, there is.** Is there a restaurant in your neighborhood? **No, there isn't.**

RULE:	*Is* does not contract with *there* in short answers.
EXAMPLE:	*Is* there a post office in your neighborhood? Yes, **there is.**

Compare the long answer, where it normally contracts:
There's a post office on Main Street.

 ON YOUR OWN *What's in Your Neighborhood?*

INTRODUCING THE MODEL

1. Have students look at the model illustration.
2. Set the scene: "Two friends are talking. One friend is asking the other about her neighborhood."
3. Present the model.
4. Ask students if they have any questions. Check understanding of vocabulary.
5. Group Choral Repetition.
6. Choral Conversation.
7. Call on one or two pairs of students to present the dialog.

(For additional practice, do Choral Conversation in small groups or by rows.)

CONVERSATION PRACTICE

1. Have students draw a simple map of their neighborhood, labeling all the buildings.
2. Divide the class into pairs, and have students ask and answer questions about each other's neighborhoods.

WORKBOOK

Pages 43–44

EXPANSION ACTIVITIES

1. Chain Game

   a. Begin the game by saying:

      "In my neighborhood there's a *drug store*."
      (You can name any place you wish.)

   b. Have each student take a turn in which he or she repeats what the person before said and adds a new place. For example:

      "In my neighborhood there's a drug store and a bank."
      "In my neighborhood there's a drug store, a bank, and a supermarket."

2. My Favorite Neighborhood Places

   a. Have students call out the words they have learned for places around town as you write them on the board.

   b. Have students make a list of their five favorite places.

   c. Have students compare their lists as a class, in pairs, or in small groups.

3. My Neighborhood

   a. Have students write several sentences about buildings in their neighborhoods.

   b. Have students draw maps to illustrate their sentences.

   c. Have pairs of students share their writing and their maps.

Text Page 59: Is There a Stove in the Kitchen?

FOCUS

- Review of: *Is there* _____*?*
  Yes, there is.
  No, there isn't.

CLOSE UP

RULE:	The indefinite article *a/an* precedes a noun. The article *a* is used when the noun begins with a consonant sound. The article *an* is used when the noun begins with a vowel sound.
EXAMPLES:	Is there **a w**indow in the kitchen?
	Is there **an e**levator in the building?

GETTING READY

1. For an object that is in the classroom, say:

   Is there a *(window)* in the room?
   Yes, there is.

   For an object that is not in the classroom, say:

   Is there a *(TV)* in the room?
   No, there isn't.

   Do Choral Repetition and Choral Conversation practice.

2. Ask about other objects.

INTRODUCING THE MODELS

There are two model conversations. Introduce and practice each separately. For each model:

1. Have students look at the model illustration.

2. Set the scene: "Someone is talking to a real estate agent about an apartment."

3. Present the model.

4. Full-Class Repetition.

5. Ask students if they have any questions. Check understanding of new vocabulary: *stove; nice; refrigerator; Oh, good.; Oh, I see.*

   ### Culture Note

   Many people in the United States rent their apartments or houses. A person who rents an apartment is called a *tenant*. A person who helps someone find an apartment to rent is called a *real estate agent* and works in a *rental office*. The person who owns the apartment building is called the *landlord*. The person who the landlord hires to live in the building and take care of it is called the *superintendent*.

6. Group Choral Repetition.

7. Choral Conversation.

8. Call on one or two pairs of students to present the dialog.

   (For additional practice, do Choral Conversation in small groups or by rows.)

SIDE BY SIDE EXERCISES

Examples

> 1. A. Is there a window in the kitchen?
>   B. Yes, there is. There's a very nice window in the kitchen.
>   A. Oh, good.
>
> 2. A. Is there a fire escape?
>   B. No, there isn't.
>   A. Oh, I see.

1. **Exercise 1:** Call on two students to present the dialog. Then do Choral Repetition and Choral Conversation practice.

2. **Exercise 2:** Introduce the new word *fire escape*. Same as above.

3. **Exercises 3–8:** Either Full-Class Practice or Pair Practice.

EXPANSION ACTIVITIES

1. Vocabulary Review

Use your own visuals from magazines, *Side by Side* Picture Cards 18–26, or the illustrations on text page 18 to review house and room vocabulary.

a. Hold up a visual and ask a question such as:

   Is there a window in the kitchen?
   Is there a closet in this room?

   Have students answer: "Yes, there is" or "No, there isn't."

b. Have pairs of students practice asking and answering questions about the visuals.

c. This is an excellent activity for introducing new household vocabulary. For example:

   Is there a *bed* in the bedroom?
   Is there a *sink* in the bathroom?
   Is there a *table* in the dining room?

2. Scrambled Sentences

a. Divide the class into teams.

b. One sentence at a time, write individual sentences out of order on the board. For example:

> the   nice   there's   in   a   living
> room   window   very
>
> building   is   fire   escape   ?
> there   the   in   a
>
> bedroom   there's   air conditioner
> the   in   an

c. The first person to raise his or her hand, come to the board, and write the sentence in the correct order earns a point for that team.

(continued)

The team with the most points wins the scrambled sentence game.

Variation: Write the words to several sentences on separate cards. Divide the class into small groups, and have students work together to put the sentences into correct order.

3. Ask Me a Question!

   a. Bring to class several pictures of rooms, number them (Picture 1, Picture 2, etc.), and place them in the front of the room.

   b. Tell students you are thinking of one of the pictures. Have students ask Yes/No questions in order to find out which of the pictures you're thinking of. For example:

      Student 1: Is there a table in the room?
      Teacher: Yes, there is.

      Student 2: Is there refrigerator in the room?
      Teacher: No, there isn't.

   Student 3: Is there a sofa in the room?
   Teacher: Yes, there is.

   Student 4: Is it Picture Number Three?
   Teacher: Yes, it is.

   c. Have students play the game in pairs, asking each other Yes/No questions.

4. My Ideal House!

   a. Have students work in pairs or in small groups to design their *ideal* house. They should draw a simple sketch and label the rooms and objects in the rooms.

   Introduce new vocabulary when necessary. For example: *patio, balcony, swimming pool, porch, study/den.*

   b. Have students ask about each other's ideal houses:

      A. Is there a _____ in the _____?
      B. Yes, there is.
         No, there isn't.

Text Page 60: How Many Bedrooms Are There in the Apartment?

FOCUS

- Introduction of: *How many _____?*
  There are _____.
- Housing

CLOSE UP

RULE:	*How many* asks about the number of a count noun.
EXAMPLE:	**How many** bedrooms are there in the apartment? There are **two** bedrooms in the apartment.
RULE:	*There is / There are* indicates the existence or location of something. The verb *to be* agrees in number with the noun that follows. If a plural noun follows, the verb *to be* is in the plural form (*are*).
EXAMPLE:	**There are** four floor**s** in the building.
RULE:	The verb *are* does not contract with *there*.
EXAMPLE:	**There are** three windows in the living room.

GETTING READY

1. Briefly introduce the final *s* for plural nouns. (Plural nouns are taught more fully in Chapter 8.) Have students listen and repeat after you:

   one student–two students
   one window–two windows
   one book–two books

2. Introduce questions with "How many _____?"

   a. Present this model and then do Choral Repetition and Choral Conversation practice:

      How many (*windows*) are there in this room?
      There are (*4*) windows.

   b. Ask other questions with *how many,* using people and objects in the room. Then have students ask each other questions.

INTRODUCING THE MODEL

1. Have students look at the model illustration.

2. Set the scene: "Someone is talking to a real estate agent about an apartment."

3. Present the model.

4. Full-Class Repetition.

5. Ask students if they have any questions. Check understanding of new vocabulary: *tell me, how many, there are, that's right.*

Language Note

In line 3 of the dialog, Speaker A repeats: "Two bedrooms?" In English it is common to repeat information with rising intonation to confirm what the other person has said.

Pronunciation Note

The pronunciation focus of Chapter 7 is **Rising Intonation to Check Understanding** (text page 66). Model this pronunciation and encourage students to incorporate it into their language practice.

Two bedrooms?

Three windows?

6. Group Choral Repetition.

7. Choral Conversation.

8. Call on one or two pairs of students to present the dialog.

(For additional practice, do Choral Conversation in small groups or by rows.)

SIDE BY SIDE EXERCISES

Examples

1. A. Tell me, how many floors are there in the building?
    B. There are four floors in the building.
    A. Four floors?
    B. Yes. That's right.

2. A. Tell me, how many windows are there in the living room?
    B. There are three windows in the living room.
    A. Three windows?
    B. Yes. That's right.

1. **Exercise 1:** Introduce the new word *floor*. Call on two students to present the dialog. Then do Choral Repetition and Choral Conversation practice.

2. **Exercise 2:** Same as above.

3. **Exercises 3–6:** Either Full-Class Practice or Pair Practice.

New Vocabulary

5. washing machines
6. a half (2 and a half)

Language Note

A "half bathroom" is the term used for a bathroom with no shower or bathtub.

WORKBOOK

Page 45

EXPANSION ACTIVITIES

1. How Many?

a. Write key words on the board or on word cards. For example:

books	students	chairs
rooms	shoes	people

b. Have students use these as cues to ask questions with "how many." For example:

A. How many students are there in this room?
B. There are (18) students in this room.

A. How many rooms are there in this building?
B. There are (25) rooms in this building.

c. Have students think of other questions to ask people in the class.

2. Match the Conversations

a. Make a set of matching cards based on the conversations in this lesson. For example:

How many rooms are there in the apartment?

There are four rooms in the apartment.

How many floors are there in the building?

There are five floors in the building.

How many bedrooms are there in the apartment?

There are two bedrooms in the apartment.

How many windows are there in the living room?

There are three windows in the living room.

How many closets are there in the apartment?

There are six closets in the apartment.

How many apartments are there in the building.

There are ten apartments in the building.

How many washing machines are there in the building?

There are three washing machines in the building.

How many bathrooms are there in the apartment?

There are two bathrooms in the apartment.

b. Distribute a card to each student.

c. Have students memorize the sentences on their cards, and then have students walk around the room saying their sentences until they find their match.

d. Then have pairs of students say their matched sentences aloud to the class.

3. Do You Remember?

a. Briefly show a picture with a scene of a classroom, a room in a home, or a neighborhood.

b. Put the picture away.

c. Ask questions to see how many details students remember about the scene. For example:

How many (desks) are there in the picture?
How many (students) are there in the picture?
Is there a (teacher) in the picture?
Where is the (computer) in this (classroom)?

(continued)

Variation: Divide the class into teams and do the activity as a game. The team with the most correct answers wins.

4. Draw, Write, and Read

a. Have students draw a picture of their house or apartment. Also, have them write a description to accompany the picture.

b. In pairs, have students describe their homes as they show their pictures.

5. True or False?

a. Bring in pictures from magazines, newspapers, or catalogs that depict rooms of the home or neighborhoods.

b. Make statements about the pictures and have students tell you "True" or "False." If the statement is false, have students correct it.

Variation: You can call on students to make true or false statements about the visuals and have other students respond.

6. Community Quiz

a. Prepare questions about your local community. For example:

How many hospitals are there?
Is there a train station?
How many bakeries are there?
Is there a book store?
How many clinics are there?
How many banks are there?

b. Divide the class into teams. Have the teams take turns answering your questions. The group that gives the most correct answers wins.

Text Pages 61–62: An Apartment Building

FOCUS

- Review of: *Is there _____?*
  Yes, there is.
  No, there isn't.

- Introduction of: *Are there any _____s?*
  Yes, there are.
  No, there aren't.

- Review of: *How many _____s are there?*
  There are _____.

GETTING READY

1. Introduce questions with "Are there _____?"

   a. Present these models, and then do Choral Repetition and Choral Conversation practice:

   Are there any *(students)* in the room?
   Yes, there are.

   Are there any *(dogs)* in the room?
   No, there aren't.

   b. Ask about other objects.

2. Introduce the following new words: *broken, cockroaches, holes, landlord, mailbox, mice, roof, satellite dish, tenant.* Use your own visuals, or have students look at the illustration on text page 61.

 ROLE PLAY *Looking for an Apartment*

1. Divide the class into groups of three. In each group, Student A is the prospective *tenant*, the person looking for an apartment. Student B is the *landlord* of the apartment building on text page 61. Student C is a *tenant* in the same building.

2. **Questions 1-8:** Student A, the prospective tenant, asks the questions. Student B, the landlord, answers them based on the illustration on text page 61.

Answer Key:

1. Is there a stove in the kitchen?
   Yes, there is.

2. Is there a refrigerator in the kitchen?
   No, there isn't.

3. Is there a superintendent in the building?
   Yes, there is.

4. Is there an elevator in the building?
   No, there isn't.

5. Is there a fire escape?
   Yes, there is.

6. Is there a satellite dish on the roof?
   Yes, there is.

7. Is there a mailbox near the building?
   Yes, there is.

8. Is there a bus stop near the building?
   Yes, there is.

3. **Questions 9-15:** Student A, the prospective tenant, asks the questions. Student C, a tenant who lives in the building, answers them based on the illustration on text page 61.

Answer Key:

9. Are there any children in the building?
   Yes, there are.

10. Are there any cats in the building?
    No, there aren't.

11. Are there any mice in the basement?
    Yes, there are.

12. Are there any cockroaches in the building?
    Yes, there are.

13. Are there any broken windows in the building?
    Yes, there are.

14. Are there any holes in the walls?
    Yes, there are.

15. Are there any washing machines in the basement?
    No, there aren't.

4. **Questions 16-19:** Student A, the prospective tenant, asks the questions. Student B, the landlord, answers them based on the illustration on text page 61.

CHAPTER 7   147

Answer Key:

16. How many rooms are there in the apartment?
There are four rooms in the apartment.

17. How many floors are there in the building?
There are three floors in the building.

18. How many closets are there in the bedroom?
There's one closet in the bedroom.

19. How many windows are there in the living room?
There are three windows in the living room.

WORKBOOK

Pages 46–49

EXPANSION ACTIVITIES

1. True or False?

Make statements about the apartment building on text page 61 and have students tell you "True" or "False." If the statement is false, have students correct it. For example:

> Teacher: There's a stove in the kitchen.
> Student: True.
>
> Teacher: There's a broken window in the bedroom.
> Student: False. There's a broken window in the living room.

Variation: You can call on students to make true or false statements about the building and have other students respond.

2. Memory Game

a. Tell students to spend three minutes looking carefully at the apartment building on text page 61.

b. Have students close their books.

c. Ask questions to see how much they remember about the building. For example:

> How many floors are there in the building?
> Is there an elevator in the building?
> Is there a closet in the living room?

> Are there any cats in the building?
> Are there any broken windows in the building?

Variation: Divide the class into teams and do the activity as a game. The team with the most correct answers wins.

3. True or False Memory Game

a. Tell students to spend three minutes looking carefully at the apartment building on text page 61.

b. Have students close their books.

c. Make true or false statements about the building.

d. Students have to decide if each statement is true or false. If the statement if false, have students try to correct it.

Variation: This can be done as a dictation with a *True* column and a *False* column. Tell students to write each statement in the appropriate column. At the end of the dictation, have students look again at the building on text page 61 to see if they were correct.

READING *The New Shopping Mall*

FOCUS

- There Is/There Are

NEW VOCABULARY

airport	more than	some
almost	now	store
because	open	town
center	outside	upset
city	owner	women
clothing store	shopping	
men	shopping mall	

READING THE STORY

Optional: Preview the story by having students talk about the story title and/or illustration. You may choose to introduce new vocabulary beforehand, or have students encounter the new vocabulary within the context of the reading.

1. Have students read the story silently, or follow along silently as the story is read aloud by you, by one or more students, or on the audio program.

2. Ask students if they have any questions. Check understanding of vocabulary.

   ### Culture Note

   Shopping malls typically have large parking areas around a main building in which many stores are located. Malls are often located on the outskirts of cities and towns. In many places, the opening of these malls has reduced the business of older stores located in downtown areas.

3. Check students' comprehension, using some or all of the following questions:

   What's everybody talking about?
   Where's the mall?
   What's in the mall?
   Who isn't happy about the new mall?
   Why?

✓ READING *CHECK-UP*

CHOOSE

1. c
2. b
3. b
4. a

READING EXTENSION

Ask students the following questions and have them review the text for the answers.

   Why aren't people shopping downtown?
   Why are people shopping at the mall?
   Why is the mall more convenient?

How About You?

Have students answer the questions in pairs or as a class.

READING *Amy's Apartment Building*

FOCUS

- Prepositions
- There Is/There Are

NEW VOCABULARY

all day	live
all night	place
convenient	sidewalk
however	

READING THE STORY

Optional: *Preview the story by having students talk about the story title and/or illustration. You may choose to introduce new vocabulary beforehand, or have students encounter the new vocabulary within the context of the reading.*

1. Have students read the story silently, or follow along silently as the story is read aloud by you, by one or more students, or on the audio program.

2. Ask students if they have any questions. Check understanding of vocabulary.

3. Check students' comprehension, using some or all of the following questions:

    Where is Amy's apartment building?
    Why is Amy very happy there?
    What's across from the building?
    What's next to the building?
    What's around the corner from the building?
    Is Amy's neighborhood quiet? Why not?
    Is Amy upset about the noise? Why not?

✓ READING *CHECK-UP*

WHAT'S THE ANSWER?

1. It's in the center of town.
2. Across from her building, there's a bank, a post office, and a restaurant.
3. Yes, there is.
4. There's a lot of noise near Amy's apartment building because there are a lot of cars on the street, and there are a lot of people on the sidewalks all day and all night.
5. She's happy there because it's a convenient place to live.

TRUE OR FALSE?

1. True
2. False
3. True
4. False
5. True

READING EXTENSION

Ask students the following questions and have them scan the text for the answers.

    What words describe Amy's neighborhood?
    What's another title for the reading?

How About You?

Have students answer the questions, in pairs or as a class.

IN YOUR OWN WORDS

1. Make sure students understand the instructions.

2. Have students do the activity as written homework, using a dictionary for any new words they wish to use.

3. Have students present and discuss what they have written, in pairs or as a class.

LISTENING

WHAT PLACES DO YOU HEAR?

Listen and choose the correct places.

Example: My neighborhood is very nice. There's a supermarket across the street, and there's a video store around the corner.

1. My neighborhood is very convenient. There's a bank around the corner and a laundromat across the street.

2. My neighborhood is very noisy. There's a fire station next to my building, and there's a gas station across the street.

3. The sidewalks in my neighborhood are very busy. There's a school across the street and a department store around the corner.

4. There are many small stores in the center of my town. There's a bakery, a drug store, and a book store.

5. My neighborhood is very busy. There's a hotel across the street, and the hotel is between a hospital and a health club.

Answers

1. b, c   4. b, c
2. a, c   5. a, c
3. a, b

TRUE OR FALSE?

Listen to the conversation. Then answer *True* or *False*.

A. Tell me about the apartment.
B. There's a large living room, a large kitchen, a nice bathroom, and a very nice bedroom.
A. How many closets are there in the apartment?
B. There's a closet in the bedroom and a closet in the living room.
A. Oh, I see. And how many windows are there in the living room?
B. There are four windows in the living room.
A. Four windows?
B. Yes. That's right.
A. Tell me. Is there a superintendent in the building?
B. Yes, there is.
A. And are there washing machines in the basement?
B. Yes, there are. There are three washing machines.
A. Oh, good. Tell me, is there an elevator in the building?
B. No, there isn't. But there's a fire escape.

Answers

1. True   4. True
2. False   5. True
3. False   6. False

PRONUNCIATION

 CHAPTER SUMMARY

> **Rising Intonation to Check Understanding:** One way to check understanding is to repeat the information with a questioning intonation. For example:
>
> Two bedrooms?

Focus on Listening

Practice the sentences in the left column. Say each sentence or play the audio one or more times. Have students listen carefully and repeat.

Focus on Pronunciation

Practice the sentences in the right column. Have students say each sentence and then listen carefully as you say it or play the audio.

If you wish, have students continue practicing the sentences to improve their pronunciation.

 JOURNAL

Have students write their journal entries at home or in class. Encourage students to use a dictionary to look up words they would like to use. Students can share their written work with other students if appropriate. Have students discuss what they have written as a class, in pairs, or in small groups.

GRAMMAR

1. Divide the class into pairs or small groups.
2. Have students take turns reading the sentences in the grammar boxes.

KEY VOCABULARY

Have students ask you any questions about the meaning or pronunciation of the vocabulary. If students ask for the pronunciation, repeat after the student until the student is satisfied with his or her pronunciation.

EXPANSION ACTIVITIES

1. Vocabulary Check

   Check students' retention of the vocabulary depicted on the opening page of Chapter 7 by doing the following activity:

   a. Have students open their books to page 55 and cover the list of vocabulary words.

   b. Either call out a number and have students tell you the word, or say a word and have students tell you the number.

   Variation: You can also do this activity as a game with competing teams.

2. Student-Led Dictation

   a. Tell each student to choose a word or phrase from the Key Vocabulary list on text page 66 and look at it very carefully.

   b. Have students take turns dictating their words to the class. Everybody writes down that student's word.

   c. When the dictation is completed, call on different students to write each word on the board to check the spelling.

3. Beanbag Toss

a. Call out a topic from the chapter—for example: *Housing*.

b. Have students toss a beanbag back and forth. The student to whom the beanbag is tossed must name a word in that category. For example:

Student 1: apartment building
Student 2: elevator
Student 3: fire escape

c. Continue until all the words in the category have been named.

END-OF-CHAPTER ACTIVITIES

1. Do You Remember?

a. Divide the class into pairs.

b. Tell students to spend three minutes looking carefully at the illustration on text page 64 or 65.

c. Have students close their books and write down what they remember about the scene.

d. Have students compare their sentences with their partner and then look at the scene in the book to see how much they remembered.

Note: This activity can also be done with any picture you bring to class from a newspaper or magazine depicting situations relevant to Chapter 7.

2. Match the Places

a. Make a set of matching cards based on places around town. For example:

library	People are reading.
cafeteria	People are eating.
movie theater	People are watching a movie.

health club	People are exercising.
park	People are feeding the birds.
laundromat	People are washing their clothes.
bakery	People are baking cakes.

b. Distribute a card to each student.

c. Have students memorize the phrase on their cards, then walk around the room saying their phrase until they find their match.

d. Then have pairs of students say their matched phrases aloud to the class.

3. Miming

a. Write down on cards the *Places Around Town* listed on text page 66.

b. Have pairs of students take turns picking a card from the pile and pantomiming activities that occur in the place written on the card. For example:

(continued)

Student picks up a card that says *fire station*:
One student mimes hitting the alarm bell.
The other student mimes running to a truck,
putting on a coat and hat, and climbing onto the
truck.

c. The class must guess where the students are.

Variation: This can be done as a game with
competing teams.

4. Category Dictation

a. Have students draw three columns on a piece
of paper. At the top of the first column, have
students write <u>Shopping</u>. At the top of the
second column, have them write
<u>Transportation</u>. At the top of the third
column, have them write <u>Food</u>.

b. Dictate various places around town from the
text that belong in one of these three
categories and have students write them in
the appropriate column. For example:

<u>Shopping</u>	<u>Transportation</u>	<u>Food</u>
department store	train station	bakery
book store	bus stop	cafeteria

5. Describe the Pictures

a. Bring in several pictures or ask students to
bring in pictures of neighborhoods.

b. Have pairs of students select a picture to
describe.

c. Have students read their descriptions aloud
as the class listens and tries to identify the
picture.

WORKBOOK ANSWER KEY AND LISTENING SCRIPTS

WORKBOOK PAGE 41

A. WHERE IS IT?

1. next to
2. across from
3. between
4. around the corner from
5. next to
6. between
7. across from
8. around the corner from
9. next to
10. between
11. across from

WORKBOOK PAGE 42

B. WHAT ARE THEY SAYING?

1. There's, next to
2. Is there, There's, around the corner from
3. there, There's, across from
4. Is there, There's, between
5. Is there, there, There's, Central, next to

WORKBOOK PAGE 43

C. LISTENING

Listen to the sentences about the buildings on the map. After each sentence, write the name on the correct building.

1. There's a bakery between the barber shop and the bank.
2. There's a school next to the church.
3. There's a department store across from the school and the church.
4. There's a library around the corner from the barber shop.
5. There's a hospital across from the library.
6. There's a police station next to the hospital.
7. There's a hair salon across from the barber shop.
8. There's a supermarket next to the hair salon.
9. There's a video store around the corner from the bank.
10. There's a park between the library and the video store.
11. There's a health club around the corner from the department store.
12. There's a train station across from the health club.

Answers

(See page 156)

D. YES OR NO?

1. No, there isn't.
2. Yes, there is.
3. No, there isn't.
4. Yes, there is.
5. Yes, there is.
6. No, there isn't.
7. No, there isn't.
8. Yes, there is.
9. No, there isn't.

WORKBOOK PAGE 45

F. WHAT ARE THEY SAYING?

1. Is there
2. there is
3. are there
4. There's, there are
5. Is there
6. there isn't, there are
7. Are there
8. there aren't, there's
9. are there
10. There are, there's

WORKBOOK PAGE 46

G. OUR APARTMENT BUILDING

1. machines
2. broken
3. mice
4. escape
5. hole
6. satellite dish
7. refrigerator
8. closets
9. cats, dogs
10. stop, mailbox

WORKBOOK PAGE 47

H. JANE'S LIVING ROOM

1. Yes, there is.
2. No, there isn't.
3. Yes, there are.
4. Yes, there is.
5. No, there aren't.
6. Yes, there are.
7. Yes, there are.
8. No, there isn't.
9. No, there aren't.
10. Yes, there is.
11. Yes, there is.
12. No, there isn't.
13. Yes, there are.
14. No, there isn't.

I. LOOKING FOR AN APARTMENT

1. Chicago
2. sunny
3. bedroom, bathroom
4. fireplaces
5. children
6. Miami
7. beautiful
8. bedrooms
9. two
10. elevator

11. New York
12. large
13. living room
14. air conditioners
15. school
16. Dallas
17. quiet
18. dining room
19. building
20. near

Answers to Page 43 Exercise C Listening

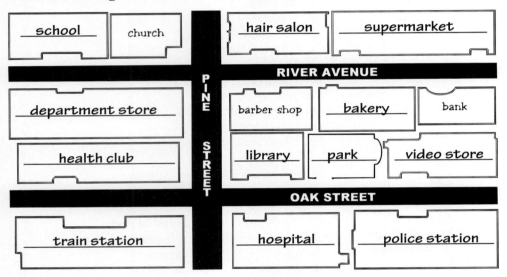

Teacher's Notes

GRAMMAR

SINGULAR/PLURAL

[s]
> I'm looking for **a** coat.
> Coat**s** are over there.

[z]
> I'm looking for **an** umbrella.
> Umbrella**s** are over there.

[ɪz]
> I'm looking for **a** dress.
> Dress**es** are over there.

THIS/THAT/THESE/THOSE

> Is **this** your umbrella?
> **That** umbrella is brown.

> Are **these** your boots?
> **Those** boots are dirty.

ADJECTIVES

> This is a **purple** jacket.
> These are **green** gloves.

FUNCTIONS

OFFERING TO HELP

May I help you?
Can I help you?
> Yes, please.

EXPRESSING WANT-DESIRE

I'm looking for a *jacket*.

I'm looking for a *brown umbrella* for *my son*.

DESCRIBING

Here's a nice *jacket*.

But this is a PURPLE *jacket!*
But these are GREEN *gloves!*

That *umbrella* is *brown*.
Those *boots* are *dirty*.

EXPRESSING AGREEMENT

You're right.

EXPRESSING DISAGREEMENT

I don't think so.

ASKING FOR AND REPORTING INFORMATION

Is this your *umbrella*?
> No, it isn't.
Are these your *boots*?
> No, they aren't.

INQUIRING ABOUT CERTAINTY

Are you sure?

EXPRESSING CERTAINTY

I think *that's my jacket*.

APOLOGIZING

I'm sorry.

ADMITTING AN ERROR

I guess I made a mistake.

ATTRACTING ATTENTION

Excuse me.

EXPRESSING SURPRISE-DISBELIEF

But this is a PURPLE jacket!

COMPLIMENTING

That's a very nice _____!
> Thanks.
Those are very nice _____!
> Thanks.

NEW VOCABULARY

Clothing

belt
blouse
boot
bracelet
briefcase
coat
dress
earring
glasses
glove
hat
jacket
jeans
mitten
necklace
pajamas
pants
pocketbook
purse
raincoat
shirt
shoe
skirt
sock
sports jacket
stocking
suit
sunglasses
sweater
tie
umbrella
watch

Colors

black
blue
brown
gold
gray
green
orange
pink
purple
red
silver
white
yellow

Adjectives

clean
dirty
empty
frustrated
inexpensive
polka dot
popular
ripped
striped
sure

People

boy
child
person

Materials

cotton
leather
vinyl
wool

Everyday Activities

getting dressed
looking for
think

Time Words

morning
year

Demonstratives

this
that
these
those

Miscellaneous

clothesline
dry cleaner's
gift
lost and found
mouse
nothing
pair (of)
something
tooth
trouble
work (n)

EXPRESSIONS

Can I help you?
having a difficult time
having a lot of trouble
I don't think so.
I guess I made a mistake.
May I help you?
Oh.
over there
please
That's okay.
You're right.

VOCABULARY PREVIEW

You may want to introduce these words before beginning the chapter, or you may choose to wait until they first occur in a specific lesson. If you choose to introduce them at this point, here are some suggestions:

1. Have students look at the illustrations on text page 67 and identify the words they already know.

2. Present the vocabulary. Say each word and have the class repeat it chorally and individually. Check students' understanding and pronunciation of the words.

3. Practice the vocabulary as a class, in pairs, or in small groups. Have students cover the word list and look at the pictures. Practice the words in the following ways:

   - Say a word and have students tell the number of the illustration.

   - Give the number of an illustration and have students say the word.

FOCUS

- Articles of Clothing
- Singular/Plural
- Indefinite Articles: *a / an*

CLOSE UP

RULE:	When a noun ends in a voiceless consonant sound [p, k, t], the plural ending is pronounced [s].
EXAMPLES:	coat**s** sock**s**

RULE:	When a noun ends in a voiced consonant [b, d, g, m, n, r, l, v], or vowel sound, the plural ending is pronounced [z].
EXAMPLES:	mitten**s** sweater**s** tie**s** umbrella**s**

RULE:	When a noun ends with a sibilant [s, z, š, ž, č, j], the plural ending is pronounced [ɪz], which forms an additional syllable on the end of the noun.
EXAMPLES:	glass**es** watch**es**

RULE:	Some nouns have irregular plural forms.
EXAMPLES:	a man – men a woman – women a child – children a person – people a tooth – teeth a mouse – mice

GETTING READY

1. Present the vocabulary on text page 68. Use the illustrations in the book, your own visuals, or real articles of clothing.

   a. Point to an article of clothing and say the new word several times. Whenever possible, also point to a student who is wearing that article of clothing.

   b. Have students repeat the new word chorally and individually.

2. Introduce the three different pronunciations of the plural as they are shown on text page 69. Practice each final sound separately.

   a. Begin with the final [s] sound. Say the singular and plural form of each noun. Then say the words again and have students repeat after you chorally and individually. Point out the articles *a* and *an*.

   b. Same as above for the words in the [z] column and the [ɪz] column.

3. Give students practice listening to singulars and plurals.

   a. Write on the board:

   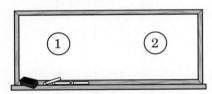

   Have students listen as you read the plural nouns at the top of text page 69 in mixed-up order. For each word, have students say:

   > "One" if they think the noun is singular.
   > "Two" if they think the noun is plural.

   b. Write on the board:

   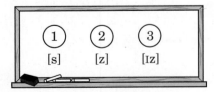

   Have students listen as you read the plural nouns at the top of text page 69 in mixed-up order. For each noun have students say:

   > "One" if they hear a final [s] sound.
   > "Two" if they hear a final [z] sound.
   > "Three" if they hear a final [ɪz] sound.

4. Give students practice saying the final plural sounds. Say the singular form of words at the top of text page 69 and call on students to give the plural.

5. Introduce irregular plurals. Point out the irregular plural nouns at the bottom of page 69. Say the singular and plural forms and have students repeat after you. Practice by saying the singular form and have students tell you the plural form and vice versa.

INTRODUCING THE MODELS

There are three model conversations. Introduce and practice each model before going on to the next. For each model:

1. Have students look at the model illustration.

2. Set the scene: "A salesperson and a customer are talking in a department store."

3. Present the model.

4. Full-Class Repetition.

5. Ask students if they have any questions. Check understanding of new vocabulary: *looking for, over there.*

6. Group Choral Repetition.

7. Choral Conversation.

8. Call on one or two pairs of students to present the dialog.

   (For additional practice, do Choral Conversation in small groups or by rows.)

SIDE BY SIDE EXERCISES

Examples

1. A. Excuse me. I'm looking for a coat.
   B. Coats are over there.
   A. Thanks.

2. A. Excuse me. I'm looking for an umbrella.
   B. Umbrellas are over there.
   A. Thanks.

3. A. Excuse me. I'm looking for a watch.
   B. Watches are over there.
   A. Thanks.

1. **Exercise 1:** Call on two students to present the dialog. Then do Choral Repetition and Choral Conversation practice.

2. **Exercise 2:** Same as above.

3. **Exercises 3–8:** Either Full Class Practice or Pair Practice.

Put These Words in the Correct Column

1. Divide the class into pairs.

2. Have pairs pronounce the words listed and write them in the appropriate columns.

3. Have the pairs share their lists with the class.

Answer Key

[s]	[z]	[ɪz]
boots	earrings	briefcases
pants	gloves	glasses
socks	shoes	purses

WORKBOOK

Pages 50–51

EXPANSION ACTIVITIES

1. Remember the Words!

   a. Tell students to spend one minute looking very carefully at text page 68.

   b. Have students close their books and write down as many words from the page as they can remember.

   c. As a class, in pairs, or in small groups, have students read their lists.

   d. Call on students to come to the board and write their list of words. Have the class check the spelling of the words.

2. Clap in Rhythm

   Object: Once a clapping rhythm is established, the students must continue naming different articles of clothing.

   a. Have students sit in a circle.

   b. Establish a steady even beat—one-two-three-four, one-two-three-four—by having students clap their hands to their laps twice and then clap their hands together twice. Repeat throughout the game, maintaining the same rhythm.

   c. The object is for each student in turn to name a clothing word each time the hands are clapped together twice. Nothing is said when students clap their hands on their laps.

Note: The beat never stops! If a student misses a beat, he or she can either wait for the next beat or else pass to the next student.

3. Drawing Game

   a. Write the names of articles of clothing on two sets of separate cards.

   b. Place the two piles of cards on a table or desk in the front of the room. Also have a pad of paper and pencil next to each team's set of cards.

   c. Divide the class into teams. Have each team sit together in a different part of the room.

   d. When you say "Go!," a person from each team comes to the front of his or her team, picks a card from the pile, and draws the article of clothing. The rest of the team then guesses what the article of clothing is.

   e. When a team correctly guesses the article of clothing, another team member picks a card and draws the item written on that card.

   f. Continue until each team has guessed all the articles of clothing in their pile.

   The team that guesses the articles of clothing in the shortest time wins the game.

(continued)

4. What's the Word?

Point to articles of clothing that people in the class are wearing. Have one student say the word for that article of clothing. Have another student give the plural form of that word.

Variation: Do the activity as a game with competing teams. Have two members of each team come to the front of the room and give the singular and plural forms of the words. The team with the most correct answers wins the game.

5. Letter Game

a. Divide the class into teams.

b. Say: "I'm thinking of an article of clothing that starts with *c.*"

c. The first person to raise his or her hand and guess correctly [*coat*] wins a point for his or her team.

d. Continue with other letters of the alphabet and clothing items.

The team that gets the most correct answers wins the game.

6. Dictation with Plurals

a. Have students draw three columns on a piece of paper. Have students write /s/ at the top of the left column, /z/ at the top of the middle column, and /ɪz/ at the top of the right column.

b. Call out plurals from pages 68–69. Have students write the word under the appropriate column. For example:

/s/	/z/	/ɪz/
shirts	shoes	dresses

7. Men, Women, or Both?

a. Have students take a piece of paper and draw two lines down the center of the page. Have them write <u>Men</u> at the top of the left column, <u>Women</u> at the top of the middle column, and <u>Both</u> at the top of the right column.

b. Dictate various clothing words. For example:

suit
dress
shirt
tie

c. Have students write the items in the appropriate columns.

d. At the end of the dictation, have students compare their lists.

8. Miming Game

a. Write down on cards the following items:

tie	belt	pants
socks	shoes	shirt
earrings	necklace	bracelet
hat	coat	gloves
purse	glasses	watch
umbrella	boots	mittens
skirt	stockings	

b. Have students take turns picking a card from the pile and pantomiming someone putting on or holding that item.

c. The class must guess what the word is.

Variation: This can be done as a game with competing teams.

FOCUS

- Colors
- Singular/Plural
- Articles of Clothing

CLOSE UP

RULE:	Adjectives and colors come before the noun they describe.
EXAMPLES:	But this is a **purple jacket**! **Purple jackets** are very popular this year.

RULE:	*This* is a demonstrative that refers to a singular object near the speaker.
EXAMPLES:	But **this** is a pink belt! *(The speaker is either holding or is very close to the belt.)*

GETTING READY

Teach the colors at the top of the page. Use visuals or real objects and clothing items in the classroom. As you say each new word, have students listen and repeat chorally and individually.

INTRODUCING THE MODEL

1. Have students look at the model illustration.
2. Set the scene: "A salesperson and a customer are talking in a department store."
3. Present the model.

   ### Pronunciation Note

   The pronunciation focus of Chapter 8 is **Emphasized Words** (text page 76). You should model this pronunciation at this point *(But this is a PURPLE jacket!)* and encourage students to incorporate it into their language practice. In this textbook, emphasized words are spelled with all capital letters as a way of visually showing their prominence in the sentence.

4. Full-Class Repetition.
5. Ask students if they have any questions. Check understanding of new vocabulary: *May I help you? please, looking for, here's, this, That's okay, popular, this year.*
6. Group Choral Repetition.
7. Choral Conversation.
8. Call on one or two pairs of students to present the dialog.

   (For additional practice, do Choral Conversation in small groups or by rows.)

SIDE BY SIDE EXERCISES

Examples

1. A. May I help you?
   B. Yes, please. I'm looking for a suit.
   A. Here's a nice suit.
   B. But this is a RED suit!
   A. That's okay. Red suits are very POPULAR this year.

2. A. May I help you?
   B. Yes, please. I'm looking for a tie.
   A. Here's a nice tie.
   B. But this is a WHITE tie!
   A. That's okay. White ties are very POPULAR this year.

1. **Exercise 1:** Call on two students to present the dialog. Then do Choral Repetition and Choral Conversation practice.

2. **Exercise 2:** Same as above.

3. **Exercises 3–8:** Either Full-Class Practice or Pair Practice.

New Vocabulary

7. striped   8. polka dot

WORKBOOK

Page 52

EXPANSION ACTIVITIES

1. What's the Color?

Point to articles of clothing or any item in the classroom. Have students tell you the color.

2. Guess What I See!

a. Divide the class into pairs or small groups.

b. Have students take turns selecting clothing that classmates are wearing and saying: "I see something _(color)_!"

c. The other student must then guess which article of clothing the other sees. For example:

   I see something red.   (Maria's belt)
   I see something green.   (Tom's shirt)

3. Listen and Match

a. Have students look at the illustrations on page 68.

b. Describe an article of clothing and its color and have students listen and point to the item you're describing.

Variation: Have students work in pairs, taking turns describing and identifying the items.

4. Department Store Role Play

a. Write the following on the board:

   A. May I . . . ?
   B. Yes, please.
   A. Here's . . .
   B. But . . .
   A. That's okay . . . .

b. Make word cards or visual of articles of clothing with unusual colors or patterns.

c. Divide the class into pairs.

d. Give each pair a word card or visual and have them create a role play between a salesperson and a customer in a store, using the dialog framework on the board as a guide.

e. Call on different pairs to present their role plays to the class.

5. Correct the Statement!

a. Make statements about students in the class. Some statements should be true, and others false. Have students respond to your statements. If a statement is false, a student should correct it. For example:

Teacher: Michael is wearing black shoes.
Student: That's right.

Teacher: Carla is wearing a red blouse.
Student: No, she isn't. She's wearing a white blouse.

Variation 1: Have students make statements for others to react to.

Variation 2: Do the activity as a game with competing teams.

6. What's Everybody Wearing?

a. Have each student choose another student to describe in writing. The student should not mention the name of the person. For example:

He's wearing black pants, a gray sweater, and white sneakers.

b. Have students take turns reading their descriptions aloud. The class must listen and identify the student being described.

Text Page 71: I'm Looking for a Pair of Gloves

FOCUS

- *A pair of* with Articles of Clothing

CLOSE UP

RULE:	*A pair* refers to a set of two. *A pair* is singular in quantity and takes a singular verb.
EXAMPLES:	Here **is** (Here's) a nice **pair** of gloves. Here **is** (Here's) a nice **pair** of pants.
RULE:	*These* is a demonstrative that refers to objects near the speaker.
EXAMPLE:	But **these** are orange earrings! *(The speaker is either holding or is very close to the earrings.)*

GETTING READY

Introduce *a pair of* by pointing out examples in the classroom. For example:

> *a pair of pants*
> *a pair of shoes*
> *a pair of socks*

Have students repeat after you chorally and individually.

INTRODUCING THE MODEL

1. Have students look at the model illustration.

2. Set the scene: "A salesperson and a customer are talking in a department store."

3. Present the model.

4. Full-Class Repetition.

5. Ask students if they have any questions. Check understanding of new vocabulary: *Can I help you? a pair of, these.*

6. Group Choral Repetition.

7. Choral Conversation.

8. Call on one or two pairs of students to present the dialog.

   (For additional practice, do Choral Conversation in small groups or by rows.)

SIDE BY SIDE EXERCISES

Examples

1. A. Can I help you?
   B. Yes, please. I'm looking for a pair of shoes.
   A. Here's a nice pair of shoes.
   B. But these are YELLOW shoes!
   A. That's okay. Yellow shoes are very POPULAR this year.

2. A. Can I help you?
   B. Yes, please. I'm looking for a pair of boots.
   A. Here's a nice pair of boots.
   B. But these are BLUE boots!
   A. That's okay. Blue boots are very POPULAR this year.

1. **Exercise 1:** Call on two students to present the dialog. Then do Choral Repetition and Choral Conversation practice.

2. **Exercise 2:** Same as above.

3. **Exercises 3-8:** Either Full-Class Practice or Pair Practice.

New Vocabulary

8. pajamas

How About You?

Have students answer the questions in pairs or as a class.

WORKBOOK

Page 53

EXPANSION ACTIVITIES

1. Describe the Picture!

Bring in pictures, from magazines, newspapers, or mail order clothing catalogs, that depict clothing items. As a class, in pairs, or in small groups, have students describe what the people in the pictures are wearing.

2. Guess Who!

a. Describe the clothing of someone else in the class. Have students listen and guess who you are describing. For example:

> She's wearing a red dress and a gold watch. He's wearing blue socks.

b. Call on students to describe the clothing of someone in the class. Have the other students guess who it is.

3. Chain Game

In this game, students practice all the vocabulary for clothing.

a. You begin the game by saying:

> "I'm in the department store and I'm looking for a (shirt)."

b. Have each student take a turn in which he or she repeats what the person before has said and adds an article of clothing. For example:

> "I'm in the department store and I'm looking for a (shirt) and a (pair of pants)."

> "I'm in the department store and I'm looking for a (shirt), a (pair of pants), and a (watch)."

4. True or False?

a. Bring in pictures from magazines, newspapers, or mail order clothing catalogs that depict clothing items.

b. Make statements about the pictures and have students tell you "True" or "False." If the statement is false, have students correct it.

Variation: You can call on students to make true or false statements about the pictures and have other students respond.

5. What's My Partner Wearing?

Have pairs of students sit back-to-back and describe what each other is wearing.

Note: To make this activity more fun, don't tell students beforehand what they're going to do so that they won't look carefully at their partner's clothes.

READING *Nothing to Wear*

FOCUS

- Singular/Plural

NEW VOCABULARY

clean	getting dressed	ripped
clothesline	having a	something
dirty	difficult time	sports jacket
dry cleaner's	morning	this morning
empty	nothing	work

READING THE STORY

Optional: *Preview the story by having students talk about the story title and/or illustration. You may choose to introduce new vocabulary beforehand, or have students encounter the new vocabulary within the context of the reading.*

1. Have students read silently, or follow along silently as the story is read aloud by you, by one or more students, or on the audio program.

2. Ask students if they have any questions. Check understanding of vocabulary.

3. Check students' comprehension, using some or all of the following questions:

   Why is Fred upset?
   Is there a clean shirt in Fred's closet?
   Why not?
   Is there a sports jacket?
   Why not?
   Is there a pair of pants for Fred to wear?
   Why not?
   Is there a pair of socks?
   Why not?

✓ READING *CHECK-UP*

CHOOSE

1. b	**4.** b
2. a	**5.** a
3. a	**6.** b

WHICH WORD DOESN'T BELONG?

Example: jeans (The others are worn on the feet.)

1. c (The others are clothing items.)
2. b (The others are jewelry items.)
3. d (The others are clothes for women.)
4. a (The others are colors.)
5. d (The others come in pairs.)

READING EXTENSION

1. Divide the class into pairs.

2. Tell students that Fred is finally going to work, and he's wearing the clothes that are in his house. Have the pairs work together to draw a picture and write a description of what Fred is wearing.

3. Have students share their ideas in small groups or with the class.

Text Page 73: Excuse Me. I Think That's My Jacket.

FOCUS

- This/That/These/Those

CLOSE UP

RULE:	*This* and *These* are demonstratives that refer to objects that are close to the speaker (usually within arm's reach).
EXAMPLES:	**This** is my jacket. *(The jacket is close to the speaker.)* **Those** are my gloves. *(The gloves are close to the speaker.)*
RULE:	*That* and *Those* are demonstratives that refer to objects that are not close to the speaker (further than arm's reach).
EXAMPLES:	**That's** my jacket. *(The jacket is not close to the speaker.)* **Those** are my gloves. *(The gloves are not close to the speaker.)*
RULE:	*That* is the only demonstrative that can contract with the verb *to be*.
EXAMPLE:	I think **that's** (that is) my coat.

GETTING READY

1. Introduce the word *this*.

   a. Hold up a book (or a pen or other object) and say: "*this* book."

   b. Give the book to several students. Have each student repeat "*this* book" while holding the book.

2. Introduce the word *that*.

   a. Put the same book (used for *this*) some distance away from you and the students. Point to the book and say: "*that* book."

   b. Have students point to the book and repeat: "*that* book" chorally and individually.

3. Introduce the words *these* and *those* the same way, using several books (or pens or other objects).

4. Put the following stick figures on the board to summarize the meanings of *this, that, these,* and *those*:

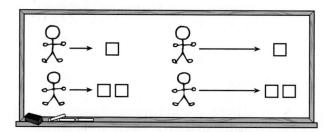

INTRODUCING THE MODELS

There are two model conversations. Introduce and practice each model before going on to the next. For each model:

1. Have students look at the model illustration.

2. Set the scene: "Two people are talking."

3. Present the model.

4. Full-Class Repetition.

5. Ask students if they have any questions. Check understanding of new vocabulary: *this, that, think, Hmm, I don't think so, Oh, You're right, I guess I made a mistake.*

   ### Language Note

   "That's my jacket" and "This is my jacket" are very direct statements. As a way of softening these statements, to make them less blunt and more polite, the speakers preface them with "I think." This way, the speakers are being polite, leaving open the possibility for correction.

6. Group Choral Repetition.

7. Choral Conversation.

8. Call on one or two pairs of students to present the dialog.

   (For additional practice, do Choral Conversation in small groups or by rows.)

SIDE BY SIDE EXERCISES

Examples

1. A. Excuse me. I think that's my hat.
   B. Hmm. I don't think so. I think this is MY hat.
   A. Oh. You're right. I guess I made a mistake.

2. A. Excuse me. I think those are my boots.
   B. Hmm. I don't think so. I think these are MY boots.
   A. Oh. You're right. I guess I made a mistake.

1. **Exercise 1:** Call on two students to present the dialog. Then do Choral Repetition and Choral Conversation practice.

2. **Exercise 2:** Same as above.

3. **Exercises 3–7:** Either Full-Class or Pair Practice.

   ### New Vocabulary

   7. sunglasses

4. **Exercise 8:** Have students use the model as a guide to create their own conversations, using vocabulary of their choice. (They can use any objects or articles of clothing they wish. Encourage students to use dictionaries to find new words they want to use.) This exercise can be done orally in class or for written homework. If you assign it for homework, do one example in class to make sure students understand what's expected. Have students present their conversations in class the next day.

WORKBOOK

Pages 54–56

EXPANSION ACTIVITIES

1. Category Dictation

a. Write on the board:

near	far
→	→

b. Have students draw two columns on a piece of paper. At the top of one column, have them write <u>near</u>, and at the top of the other column, have them write <u>far</u>.

c. Dictate phrases and have students write them in the appropriate column. For example:

<u>near</u>	<u>far</u>
this hat	those boots
these blouses	that shirt
this boot	those socks

2. Role Play

a. Review the model conversations on text page 73 and then have students close their books.

b. Call on different pairs of students to come to the front of the class and act out similar conversations, using real objects for props (for example: gloves, a hat, an umbrella, a purse, a book, a pair of glasses).

FOCUS

* Review of This/That/These/Those

GETTING READY

Using visuals or realia, review the following adjectives:

new–old
beautiful–ugly
large/big–small/little
expensive–cheap

INTRODUCING THE MODELS

There are two model conversations. Introduce and practice each model before going on to the next. For each model:

1. Have students look at the model illustration.

2. Set the scene: "People are at the Lost and Found department."

3. Present the model.

4. Full-Class Repetition.

5. Ask students if they have any questions. Check understanding of new vocabulary: *sure*.

Culture Note

Lost and Found: Many restaurants, large stores, and other public buildings in the United States have *Lost and Found* departments where people may turn in and pick up lost items.

6. Group Choral Repetition.

7. Choral Conversation.

8. Call on one or two pairs of students to present the dialog.

(For additional practice, do Choral Conversation in small groups or by rows.)

SIDE BY SIDE EXERCISES

Examples

In these exercises, students use colors or adjectives of their choice.

Possible Conversations:

1. A. Is this your watch?
   B. No, it isn't.
   A. Are you sure?
   B. Yes. THAT watch is OLD, and MY watch is NEW. /
   Yes. THAT watch is SILVER, and MY watch is GOLD.

2. A. Are these your gloves?
   B. No, they aren't.
   A. Are you sure?
   B. Yes. THOSE gloves are BROWN, and MY gloves are BLACK. /
   Yes. THOSE gloves are SMALL, and MY gloves are LARGE.

1. **Exercise 1:** Call on two students to present the dialog. Then do Choral Repetition and Choral Conversation practice.

2. **Exercise 2:** Same as above.

3. **Exercises 3–4:** Either Full-Class Practice or Pair Practice.

4. **Exercise 5:** Have students create two dialogs, using the models as a guide and using vocabulary of their choice, one dialog using *this* and *that*, the other using *these* and *those*. Encourage students to use dictionaries to find new words they want to use. This exercise can be done orally in class or for written homework. If you assign it for homework, do one example in class to make sure students understand what's expected. Have students present their conversations in class the next day.

WORKBOOK

Pages 57–59

EXPANSION ACTIVITIES

1. Scrambled Dialog

a. Write each line of the two model conversations from page 74 on a separate card. Scramble the cards.

b. Give the cards to eight students. Have them unscramble the lines and put together the two conversations.

c. Form pairs and have each pair read a conversation.

2. Pronunciation Practice

The following groups of words have the sound [I] as in *this* and [i] as in *these*. Write some or all of these words on the board and have students practice saying these sounds.

[I] – "this"		[i] – "these"
single	sister	she
sit	hospital	he
mistake	it's	sleeping
swimming	little	reading
big		eating
in		feeding
thin		easy
kitchen		cleaning
sink		teeth
living room		cheap
miss		beach
busy		between

3. Listening Practice

Write on the board:

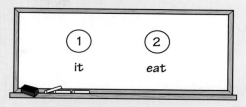

Have students listen as you read the following words. For each word, have students say "one" if the word has the same sound as in *it*, or "two" if the word has the same sound as in *eat*.

big, miss, he, cheap, sister, beach, she, thin, sink, teeth, swimming, easy

4. Role Play

a. Review the model conversations on text page 74 and then have students close their books.

b. Call on different pairs of students to come to the front of the class and act out conversations, using real objects belonging to them. Encourage students to expand the conversations any way they wish.

How to Say It!

> **Complimenting:** "That's a very nice _____!" is a common way to compliment. It is customary to respond to a compliment by saying "Thank you" or "Thanks."

1. Have students look at the illustration.

2. Set the scene: "Two friends are talking."

3. Present the first model.

4. Full-Class Repetition.

5. Group Choral Repetition.

6. Choral Conversation.

7. Call on one or two pairs of students to present the dialog.

8. Present and practice the second conversation in the same way.

9. Have students walk around the classroom complimenting each other.

10. Call on several pairs of students to present their *complimentary* conversations to the class.

📖 READING *Holiday Shopping*

FOCUS

- Singular/Plural

NEW VOCABULARY

cotton	inexpensive	vinyl
frustrated	leather	wool
gift	raincoat	
holiday	trouble	

READING THE STORY

Optional: Preview the story by having students talk about the story title and/or illustration. You may choose to introduce new vocabulary beforehand, or have students encounter the new vocabulary within the context of the reading.

1. Have students read silently, or follow along silently as the story is read aloud by you, by one or more students, or on the audio program.

2. Ask students if they have any questions. Check understanding of vocabulary.

✔ READING *CHECK-UP*

Q & A

1. Call on a pair of students to present the model.

2. Have students work in pairs to create new dialogs.

3. Call on pairs to present their new dialogs to the class.

READING EXTENSION

Ask students the following questions:

> What's another title for the story?
> What's the big *shopping* holiday in your country?
> What's your favorite store for buying gifts?

LISTENING

WHAT'S THE WORD?

Listen and choose the correct answer.

1. A. May I help you?
   B. Yes, please. I'm looking for a blouse.

2. A. Can I help you?
   B. Yes, please. I'm looking for a pair of boots.

3. A. May I help you?
   B. Yes, please. I'm looking for a necklace.

4. A. Can I help you?
   B. Yes, please. I'm looking for a raincoat.

5. A. May I help you?
   B. Yes, please. I'm looking for a pair of stockings.

6. A. Can I help you?
   B. Yes, please. I'm looking for a shirt.

Answers

1. a		4. b	
2. b		5. b	
3. a		6. a	

WHICH WORD DO YOU HEAR?

Listen and choose the correct answer.

1. These jackets are expensive.

2. I'm looking for a leather belt.

3. I'm wearing my new wool sweater.
4. Suits are over there.
5. Is this your shoe?
6. Polka dot ties are very popular this year.

Answers

1. b		**4.** b	
2. a		**5.** a	
3. a		**6.** b	

PRONUNCIATION

> **Emphasized Words:** A speaker can give emphasis to certain words to stress their importance or to contrast information. To give emphasis to a word, the speaker says it louder and with a higher pitch than the other words in the sentence. For example:
>
> THAT umbrella is BROWN, and MY umbrella is BLACK.

Focus on Listening

Practice the sentences in the left column. Say each sentence or play the audio one or more times. Have students listen carefully and repeat.

Focus on Pronunciation

Practice the sentences in the right column. Have students say each sentence and then listen carefully as you say it or play the audio.

If you wish, have students continue practicing the sentences to improve their pronunciation.

 JOURNAL

Have students write their journal entries at home or in class. Encourage students to use a dictionary to look up words they would like to use. Students can share their written work with other students if appropriate. Have students discuss what they have written as a class, in pairs, or in small groups.

WORKBOOK

Check-Up Test: Pages 60–61

 CHAPTER SUMMARY

GRAMMAR

1. Divide the class into pairs or small groups.
2. Have students take turns reading the sentences in the grammar boxes.

KEY VOCABULARY

Have students ask you any questions about the meaning or pronunciation of the vocabulary. If students ask for the pronunciation, repeat after the student until the student is satisfied with his or her pronunciation.

EXPANSION ACTIVITIES

1. Do You Remember the Words?

   Check students' retention of the vocabulary depicted on the opening page of Chapter 8 by doing the following activity:

   a. Have students open their books to page 67 and cover the list of vocabulary words.

   b. Either call out a number and have students tell you the word, or say a word and have students tell you the number.

   Variation: You can also do this activity as a game with competing teams.

2. Student-Led Dictation

   a. Tell each student to choose a word from the Key Vocabulary list on text page 76 and look at it very carefully.

   b. Have students take turns dictating their words to the class. Everybody writes down that student's word.

c. When the dictation is completed, call on different students to write each word on the board to check the spelling.

3. Beanbag Toss

a. Call out a topic from the chapter—for example: *Clothing.*

b. Have students toss a beanbag back and forth. The student to whom the beanbag is tossed must name a word in that category. For example:

Student 1:   shirt
Student 2:   pants
Student 3:   tie

c. Continue until all the words in the category have been named.

END-OF-CHAPTER ACTIVITIES

1. Remember the Words!

a. Bring in pictures depicting clothing items from magazines, newspapers, or mail order clothing catalogs. Choose one picture and show it to class for one minute.

b. Have students write down as many words from the picture as they can remember.

c. Have students read their lists as a class, in pairs, or in small groups.

d. Call on students to come to the board and write their list of words. Have the class check the spelling of the words.

2. Correct the Teacher!

a. Make statements about students and objects in the class. Some statements should be true and others false.

b. Have students respond to the statements. If the statement is false, have students correct it. For example:

Teacher (pointing):   Those books are blue.
        Student: True.

Teacher (pointing):   These shoes are brown.
Student (pointing):   False. Those shoes are black.

Variation: Do the activity as a game with competing teams.

WORKBOOK PAGE 50

A. WHAT'S THE WORD?

1. tie	16. dress
2. shirt	17. coat
3. jacket	18. purse
4. pants	19. stocking
5. umbrella	20. hat
6. earring	21. watch
7. necklace	22. glove
8. blouse	23. briefcase
9. bracelet	24. mitten
10. skirt	25. sweater
11. glasses	26. jeans
12. suit	27. boot
13. belt	
14. sock	
15. shoe	

WORKBOOK PAGE 51

B. A OR AN?

1. a	13. an
2. an	14. a
3. a	15. a
4. an	16. a
5. a	17. an
6. an	18. a
7. a	19. an
8. an	20. an
9. an	21. a
10. a	22. an
11. a	23. a
12. a	24. a

C. SINGULAR/PLURAL

1. a hat	10. a room
2. a basement	11. earrings
3. dresses	12. a purse
4. bosses	13. nieces
5. exercises	14. women
6. a watch	15. a child
7. a glove	16. mice
8. socks	17. a tooth
9. drums	18. a person

D. LISTENING

Listen to each word. Put a circle around the word you hear.

1. umbrellas	4. computer
2. blouses	5. shoes
3. coats	6. exercises

7. dress	12. watches
8. restaurants	13. nieces
9. necklaces	14. nephew
10. earring	15. shirts
11. belt	16. tie

Answers

1. umbrellas	9. necklaces
2. blouses	10. earring
3. coats	11. belt
4. computer	12. watches
5. shoes	13. nieces
6. exercises	14. nephew
7. dress	15. shirts
8. restaurants	16. tie

WORKBOOK PAGE 52

E. LISTENING

Listen and circle the color you hear.

1. My favorite color is blue.
2. My favorite color is green.
3. My favorite color is gray.
4. My favorite color is silver.
5. My favorite color is yellow.
6. My favorite color is orange.

Answers

1. blue	4. silver
2. green	5. yellow
3. gray	6. orange

WORKBOOK PAGE 53

G. WHAT ARE THEY LOOKING FOR?

1. a pair of pants
2. a pair of gloves
3. a pair of shoes
4. a pair of jeans
5. a pair of mittens
6. a pair of boots
7. a pair of stockings
8. a pair of earrings
9. a pair of pajamas

WORKBOOK PAGE 54

H. LISTENING

Listen and put a check under the correct picture.

1. I'm washing these socks.
2. He's reading this book.

3. I'm looking for these men.
4. They're using these computers.
5. We're vacuuming this rug.
6. She's playing with these dogs.
7. We're painting this garage.
8. They're listening to these radios.

Answers

1. ___ ✔   2. ✔ ___
3. ___ ✔   4. ___ ✔
5. ✔ ___   6. ___ ✔
7. ✔ ___   8. ___ ✔

I. LISTENING

Listen and circle the correct word to complete the sentence.

1. This bicycle . . .
2. These exercises . . .
3. These apartment buildings . . .
4. This bracelet . . .
5. These women . . .
6. These sunglasses . . .
7. This car . . .
8. These jeans . . .
9. This refrigerator . . .

Answers

1. is   6. are
2. are   7. is
3. are   8. are
4. is   9. is
5. are

WORKBOOK PAGE 55

J. THIS/THAT/THESE/THOSE

1. This hat is orange.
2. That hat is yellow.
3. These boots are brown.
4. Those boots are black.
5. This computer is expensive.
6. That computer is cheap.
7. These gloves are small.
8. Those gloves are large.
9. This tie is pretty.
10. That tie is ugly.
11. These earrings are gold.
12. Those earrings are silver.

WORKBOOK PAGE 56

K. SINGULAR → PLURAL

1. Those coats are blue.
2. These bracelets are new.

3. Those watches are beautiful.
4. These are Tom's jackets.
5. These aren't your shoes.
6. Are those your earrings?
7. Those aren't your notebooks.
8. There people aren't rich.

L. PLURAL → SINGULAR

1. This sweater is pretty.
2. That purse is expensive.
3. Is this your neighbor?
4. Is that your dress?
5. That's Bill's shirt.
6. This woman is my friend.
7. This isn't my glove.
8. That's her cat

M. SCRAMBLED SENTENCES

1. I think that's my jacket.
2. These are my new gloves.
3. Those aren't your black boots.
4. Blue suits are very popular this year.
5. Here's a nice pair of sunglasses.
6. That's my brother's old car.

WORKBOOK PAGE 58

P. THIS/THAT/THESE/THOSE

1. This, These, this
2. That, those
3. This, This, these
4. those, that
5. This, This, these
6. those, that

WORKBOOK PAGE 59

Q. GRAMMARSONG

1. this   14. these
2. this   15. Are
3. shirt   16. boots
4. That's   17. Those
5. skirt   18. suits
6. this   19. are
7. hat   20. these
8. this   21. those
9. that   22. This
10. This   23. that
11. that   24. These
12. This   25. those
13. that   26. that

CHECK-UP TEST: Chapters 7-8

A.

1. these
2. of
3. Is there
4. earring
5. How
6. people
7. there
8. No, there isn't.

B.

1. It's around the corner from the barber shop.
2. It's across from the library.
3. It's between the clinic and the drug store.

C.

1. their (The others are demonstratives.)
2. striped (The others are colors.)
3. closet (The others are places in the community.)
4. necklace (The others are worn on the feet.)

D.

1. These gloves are large.
2. That table is broken.
3. Those shoes are black.

E.

1. These rooms are small.
2. Those aren't my pencils.
3. Are these your boots?

F.

Listen and circle the correct word to complete the sentence.

Ex. These dresses . . .

1. That house . . .
2. Those people . . .
3. These flowers . . .
4. This blouse . . .

Answers

1. is
2. are
3. are
4. is

FEATURE ARTICLE
Clothing, Colors, and Cultures

PREVIEWING THE ARTICLE

1. Have students talk about the title of the article and the accompanying photographs.

2. You may choose to introduce the following new vocabulary beforehand, or have students encounter it within the context of the article:

culture	meanings
for example	sad
lucky	traditional

READING THE ARTICLE

1. Have students read silently, or follow along silently as the article is read aloud by you, by one or more students, or on the audio program.

2. Ask students if they have any questions. Check understanding of new vocabulary.

3. Check students' comprehension by having students decide whether the following statements are true or false:

Blue is a color for boys all around the world. *(False)*
In some countries, pink is a color for girls. *(True)*
White is the color for wedding dresses all around the world. *(False.)*
Red is a lucky color in all cultures. *(False.)*

4. Discuss the question at the end of the article.

  a. With student input, write the names of colors on the board.

  b. Divide the class into groups, and have students talk about each color.

  c. Then have the groups share their ideas with the class. Write students' ideas on the board, explaining new vocabulary as it comes up.

5. If possible, bring in pictures of flags from different countries. Have students explain the meaning of the colors in their country's flag.

EXPANSION ACTIVITY

Associations

This activity gets students thinking about the different uses of colors in their cultures.

1. Divide the class into pairs or small groups.

2. Call out a color.

3. Have the students in each pair or group work together to see how many words they can associate with that color. For example:

  white: wedding dress, doctor's coat, snow

  green: plants, money

4. Have students share their words with the class.

Variation: You can do the activity as a game with several competing teams. The team with the most items wins.

 LISTENING *Attention, J-Mart Shoppers!*

1. Set the scene: "You're shopping at J-Mart."

2. Introduce new vocabulary: *attention, shoppers, aisle.*

LISTENING SCRIPT

Listen to these announcements in a clothing store. Match the clothing and the aisles.

Attention, J-Mart shoppers! Are you looking for a black leather jacket? Black leather jackets are very popular this year! There are a lot of black leather jackets at J-Mart today! They're in Aisle 9, next to the coats.

Attention, J-Mart shoppers! Are you looking for a pair of vinyl gloves? Vinyl gloves are very popular this year! Well, there are a lot of vinyl gloves at J-Mart today! They're in Aisle 5, across from the hats.

Attention, J-Mart shoppers! Are you looking for a blouse? Is red your favorite color? Red blouses are very popular this year! There are a lot of red blouses at J-Mart today. They're in Aisle 7, next to the dresses.

Attention, J-Mart shoppers! Are you looking for a special gift for your mother, your wife, or your sister? A silver bracelet is a special gift for that special person. All our silver bracelets are in Aisle 1, across from the earrings.

Attention, J-Mart shoppers! Are you looking for a special gift for your father, your husband, or your brother? A polka dot tie is a special gift for that special person. All our polka dot ties are in Aisle 11, next to the belts.

Answers

1. c

2. e

3. b

4. a

5. d

 BUILD YOUR VOCABULARY!
Clothing

bathrobe	sandals
tee shirt	slippers
scarf	sneakers
wallet	shorts
ring	sweat pants

1. Have students look at the illustrations and identify any words they already know.

2. Present the vocabulary. Say each word and have the class repeat it chorally and individually. Check students' understanding and pronunciation of the words.

EXPANSION ACTIVITIES

1. **Clap in Rhythm**

   Object: Once a clapping rhythm is established, the students must continue naming different articles of clothing.

   a. Have students sit in a circle.

   b. Establish a steady even beat—one-two-three-four, one-two-three-four—by having students clap their hands to their laps twice and then clap their hands together twice. Repeat throughout the game, maintaining the same rhythm.

   c. The object is for each student in turn to name a clothing word each time the hands are clapped together twice. Nothing is said when students clap their hands on their laps.

   Note: The beat never stops! If a student misses a beat, he or she can either wait for the next beat or pass to the next student.

2. **Drawing Game**

   a. Write the names of articles of clothing from text pages 68 and 77 on two sets of separate cards.

   b. Place the two piles of cards on a table or desk in the front of the room. Also have a pad of paper and pencil next to each team's set of cards.

   c. Divide the class into teams. Have each team sit together in a different part of the room.

   d. When you say "Go!", a person from each team comes to the front of his or her team, picks a card from the pile, and draws the article of clothing. The rest of the team then guesses what the article of clothing is.

   e. When a team correctly guesses the article of clothing, another team member picks a card and draws the item written on that card.

   f. Continue until each team has guessed all the articles of clothing in their pile.

   The team that guesses the articles of clothing in the shortest time wins the game.

3. Letter Game

a. Divide the class into teams.

b. Say; "I'm thinking of a piece of clothing that starts with *b*."

c. The first person to raise his or her hand and guess correctly [bathrobe] wins a point for that team.

d. Continue with other letters of the alphabet and clothing items.

   The team that gets the most correct answers wins the game.

4. Category Dictation

a. Have students draw the following columns on a piece of paper:

   <u>Cold Weather</u> <u>Hot Weather</u> <u>Jewelry</u> <u>Feet</u>

   Introduce the words *jewelry* and *feet*.

b. Dictate various clothing items from text pages 68 and 77 and have students write them in the appropriate column. For example:

Cold Weather	Hot Weather	Jewelry	Feet
scarf	shorts	ring	sandals
mittens	tee shirt	necklace	slippers

AROUND THE WORLD
People's Homes

1. Have students read silently or follow along silently as the text is read aloud by you, by one or more students, or on the audio program. Check understanding of new vocabulary:

farmhouse	mobile home
houseboat	trailer
hut	

2. Have students first work in pairs or small groups, reacting to the photographs and responding to the question. Then have students tell the class what they talked about. Write any new vocabulary on the board.

Option: You might want to see if your students can guess the location of the family in the hut (Kenya) and the family in the houseboat (Hong Kong).

EXPANSION ACTIVITIES

1. Be an Observer!

Have students take a tour of their neighborhoods, describe the types of homes they find, and then report back to class.

2. Tell a Story

Have each student choose one of the photographs on text page 78 and write about what the people in that home are doing. Encourage students to use a dictionary to look up words they would like to use in their stories.

FACT FILE
Urban, Suburban, and Rural

1. Read the text aloud as students follow along. Explain new vocabulary: *urban, suburban, rural, countryside, far from, about, percent, population.*

2. Ask students if their home is in an *urban*, *suburban*, or *rural* area.

3. For additional practice, do either or both of the following:

   a. Have students look at the photographs in *Around the World* and decide whether the homes are in urban, suburban, or rural areas.

   b. Bring pictures of different homes to class. Have students decide if the homes are in an urban, suburban, or rural areas.

   c. Write *urban* on the board. Ask students:

      What's good about living in an urban area?
      What's bad?

   Write students' ideas on the board. Do the same for *suburban* and *rural*.

GLOBAL EXCHANGE

1. Set the scene: "RosieM is writing to her keypal."

2. Have students read silently or follow along silently as the message is read aloud by you, by one or more students, or on the audio program.

3. Ask students if they have any questions. Check understanding of vocabulary.

4. Options for additional practice:

   • Have students write a response to RosieM and share their writing in pairs.

   • Have students correspond with a keypal on the Internet and then share their experience with the class.

WHAT ARE THEY SAYING?

FOCUS

• Article of Clothing
• This/That/These/Those

Have students talk about the people and the situation, and then create role plays based on the scene. Students may refer back to previous lessons as a resource, but they should not simply reuse specific conversations.

Note: You may want to assign this exercise as written homework, having students prepare their role plays, practice them the next day with the other students, and then present them to the class.

Teacher's Notes

GRAMMAR

SIMPLE PRESENT TENSE

Where	do	I we you they	live?
	does	he she it	

I We You They	live	in Rome.
He She It	lives	

FUNCTIONS

ASKING FOR AND REPORTING INFORMATION

What's your name?
    My name is *Antonio*.
Where do you live?
    I live in *Rome*.
What language do you speak?
    I speak *Italian*.
What do you do every day?
    I *eat Italian food*.

Tell me, _____?

NEW VOCABULARY

Everyday Activities

call
do/does
drive
forget
live
sell
shop
speak
visit
work

Languages

Arabic
English
French
German
Polish
Portuguese
Russian
Spanish

Nationalities

Brazilian
Canadian
Egyptian
French
German
Polish
Russian
Spanish

Places Around the World

Berlin
Boston
Buffalo
Cairo
Chicago
Cleveland
Hong Kong
London
Madrid
Moscow
Rio de Janeiro
San Diego
Tampa
Toronto

Time Words

every day
weekend

Question Words

When

Adverbs of Frequency

always
usually

Miscellaneous

a little
afraid
bus
grocery store
language
office
program
so
song
suburb
taxi
telephone
TV show

EXPRESSIONS

Hesitating

Hmm. Well . . .

VOCABULARY PREVIEW

You may want to introduce these words before beginning the chapter, or you may choose to wait until they first occur in a specific lesson. If you choose to introduce them at this point, here are some suggestions:

1. Have students look at the illustrations on text page 79 and identify the words they already know.

2. Present the vocabulary. Say each word and have the class repeat it chorally and individually. Check students' understanding and pronunciation of the words.

3. Practice the vocabulary as a class, in pairs, or in small groups. Have students cover the word list and look at the pictures. Practice the words in the following ways:

   • Say a word and have students tell the number of the illustration.

   • Give the number of an illustration and have students say the word.

FOCUS

- Simple Present Tense with *I, we, you, they*
- Questions with *Where* and *What*
- Nationalities

The focus of the lesson on text page 80 is the non-3rd person singular forms of the simple present. The 3rd person singular form is introduced on text page 81.

CLOSE UP

RULE:	The simple present tense describes habitual activities.

EXAMPLES:	What do you do every day?
	    I **eat** Italian food.
	    I **sing** Italian songs.

RULE:	The simple present tense also describes a generally known fact.
EXAMPLES:	I **live** in Rome. I **speak** Italian.
RULE:	For the subjects *I, we, you,* and *they,* the simple present tense uses the base form of the verb.
EXAMPLES:	I **eat**. You **eat**. We **eat**. They **eat**.
RULE:	The word order of a question in the simple present tense is: Question word + auxiliary + subject + base form of the verb. The auxiliary for *I, you, we,* and *they* in the simple present tense is *do*.
EXAMPLES:	**Where + do + you + live?** **What language + do + you + speak?** **What + do + you + do every day?**

GETTING READY

1. Introduce yourself this way. Say:

   My name is (*your name*).
   I live in (*city*).
   I speak (*native language*).

2. Write the following categories on the board. Under each one write the correct information about yourself.

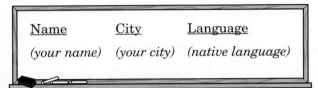

Name	City	Language
(*your name*)	(*your city*)	(*native language*)

3. Repeat your introduction as in 1 above, then call on students to introduce themselves the same way. Add their information to the chart. (Leave the chart on the board. You will use it again for the exercises.)

   ### *Language Note*

   In English, the names of languages and nationalities are capitalized.

INTRODUCING THE MODEL

1. Have students look at the model illustration.

2. Set the scene: "A TV reporter is interviewing somebody in Rome." (Use a world map to show where Rome, Italy is.)

3. Present the model.

4. Full-Class Repetition.

5. Write the information about Antonio on the board, under the same three categories: *Name, City,* and *Language.*

6. Ask students if they have any questions. Check understanding of new vocabulary: *live, speak, Italian, language, every day, songs, TV shows.*

7. Group Choral Repetition.

8. Choral Conversation.

9. Call on one or two pairs of students to present the dialog.

   (For additional practice, do Choral Conversation in small groups or by rows.)

10. Practice the questions in the green shaded box above the exercises. Write them on the board, say each question, and have students repeat after you chorally and individually.

SIDE BY SIDE EXERCISES

Examples

1. A. What's your name?
   B. My name is Carmen.
   A. Where do you live?
   B. I live in Madrid.
   A. What language do you speak?
   B. I speak Spanish.
   A. What do you do every day?
   B. I eat Spanish food, I sing Spanish songs, and I watch Spanish TV shows.

2. A. What's your name?
   B. My name is Kenji.
   A. Where do you live?
   B. I live in Tokyo.
   A. What language do you speak?
   B. I speak Japanese.
   A. What do you do every day?
   B. I eat Japanese food, I sing Japanese songs, and I watch Japanese TV shows.

Note: Before doing the exercises, point out the locations of the cities on a world map.

1. **Exercise 1:** Introduce *Madrid, Spanish.* Call on two students to present the interview. Then do Choral Repetition and Choral Conversation practice.

2. **Exercise 2:** Same as above.

3. **Exercises 3-6:** Either Full-Class Practice or Pair Practice.

New Vocabulary	

3. Paris
  French
	6. Moscow
	  Russian

4. Berlin German	

WORKBOOK

Pages 62–63 Exercises A, B

EXPANSION ACTIVITIES

1. Clap and Listen

a. With students' books closed, read the model conversation.

b. Read it again, this time clapping your hands or tapping on the desk to indicate missing words. For example: "[*clap*] your name?" Have students respond, "What's."

c. Read, "My [*clap*] is Antonio." Have students respond "name."

d. Continue in the same way with the other lines of the conversation.

2. Scrambled Dialog

a. Write each line of the model conversation from page 80 on a separate card. Scramble the cards.

b. Give the cards to 8 students. Have them unscramble the lines, put together the conversation, and then present it to the class.

3. Interview These People!

a. Make up cards with information about new people. On each card write a new name, city, and language. For example:

Mrs. Ponti	Fernando	Mr. and Mrs. Kitano
Venice	Caracas	Kyoto
Italian	Spanish	Japanese

b. Have some students draw cards and pretend to be those people. Have other students interview them, using the questions on text page 80. You can do the activity as Full-Class Practice or Pair Practice.

4. Who Are They?

a. Write the following questions on the board:

> What are their names?
> Where do they live?
> What language do they speak?
> What do they do every day?

b. Make up cards that show two or more people. Include their names, a city, and a language. For example:

Nicole and Paul	Mr. and Mrs. Park
Paris	Seoul
French	Korean

Carlos and Maria	Boris and Natasha
Barcelona	Moscow
Spanish	Russian

c. Have students ask and answer about the people on the cards. You can do this as Full-Class Practice or Pair Practice.

5. What's My Name?

Call on two students. Have Student A pretend to be in the hospital with *amnesia*, a condition that causes a person to forget things. Have Student B pretend to be a friend, relative, or doctor. Have Student A ask the questions on text page 80 with *I*. For example:

> What's my name?
> Where do I live?

Have Student B answer, using any information he or she wishes.

6. Question the Answers!

a. Dictate answers such as the following to the class:

> My name is Carla.
> I'm from Rome.
> I speak Italian.
> Every day I eat Italian food and I watch Italian TV shows.

b. Have students write questions for which these answers would be correct.

Variation: Write the answers on cards. Divide the class into groups and give each group a set of cards.

Text Page 81: People Around the World

FOCUS

- Simple Present Tense with *he* and *she*
- Nationalities

CLOSE UP

RULE:	The 3rd person singular of the simple present tense is formed with the base verb + *s*-ending.
EXAMPLES:	He live**s**. She eat**s**.
Note:	The three different pronunciations of the 3rd person singular ending are presented in Chapter 11 on text page 101.

RULE:	The auxiliary for the 3rd person singular in the simple present tense is *does*.
EXAMPLES:	Where **does** he live? What language **does** she speak?

INTRODUCING THE MODEL

1. Have students look at the model illustration.
2. Set the scene: "Two people are talking about Miguel."
3. Present the model.
4. Full-Class Repetition.

Pronunciation Note

The pronunciation focus of Chapter 9 is **Blending with does** (text page 86). You may wish to model this pronunciation at this point and encourage students to incorporate it into their language practice.

Where does she live?

What does he do every day?

5. Put the following chart on the board and write the information about Miguel (note that language and nationality are different).

Name	City	Language	Nationality
Miguel	Mexico City	Spanish	Mexican

6. Ask students if they have any questions. Check understanding of new vocabulary: *Mexico City, Spanish, Mexican.*
7. Group Choral Repetition.
8. Choral Conversation.
9. Call on one or two pairs of students to present the dialog.

   (For additional practice, do Choral Conversation in small groups or by rows.)

SIDE BY SIDE EXERCISES

Before doing each exercise, use the chart on the board to write in the new information for that exercise. Use a world map to show where the cities are. Your chart should look like this:

	Name	City	Language	Nationality
	Miguel	Mexico	Spanish	Mexican
1.	Kate	Toronto	English	Canadian
2.	Carlos	San Juan	Spanish	Puerto Rican
3.	Anna	Athens	Greek	Greek
4.	Ming	Hong Kong	Chinese	Chinese
5.	Sonia	Rio de Janeiro	Portuguese	Brazilian
6.	Omar	Cairo	Arabic	Egyptian

Examples

1. A. What's her name?
   B. Her name is Kate.
   A. Where does she live?
   B. She lives in Toronto.
   A. What language does she speak?
   B. She speaks English.
   A. What does she do every day?
   B. She eats Canadian food, she reads Canadian newspapers, and she listens to Canadian music.

2. A. What's his name?
   B. His name is Carlos.
   A. Where does he live?
   B. He lives in San Juan.
   A. What language does he speak?
   B. He speaks Spanish.
   A. What does he do every day?
   B. He eats Puerto Rican food, he reads Puerto Rican newspapers, and he listens to Puerto Rican music.

1. Model the questions in the green shaded box above the exercises and have students repeat chorally and individually.

2. **Exercise 1:** Introduce *Canadian*. Call on two students to present the dialog. Then do Choral Repetition and Choral Conversation practice.

3. **Exercise 2:** Same as above.

4. **Exercises 3–6:** Either Full-Class Practice or Pair Practice.

New Vocabulary

4. Hong Kong
5. Rio de Janeiro
   Portuguese
   Brazilian

6. Cairo
   Arabic
   Egyptian

WORKBOOK

Pages 63 Exercise C–66

1. Pronunciation Practice

Practice the final s sound. Write on the board and have students repeat chorally and individually (read from left to right):

I live	he lives	she lives
I speak	he speaks	she speaks
I eat	he eats	she eats
I sing	he sings	she sings
I read	he reads	she reads

2. Interviews

a. Write the following cues on the board:

name?   language?   live?   every day?

b. Make up word cards with information about people from different countries. Include the person's name, city, language, and nationality. For example:

Sung Hee	Marco	Mr. Garcia	Mrs. Wong
Seoul	Florence	Cancun	Shanghai
Korean	Italian	Spanish	Chinese
Korean	Italian	Mexican	Chinese

c. Divide the class into pairs.

d. Give one member of each pair a card, and have the other student ask that person questions based on the cues on the board.

e. Have the interviewer report to the class about the person he or she just interviewed. For example:

> Her name is Sung Hee. She lives in Seoul. She speaks Korean. Every day she eats Korean food, and she reads Korean newspapers.

3. Listening Practice: I or She?

Have students listen as you read each of the following words. Have students say "she" (for 3rd person) if they hear a final s sound. Have students say "I" (for non-3rd person) if they do not hear a final s sound.

live	listen	do	speaks
sings	listens	does	lives
eats	read	eat	sing

4. Dictation

Read these sentences slowly and have students write them on a separate piece of paper. When you have finished, you can either collect them and correct them later or write the sentences on the board and have students correct their own papers.

1. She speaks English.
2. He eats Italian food.
3. She reads the newspaper.
4. He lives in Toronto.
5. She listens to music.
6. He sings songs.

5. Talk About Students in the Class

Use the questions in the green shaded box on text page 81 to answer questions about students in the class. You can begin by asking about one student. Then call on pairs of students to ask and answer questions about someone else in the class. Encourage students to use any vocabulary they wish to answer the last question, "What does he/she do every day?"

6. Board Game

a. On poster boards or on manila file folders, make up game boards with a pathway consisting of separate spaces. You may use any theme or design you wish.

b. Divide the class into groups of 2 to 4 students and give each group a game board, a die, and something to be used as a playing piece.

c. Give each group a pile of cards face down with sentences written on them. Some sentences should be correct, and others incorrect. For example:

She lives in Hong Kong.
He read the newspaper every day.
I listens to Italian music.
They eat Greek food.
We speaks Japanese.

d. Each student in turn rolls the die, moves the playing piece along the game path, and after landing on a space, picks a card, reads the sentence, and says if it is *correct* or *incorrect*. If the sentence is incorrect and the student is able to give the correct version, that student takes an additional turn.

e. The first student to reach the end of the pathway is the winner.

7. Concentration

a. Write 16 sentences based on the nationalities and origins of characters on text pages 80 and 81. For example:

Henry is from Shanghai.	He's Chinese.
Carmen is from San Juan.	She's Puerto Rican.
Michael is from Athens.	He's Greek.
Sonia is from Rio de Janeiro.	She's Brazilian.
Mohammed is from Cairo.	He's Egyptian.
Laura is from Toronto.	She's Canadian.
Toshi is from Tokyo.	He's Japanese.
Anna is from Berlin.	She's German.

b. Shuffle the cards and place them face down in four rows of four each.

c. Divide the class into two teams. The object of the game is for students to find the matching cards. Both teams should be able to see all the cards, since *concentrating* on

their location is an important part of playing the game.

d. A student from Team 1 turns over two cards. If they match, the student picks up the cards, that team gets a point, and the student takes another turn. If the cards don't match, the student turns them face down, and a member of Team 2 takes a turn.

e. The game continues until all the cards have been matched. The team with the most correct matches wins the game.

Variation: This game can also be played in groups and pairs.

8. Scrambled Conversations

a. Make a set of matching cards based on the conversations on text page 81. For example:

What's his name?	His name is Toshi.
Where does he live?	He lives in Tokyo.
What language does he speak?	He speaks Japanese.
What does he do every day?	He listens to Japanese music.
What's her name?	Her name is Marie.
Where does she live?	She lives in Paris.
What language does she speak?	She speaks French.
What does she do every day?	She listens to French music.

b. Distribute a card to each student.

c. Have students memorize the sentence on their cards, and then have students walk around the room saying their sentence until they find their match.

d. Then have pairs of students say their matched sentences aloud to the class.

TALK ABOUT IT! *Where Do They Live, and What Do They Do?*

FOCUS

- Review of the Simple Present Tense
- Daily Activities

GETTING READY

1. Bring a map or atlas to class and point out the following locations:

   Boston (USA–Massachusetts)
   Buffalo (USA–New York)
   Cleveland (USA–Ohio)
   Honolulu (USA–Hawaii)
   London (England)
   San Diego (USA–California)
   Tampa (USA–Florida)
   Vancouver (Canada)
   Washington, D.C. (USA)

2. Have students practice pronouncing the names of these cities.

INTRODUCING THE PEOPLE

Call on individual students to read each person's statements. Check understanding of new vocabulary:

> Linda: *work*
> Walter and Wendy: *office*
> Bob: *drive, bus*
> Tina: *taxi*
> Susan: *sell*

Language Note

The question *What do you do?* refers to what people do as their job. For example: *What do you do? (I work in a bank. / I drive a taxi. / We paint houses.)*

CONVERSATION PRACTICE

1. There are two conversational models for talking about the characters. Call on a few pairs of students to present each model.

2. Divide the class into pairs and have students take turns using the models to ask and answer questions about the people on the page.

3. Call on pairs to present their conversations to the class.

How About You?

Have students answer the questions, in pairs or as a class.

WORKBOOK

Pages 67–68

EXPANSION ACTIVITIES

1. True or False?

   a. Have students open their books to text page 82.

   b. Make statements about the characters on text page 82 and have students tell you "True" or "False." If the statement is false, have students correct it. For example:

      Teacher: Brian works in a bank.
      Student: True.

      Teacher: Walter and Wendy live in New York.
      Student: False. Walter and Wendy live in Washington, D.C.

   Variation: You can call on students to make true or false statements about the characters on the page and have other students respond.

2. Guess Who!

a. Have students look at the illustration on text page 82.

b. Make statements about the people and have students identify who they are. For example:

> They live in Honolulu. *(Howard and Henry)*
> He plays the violin. *(Victor)*
> She works in a library. *(Linda)*

3. Memory Game

a. Have students look carefully at text page 82 and then close their books.

b. Make two statements about each of the people on the page and ask a question about the missing information. For example:

> Teacher: He lives in Boston. He works in a bank. What's his name?
> Student: His name is Brian.
>
> Teacher: Her name is Susan. She lives in San Diego. What does she do?
> Student: She sells cars.
>
> Teacher: Their names are Carol and Ray. They cook in a restaurant. Where do they live?
> Student: They live in Cleveland.

If you wish, you can do the activity as a game with competing teams.

Variation: Call on students to lead the activity.

READING *Mr. and Mrs. DiCarlo*

FOCUS

- Simple Present Tense
- Daily Activities

NEW VOCABULARY

a little	program
afraid	suburb
always	telephone
culture	time
forget	usually
grocery store	visit
life back in the	weekend
"old country"	when

READING THE STORY

Optional: *Preview the story by having students talk about the story title and/or illustrations. You may choose to introduce new vocabulary beforehand, or have students encounter the new vocabulary within the context of the reading.*

1. Have students read the story silently, or follow along silently as the story is read aloud by you, by one or more students, or on the audio program.

2. Ask students if they have any questions. Check understanding of vocabulary.

   ### Culture Note

   Many large American cities have ethnic neighborhoods where many people of one nationality live (Chinese, Italian, Polish, Cuban, etc.). These neighborhoods often have grocery stores that sell ethnic food, as well as other businesses that provide services in the customers' native language. These communities often resemble neighborhoods back in the native country.

3. Check students' comprehension, using some or all of the following questions:

   Where do Mr. and Mrs. DiCarlo live?
   How much English do they speak?
   What language do they usually speak?
   What do they read?
   What do they listen to?
   Where do they shop?
   Who do they visit every day?
   What do they talk about?
   Who are Mr. and Mrs. DiCarlo upset about? Why?
   What does Joe read?
   What does he listen to?
   Where does he shop?
   Who does he visit? What language does he speak?
   When does Joe speak Italian?
   Why are Mr. and Mrs. DiCarlo sad?

✓ READING CHECK-UP

WHAT'S THE ANSWER?

1. They live in an old Italian neighborhood in New York City.

2. He lives in a small suburb outside the city.

3. They usually speak Italian.

4. He usually speaks English.

5. They read the Italian newspaper.

6. He reads American newspapers.

7. They listen to Italian radio programs.

8. He listens to American radio programs.

9. They shop at the Italian grocery store around the corner from their apartment building.

10. He shops at big suburban supermarkets and shopping malls.

1. reads
2. shops
3. live
4. lives
5. speaks
6. listen
7. visit
8. talk
9. calls
10. speak

READING EXTENSION

Ask students the following questions and have them review the text for the answers.

What's another title for this reading?
Why does Joe usually speak English?
Why do Mr. and Mrs. DiCarlo usually speak Italian?

 LISTENING

Listen and choose the correct answer.

1. My brother lives in Chicago.
2. My name is Peter. I work in an office.
3. This is my friend Carla. She speaks Italian.
4. My sister drives a bus in Chicago.
5. We read the newspaper every day.
6. My parents visit their friends every weekend.
7. Charlie cooks in a Greek restaurant.
8. My brother and I paint houses.
9. My friend Betty calls me every day.
10. My parents usually shop at the mall.

Answers

1. b
2. a
3. b
4. b
5. a
6. a
7. b
8. a
9. b
10. a

How to Say It!

> **Hesitating:** *Hmm, well,* is one way to express hesitation before speaking. English speakers are not accustomed to silent pauses in spoken conversation. A way to gain time to think and also keep the conversation going is to hesitate verbally and then speak when ready.

1. Set the scene: "Two co-workers are talking."
2. Present the conversation.
3. Full-Class Repetition.
4. Ask students if they have any questions. Check understanding of new vocabulary: *Hmm, well*.
5. Group Choral Repetition.
6. Choral Conversation.
7. Call on one or two pairs to present the dialog.
8. Have students practice in pairs asking the question "What do you do every day?" and hesitating as they answer.
9. Call on several pairs of students to present their conversations to the class.

IN YOUR OWN WORDS

1. Make sure students understand the instructions.
2. Have students do the activity as written homework, using a dictionary for any new words they wish to use.
3. Have students present and discuss, in pairs or as a class, what they have written.

INTERVIEW

THE QUESTIONS

Have the class practice saying the three interview questions:

  Where do you live?
  What language do you speak?
  What do you do every day?

THE MODEL INTERVIEW

1. Have students look at the model illustration. Set the scene. "One person is interviewing another."
2. Call on a pair of students to present the interview. Student A asks the three interview questions, and Student B reads the answers.
3. Then have Student A tell the class about the person in the model interview.

STUDENT INTERVIEWS

1. Brainstorm daily activities with the class. Write them on the board for student reference during their interviews.
2. Have pairs of students interview each other, using the three interview questions.
3. Call on students to report to the class about the person they interviewed.

PRONUNCIATION

> **Blending with _does_:** When the word _does_ occurs in the middle of a question, it blends with the sounds surrounding it. The final /t/ of _what_ turns into the /d/ of _does_. The final /s/ sound of _does_ blends with the initial /s/ sound of _she_. The initial /h/ sound of _he_ is deleted so _does_ blends with _he_.

Focus on Listening

Practice the sentences in the left column. Say each sentence or play the audio one or more times. Have students listen carefully and repeat.

Focus on Pronunciation

Practice the sentences in the right column. Have students say each sentence and then listen carefully as you say it or play the audio.

If you wish, have students continue practicing the sentences to improve their pronunciation.

 **JOURNAL**

Have students write their journal entries at home or in class. Encourage students to use a dictionary to look up words they would like to use in their descriptions. They can share their written work with other students if appropriate. As a class, in pairs, or in small groups, have students discuss what they have written.

 CHAPTER SUMMARY

GRAMMAR

1. Divide the class into pairs or small groups.
2. Have students take turns forming sentences from the grammar boxes. Student A says a sentence, and Student B points to the words from each column that are in the sentence. Then have students switch: Student B says a sentence, and Student A points to the words.

KEY VOCABULARY

Have students ask you any questions about the meaning or pronunciation of the vocabulary. If students ask for the pronunciation, repeat after the student until the student is satisfied with his or her pronunciation.

EXPANSION ACTIVITIES

1. Vocabulary Check

   Check students' retention of the vocabulary depicted on the opening page of Chapter 9 by doing the following activity:

   a. Have students open their books to page 79 and cover the list of vocabulary words.

   b. Either call out a number and have students tell you the word, or say a word and have students tell you the number.

   Variation: You can also do this activity as a game with competing teams.

2. Student-Led Dictation

   a. Tell each student to choose a word from the Key Vocabulary list on text page 86 and look at it very carefully.

   b. Have students take turns dictating their words to the class. Everybody writes down that student's word.

   (continued)

EXPANSION ACTIVITIES (Continued)

c. When the dictation is completed, call on different students to write each word on the board to check the spelling.

3. Beanbag Toss

a. Call out a topic from the chapter—for example: *Everyday Activities*.

b. Have students toss a beanbag back and forth. The student to whom the beanbag is tossed must name a word in that category. For example:

> Student 1: cook
> Student 2: sell
> Student 3: work

c. Continue until all the words in the category have been named.

END-OF-CHAPTER ACTIVITIES

1. Do You Remember?

a. Divide the class into pairs.

b. Tell students to spend three minutes looking carefully at the illustrations on page 83.

c. Have students close their books and write down what they remember about the story.

d. Have students compare their sentences with their partner and then look back at the story to see how much they remembered.

2. Miming

a. Write down on cards the *Everyday Activities* listed on text page 86.

b. Have pairs of students take turns picking a card from the pile and pantomiming the action.

c. The class must guess what the action is.

Variation: This can be done as a game with competing teams.

3. Finish the Sentence!

Begin a sentence and have students repeat what you said and add appropriate endings to the sentence. For example:

Teacher	Students
I wash . . .	I wash my car.
	I wash my windows.
	I wash my clothes.
We visit . . .	We visit our family.
	We visit our friends.
	We visit our old neighborhood.
She calls . . .	She calls her mother.
	She calls the school.
	She calls her friends.
They sell . . .	They sell clothing.
	They sell refrigerators.
	They sell cars.

Variation: This activity may be done as a class, in pairs or small groups, or as a game with competing teams.

4. Sense or Nonsense?

a. Divide the class into four groups.

b. Make four sets of split sentence cards with beginnings and ends of sentences. For example:

She works . . .	in a bank.
He calls . . .	his mother every day.
They live . . .	in a suburb.
I watch . . .	TV shows in Spanish.
I speak . . .	a little French.
You listen . . .	to the radio.
She shops . . .	in a small grocery store.
He drives . . .	a taxi.
We sing . . .	songs together.
I cook . . .	dinner for my family.

c. Mix up the cards and distribute sets of cards to each group, keeping the beginnings and endings cards in different piles.

d. Have students take turns picking up one card from each pile and reading the sentence to the group. For example:

We sing . . .	dinner for my family.

e. The group decides if the sentence makes *sense* or is *nonsense*.

f. After all the cards have been picked, have the groups lay out all the cards and put together all the sentence combinations that make sense.

5. What's Wrong?

a. Divide the class into pairs or small groups.

b. Write several sentences such as the following on the board or on a handout. Some of the sentences should be correct, and others incorrect. For example:

> We eat in an Italian restaurant.
> I cooks breakfast every day.
> She are from Rome.
> He speaks Mexican.
> She works in an office.
> They listen the radio.
> I watch to TV every day.
> They calls their parents every weekend.
> He visits his friends every weekend.

c. The object of the activity is for students to identify which sentences are incorrect and then correct them.

d. Have students compare their answers.

Variation: Do the activity as a game with competing teams. The team that successfully completes the task in the shortest time is the winner.

6. Question the Answers!

a. Dictate answers such as the following to the class:

> She lives in Toronto.
> They paint houses.
> She's from Mexico.
> He speaks English.
> My name is Anna.
> We work in an office.

b. Have students write questions for which these answers would be correct. For example:

Answers	Questions
She lives in Toronto.	Where does she live?
They paint houses.	What do they do?

c. Have students compare their questions with one another.

Variation: Write the answers on cards. Divide the class into groups and give each group a set of cards.

WORKBOOK ANSWER KEY AND LISTENING SCRIPTS

A. INTERVIEWS AROUND THE WORLD

1.	What's	26.	do
2.	name	27.	we
3.	is	28.	sing
4.	do	29.	read
5.	you	30.	What
6.	live	31.	are
7.	What	32.	Their
8.	language	33.	names
9.	speak	34.	are
10.	do	35.	Where
11.	you	36.	do
12.	eat	37.	They
13.	watch	38.	live
14.	are	39.	What
15.	Our	40.	language
16.	names	41.	do
17.	do	42.	they
18.	you	43.	speak
19.	We	44.	do
20.	live	45.	do
21.	What	46.	they
22.	do	47.	eat
23.	you	48.	they
24.	speak	49.	watch
25.	do		

B. LISTENING

Listen and choose the correct response.

1. What's your name?
2. What language do you speak?
3. What do they do every day?
4. Where do you live?
5. What language do you speak?
6. What do you do every day?

Answers

1.	a	4.	a
2.	b	5.	b
3.	a	6.	b

C. PEOPLE AROUND THE WORLD

1. Her name is Jane.
2. She lives in Montreal.
3. She plays the piano, and she listens to Canadian music.
4. What's his name?
5. Where does he live?
6. He speaks Arabic.

7. does he do
   eats, he reads Egyptian newspapers
8. Her name is Sonia.
9. Where does
   She lives in Sao Paolo.
10. does she speak
    She speaks Portuguese.
11. does she do
    She does exercises, and she plays soccer.

F. EDUARDO'S FAMILY

1. live
2. speak
3. speaks
4. speak
5. read
6. live
7. reads
8. works
9. cook
10. work
11. clean
12. shop
13. plays
14. play
15. do
16. do

G. LISTENING

Listen and circle the word you hear.

1. We live in Paris.
2. Where do you live?
3. What language does he speak?
4. Every day I listen to Greek music.
5. Every day she watches English TV shows.
6. What do they eat every day?
7. Every day I sing Korean songs.
8. Every day she eats Chinese food.
9. Every day he reads Mexican newspapers.

Answers

1. live
2. do
3. does
4. listen
5. watches
6. eat
7. sing
8. eats
9. reads

H. WHAT'S THE WORD?

1. does, lives
2. do, paint
3. does, drives
4. do, live
5. do, cook
6. does, do, sells

I. WHAT'S THE DIFFERENCE?

1. drives
2. work
3. plays
4. sells
5. paints
6. lives

K. LOUD AND CLEAR

1. Charlie, chair, kitchen, Chinese
2. Shirley, short, shoes
3. Richard, cheap, French, watch
4. washing, shirt, washing machine
5. Chen, children, bench, church
6. Sharp, English, station

GRAMMAR

SIMPLE PRESENT TENSE:
YES/NO QUESTIONS

Do	I we you they	work?
Does	he she it	

SHORT ANSWERS

Yes,	I we you they	do.
	he she it	does.

No,	I we you they	don't.
	he she it	doesn't.

SIMPLE PRESENT TENSE:
NEGATIVES

I We You They	don't	work.
He She It	doesn't	

FUNCTIONS

ASKING FOR AND REPORTING INFORMATION

What *do you do there*?
What kind of *food does Stanley cook on Monday*?
When *does he cook Japanese food*?

Do you *go to Stanley's Restaurant*?
    Yes, I do.
    No, I don't.
Does *Stanley cook Greek food on Tuesday*?
    Yes, *he* does.
    No, *he* doesn't.

INQUIRING ABOUT LIKES/DISLIKES

What kind of *movies* do you like?

Who's your favorite *movie star*?
What's your favorite *team*?

EXPRESSING LIKES

I like *comedies*.

EXPRESSING DISLIKES

I don't like *American food*.

STARTING A CONVERSATION

Tell me, . . .

NEW VOCABULARY

Everyday Activities

baby-sit
do yoga
go dancing
play volleyball
ride a bicycle
see a play
stay home

Days of the Week

Sunday
Monday
Tuesday
Wednesday
Thursday
Friday
Saturday

Movies

adventure movies
cartoons
comedies
dramas
movie
movie star
science fiction movies
videos
westerns

Books

author
biographies
non-fiction
novels
poetry
short stories

TV

game shows
news programs
TV star

Music

choir
classical music
concert
country music
jazz
musical instrument
orchestra
performer
popular music
rock music

Sports

athlete
bike
exercise
football
golf
hockey
jog
karate
sport
volleyball
yoga

Nationalities

Ethiopian
Thai
Vietnamese

Adjectives

active
athletic
important
international
outgoing
shy

Time Words

evening
afternoon
week

Question Words

What kind of
Why
Why not

Miscellaneous

activity
alone
ask
doesn't
don't
during
garden
kind (n)
lesson
like
much
often
spend time
well

Text Page 87: Chapter Opening Page

VOCABULARY PREVIEW

You may want to introduce these words before beginning the chapter, or you may choose to wait until they first occur in a specific lesson. If you choose to introduce them at this point, here are some suggestions:

1. Have students look at the illustrations on text page 87 and identify the words they already know.

2. Present the vocabulary. Say each word and have the class repeat it chorally and individually. Check students' understanding and pronunciation of the words.

3. Practice the vocabulary as a class, in pairs, or in small groups. Have students cover the word list and look at the pictures. Practice the words in the following ways:

   - Say a word and have students tell the number of the illustration.
   - Give the number of an illustration and have students say the word.

FOCUS

- Simple Present Tense with *he*
- Days of the Week
- Yes/No Questions with *does*
- Short Answers: *Yes, he does. / No, he doesn't.*
- Questions with *When* and *What Kind of*

CLOSE UP

RULE:	The word order of a WH-question in the simple present tense is: Question word + auxiliary verb *(does / do)* + subject + base verb + complement.
EXAMPLES:	**What kind of food + does + Stanley + cook + on Saturday?** **When + does + he + cook + Japanese food?**
RULE:	The word order of a Yes/No question in the simple present tense is: Auxiliary verb *(Does / Do)* + subject + base verb + complement.
EXAMPLE:	**Does + Stanley + cook + Greek food on Tuesday?**
RULE:	It is common to respond to Yes/No questions with a short answer. A short answer includes the subject and the auxiliary verb.

EXAMPLES:	Does Stanley cook Puerto Rican food on Thursday?
	  Yes, he does.
	Does Stanley cook Mexican food on Tuesday?
	  No, he doesn't.

RULE:	In spoken and informal written English, the auxiliary verb *does* contracts with *not*.
EXAMPLE:	Stanley (does not) **doesn't** cook Russian food.
RULE:	In negative statements, the negative comes before the base form of the verb.
EXAMPLE:	He cooks Japanese food on Friday. He **doesn't** cook Japanese food on Sunday.

GETTING READY

1. If you did not introduce the days of the week on the Chapter Opening page, introduce them at this point. Write them on the board, or use word cards or a calendar. Say each day and have students repeat after you chorally and individually.

2. Review the nationalities: *Italian, Greek, Chinese, Puerto Rican, Japanese, Mexican, American.*

STANLEY'S INTERNATIONAL RESTAURANT

Text pages 88–89 are about a chef named Stanley and his restaurant, called Stanley's International Restaurant. For the exercises on these pages, students will need to look at the illustration of Stanley's menu, which shows each day of the week with the type of food served on that day. You can have students look at the illustration on text page 88, or you can draw a simple version of Stanley's menu on the board.

There are three model conversations on text page 88, each followed by exercises.

INTRODUCING THE 1ST MODEL

1. Have students look at Stanley's menu.

2. Set the scene: "Stanley's International Restaurant is a very special place. Every day Stanley cooks a different kind of food. On Monday he cooks Italian food. On Tuesday he cooks Greek food. On Wednesday he cooks Chinese food. On Thursday he cooks Puerto Rican food. On Friday he cooks Japanese food. On Saturday he cooks Mexican food. And on Sunday he cooks American food."

3. Present the model:
   A. What kind of food does Stanley cook on Monday?
   B. On Monday he cooks Italian food.

   ### Spelling Note

   Days of the week are capitalized in English.

Pronunciation Note

The pronunciation focus of Chapter 10 is **Reduced of** (text page 96). You may wish to model this pronunciation at this point and encourage students to incorporate it into their language practice.

   What kind of food does Stanley cook on Monday?

4. Full-Class Repetition.

5. Have students open their books. Check understanding of new vocabulary: *international, kind, what kind of.*

6. Group Choral Repetition.

7. Choral Conversation.

8. Call on one or two pairs of students to present the model.

   (For additional practice, do Choral Conversation in small groups or by rows.)

SIDE BY SIDE EXERCISES

Examples

> A. What kind of food does Stanley cook on Tuesday?
> B. On Tuesday he cooks Greek food.
>
> A. What kind of food does Stanley cook on Wednesday?
> B. On Wednesday he cooks Chinese food.

1. **Tuesday:** Call on two students to ask and answer about Tuesday. Then do Choral Repetition and Choral Conversation practice.

2. **Wednesday:** Same as above.

3. **Thursday-Sunday:** Either Full-Class Practice or Pair Practice.

INTRODUCING THE 2ND MODEL

1. Have students look at Stanley's menu.

2. Set the scene: "Somebody is calling Stanley's International Restaurant."

3. Present the model.
   A. Does Stanley cook Greek food on Tuesday?
   B. Yes, he does.
4. Full-Class Repetition.
5. Have students open their books and look at the dialog. Ask if there are any questions.
6. Group Choral Repetition.
7. Choral Conversation.
8. Call on one or two pairs of students to present the dialog.

   (For additional practice, do Choral Conversation in small groups or by rows.)

SIDE BY SIDE EXERCISES

Examples

> A. Does Stanley cook Chinese food on Wednesday?
> B. Yes, he does.
> A. Does Stanley cook Puerto Rican food on Thursday?
> B. Yes, he does.

1. **Wednesday:** Call on two students to ask and answer about Wednesday. Then do Choral Repetition and Choral Conversation practice.
2. **Thursday:** Same as above.
3. **Friday-Monday:** Either Full-Class Practice or Pair Practice.

INTRODUCING THE 3RD MODEL

1. Have students look at Stanley's menu.
2. Set the scene: "A customer is talking to a waiter at Stanley's International Restaurant."
3. Present the model.

4. Full-Class Repetition.
5. Have students open their books and look at the dialog. Check understanding of *doesn't, when.*
6. Group Choral Repetition.
7. Choral Conversation.
8. Call on one or two pairs of students to present the dialog.

   (For additional practice, do Choral Conversation in small groups or by rows.)

SIDE BY SIDE EXERCISES

Students can ask about any food and any day. For example:

> A. Does Stanley cook Mexican food on Tuesday?
> B. No, he doesn't.
> A. When does he cook Mexican food?
> B. He cooks Mexican food on Saturday.
> A. Does Stanley cook Puerto Rican food on Sunday?
> B. No, he doesn't.
> A. When does he cook Puerto Rican food?
> B. He cooks Puerto Rican food on Thursday.

1. Call on two students to create a dialog. Then do Choral Repetition and Choral Conversation practice.
2. Call on two other students to create a dialog. Then do Choral Repetition and Choral Conversation practice.
3. Have pairs of students create 4 more dialogs. This can be done as Full-Class Practice or Pair Practice.

WORKBOOK

Page 69

1. Scrambled Dialogs

a. Write each line of the three model conversations from text page 88 on a separate card. Scramble the cards.

b. Give the cards to 8 students. Have them unscramble the lines and put together the three conversations.

c. Form pairs and have each pair read a conversation.

2. True or False?

Make statements about Stanley's menu and have students tell you "True" or "False." If the statement is false, have students correct it. For example:

Teacher: Stanley cooks Japanese food on Friday.

Student: True.

Teacher: Stanley cooks Puerto Rican food on Monday.

Student: False. He doesn't cook Puerto Rican food on Monday. He cooks Puerto Rican food on Thursday.
   (or)
False. He doesn't cook Puerto Rican food on Monday. He cooks Italian food on Monday.

Variation: You can call on students to make true or false statements about the menu and have other students respond.

3. Role Play: Calling Stanley's International Restaurant

a. Write Stanley's menu (see below) on the board.

b. Write the following skeletal dialog on the board:

(ring, ring)
A. Hello. Stanley's International Restaurant. May I help you?
B. Yes, please. _____?
A. _____.
B. Thank you very much.
A. You're welcome.

c. Divide the class into pairs. One member of the pair works at Stanley's Restaurant. The other is calling the restaurant for information about Stanley's menu. The caller can ask questions such as the following:

What kind of food does Stanley cook on Friday?
Does Stanley cook *Italian* food on *Thursday?*
When does he cook *Italian* food?

d. Call on pairs to present a few of their telephone conversations.

MON	TUE	WED	THU	FRI	SAT	SUN
Italian	Greek	Chinese	Puerto Rican	Japanese	Mexican	American

4. Information Gap: Gloria's World Restaurant

a. Tell students: Across the street from *Stanley's International Restaurant* is *Gloria's World Restaurant*. Every day Gloria also cooks a different kind of international food.

b. Make up a menu schedule for Gloria's restaurant , but divide the information between two different schedules. For example (see below):

c. Divide the class into pairs. Give each member of the pair a different schedule. Have students share their information and fill in their schedules. For example:

Student A: What kind of food does Gloria cook on Monday?

Student B: On Monday she cooks Brazilian food.

Student A: [writes the information in Schedule A].

d. The pairs continue until each has a filled schedule.

e. Have students look at their partner's schedule to make sure that they have written the information correctly.

Schedule A:

MON	TUE	WED	THU	FRI	SAT	SUN
	Italian		German		Spanish	

Schedule B:

MON	TUE	WED	THU	FRI	SAT	SUN
Brazilian		Greek		Russian		French

Text Page 89: Stanley's International Restaurant (continued)

FOCUS

- Simple Present Tense with *I, you, we* (non-3rd person singular)
- Yes/No Questions with *do*
- Short Answers: *Yes, I do./No, I don't.*
- Questions with *When* and *What kind of*
- Likes and Dislikes

CLOSE UP

RULE: In spoken and informal written English, the auxiliary verb *do* contracts with *not.*

EXAMPLES: I (do not) **don't** like American food.
No, we (do not) **don't**.

GETTING READY

Briefly review Stanley's menu.

INTRODUCING THE 1st MODEL

1. Have students look at Stanley's menu.
2. Set the scene: "A TV reporter is interviewing somebody."
3. Present the model.
4. Full-Class Repetition.
5. Ask students if they have any questions. Check understanding of new vocabulary: *do, go, to, why, because, like.*
6. Group Choral Repetition.
7. Choral Conversation.
8. Call on one or two pairs of students to present the dialog.

   (For additional practice, do Choral Conversation in small groups or by rows.)

SIDE BY SIDE EXERCISES

Examples

1. A. Do you go to Stanley's Restaurant on Monday?
   B. Yes, I do.
   A. Why?
   B. Because I like Italian food.
2. A. Do you go to Stanley's Restaurant on Thursday?
   B. Yes, we do.
   A. Why?
   B. Because we like Puerto Rican food.

1. **Exercise 1:** Call on two students to present the dialog. Then do Choral Repetition and Choral Conversation practice.
2. **Exercise 2:** Same as above.
3. **Exercises 3–4:** Either Full-Class Practice or Pair Practice.

216 CHAPTER 10

INTRODUCING THE 2ND MODEL

Same as above. Check understanding of *don't, why not.*

SIDE BY SIDE EXERCISES

Examples

> 5. A. Do you go to Stanley's Restaurant on Tuesday?
>   B. No, I don't.
>   A. Why not?
>   B. Because I don't like Greek food.
> 6. A. Do you go to Stanley's Restaurant on Wednesday?
>   B. No, we don't.
>   A. Why not?
>   B. Because we don't like Chinese food.

1. **Exercise 5:** Call on two students to present the dialog. Then do Choral Repetition and Choral Conversation practice.
2. **Exercise 6:** Same as above.
3. **Exercises 7–8:** Either Full-Class Practice or Pair Practice.

INTRODUCING THE 3RD MODEL

Same as above. Check understanding of *there.*

SIDE BY SIDE EXERCISES

Examples

> 9. A. What kind of food do you like?
>   B. I like French food.
>   A. When do you go to Stanley's Restaurant?
>   B. I don't go there.
>   A. Why not?
>   B. Because Stanley doesn't cook French food.
> 10. A. What kind of food do you like?
>   B. We like Ethiopian food.
>   A. When do you go to Stanley's Restaurant?
>   B. We don't go there.
>   A. Why not?
>   B. Because Stanley doesn't cook Ethiopian food.

1. **Exercise 9:** Call on two students to present the dialog. Then do Choral Repetition and Choral Conversation practice.
2. **Exercise 10:** Same as above.
3. **Exercises 11–12:** Either Full-Class Practice or Pair Practice.

> **New Vocabulary**
>
> 10. Ethiopian   12. Vietnamese
> 11. Thai

WORKBOOK

Pages 70–71

EXPANSION ACTIVITIES

1. Scrambled Dialog

a. Write each line of the 3rd model conversation from text page 89 on a separate card. Scramble the cards.

b. Give the cards to 6 students. Have them unscramble the lines and put together the conversation.

c. Have them read the conversation to the class.

2. Going to Stanley's International Restaurant

Have students create "Stanley's Restaurant" conversations about themselves.

a. Write the following conversation cues on the board as a guide:

> A. Do you go to Stanley's Restaurant on _____?
> B. _____.
> A. Why/Why not?
> B. Because _____.
>
> A. What kind of food do you like?
> B. _____.
> A. When do you go _____?
> B. I go _____/I don't go because _____.

b. Have pairs of students ask and answer questions according to their own likes and dislikes. You can do this as Full-Class Practice or Pair Practice.

3. International Foods

If you feel it is appropriate for your class, name different kinds of international foods and have students tell you what kind of food each one is. For example:

tacos	(Mexican)	sushi	(Japanese)
lasagna	(Italian)	hot dogs	(American)
chop suey	(Chinese)	moussaka	(Greek)

Have students tell the names of popular foods from their countries.

4. Question the Answers!

a. Dictate answers such as the following to the class:

> Italian food.
> Every Monday.
> Yes, he does.
> No, she doesn't.
> Yes, I do.
> Because I like the clothing they sell.

b. Have students write questions for which these answers would be correct. For example:

Answers	Questions
Italian food.	What kind of food do you like?
Every Monday.	When do you go to the bank?
Yes, he does.	Does your brother play the guitar?
No, she doesn't.	Does your wife work there?
Yes, I do.	Do you study every day?
Because I like the clothing they sell.	Why do you shop at that store?

c. Have students compare their questions with each other.

Variation: Write the answers on cards. Divide the class into groups and give each group a set of cards.

5. Questions Alive!

a. Make up several questions using the simple present tense. For example:

> What kind of food do you like?
> Does your brother work at the bank on Saturday?
> Do your children go to school every day?
> Why do you shop at that store?
> When does Stanley cook American food?
> Do you and your friends play soccer in the park?
> Where do you and your wife live?

b. Write the words to each of these questions on separate cards.

c. One sentence at a time, distribute the cards randomly to students in the class.

d. Have students decide on the correct word order of the sentence and then come to the front of the room, and make the question *come alive* by standing in order while holding up their cards and saying the sentence aloud one word at a time.

6. Question Game

a. Write the following sentence on the board:

> I go to Stanley's Restaurant on Saturday because I like Mexican food.

b. Underline different elements of the sentence, and have students create a question based on that portion of the sentence. For example:

> I go to <u>Stanley's Restaurant</u> on Saturday because I like Mexican food.

Where do you go on Saturday?

> I go to Stanley's Restaurant <u>on Saturday</u> because I like Mexican food.

When do you go to Stanley's Restaurant?

> I go to Stanley's Restaurant on Saturday <u>because I like Mexican food</u>.

Why do you go to Stanley's Restaurant on Saturday?

c. Continue with other sentences.

7. Expand the Sentence!

Tell students that the object of the activity is to build a long sentence on the board, one word at a time.

a. Call on a student to write a pronoun or someone's name on the far left side of the board. For example:

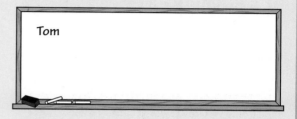

Tom

b. Have another student come to the board and add a word. For example:

Tom doesn't

c. Have a third student add a third word. For example:

Tom doesn't go

d. Continue until each student in the class has had one or more turns to add a word to expand the sentence into the longest one they can think of. For example:

> Tom doesn't go to that supermarket because the food is very expensive and the supermarket isn't in his neighborhood.

Text Pages 90-91: Busy People

FOCUS

- Simple Present Tense
- Daily Activities

NEW VOCABULARY

active	go/goes
activity	jog
athletic	karate
baby-sit	lesson
bike	movie
choir	orchestra
concert	sport
do yoga	volleyball
exercise (n)	
go dancing	

READING THE STORIES

Optional: Preview the stories by having students talk about the story title and/or illustrations. You may choose to introduce new vocabulary beforehand, or have students encounter the new vocabulary within the context of the reading.

1. Have students read the stories silently, or follow along silently as the stories are read aloud by you, by one or more students, or on the audio program.

2. Ask students if they have any questions. Check understanding of vocabulary.

3. Check students' comprehension, using some or all of the following questions:

   What does Jeff do on Monday?
   What does Jeff do on Tuesday?
   What does Jeff do on Wednesday?
   What does Jeff do on Thursday?
   What does Jeff do on Friday?
   What does Jeff do on Saturday?
   What does Jeff do on Sunday?

   What does Julie do on Monday?
   What does Julie do on Tuesday?
   What does Julie do on Wednesday?
   What does Julie do on Thursday?
   What does Julie do on Friday?
   What does Julie do on Saturday?
   What does Julie do on Sunday?

   What do the Bakers do on Monday?
   What do the Bakers do on Tuesday?
   What do the Bakers do on Wednesday?
   What do the Bakers do on Thursday?
   What do the Bakers do on Friday?
   What do the Bakers do on Saturday?
   What do the Bakers do on Sunday?

SHORT ANSWERS

Have students practice the short answers at the top of text page 91. Say each one and have students repeat after you. For example:

   Yes, I do.
   Yes, we do.
   Yes, you do.

INTRODUCING THE MODELS WITH "YES" ANSWERS

1. Have students look at the three illustrations in the top row.

2. Set the scene: "Someone is talking about Jeff, Julie, and Mr. and Mrs. Baker."

3. Present the models.

4. Full-Class Repetition.

5. Ask students if they have any questions.

6. Group Choral Repetition.

7. Choral Conversation.

8. Call on one or two pairs of students to present each dialog.

QUESTIONS WITH "YES" ANSWERS

Have pairs of students ask and answer questions with "yes" answers. For example:

A. Does Jeff jog on Monday?
B. Yes, he does.

A. Does Julie play volleyball on Thursday?
B. Yes, she does.

A. Do Mr. and Mrs. Baker go dancing on Friday?
B. Yes, they do.

This can be done as Full-Class Practice or Pair Practice.

INTRODUCING THE MODELS WITH "NO" ANSWERS

1. Have students look at the three illustrations in the second row.
2. Set the scene: "Someone is talking about Jeff, Julie, and Mr. and Mrs. Baker."
3. Present the models.
4. Full-Class Repetition.
5. Ask students if they have any questions.
6. Group Choral Repetition.
7. Choral Conversation.
8. Call on one or two pairs of students to present each dialog.

QUESTIONS WITH "NO" ANSWERS

Have pairs of students ask and answer questions with "no" answers. For example:

A. Does Jeff go to a health club on Tuesday?
B. No, he doesn't.

A. Does Julie visit her grandparents on Wednesday?
B. No, she doesn't.

A. Do Mr. and Mrs. Baker go to a museum on Saturday?
B. No, they don't.

This can be done as Full-Class Practice or Pair Practice.

INTRODUCING THE INTERVIEWS

1. Have students look at the last four illustrations.
2. Set the scene: "Someone is asking Jeff, Julie, and Mr. and Mrs. Baker about their activities."
3. Present the models.
4. Full-Class Repetition.
5. Ask students if they have any questions.
6. Group Choral Repetition.
7. Choral Conversation.
8. Call on one or two pairs of students to present each dialog.

PRACTICING THE INTERVIEWS

Divide the class into groups of five. Student 1 is the *interviewer*. Student 2 is *Jeff*. Student 3 is *Julie*. Students 4 and 5 are *Mr.* and *Mrs. Baker*. The interviewer asks the others questions. For example:

[to Jeff]
A. Do you play tennis on Tuesday?
B. Yes, I do.

A. Do you play basketball on Friday?
B. No, I don't.

[to Julie]
A. Do you sing in the choir on Monday?
B. Yes, I do.

A. Do you work at the mall on Thursday?
B. No, I don't.

[to Mr. and Mrs. Baker]
A. Do you see a play on Tuesday?
B. Yes, we do.

A. Do you see a movie on Thursday?
B. No, we don't.

WORKBOOK

Pages 72–73

EXPANSION ACTIVITIES

1. **Guess Who!**

   a. Have students look at the illustrations on text page 90.

   b. Describe a character and have students identify that person. For example:

   > Teacher: This person works in the mall.
   > Student: Julie.

   > Teacher: These people go to a museum.
   > Student: Mr. and Mrs. Baker.

   > Teacher: This person goes to a health club.
   > Student: Jeff.

2. **Correct the Statement!**

   Make statements about the characters in the stories. Some statements should be true, and others false. Have students respond to your statements. If a statement is false, a student should correct it. For example:

   > Teacher: Jeff jogs on Monday.
   > Student: That's right.

   > Teacher: Jeff plays baseball on Tuesday.
   > Student: No, he doesn't play baseball on Tuesday. He plays tennis.

   Variation 1: Have students make statements for others to react to.

   Variation 2: Do the activity as a game with competing teams.

3. **Chain Story: Arthur's Busy Life!**

   a. Begin by saying "Arthur is very busy. On Sunday he sees a movie."

   b. Student 1 repeats what you said and adds another day and another activity. For example: "Arthur is very busy. On Sunday he sees a movie. On Monday he sings in the choir."

   c. Continue around the room in this fashion, with each student repeating what the previous one said and adding another sentence until Arthur's whole week has been described.

   d. Start a new story, beginning and ending with different students.

If the class is large, you may want to divide students into groups of six to give students more practice.

4. **Associations**

   a. Divide the class into pairs or small groups.

   b. Call out a verb and tell students to write down all the words they associate with that verb. For example:

   > play: cards, basketball, the piano
   > do: exercises, yoga
   > see: a friend, a play, a movie

   c. Have a student from each pair or group come to the board and write their words.

   Variation: Do the activity as a game in which you divide the class into teams. The team with the most number of associations is the winner.

5. **Scrambled Sentences**

   a. Divide the class into two teams.

   b. Write individual sentences out of order on the board. For example:

   ```
   Mr.    Mrs.    are    and    Lee
   people busy    very

   go     Wednesday they    to
   concert a      on

   visit  on      grandchildren  they
   their  Saturday
   ```

   c. The first person to raise his or her hand, come to the board, and write the sentence in the correct order earns a point for that team.

   d. The team with the most points wins the scrambled sentence game.

Variation: Write the words to several sentences on separate cards. Divide the class into small groups, and have students work together to put the sentences into correct order.

6. Ranking

a. Dictate the following weekend activities to the class:

> see a movie
> go to a museum
> go to a restaurant
> go to a health club
> go dancing
> visit friends

b. Have students rank these activities in the order of preference.

c. As a class, in pairs, or in small groups, have students compare their lists.

Variation: You could also dictate sports activities (jog, play tennis, play golf, play basketball, do yoga, swim, ride a bike) or after-school activities (sing in a choir, play in the orchestra, write for a school newspaper, play on a school team, study at the library).

7. Information Gap Handouts: Sally's Busy Week

a. Tell students: "Sally is a very busy person." Make up a schedule for Sally's week, but divide the information between two different schedules. For example (see below):

b. Divide the class into pairs. Give each member of the pair a different schedule. Have students share their information and fill in their schedules. For example:

> Student A: What does Sally do on Sunday?
> Student B: She visits her friends.
> Student A: [writes the information in Schedule A].

c. The pairs continue until each has a filled schedule.

d. Have students look at their partner's schedule to make sure that they have written the information correctly.

Schedule A:

SUN	MON	TUE	WED	THU	FRI	SAT
	play in the orchestra		take a karate lesson		go dancing	

Schedule B:

SUN	MON	TUE	WED	THU	FRI	SAT
visit her friends		do yoga		go to a health club		play tennis

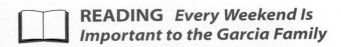

READING *Every Weekend Is Important to the Garcia Family*

FOCUS

- Simple Present Tense

NEW VOCABULARY

afternoon	much
alone	musical instrument
during	spend time
evening	stay home
garden	videos
important	week

READING THE STORY

Optional: Preview the story by having students talk about the story title and/or illustrations. You may choose to introduce new vocabulary beforehand, or have students encounter the new vocabulary within the context of the reading.

1. Have students read the story silently, or follow along silently as the story is read aloud by you, by one or more students, or on the audio program.

2. Ask students if they have any questions. Check understanding of vocabulary.

3. Check students' comprehension, using some or all of the following questions:

> Do the Garcias spend a lot of time together during the week?
> When do they spend a lot of time together?
> Where does Mr. Garcia work?
> Does he work on the weekend?
> When does he work?
> Where does Mrs. Garcia work?
> Does she work on the weekend?
> When does she work?

> Where do Jennifer and Jonathan Garcia go to school?
> Do they go to school on the weekend?
> When do they go to school?
> Where does the Garcias' dog Max stay?
> Does he stay home alone on the weekend?
> When does he stay home alone?
> What do the Garcias do on Saturday morning? on Saturday afternoon? on Saturday evening?
> What do the Garcias do on Sunday morning? on Sunday afternoon? on Sunday evening?

✓ READING *CHECK-UP*

Q & A

1. Call on a pair of students to present each model.

2. Have students work in pairs to create new dialogs.

3. Call on pairs to present their new dialogs to the class.

WHAT'S THE ANSWER?

1. Yes, he does.

2. Yes, they do.

3. No, she doesn't.

4. No, they don't.

5. Yes, she does.

6. Yes, they do.

7. No, he doesn't.

DO OR DOES?

1. Does

2. Do

3. do

4. does

5. Do

6. does

DON'T OR DOESN'T?

1. don't
2. doesn't
3. don't
4. doesn't
5. don't
6. doesn't

READING EXTENSION

1. Ask students the following questions and have them review the reading passage for the answers.

   What's another title for this reading?
   Why don't the Garcias have time together during the week?
   Why is every weekend important to the Garcias?

2. As a class or in small groups, have students discuss the following questions:

   When do you spend time with your family?
   What family activities do you do?

 LISTENING

WHAT'S THE WORD?

Listen and choose the word you hear.

1. Do you work on Monday?
2. Does your daughter go to this school?
3. We do a different activity every Sunday.
4. Larry doesn't play a sport.
5. We don't go to Stanley's Restaurant.
6. Sally goes to a health club every week.
7. She baby-sits for her neighbors every Thursday.
8. They go to work every morning.

Answers

1. a
2. b
3. a

4. b
5. a
6. b
7. b
8. a

WHAT'S THE ANSWER?

Listen and choose the correct response.

1. Do you speak Korean?
2. Does Mrs. Wilson go to Stanley's Restaurant?
3. Does your sister live in Los Angeles?
4. Do you and your brother clean the house together?
5. Does your husband like American food?
6. Do you go to school on the weekend?
7. Do you and your friends play tennis?
8. Does your cousin live in this neighborhood?

Answers

1. a
2. b
3. a
4. b
5. b
6. a
7. a
8. b

How About You?

Have students answer the questions in pairs or as a class.

 **READING** *A Very Outgoing Person*

FOCUS

- Simple Present Tense

NEW VOCABULARY

often
outgoing

READING THE STORY

Optional: Preview the story by having students talk about the story title and/or illustration. You may choose to introduce new vocabulary beforehand, or have students encounter the new vocabulary within the context of the reading.

1. Have students read the story silently, or follow along silently as the story is read aloud by you, by one or more students, or on the audio program.

2. Ask students if they have any questions. Check understanding of vocabulary.

3. Check students' comprehension, using some or all of the following questions:

   Is Alice an outgoing person?
   Where does she go with her friends?
   Is she popular?
   Does she like sports?
   Which sports does she play?
   Is she athletic?
   Does Alice stay home alone very often?
   Does she read many books?
   Does she watch TV?
   Does she listen to music?
   Is she active?

 IN YOUR OWN WORDS

1. Make sure students understand the instructions. Introduce the word *shy*.

2. Have students do the activity as written homework, using a dictionary for any new words they wish to use.

3. Have students present and discuss what they have written, in pairs or as a class.

How About You?

Have students answer the questions in pairs or as a class.

FOCUS

- Simple Present Tense
- Likes and Dislikes

CLOSE UP

RULE:	*Who* refers to a person. The word order of a question with *who* as subject is: Who + verb + complement.
EXAMPLE:	**Who + is + your favorite movie star?**
RULE:	In spoken and informal written English, *who* usually contracts with *is.*
EXAMPLE:	(Who is) **Who's** your favorite author?

How to Say It!

Starting a Conversation: In English-speaking cultures, it is common to start a conversation with a question. The question may be about shared interests such as movies, books, or television programs. Prefacing a question with *Tell me,* expresses warmth and interest in the other person's answer.

1. Set the scene: "Two co-workers are talking."
2. Present the conversation.

3. Full-Class Repetition.
4. Ask students if they have any questions. Check understanding of new vocabulary: *comedies, movie star.*
5. Group Choral Repetition.
6. Choral Conversation.

INTERVIEW

1. Go over the questions. Introduce the new vocabulary:

> *movies:* comedies (comedy), dramas, westerns, adventure movies, science fiction movies, cartoons, movie star
>
> *books:* novels, poetry, short stories, non-fiction, biographies, author
>
> *TV programs:* game shows, news programs, TV star
>
> *music:* classical music, popular music, jazz, rock music, country music, performer
>
> *sports:* football, golf, hockey, athlete, team

2. First, have students answer the questions about themselves.
3. Divide the class into pairs and have students interview each other.
4. Have students report back to the class about their interviews.

WORKBOOK

Page 74

1. Do You Remember?

a. Divide the class into pairs.

b. Tell students to spend three minutes looking carefully at the illustrations and vocabulary on text page 95.

c. Have students close their books and write a list of all the vocabulary they can remember from the page.

d. Have students compare their lists with their partner and then look at the page to see how much they remembered.

2. Memory Chain

a. Write the following on the board:

I like _____ .

b. Divide the class into groups of 5 or 6 students each.

c. One group at a time, Student 1 begins by making a true statement about himself or herself beginning with "I like." For example:

I like adventure movies.

d. Student 2 repeats what Student 1 said and adds a statement about himself or herself. For example:

Robert likes adventure movies. I like jazz.

e. Student 3 continues in the same way. For example:

Robert likes adventure movies. Maria likes jazz. I like hockey.

f. Continue until everyone has had a chance to play the *memory chain*.

3. Match the Conversations

a. Make the following set of matching cards:

What kind of movies do you like?	I like adventure movies.
What kind of books do you like?	I like novels.
What kind of TV programs do you like?	I like game shows.
What kind of music do you like?	I like jazz.
What kind of sports do you like?	I like hockey.

b. Distribute a card to ten different students.

c. Have students memorize the sentence on their cards, and then have students walk around the room saying their sentence until they find their match.

d. Then have pairs of students say their matched sentences aloud to the class.

4. Tic Tac Question Formation

a. Draw a tic tac grid on the board and fill it with question words. For example:

When?	Who?	Does?
What?	Is?	When?
What kind?	Do?	Why?

b. Divide the class into two teams. Give each team a mark: X or O.

c. Have each team ask a question that begins with one of the question words and then provide the answer to the question. If the question and answer are correct, the team gets to put its mark in that space. For example:

X Team: What kind of books do you like?
I like novels.

When?	Who?	Does?
What?	Is?	When?
X	Do?	Why?

d. The first team to mark out three boxes in a straight line—vertically, horizontally, or diagonally—wins.

Text Page 96

 PRONUNCIATION

> **Reduced *of*:** The final "v" sound in the word *of* is usually not pronounced before words beginning with a consonant.

Focus on Listening

Practice the sentences in the left column. Say each sentence or play the audio one or more times. Have students listen carefully and repeat.

Focus on Pronunciation

Practice the sentences in the right column. Have students say each sentence and then listen carefully as you say it or play the audio.

If you wish, have students continue practicing the sentences to improve their pronunciation.

 JOURNAL

Have students write their journal entries at home or in class. Encourage students to use a dictionary to look up words they would like to use in their descriptions. They can share their written work with other students if appropriate. As a class, in pairs, or in small groups, have students discuss what they have written.

WORKBOOK

Check-Up Test: Page 75

 CHAPTER SUMMARY

GRAMMAR

1. Divide the class into pairs or small groups.
2. Have students take turns forming sentences from the grammar boxes. Student A says a sentence, and Student B points to the words from each column that are in the sentence. Then have students switch: Student B says a sentence, and Student A points to the words.

KEY VOCABULARY

Have students ask you any questions about the meaning or pronunciation of the vocabulary. If students ask for the pronunciation, repeat after the student until the student is satisfied with his or her pronunciation.

EXPANSION ACTIVITIES

1. **Vocabulary Check**

   Check students' retention of the vocabulary depicted on the opening page of Chapter 10 by doing the following activity:

   a. Have students open their books to page 87 and cover the list of vocabulary words.

   b. Either call out a number and have students tell you the word, or say a word and have students tell you the number.

   Variation: You can also do this activity as a game with competing teams.

2. **Student-Led Dictation**

   a. Tell each student to choose a word or phrase from the Key Vocabulary list on text page 96 and look at it very carefully.

   b. Have students take turns dictating their words to the class. Everybody writes down that student's word.

c. When the dictation is completed, call on different students to write each word on the board to check the spelling.

3. Beanbag Toss

   a. Call out a topic from the chapter—for example: *Everyday Activities*.

   b. Have students toss a beanbag back and forth. The student to whom the beanbag is tossed must name a word in that category. For example:

      Student 1: baby-sit
      Student 2: see a movie
      Student 3: play volleyball

   c. Continue until all the words in the category have been named.

END-OF-CHAPTER ACTIVITIES

1. Board Game

   a. On poster boards or on manila file folders, make up game boards with a pathway consisting of separate spaces. You may use any theme or design you wish.

   b. Divide the class into groups of 2 to 4 students and give each group a game board, a die, and something to be used as a playing piece.

   c. Give each group a pile of cards face-down with challenges written on them. For example:

      Name three different kinds of books.
         (novels, short stories, non-fiction)
      Names four different kinds of movies.
         (dramas, westerns, science fiction, comedies)
      Name four kinds of TV programs.
         (comedies, game shows, news programs, cartoons)
      Name four kinds of music.
         (jazz, classical, country, rock)
      Name five different sports.
         (basketball, baseball, volleyball, golf, soccer)
      Name the days of the week.
      Name six different nationalities.

   d. Each student in turn rolls the die, moves the playing piece along the game path, and after landing on a space, picks a card, reads the challenge, and answers it. If the student is correct, that student takes an additional turn.

   e. The first student to reach the end of the pathway is the winner.

2. Find the Right Person!

   a. Collect some information about students in your class. Have them write answers to the following questions:

      What musical instruments do you play?
      Where do you work?
      What sports do you play?
      What kind of food do you like?
      What kind of movies do you like?
      What do you do on the weekend?

   b. Based on their answers, put the information on a handout in the following form:

      Find someone who . . .

      1. plays the guitar.   _____
      2. works at a mall.   _____
      3. plays golf.   _____
      4. likes Chinese food.   _____
      5. likes science fiction movies. _____
      6. goes to the park on Saturday. _____

   c. Have students circulate around the room, asking each other questions to identify the above people.

(continued)

d. The first student to find all the people, raise his or her hand, and tell the class who they are, is the winner of the game.

3. Miming

a. Write down on cards the *Everyday Activities* listed on text page 96.

b. Have pairs of students take turns picking a card from the pile and pantomiming the action.

c. The class must guess what the action is.

Variation: This can be done as a game with competing teams.

4. Finish the Sentence!

Begin a sentence and have students repeat what you said and add appropriate endings to the sentence. For example:

Teacher	Students
I play . . .	I play golf. I play in the orchestra. I play cards.
We see . . .	We see a play. We see a movie. We see our friends.
She goes to . . .	She goes to a museum. She goes to a concert. She goes to the mall.

Variation: This activity may be done as a class, in pairs or small groups, or as a game with competing teams.

5. Sense or Nonsense?

a. Divide the class into four groups.

b. Make four sets of split sentence cards with beginnings and endings of sentences. For example:

She reads . . .	novels and short stories.
He watches . . .	news programs on TV.
I visit . . .	my grandparents.
They go . . .	dancing on the weekend.
She eats . . .	Italian food.
We do . . .	yoga.
She works . . .	at the bank.
He plays . . .	baseball and football.
The children ride . . .	their bikes.
He cleans . . .	the house on Saturday.

c. Mix up the cards and distribute sets of cards to each group, keeping the beginning and ending cards in different piles.

d. Have students take turns picking up one card from each pile and reading the sentence to the group. For example:

She eats . . .	adventure movies.

e. That group decides if the sentence makes *sense* or is *nonsense*.

f. After all the cards have been picked, have the groups lay out all the cards and put together all the sentence combinations that make sense.

6. **What's Wrong?**

   a. Divide the class into pairs or small groups.

   b. Write several sentences such as the following on the board or on a handout. Some of the sentences should be correct, and others incorrect. For example:

   > Stanley cook Greek food on Tuesday.
   > He don't like science fiction movies.
   > I don't like american food.

   > She sings in the choir on Monday.
   > What kind of movies do you like?
   > Does she work on friday?
   > Does Mr. and Mrs. Garcia go to the mall on Saturday?
   > Who's your favorite author?

   c. The object of the activity is for students to identify which sentences are incorrect and then correct them.

   d. Have students compare their answers.

   Variation: Do the activity as a game with competing teams. The team that successfully completes the task in the shortest time is the winner.

WORKBOOK ANSWER KEY AND LISTENING SCRIPTS

WORKBOOK PAGE 69

A. WHAT'S THE DAY?

1. Tuesday
2. Saturday
3. Wednesday
4. Sunday
5. Friday
6. Monday

B. WHAT ARE THEY SAYING?

1. Does, he does
2. Does, she does
3. Does, he doesn't
4. What kind of
5. Does, doesn't
6. Does, he does
7. Does, she doesn't
8. When

WORKBOOK PAGE 70

C. WHAT ARE THEY SAYING?

1. Do, I do
2. Do, they don't
3. Do, we do
4. Do, we don't
5. Do, I don't
6. Do, they do

D. LISTENING

Listen and choose the correct response.

1. What kind of food do you like?
2. Do they paint houses?
3. Why does he go to that restaurant?
4. When does Mrs. Miller cook dinner?
5. Do you work in a bank?
6. Where do they live?
7. What do your children do in the park?
8. Does your friend Patty drive a taxi?
9. Why do they shop in that store?

Answers

1. b
2. c   6. a
3. b   7. b
4. a   8. c
5. c   9. a

WORKBOOK PAGE 71

E. YES AND NO

1. doesn't cook
2. doesn't drive
3. don't play
4. don't work
5. doesn't live
6. don't exercise
7. goes
8. shop
9. wears
10. speaks
11. doesn't sing

F. WHAT'S THE WORD?

1. do
2. does
3. do
4. does
5. do
6. does
7. Do
8. Does
9. do
10. Do
11. does
12. does
13. do

WORKBOOK PAGE 72

H. YES OR NO?

1. Yes, she does.
2. No, they don't. The play volleyball.
3. Yes, we do.
4. No, he doesn't. He sings in the choir.
5. No, I don't. I see a play.
6. Yes, they do.
7. Yes, he does.
8. No, we don't. We do yoga.

I. LISTENING

Listen and choose the correct response.

1. Do you do a different kind of sport every day?
2. Does Bob write for the school newspaper?
3. Do Mr. and Mrs. Chang live near a bus stop?
4. Does your sister baby-sit every weekend?

5. Does Timmy do a different activity every day?
6. Do your children play in the orchestra?
7. Does your son sing in the choir?
8. Do your parents go to the park every day?
9. Do you play cards with your friends?

Answers

1. b
2. a
3. b
4. a
5. b
6. b
7. b
8. a
9. a

WORKBOOK PAGE 75

CHECK-UP TEST: Chapters 9–10

A.

1. plays
2. shop
3. doesn't
4. do
5. stay
6. does

B.

1. Where
2. What
3. Does
4. Why
5. When
6. What

C.

1. lives
2. does
3. cleans
4. plays
5. takes
6. rides
7. goes
8. eats

D.

Listen and choose the correct response.

Ex. What do Patty and Peter do during the week?

1. When do you watch your favorite TV program?
2. Why do you eat Italian food?
3. Does Carlos visit his grandparents in Puerto Rico?
4. What kind of books do you like?
5. Where do your nephews live?

Answers

1. c
2. b
3. b
4. a
5. c

FEATURE ARTICLE
Language

PREVIEWING THE ARTICLE

1. Tell students that the article is about some very common languages—languages that a lot of people around the world speak. Ask them to tell you which languages they think are mentioned in the article, and write their ideas on the board. As they read the article, they can see if their predictions were correct.

2. You may choose to introduce the following new vocabulary beforehand, or have students encounter it within the context of the article:

borrow	on the other hand
change	rare
come from	recent
grow	relate
million	

READING THE ARTICLE

1. Have students read silently or follow along silently as the article is read aloud by you, by one or more students, or on the audio program.

2. Ask students if they have any questions. Check understanding of vocabulary.

3. Check students' comprehension, using some or all of the following questions:

> How many languages are there in the world?
> What are three examples of common languages?
> What is one example of a rare language?
> How many people speak Bahinemo?
> What language does the word *rodeo* come from?
> What language does the word *cafe* come from?
> What language does the word *ketchup* come from?

> What language does the word *sofa* come from?
> What language does the word *potato* come from?
> What are two examples of words from the Internet?

FACT FILE *Common Languages*

1. Tell students to look at the map. Explain that the color next to each language corresponds to the color on the map. Each corresponding color shows where people speak that language.

2. Read aloud the list of languages, and have students point to the corresponding language area on the map.

3. Have students practice pronouncing the names of the languages depicted on the map.

4. Write some of the numbers on the board. For example:

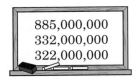

> 885,000,000
> 332,000,000
> 322,000,000

Explain that the numbers in the table are in *millions*. Have students practice saying the different numbers.

EXPANSION ACTIVITIES

1. **My Country**

   Have students identify their own country of origin on the map and tell the class the languages people speak in that country.

2. **What's the Country?**

   a. Write on the board:

   > They speak _____ in _____.

b. See if students can tell you where different languages depicted in the map are spoken. For example:

> They speak Japanese in Japan.
> They speak Spanish in Mexico.
> They speak English in Australia.
> They speak Arabic in Egypt.

3. What's the Language?

Name a country or region depicted on the map and see if students can name the language and point to the country on the map. For example:

India	(Hindi)
Brazil	(Portuguese)
Russia	(Russian)

4. Class Survey

Have students take a classroom survey of all the languages students speak.

 BUILD YOUR VOCABULARY!
Everyday Activities

get up	go to school
take a shower	go to work
brush my teeth	eat
comb my hair	take a bath
get dressed	go to bed

1. Have students look at the illustrations and identify any words they already know.

2. Present the vocabulary. Say each word and have the class repeat it chorally and individually. Check students' understanding and pronunciation of the words.

EXPANSION ACTIVITIES

1. Clap in Rhythm

Object: Once a clapping rhythm is established, the students must continue naming different daily activities.

a. Have students sit in a circle.

b. Establish a steady even beat—one-two-three-four, one-two-three-four—by having students clap their hands to their laps twice and then clap their hands together twice. Repeat throughout the game, maintaining the same rhythm.

c. The object is for each student in turn to name a daily activity each time the hands are clapped together twice. Nothing is said when students clap their hands on their laps.

Note: The beat never stops! If a student misses a beat, he or she can either wait for the next beat or pass to the next student.

2. Miming

a. Write down on cards the activities from text page 97.

b. Have students take turns picking a card from the pile and pantomiming the action on the card.

c. The class must guess what the person is doing.

Variation: This can be done as a game with competing teams.

3. Chain Game

a. Begin the game by saying:

> "I get up in the morning and I take a shower."

b. Student 1 repeats what you said and adds another activity. For example:

> "I get up in the morning, I take a shower, and I brush my teeth."

c. Continue around the room in this fashion, with each students repeating what the previous said and adding another activity.

(continued)

EXPANSION ACTIVITIES (Continued)

4. Category Dictation

a. Have students make three columns on a piece of paper.

b. At the top of the first column, have students write <u>take</u>. At the top of the second column, have them write <u>get</u>. And at the top of the third column, have them write <u>go</u>.

c. Dictate object words that can follow these verbs. For example:

up	to work
a shower	a bath
dressed	to bed
to school	

d. Have students write the words in the correct category. For example:

<u>take</u>	<u>get</u>	<u>go</u>
a shower	up	to school
a bath	dressed	to work
		to bed

AROUND THE WORLD
Exercising

1. Have students read silently or follow along silently as the text is read aloud by you, by one or more students, or on the audio program. Check understanding of new vocabulary:

go hiking	outdoors

2. Have students first work in pairs or small groups, responding to the question. Then have students tell the class what they talked about. Write any new vocabulary on the board.

Option: You might want to see if your students can guess the country where people in the photograph are exercising outdoors (China) and the type of exercise they're doing (Tai Chi).

EXPANSION ACTIVITY

Interview

1. Write the following on the board:

> Do you like to exercise? Why or why not?
> What is your favorite way to exercise?

2. Have pairs of students interview each other and then report back to the class about their partners.

GLOBAL EXCHANGE

1. Set the scene: "Jogger9 is writing to his keypal."

2. Have students read silently or follow along silently as the message is read aloud by you, by one or more students, or on the audio program.

3. Ask students if they have any questions. Check understanding of vocabulary.

4. Suggestions for additional practice:

   • Have students write a response to Jogger9 and share their writing in pairs.

   • Have students correspond with a keypal on the Internet and then share their experience with the class.

LISTENING *Hello! This Is the International Cafe!*

Set the scene: "This is a telephone recording at the International Cafe."

LISTENING SCRIPT

You're calling the International Cafe!
Listen to the recorded announcement.
Match the day of the week and the kind of
entertainment.

Hello! This is the International Cafe—your
special place for wonderful entertainment every
day of the week! Every day the International
Cafe presents a different kind of entertainment.
On Monday, Antonio Bello plays Italian classical
music. On Tuesday, Miguel Garcia reads
Spanish poetry. On Wednesday, Amanda Silva
sings Brazilian jazz. On Thursday, Nina
Markova reads Russian short stories. On
Friday, Hiroshi Tanaka plays Japanese rock
music. On Saturday, Rita Rivera sings Mexican
popular music. And on Sunday, Slim Wilkins
sings American country music. So come to the
International Cafe—your special place for
wonderful entertainment—every day of the
week!

Answers

1. c
2. e
3. a
4. g
5. b
6. d
7. f

 ## WHAT ARE THEY SAYING?

FOCUS

- Everyday Activities and Interests
- Simple Present Tense

Have students talk about the people and the
situation, and then create role plays based on
the scene. Students may refer back to previous
lessons as a resource, but they should not
simply reuse specific conversations.

Note: You may want to assign this exercise as
written homework, having students prepare
their role plays, practice them the next day with
other students, and then present them to the
class.

CHAPTER 11 OVERVIEW: Text Pages 99–106

GRAMMAR

OBJECT PRONOUNS

He calls	me him her it us you them	every night.

HAVE/HAS

I We You They	have	brown eyes.
He She It	has	

SIMPLE PRESENT TENSE: S VS. NON-S ENDINGS

He She It	eats. reads. washes.	[s] [z] [ɪz]

I We You They	eat. read. wash.

ADVERBS OF FREQUENCY

I	always usually sometimes rarely never	wash my car.

FUNCTIONS

ASKING FOR AND REPORTING INFORMATION

How often *does your boyfriend call you?*
  He calls me every night.

Does *Carmen* usually *study in her room?*
  No. *She* rarely *studies in her room.*
  She usually *studies in the library.*

Do you have *quiet neighbors*?

I'm a *teacher*.
I live in *Miami*.
I have a *large house*.
I'm *married*.
I play *golf*.
I play *the piano*.
I usually *watch videos* and rarely *go out*.

DESCRIBING

We *have noisy neighbors*.
They have an old TV antenna.

My brother and I look very different.
I don't look like *my brother*.

My sister and I are very different.

I have *brown eyes*.
He has *blue eyes*.

I have *short, curly* hair.
He has *long, straight* hair.

I'm *tall* and *thin*.
He's *short* and *heavy*.

REACTING TO INFORMATION

Oh, really? That's interesting.

240   CHAPTER 11

NEW VOCABULARY

Everyday Activities

get together
go out
make
say
travel
use

Describing People

blond
curly
famous
long
straight

Occupations

journalist
scientist
television news reporter

People

baby
boyfriend
girlfriend

Time Expressions

after
all the time

Adverbs of Frequency

always
never
rarely
sometimes

Object Pronouns

her
him
them
us

Question Words

How often

Miscellaneous

after
animal
as
bark
both
close (adj)
conversation
escalator
experiment
eye
Hollywood
laboratory
look like
magazine
TV antenna
unfortunately

VOCABULARY PREVIEW

You may want to introduce these words before beginning the chapter, or you may choose to wait until they first occur in a specific lesson. If you choose to introduce them at this point, here are some suggestions:

1. Have students look at the illustrations on text page 99 and identify the words they already know.

2. Present the vocabulary. Say each word and have the class repeat it chorally and individually. Check students' understanding and pronunciation of the words.

3. Practice the vocabulary as a class, in pairs, or in small groups. Have students cover the word list and look at the pictures. Practice the words in the following ways:

   - Say a word and have students tell the number of the illustration.
   - Give the number of an illustration and have students say the word.

Text Page 100: How Often?

FOCUS

- Object Pronouns
- Time Expressions with *every*
- Review of Possessive Adjectives: *my, his, her, our your, their*

CLOSE UP

RULE:	*How often* refers to the frequency of an activity.
EXAMPLE:	**How often** does your boyfriend call you? He calls me **every night**.

RULE:	Time expressions are usually placed at the end of a sentence.
EXAMPLES:	I write to him **every week**. I visit her **every year**. I think about you **all the time**.

GETTING READY

Introduce the object pronouns.

1. Read the words in the grammar box at the top of text page 100 and have students repeat after you chorally and individually.

2. Draw a face on the board and say: "This is George." Then say these sentences and have students repeat:

   (Point to yourself.) George likes *me*.
   (Point to a female student.) George likes *her*.
   (Point to a male student.) George likes *him*.
   (Gesture to everyone.) George likes *us*.
   (Point to one student and say to that student)
      George likes *you*.
   (Point to 2 students.) George likes *them*.

INTRODUCING THE MODEL

1. Have students look at the model illustration.

2. Set the scene: "Two friends are talking."

3. Present the model.

4. Full-Class Repetition.

5. Ask students if they have any questions. Check understanding of new vocabulary: *how often? boyfriend.*

6. Group Choral Repetition.

7. Choral Conversation.

8. Call on one or two pairs of students to present the dialog.

   (For additional practice, do Choral Conversation in small groups or by rows.)

SIDE BY SIDE EXERCISES

Examples

> 1. A. How often do you use your computer?
>   B. I use it every day.
>
> 2. A. How often do you write to your son?
>   B. I write to him every week.

1. **Exercise 1:** Introduce the new word *use*. Call on two students to present the dialog. Then do Choral Repetition and Choral Conversation practice.

2. **Exercise 2:** Same as above.

3. **Exercises 3–9:** Either Full-Class Practice or Pair Practice.

New Vocabulary

3. month	8. animal
4. Minnesota	9. all the time
7. say	

Pronunciation Note

The pronunciation focus of Chapter 11 is on **Deleted h** (text page 106). You may wish to model this pronunciation at this point and encourage students to incorporate it into their language practice.

I write to h́im every week.

I visit h́er every year.

WORKBOOK

Pages 76–77

EXPANSION ACTIVITIES

1. Category Dictation

a. Have students draw two columns on a piece of paper. At the top of one column, have students write <u>Every day</u>. At the top of the other column, have them write <u>Every month</u>.

b. Dictate various activities from the text and have students write them in the appropriate column. For example:

<u>Every day</u>	<u>Every month</u>
brush my teeth	wash my car
study English	see a movie in English
watch TV	see a play

2. Class Interviews

a. Write the following verbs on the board:

watch	read	brush
sleep	write	clean
study	eat	wash
play	drink	call
speak	listen to	feed

b. Divide the class into pairs. Have students ask each other questions with *How often* and the list of verbs on the board. Students should answer the questions as truthfully as possible.

3. Grammar Chain

a. Write activities such as the following on the board:

> use your computer
> read the newspaper
> call your grandparents
> do your homework
> wash your clothes
> play soccer
> see a movie in English

b. Start the chain game by saying:

> Teacher (to Student A): How often do you use your computer?

c. Student A answers truthfully and then forms a new question using another activity.

Student A asks the new question to Student B, who then continues the chain. For example:

Student A: I use my computer every afternoon.
(to Student B): How often do you read the newspaper?

Student B: I read the newspaper every morning.
(to Student C): How often do you call your grandparents?

Etc.

4. Find the Right Person!

a. Collect some information about students' habits.

b. Put the information on a handout in the following form:

> Find someone who . . .
>
> 1. reads the newspaper every day. _____
> 2. writes to a friend every month. _____
> 3. goes to the supermarket every _____ Saturday.
> 4. washes the car every weekend. _____
> 5. uses the computer every night. _____

c. Have students circulate around the room, asking each other questions to identify the above people. For example:

> Do you read the newspaper every day?
> Do you write to a friend every month?

d. The first student to find all the people, raise his or her hand, and tell the class who they are, is the winner of the game.

5. Concentration

a. Write 12 sentences using nouns, and then their equivalents with pronouns. For example:

> My sister writes to her boyfriend every week.

> She writes to him every week.

> Linda writes to her parents every week.

> She writes to them every week.

> Diane washes her car on Sunday.

> She washes it on Sunday.

> David washes the dishes on Sunday.

> He washes them on Sunday.

> My husband and I visit our grandchildren every weekend.

> We visit them every weekend.

> My niece and nephew visit my wife and me every weekend.

> They visit us every weekend.

b. Shuffle the cards and place them face down in three rows of 4 each.

c. Divide the class into two teams. The object of the game is for students to find the matching cards. Both teams should be able to see all the cards, since *concentrating* on their location is an important part of playing the game.

d. A student from Team 1 turns over two cards. If they match, the student picks up the cards, that team gets a point, and the student takes another turn. If the cards don't match, the student turns them face down, and a member of Team 2 takes a turn.

e. The game continues until all the cards have been matched. The team with the most correct matches wins the game.

Variation: This game can also be played in groups and pairs.

Text Page 101: She Usually Studies in the Library

FOCUS

- Simple Present Tense: Contrast of -*s* and non-*s* Endings
- Adverbs of Frequency
- Daily Activities

CLOSE UP

RULE:	When a verb ends in a voiceless consonant sound [p, k, t], the ending is pronounced [s] in the 3rd-person singular form.
EXAMPLES:	[**p**] helps [**t**] sits [**k**] thinks
RULE:	When a verb ends in a voiced consonant [b, d, g, l, m, n, r, v], or a vowel sound, the ending is pronounced [z] in the 3rd-person singular form.
EXAMPLES:	[**d**] reads [**v**] loves [**n**] listens [**l**] calls [**o**] goes
RULE:	When a verb ends with a sibilant [s, z, š, ž, č, j], the ending of the 3rd-person singular form is pronounced [ɪz] and forms an additional syllable.
EXAMPLES:	[**z**] uses [**č**] watches [**š**] washes
SPELLING RULE:	Verbs ending with the letter *s, sh, ch,* or *x*, add es in the 3rd-person singular form.
EXAMPLES:	watch–watches miss–misses
SPELLING RULE:	When a verb ends in *y* and is preceded by a consonant, the 3rd-person singular form ends in *ies*. When a verb ends in *y* and is preceded by a vowel, the verb ends in *s*.
EXAMPLES:	study–studies say–says

SPELLING RULE:	When a verb ends in *o*, *es* is added in the 3rd-person singular form.
EXAMPLES:	g<u>o</u>—g<u>o</u>es d<u>o</u>—d<u>o</u>es
RULE:	In sentences, adverbs of frequency are placed between the subject and the verb. In questions, they are placed between the subject and base verb.
EXAMPLES:	She **rarely** studies in her room. He **never** watches the news after dinner. Does Henry **usually** wash his car on Sunday?

GETTING READY

1. Form sentences using the *s* and non-*s* endings for each verb in the grammar boxes. For example, have students listen and repeat:

   I eat. – He eats.
   I write. – He writes.

2. Give students listening practice distinguishing between the -*s* and non-*s* forms of a verb.

   a. Write the following on the board:

   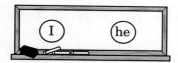

   b. Have students listen as you read these -*s* and non-*s* verbs: s*peaks, clean, watches, reads, eat.*

   c. For each verb, have students say "I" if they don't hear a final *s* sound and say "he" if they hear a final *s* sound.

3. Give students practice distinguishing between the three different pronunciations of the 3rd person singular.

   a. Write on the board:

   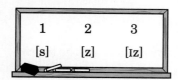

   b. Have students listen as you read the verbs at the top of text page 101 in mixed-up order. For each verb have students say:

   "One" if they hear a final [s] sound.
   "Two" if they hear a final [z] sound.
   "Three" if they hear a final [ɪz] sound.

4. Give students practice saying the final verb sounds. Say the "I" form of verb at the top of text page 101 and call on students to give the form with "he" or "she."

5. Introduce the adverbs *always, usually, sometimes, rarely, never.*

   a. Have students read these words in the box at the top of the page.

   b. Say each word and have students repeat chorally and individually.

   c. Make a sentence with each word to show the meaning. Describe yourself. For example, describe your clothing habits:

   I *always* wear shoes.
   I *usually* wear a watch.
   I *sometimes* wear gloves.
   I *rarely* wear a hat.
   I *never* wear a tie.

   d. For each adverb, call on a student to make a sentence describing himself or herself.

INTRODUCING THE MODEL

1. Have students look at the model illustration.

2. Set the scene: "Two students are talking about their friend."

3. Present the model.

4. Full-Class Repetition.

5. Have students open their books and look at the model. Ask if there are any questions. Check understanding of vocabulary.

6. Group Choral Repetition.

7. Choral Conversation.

8. Call on one or two students to present the model.

(For additional practice, do Choral Repetition in small groups or by rows.)

SIDE BY SIDE EXERCISES

Examples

> 1. A. Does Linda usually eat lunch in her office?
>   B. No. She rarely eats lunch in her office. She usually eats lunch in the cafeteria.
>
> 2. A. Does Alan always watch the news after dinner?
>   B. No. He never watches the news after dinner. He always watches game shows.

1. Exercise 1: Call on two students to present the dialog. Then do Choral Repetition and Choral Conversation practice.

2. Exercise 2: Introduce the new words *the news, after*. Same as above.

3. Exercises 3–6: Either Full-Class Practice or Pair Practice.

> **New Vocabulary**
>
> 3. magazine   5. girlfriend

Culture Note

The *National Star* (Exercise 3) is an invented name of a type of weekly newspaper that contains sensational news stories and gossip about famous personalities. *Time* Magazine is a real weekly news magazine with world news, national U.S. news, sports, movies, science, and other topical concerns.

WORKBOOK

Pages 78–79

EXPANSION ACTIVITIES

1. Correct the Statement!

a. Write on the board:

> always   usually   sometimes
>
> rarely   never

b. Call on students to make statements about others in the class, using one of the words on the board.

c. Have people respond "That's true" or "That's not true" after each statement. If someone responds "That's not true," then he or she must *correct* the statement. For example:

> A. Maria usually *comes* to class on time.
> B. That's true.
>
> A. Robert rarely *does* his English homework.
> B. That's not true. He always does his English homework.

If students need ideas, write key words on the board. For example:

wears _____	works _____
eats _____	watches TV _____
reads _____	dances _____
studies _____	drinks _____
sings _____	plays _____

2. It's the Truth!

a. Write the following cues on the board:

> always
> usually
> sometimes
> rarely
> never

movies	TV	my parents
beach	visit	on Sunday
eat	bored	breakfast
homework	on Saturday	clean

b. Have students make true statements about themselves, using an adverb of frequency and one of the cues. For example:

I always do my homework after dinner.
I never watch cartoons on TV.
My parents are rarely angry at me.

3. Sentence Cues

a. On separate cards, write key words that can be put together to form sentences. Clip together the cards for each sentence. For example:

I	speak	grandparents	every weekend
My sister	talk	boyfriend	every day
Our boss	never	say hello	us
Alan and Tom	rarely	study	library
Richard	read	newspaper	every morning
Our neighbor's dog	always	bark	night

b. Divide the class into small groups and give a clipped set of cards to each group.

c. Have each group write a sentence based on their set of cards.

d. Have one member of each group write that group's sentence on the board and compare everybody's sentences.

4. Category Dictation

a. Have students take a piece of paper and draw a line down the center of the page. At the top of the left column, have them write I usually, and on the top of the right column, have them write I rarely.

b. Dictate various daily activities. For example:

read a magazine
clean the basement
speak English at home
fix my car
wash windows
eat Italian food
watch TV in the morning
take a shower at night

c. Have students write down the activities in either the left or right columns, depending on how often they do them. Some students may write the item under I usually, and others may write it under I rarely.

d. At the end of the dictation, have students compare their lists to see what people usually and rarely do.

5. Survey

a. Using the information developed from the above activity, have students interview each other about their daily activities.

b. Have students report back to the class about their interviews.

6. Memory Chain

a. Divide the class into groups of 5 or 6 students each.

b. Tell each student to think of something that he or she always, usually, sometimes, rarely, or never does.

c. One group at a time, have Student 1 begin. For example:

I usually watch TV after dinner.

(continued)

d. Student 2 repeats what Student 1 said and adds a statement about himself or herself. For example:

> Robert usually watches TV after dinner.
> I never drink lemonade.

e. Student 3 continues in the same way. For example:

> Robert usually watches TV after dinner.
> Linda never drinks lemonade.
> I sometimes wash my car at night.

f. Continue until everyone has had a chance to play the *Memory Chain*.

7. **Which One Isn't True?**

a. Tell students to write three true statements and one false statement about themselves. For example:

> I usually jog in the evening.
> I never eat breakfast.
> I often watch cartoons on TV.
> I always study in the library.

b. Have students take turns reading their statements to the class and have the class guess which statement isn't true.

Text Page 102: We Have Noisy Neighbors

FOCUS

- Have/Has

CLOSE UP

RULE:	The verb *have* is an irregular verb in the simple present tense.
EXAMPLES:	I **have** a brother. We **have** a cat. They **have** an old TV antenna. He **has** brown hair. She **has** curly hair. It **has** an escalator.

GETTING READY

Introduce the forms of the verb *have*. Read the forms in the box at the top of page 102 and have students repeat chorally and individually. For example:

> I have brown eyes.
> You have brown eyes.
> He has brown eyes.

Have students use other eye colors, depending on the color of their eyes and their friends' eyes: brown, blue, green.

INTRODUCING THE MODEL

1. Have students look at the model illustration.
2. Set the scene: "Friends are talking."
3. Present the model.
4. Full-Class Repetition.
5. Have students open their books and look at the dialog. Ask students if they have any questions.
6. Group Choral Repetition.

7. Choral Conversation.
8. Call on one or two pairs of students to present the dialog.

   (For additional practice, do Choral Conversation in small groups or by rows.)

9. Ask students: "How about you? Do you have quiet neighbors or noisy neighbors?"

SIDE BY SIDE EXERCISES

Examples

1.	A. Do you have a sister? B. No. I have a brother.
2.	A. Does this store have an elevator? B. No. It has an escalator.

1. **Exercise 1:** Call on two students to present the dialog. Then do Choral Repetition and Choral Conversation practice. Then personalize the lesson and ask students: "How about you? Do you have brother or a sister? What's your brother's/sister's name?"

2. **Exercise 2:** Introduce the new word *escalator*. Same as above.

3. Exercises 3–8: Either Full-Class Practice or Pair Practice.

> **New Vocabulary**
>
> 3. straight   7. TV antenna
>   curly
> 4. blond   8. motorcycle
> 6. baby
>   eyes

4. Personalize the lesson. As students are presenting the exercises, ask them about things *they* have. For example:

> Exercise 3: How about you? Do you have curly hair or straight hair?

Exercise 4: How about you? What color hair do you have?

Exercise 5: How about you? Do you have a cat or a dog? What's your cat's/dog's name?

Exercise 6: How about you? What color eyes do you have?

Exercise 7: How about you? Do you have a satellite dish or a TV antenna?

Exercise 8: How about you? Do you have a car, a motorcycle, or a bicycle?

WORKBOOK

Page 80

EXPANSION ACTIVITIES

1. Correct the Statement!

a. Make true and false statements about students.

b. Have students respond "That's true" or "That's not true" after each statement. If someone responds "That's not true," then he or she must correct the statement. For example:

> A. Diana has brown hair.
> B. That's true.
>
> A. Robert has green eyes.
> B. That's not true. He has brown eyes.

2. What Do They "Have"?

Make negative and have students respond with an appropriate positive sentence. For example:

Teacher	Students
She doesn't have a car.	She has a motorcycle.
He doesn't have straight hair.	He has curly hair.
We don't have noisy neighbors.	We have quiet neighbors.
The mall doesn't have an escalator.	It has an elevator.
He doesn't have blond hair.	He has black hair.

Their baby girl doesn't have blue eyes.	She has brown eyes.
We don't have a TV antenna.	We have a satellite dish.

3. Find the Right Person!

a. Collect some information about what students *have*.

b. Put the information on a handout in the following form:

> Find someone who . . .
>
> 1. has a new computer. _____
> 2. has a large dog. _____
> 3. has noisy neighbors. _____
> 4. has three sisters. _____
> 5. has a guitar. _____

c. Have students circulate around the room, asking each other questions to identify the above people. For example:

> Do you have a new computer?
> Do you have a large dog?

d. The first student to find all the people, raise his or her hand, and tell the class who they are, is the winner of the game

252   CHAPTER 11

4. Same and Different

a. Put the following on the board:

I _____.
He _____.
She _____.
We both _____.

b. Write a list of questions such as the following on the board or on a handout for students:

Where are you from?
Where do you live now?
What languages do you speak?
How many brothers and sisters do you have?
What do you usually have for breakfast?
What newspaper do you usually read?

c. Divide the class into pairs.

d. Have students interview each other and then report to the class about the ways in which they're *the same* and the ways in which they're *different*. For example:

I'm from Japan. I speak Japanese. I have two sisters. I live in Centerville.
Marta is from Colombia. She speaks Spanish. She has four brothers. She lives in Greenville.
We both speak English. We both read the *Daily Times*.

5. Which One Isn't True?

a. Tell students to write three true statements and one false statement about things they *have*. For example:

I have two sisters.
My grandfather has a motorcycle.
Our apartment has five rooms.
I have a large dog.

b. Have students take turns reading their statements to the class and have the class guess which statement isn't true.

ON YOUR OWN *Very Different*

FOCUS

- Review of *have / has*
- Simple Present Tense: Contrast of *-s* and non-*s* Endings
- Describing People

INTRODUCING THE MODELS

There are two models, one in which a man compares himself to his brother, and a second in which a woman compares herself to her sister. Introduce and practice the comparison of the two brothers before going on to the comparison of the two sisters. For each model:

1. Have students look at the illustration.

2. Set the scene:

   1st model: "A man is comparing himself to his brother."
   2nd model: "A woman is comparing herself to her sister."

3. Have students read silently, or follow along silently as the model is read aloud by you, by one or more students, or on the audio program.

4. Ask students if they have any questions. Check understanding of vocabulary:

   1st model: *both, long, look like*
   2nd model: *journalist, go out*

ON YOUR OWN ACTIVITY

Model 1

In this exercise students say or write sentences in which they compare themselves to two people: someone they look like and someone they don't look like. Students can compare themselves to family members, friends, other students in class, or famous people.

1. Give some examples. Make up sentences about yourself or read these:

   A. Who do you look like?
   B. I look like my father.
      We both have brown eyes and black hair.
      We're both tall and thin.

   A. Who *don't* you look like?
   B. I don't look like my mother.
      I have brown eyes, and she has blue eyes.
      I'm tall, and she's short.

2. Have students write similar sentences for homework and then present them in class the next day.

Model 2

In this exercise, students again compare themselves to someone else. Write on the board:

	You	Another Person
occupation?		
city?		
house? apartment?		
single? married? divorced?		
play a sport?		
play an instrument?		
on the weekend?		

The cues on the board are suggested topics for students' comparisons. Introduce the new words *occupation, divorced.*

1. For homework, have students choose a person to compare themselves with, and then write at least five sentences. They can use some or all of the suggested topics.

2. Have students present their comparisons in the next class.

WORKBOOK

Pages 81–82

EXPANSION ACTIVITIES

1. Carol and Jane

Practice the verb *have* and new vocabulary by telling this story.

a. Draw two people on the board and tell about them:

Carol and Jane are sisters.
Carol has short, curly brown hair.
She has brown eyes.

Jane has long, straight brown hair.
She has brown eyes.

b. Point to Carol and ask students: "Tell me about Carol." Students answer, using the drawing as a cue.

c. Next, point to Jane and ask students: "Tell me about Jane."

d. Ask students: "Does Jane look like her sister?" "Does Carol look like her sister?" Students answer "Yes" or "No" and explain why. For example:

Carol has short hair, and Jane has long hair.
They both have brown eyes and brown hair.

2. Describe the Pictures

a. Bring in several pictures or ask students to bring in pictures of people.

b. In pairs, have students select a picture to describe in writing.

c. Have students read their descriptions aloud as the class listens and tries to identify the picture.

3. Mystery Student!

Have students take turns describing someone in the class. Others have to guess which student is being described. For example:

A. She has long, curly black hair. She has brown eyes.
B. It's (name)!

4. True or False?

Talk about the two brothers or the two sisters on text page 103.

a. Give the brothers and sisters names. Write them on the board or have the students write the names in their books. For example: *Tom* and *Jim, Carmen* and *Maria.*

b. Make true and false statements about the brothers and sisters. Have students respond "That's true" or "That's not true." If students respond "That's not true." they must correct the statement. For example:

Teacher	Students
Carmen lives in Miami.	That's true.
She's a journalist.	That's not true.
	She's a teacher.
Maria has a small house.	That's not true.
	She has a small apartment.
She plays tennis.	That's true.
Tom has brown hair.	That's true.
Tom is short and heavy.	That's not true.
	He's tall and thin.

c. Have students make true and false statments. Have other students answer as before.

5. Information Gap: George and John

a. Tell students that *George* and *John* are good friends, but they're very different.

b. Make up a description of *George* and a description of *John*, but divide the information between two different charts. Provide example questions. For example:

George's Chart:

	George	John
occupation	actor	
city	Los Angeles	
sport	golf	
weekend activities	go to parties	
hair and eyes	blond hair blue eyes	

(continued)

John's Chart:

	George	John
occupation		teacher
city		Boston
sport		tennis
weekend activities		visit the library
hair and eyes		brown hair green eyes

c. Write the following questions on the board:

Questions to Ask:
What does he do?
Where does he live?
What's his favorite sport?
What does he do on the weekend?
What color hair does he have?
What color eyes does he have?

d. Divide the class into pairs. Give each member of the pair a different chart. Have students ask and answer the questions and fill in their charts.

e. The pairs continue until each has a filled chart.

f. Have students look at their partner's chart to make sure that they have written the information correctly.

6. Chain Story

a. Begin by saying "Michael and his brother are very different."

b. Student 1 repeats what you said and adds more information. For example:

"Michael and his brother are very different. Michael has blue eyes, and his brother has brown eyes."

c. Student 3 repeats what was said before and adds more information. For example:

"Michael and his brother are very different. Michael has blue eyes, and his brother has brown eyes. Michael lives in a small house in Chicago. His brother lives in a large apartment in Los Angeles."

d. Continue around the room in this fashion, with each student repeating what the previous one said and adding additional information.

e. You can do the activity again, beginning and ending with different students.

If the class is large, you may want to divide students into groups to give students more practice.

WORKBOOK

Pages 81–82

How to Say It!

Reacting to Information: It is considered polite and appropriate to react when the person you are speaking with tells you something you didn't know before. The expression "Oh, really? That's interesting" is a common way to react to news. Speakers use the phrase "That's interesting" not so much to say how *interesting* the news is, but rather to indicate simply that they have heard the information.

1. Set the scene: "A friend and one of the 'sisters' on this page are talking."

2. Present the conversation.

3. Full-Class Repetition.

4. Ask students if they have any questions. Check understanding of the expression *Oh, really?*

5. Group Choral Repetition.

6. Choral Conversation.

7. Have pairs of students talk with each other, telling about people they know. Remind the listener to react with *interest* to the other person's information.

READING *Close Friends*

FOCUS

- Object Pronouns
- Simple Present Tense
- Adverbs of Frequency

NEW VOCABULARY

as	make
close	television news
conversation	reporter
experiment	scientist
famous	travel
get together	unfortunately
Hollywood	world
laboratory	

READING THE STORY

Optional: *Preview the story by having students talk about the story title and/or illustrations. You may choose to introduce new vocabulary beforehand, or have students encounter the new vocabulary within the context of the reading.*

1. Have students read silently, or follow along silently as the story is read aloud by you, by one or more students, or on the audio program.

2. Ask students if they have any questions. Check understanding of vocabulary.

3. Check students' comprehension, using some or all of the following questions:

   Why are they so lucky?
   What does Greta do?
   When do they see her?
   What does she tell them about?
   What does Dan do?
   When do they see him?
   What does he tell them about?

What do Bob and Carol do?
When do they see them?
What do they tell them about?
Why don't they see Greta, Dan, Bob, or Carol very often?

✔ READING *CHECK-UP*

WHAT'S THE WORD?

1. She		**11.** he	
2. Her		**12.** his	
3. she		**13.** him	
4. her		**14.** He	
5. her		**15.** Their	
6. her		**16.** them	
7. He		**17.** they	
8. his		**18.** them	
9. him		**19.** They	
10. him		**20.** their	

READING EXTENSION

Ask students the following questions.

   What's another title for this reading?
   Do you think their friends are interesting?
   Do very busy people have time to be close friends?

EXPANSION ACTIVITY

Tic Tac Question Formation

1. Draw a tic tac grid on the board and fill it with question words. For example:

Where?	Who?	How often?
What?	Does?	When?
Is?	Do?	Why?

(continued)

EXPANSION ACTIVITY (Continued)

2. Divide the class into two teams. Give each team a mark: X or O.

3. Have each team ask a question about the reading on text page 104 that begins with one of the question words and then provide the answer to the question. If the question and answer are correct, the team gets to put its mark in that space. For example:

   X Team: Is Dan a teacher?
   　　　　No. He's a scientist.

Where?	Who?	How often?
What?	Does?	When?
X	Do?	Why?

4. The first team to mark out three boxes in a straight line—vertically, horizontally, or diagonally—wins.

 LISTENING

Listen to the conversations. Who and what are they talking about?

1. A. How often do you visit him?
   B. I visit him every week.

2. A. How often do you wash them?
   B. I wash them every year.

3. A. Do you write to her very often?
   B. I write to her every month.

4. A. Is it broken?
   B. Yes. I'm fixing it now.

5. A. How often do you see them?
   B. I see them every day.

6. A. How often do you use it?
   B. I use it all the time.

7. A. When does he wash it?
   B. He washes it every Sunday.

8. A. Do you see him very often?
   B. No. I rarely see him.

9. A. Do you study with them very often?
   B. Yes. I study with them all the time.

Answers

1. a
2. b
3. b
4. a
5. b
6. a
7. b
8. b
9. b

 IN YOUR OWN WORDS

1. Make sure students understand the instructions.

2. Have students do the activity as written homework, using a dictionary for any new words they wish to use.

3. Have students present and discuss what they have written, in pairs or as a class.

PRONUNCIATION

> **Deleted h:** The initial /h/ sound in the object pronouns *her* and *him* is not pronounced.

Focus on Listening

Practice the sentences in the left column. Say each sentence or play the audio one or more times. Have students listen carefully and repeat.

Focus on Pronunciation

Practice the sentences in the right column. Have students say each sentence and then listen carefully as you say it or play the audio.

If you wish, have students continue practicing the sentences to improve their pronunciation.

 JOURNAL

Have students write their journal entries at home or in class. Encourage students to use a dictionary to look up words they would like to use in their descriptions. They can share their written work with other students if appropriate. As a class, in pairs, or in small groups, have students discuss what they have written.

 CHAPTER SUMMARY

GRAMMAR

1. Divide the class into pairs or small groups.
2. Have students take turns forming sentences from the grammar boxes. Student A says a sentence, and Student B points to the words from each column that are in the sentence. Then have students switch: Student B says a sentence, and Student A points to the words.

KEY VOCABULARY

Have students ask you any questions about the meaning or pronunciation of the vocabulary. If students ask for the pronunciation, repeat after the student until the student is satisfied with his or her pronunciation.

EXPANSION ACTIVITIES

1. Vocabulary Check

   Check students' retention of the vocabulary depicted on the opening page of Chapter 11 by doing the following activity:

   a. Have students open their books to page 99 and cover the list of vocabulary words.

   b. Either call out a number and have students tell you the word, or say a word and have students tell you the number.

   Variation: You can also do this activity as a game with competing teams.

2. Student-Led Dictation

   a. Tell each student to choose a word or phrase from the Key Vocabulary list on text pge 106 and look at it very carefully.

   b. Have students take turns dictating their words to the class. Everybody writes down that student's word.

3. Beanbag Toss

   a. Call out a topic from the chapter—for example: *Time Expressions.*

   b. Have students toss a beanbag back and forth. The student to whom the beanbag is tossed must name a word in that category. For example:

      Student 1: morning
      Student 2: evening
      Student 3: afternoon

   c. Continue until all the words in the category have been named.

1. Board Game

a. On poster boards or on manila file folders, make up game boards with a pathway consisting of separate spaces. You may use any theme or design you wish.

b. Divide the class into groups of 2 to 4 students and give each group a game board, a die, and something to be used as a playing piece.

c. Give each group a pile of cards face down with sentences written on them. Some sentences should be correct and others incorrect. For example:

How often do you clean your apartment?
Does she has brown eyes?
He sometimes washs his car on the weekend.
I rarely watch videos.
We always does the dishes after dinner.
She is curly hair and blue eyes.
He me calls every night.
Does Henry every morning jog?
Do you always sleep in the afternoon?
They visit rarely their parents.

d. Each student in turn rolls the die, moves the playing piece along the game path, and after landing on a space, picks a card, reads the sentence, and says if it is correct or incorrect. If the sentence is incorrect and the student is able to give the correct version, that student takes an additional turn.

e. The first student to reach the end of the pathway is the winner.

2. Scrambled Sentences

This activity helps students practice placing adverbs of frequency and time expression in a sentence correctly.

a. Divide the class into two teams.

b. One sentence at a time, write individual sentences out of order on the board. For example:

usually goes work he in morning the to

every they their visit month grandchildren

barks in dog always the neighbors' evening the

usually she afternoon does ? play in piano the the

c. The first person to raise his or her hand, come to the board, and write the sentence or question in the correct order earns a point for that team.

d. The team with the most points wins the scrambled sentence game.

Variation: Write the words to several sentences on separate cards. Divide the class into small groups, and have students work together to put the sentences into correct order.

WORKBOOK ANSWER KEY AND LISTENING SCRIPTS

WORKBOOK PAGE 76

A. WHAT ARE THEY SAYING?

1. you
2. them
3. her
4. him
5. them
6. it
7. us
8. it
9. me

WORKBOOK PAGE 77

B. WHAT'S THE WORD?

1. it
2. her
3. them
4. him
5. it
6. them

C. LISTENING

Listen and put a check under the correct picture.

1. How often do you read them?
2. I call her every day.
3. I don't like him.
4. I wash it every weekend.
5. He call us all the time.
6. I say hello to them every morning.

Answers

1. ___ ✔   2. ✔ ___   3. ___ ✔
4. ___ ✔   5. ✔ ___   6. ___ ✔

WORKBOOK PAGE 78

E. WRITE IT AND SAY IT

1. eats
2. barks
3. cleans
4. washes
5. jogs
6. reads
7. shops
8. watches
9. speaks
10. plays

F. MATCHING

1. c
2. e
3. a
4. g
5. b
6. f
7. d
8. h

G. LISTENING

Listen and choose the correct answer.

1. Henry's car is always very dirty.
2. My husband sometimes makes dinner.
3. My neighbors play loud music at night.
4. My grandparents rarely speak English.
5. Jane always spends a lot of time with her friends.
6. I rarely study in the library.

Answers

1. b
2. a
3. b
4. a
5. b
6. a

WORKBOOK PAGE 80

J. WHAT'S THE WORD?

1. have
2. has
3. have
4. have
5. has
6. have
7. has
8. have

K. WHAT ARE THEY SAYING?

1. Does, have, doesn't have, has
2. don't have, have
3. have, have
4. do, have, have
5. Do, have, don't have, have
6. Does, have, doesn't have, has

WORKBOOK PAGE 81

L. WHAT'S THE WORD?

1. long
2. curly
3. short
4. single
5. hair
6. brown
7. suburbs

M. TWO BROTHERS

1. short
2. have
3. has
4. have
5. short
6. curly
7. tall

8. thin
9. he's
10. lives
11. has
12. in
13. plays
14. play/have
15. go
16. go
17. watches
18. reads

N. LISTENING

Listen and choose the correct response.

1. Do you have curly hair?
2. Are you married?
3. Does he have brown eyes?
4. Do you have a brother?
5. Do you usually go out on weekends?
6. Is your husband heavy?
7. Do you live in the city?
8. Do you have short hair?

Answers

1.	b	5.	a
2.	a	6.	b
3.	a	7.	b
4.	b	8.	a

O. WHAT'S THE WORD?

1. in
2. on
3. on
4. in
5. about
6. for
7. in
8. to
9. at
10. of
11. to, on
13. to

Teacher's Notes

GRAMMAR

SIMPLE PRESENT TENSE

> I always **cry** when I'm sad.
>
> I never **wash** the dishes in the bathtub.

PRESENT CONTINUOUS TENSE

> I'm **crying** because I'm sad.
>
> I'm **washing** the dishes in the bathtub today.

FUNCTIONS

ASKING FOR AND REPORTING INFORMATION

Why *are you crying*?
  I'm crying because *I'm sad.*

What are you doing?
  I'm *washing the dishes in the bathtub.*

Do you usually *wash the dishes in the bathtub?*

My *sink* is broken.

DESCRIBING FEELINGS–EMOTIONS

I'm *angry / cold / embarrassed / happy / hot / hungry / nervous / sad / scared / sick / thirsty / tired.*

When I'm *nervous,* I *bite my nails.*

EXPRESSING SURPRISE–DISBELIEF

That's strange!

REACTING TO BAD NEWS

I'm sorry to hear that.
That's too bad!
What a shame!

NEW VOCABULARY

Everyday Activities

deliver
direct
rush (v)
sweep
take the bus
walk

Office Activities

answer the telephone
sort the mail
type letters

Describing Feelings and Emotions

angry
cold
embarrassed
happy
hot
hungry
nervous
sad
scared
sick
thirsty
tired

Actions Related to Feelings and Emotions

bite *my* nails
blush
cover *my eyes*
perspire
shiver
shout
smile
walk back and forth
yawn

Occupations

custodian
doctor
mail carrier
office assistant
police officer
receptionist
secretary

Time Expressions

early
all the time

Miscellaneous

(to be) out
bad
bathtub
business
by
company
dish
energetic
flashlight
flu
hard (adv)
job
lamp
letter
school bus
staff
traffic
truck
typewriter
unusual

EXPRESSIONS

as a result
have a bad day
it's snowing very hard
That's strange!

Text Page 107: Chapter Opening Page

VOCABULARY PREVIEW

You may want to introduce these words before beginning the chapter, or you may choose to wait until they first occur in a specific lesson. If you choose to introduce them at this point, here are some suggestions:

1. Have students look at the illustrations on text page 107 and identify the words they already know.

2. Present the vocabulary. Say each word and have the class repeat it chorally and individually. Check students' understanding and pronunciation of the words.

3. Practice the vocabulary as a class, in pairs, or in small groups. Have students cover the word list and look at the pictures. Practice the words in the following ways:

   - Say a word and have students tell the number of the illustration.

   - Give the number of an illustration and have students say the word.

FOCUS

- Contrast: Simple Present and Present Continuous Tenses
- *Why* Questions with the Present Continuous Tense
- Feelings and Emotions

CLOSE UP

RULE:	The simple present tense is used to describe habitual actions.
EXAMPLE:	I **always shout** when I'm angry.

RULE:	The present continuous tense describes an action in progress at the moment of speaking.
EXAMPLES:	Why **are** you **shouting**? I'**m shouting** because I'm angry.

GETTING READY

1. Introduce or review the vocabulary for feelings and emotions depicted on the text page 107. If you are introducing the vocabulary for the first time, refer to the suggestions for presenting it on the previous page.

2. Review and contrast the present continuous and simple present tense forms.

   a. Write on the board:

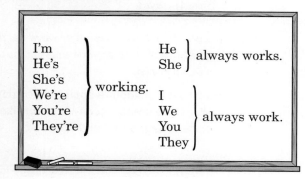

b. Make sentences using these forms. Have students repeat chorally. For example:

   He's working now.   He always works.
   We're working now.   We always work.

c. Do the same with the verbs *go* and *study*.

INTRODUCING THE MODELS

There are two model conversations. Introduce and practice the first before going on to the next. For each model:

1. Have students look at the illustration.
2. Set the scene: "Two people are talking."
3. Present the model.
4. Full-Class Repetition.
5. Ask students if they have any questions. Check understanding of *cry, sad, smile, happy*.
6. Group Choral Repetition.

7. Choral Conversation.

8. Call on one or two pairs of students to present the dialog.

(For additional practice, do Choral Conversation in small groups or by rows.)

SIDE BY SIDE EXERCISES

Examples

1. A. Why are you shouting?
   B. I'm shouting because I'm angry. I always shout when I'm angry.

2. A. Why is he biting his nails?
   B. He's biting his nails because he's nervous. He always bites his nails when he's nervous.

In the following exercises, use the illustrations in the text or *Side by Side* Picture Cards 122–130 to introduce the new vocabulary.

1. Exercise 1: Introduce the new words *shout, angry*. Call on two students to present the dialog. Then do Choral Repetition and Choral Conversation practice.

2. Exercise 2: Introduce the new words *bite, nails, nervous*. Same as above.

3. Exercises 3–10: Either Full-Class Practice or Pair Practice.

New Vocabulary	
3. thirsty	7. perspire, hot
4. shiver, cold	8. blush, embarrassed
5. hungry	9. yawn, tired
6. doctor, sick	10. cover, scared

WORKBOOK

Pages 83–86

EXPANSION ACTIVITIES

1. Adjective Review

Review the vocabulary for feelings and emotions using your own visuals, *Side by Side* Picture Cards 110–121, or the illustrations on text page 107. Point to a visual and ask a Yes/No question. If the answer is "No," have students give the correct adjective. For example:

Teacher: Is he happy?
Student: Yes, he is.

Teacher: Is she angry?
Student: No, she isn't. She's tired.

Variation: You can do this activity as a game with competing teams.

2. Act It Out!

a. Use *Side by Side* Picture Cards 46, 122–130, or make word cards for the following actions:

cry	smile	drink	shiver
smile	bite nails	perspire	blush
yawn	cover eyes		

b. Have a student take a visual or word card without showing it to anyone and act out the action on the card.

c. Based on that student's action, call on a pair of students to create a conversation like the ones on text pages 108 and 109.

3. Mystery Word

a. Divide the class into pairs.

b. Give each pair a card with one of the following *mystery words* written on it:

nervous	tired	happy
cold	hungry	hot
angry	thirsty	sad
sick	embarrassed	scared

c. Have each pair create a sentence in which that word is in final position. For example:

   I'm biting my nails because I'm _____.
   (nervous)
   I shout at people when I'm _____. *(angry)*

d. One student from each pair then reads aloud the sentence with the final word missing. The other pairs of students try to guess the missing word.

Variation: Do the activity as a game, in which each pair scores a point for identifying the correct mystery word. The pair with the most points wins the game.

4. Tic Tac Vocabulary

a. Have students draw a tic tac grid and fill it in with the following words:

thirsty	angry
cold	sick
tired	hot
embarrassed	nervous
hungry	

b. Say the beginnings of the following sentences and tell students to cross out the word that finishes each sentence:

   I always shiver when I'm . . .
   I'm shouting because I'm . . .
   I always blush when I'm . . .
   I'm going to the doctor because I'm . . .
   I always bite my nails when I'm . . .
   I'm drinking because I'm . . .
   I'm eating because I'm . . .
   I always perspire when I'm . . .
   I'm yawning because I'm . . .

c. The first student to cross out three words in a straight line—either horizontally, vertically, or diagonally—wins the game.

d. Have the winner call out the words to check for accuracy.

5. Match the Sentences

a. Make a set of split sentence cards such as the following:

Why are you shouting?	Because I'm angry.
Why are you biting your nails?	Because I'm nervous.
Why are you perspiring?	Because I'm hot.
Why are you drinking water?	Because I'm thirsty.
Why are you yawning?	Because I'm tired.
Why are you covering your eyes?	Because I'm scared.
Why are you shivering?	Because I'm cold.
Why are you blushing?	Because I'm embarrassed.

b. Distribute a card to each student.

c. Have students memorize the sentences on their cards, then walk around the room trying to find their corresponding match.

d. Then have pairs of students say their completed sentences aloud to the class.

(continued)

6. Concentration

a. Use the sentence cards from the above activity.

b. Shuffle the cards and place them face down in four rows of 4 each.

c. Divide the class into two teams. The object of the game is for students to find the matching cards. Both teams should be able to see all the cards, since *concentrating on their location* is an important part of playing the game.

d. A student from Team 1 turns over two cards. If they match, the student picks up the cards, that team gets a point, and the student takes another turn. If the cards don't match, the student turns them face down, and a member of Team 2 takes a turn.

e. The game continues until all the cards have been matched. The team with the most correct matches wins the game.

Variation: This game can also be played in groups and pairs.

ON YOUR OWN *What Do You Do When You're Nervous?*

GETTING READY

1. Write on the board:

> A. What do you do when you're nervous?
> B. When I'm nervous, I _____.

2. Call on pairs of students to present the three dialog models in the text:

A. What do you do when you're nervous?
B. When I'm nervous, I perspire.

A. What do you do when you're nervous?
B. When I'm nervous, I bite my nails.

A. What do you do when you're nervous?
B. When I'm nervous, I walk back and forth.

ON YOUR OWN ACTIVITY

1. Write on the board:

> A. What do you do when you're _____?
> B. When I'm _____, I _____.

2. Have students answer questions 1–12 in class or for homework, using the model on the board as a guide. Encourage students to use dictionaries to find new words they would like to use to describe themselves.

3. After students have completed their answers, divide the class into pairs, and have the pairs ask each other the questions.

4. Compare the different responses to the questions.

Culture Note

In this activity, students tell how they personally react to different emotional and physical states. You may want to discuss cultural differences in these reactions. For example, a common reaction to angry feelings in one culture may be shouting; in another it may be silence. You may also want to discuss differences in male and female expression of emotion. For example, in one culture, men and women may often cry when they are sad; in another culture, men may not usually cry.

Text Pages 110–111: I'm Washing the Dishes in the Bathtub

FOCUS

- Contrast: Simple Present and Present Continuous Tenses

INTRODUCING THE MODEL

1. Have students look at the model illustration.

2. Set the scene: "Two friends are talking. One is surprised because the other is doing something very strange."

3. Present the model.

4. Full-Class Repetition.

5. Ask students if they have any questions. Check understanding of new vocabulary: *dish, bathtub, That's strange!*

6. Group Choral Repetition.

7. Choral Conversation.

8. Call on one or two pairs of students to present the dialog.

   (For additional practice, do Choral Conversation in small groups or by rows.)

SIDE BY SIDE EXERCISES

Examples

1. A. What are you doing?!
   B. I'm sleeping on the floor.
   A. That's strange! Do you USUALLY sleep on the floor?
   B. No. I NEVER sleep on the floor, but I'm sleeping on the floor TODAY.
   A. Why are you doing THAT?!
   B. Because my BED is broken.
   A. I'm sorry to hear that.

2. A. What are you doing?!
   B. I'm studying with a flashlight.
   A. That's strange! Do you USUALLY study with a flashlight?
   B. No. I NEVER study with a flashlight, but I'm studying with a flashlight TODAY.
   A. Why are you doing THAT?!
   B. Because my lamp is broken.
   A. I'm sorry to hear that.

1. **Exercise 1:** Call on two students to present the dialog.

2. **Exercise 2:** Introduce the new words *flashlight, lamp.* Same as above.

3. **Exercises 3–5:** Either Full-Class Practice or Pair Practice.

   New Vocabulary

   3. walk
   4. typewriter
   5. sweep

4. **Exercise 6:** Have students use the model as a guide to create their own conversations using vocabulary of their choice. Encourage students to use dictionaries to find new words they want to use. This exercise can be done orally in class or for written homework. If you assign it for homework, do one example in class to make sure students understand what's expected. Have students present their conversations in class the next day. (They can bring in *props* if they wish.)

WORKBOOK

Pages 87–90

EXPANSION ACTIVITIES

1. Scrambled Dialog

a. Write each line of the model dialog on text page 110 a separate card.

b. Distribute the cards to students and have them practice saying their lines, then talk with each other to figure out what the correct order of the lines should be.

c. Have them present the dialog to the class, each student in turn reading his or her line. Have the class decide if it's in the correct order. Then practice the dialog with the class.

2. Can You Hear the Difference?

a. Write on the board:

Today	Usually
I'm walking to work.	I walk to work.
He's sweeping the carpet.	He sweeps the carpet.
We're using a computer.	We use a computer.
They're studying with a flashlight.	They study with a flashlight.

b. Choose a sentence from one of the two columns and say it to the class. Have the class listen and identify whether the sentence is telling about *today* or *usually*.

c. Have students continue the activity in pairs. One student says a sentence, and the other identifies whether it's *today* or *usually*. Then have them reverse roles.

d. Write other similar sentences on the board and continue the practice.

3. Pantomime the Situation

a. Make up situation cards such as the following:

> You're walking to work because your car is broken.

> You're sweeping the carpet because your vacuum is broken.

> You're studying English with a flashlight because your lamp is broken.

b. Have a pair of students come to the front of the class. One student (Student A) looks at the card and pantomimes the situation on the card. The other (Student B) must guess the situation and then create a conversation with Student A based on what Student A is doing.

4. Practice /sh/ and /s/ Sounds

a. Have students practice saying these words with *sh* sounds. Write some or all of them on the board and have students repeat after you.

shout	wash
shiver	dishes
shirt	international
short	Russian
sure	station
blush	fiction

b. Have students practice saying these words with *s* sounds. Write some or all of them on the board and have students repeat after you.

sing	Miss
sad	fix
listen	what's
hospital	sports
baseball	study
office	sleeps

5. Sentences Alive!

a. Make up several sentences based on this lesson. For example:

> I never use a typewriter, but I'm using a typewriter today because my computer is broken.

(continued)

I never walk to work, but I'm walking to work today because my car is broken.

b. Write the words to each of these sentences on separate cards.

c. One sentence at a time, distribute the cards randomly to students in the class.

d. Have students decide on the correct word order of the sentence and then come to the front of the room, and make the sentence *come alive* by standing in order while holding up their cards and saying the sentence aloud one word at a time.

6. Dictate and Discuss

   a. Divide the class into pairs or small groups.

   b. Dictate sentences such as the following:

   He never watches TV in the basement, but he's watching TV in the basement today.

They never ride their bicycles to work, but they're riding their bicycles to work today.

She never washes her hair in the sink, but she's washing her hair in the sink today.

We never eat pizza for breakfast, but we're eating pizza for breakfast today.

c. Have students discuss possible reasons for the strange behavior. For example:

   He's watching TV in the basement because his wife is talking with her friends in the living room.

   They're riding their bicycles to work today because it's a beautiful day.

d. Call on students to share their ideas with the rest of the class.

How to Say It!

> **Reacting to Bad News:** There are many ways to respond with sympathy to bad news. "I'm sorry to hear that," "That's too bad!" and "What a shame!" are three common sympathetic responses.

1. Set the scene: "Two friends are talking on the phone. One has a problem."

2. Present the conversation.

3. Full-Class Repetition.

   Pronunciation Note

   The pronunciation focus of Chapter 12 is **Reduced *to*** (text page 114). You may wish to model this pronunciation at this point and encourage students to incorporate it into their language practice:

   I'm sorry to hear that.

4. Ask students if they have any questions. Check understanding of vocabulary.

5. Group Choral Repetition.

6. Choral Conversation.

7. Brainstorm *bad news* items with the class and write students' ideas on the board.

8. Have pairs of students practice conversations in which they share bad news. Remind students to react to each other other's bad news with sympathy.

Text Page 112

READING *A Bad Day at the Office*

FOCUS

- Contrast: Simple Present and Present Continuous Tenses

NEW VOCABULARY

answer (v)	flu	receptionist
as a result	job	secretary
bad	letter	sort the mail
company	nobody	staff
custodian	office assistant	type
employee	on strike	
energetic	out	

READING THE STORY

Optional: Preview the story by having students talk about the story title and/or illustration. You may choose to introduce new vocabulary beforehand, or have students encounter the new vocabulary within the context of the reading.

1. Have students read the story silently, or follow along silently as the story is read aloud by you, by one or more students, or on the audio program.

2. Ask students if they have any questions. Check understanding of vocabulary.

   ### Culture Note

   Strikes are common in the United States. Employees may go on strike if they are unable to reach an agreement with their company regarding pay raises, benefits, working conditions, and other issues.

3. Check students' comprehension, using some or all of the following questions:

   What does Mr. Blaine do?

What kind of staff does he have?
Where are Mr. Blaine's employees today?
Who is there?
Why is Mr. Blaine answering the telephone?
Why is he typing letters?
Why is he sorting the mail?
Why is he cleaning the office?

✓ READING *CHECK-UP*

TRUE OR FALSE?

1. False   4. False
2. False   5. True
3. True   6. True

READING EXTENSION

Ask students the following questions:

What's another title for this reading?
Do the employees at Acme Internet Company usually work hard?
Is Mr. Blaine doing a good job today?

EXPANSION ACTIVITY

Finish the Sentence

1. Write the following words on the board:

office	office assistant
employee	on strike
secretary	custodian
receptionist	

2. Say the beginnings of the following sentences and have students complete them with the correct word on the board:

   A person who works in a company is an . . .
   The employee who answers the telephone and greets people is the . . .
   The employee who cleans a building is the . . .
   The employee who sorts the mail is the . . .
   The employee who types letters is the . . .
   All these people work in an . . .
   The employees aren't working today because they're all . . .

 **LISTENING**

Listen and choose the correct answer.

1. What are you doing?

2. What does the office assistant do?

3. What's the receptionist doing?

4. Is he tired?

5. What do you do when you're scared?

6. Where do you usually study?

Answers

1. b

2. a

3. b

4. b

5. b

6. a

READING *Early Monday Morning in Centerville*

FOCUS

- Contrast: Simple Present and Present Continuous Tenses

NEW VOCABULARY

business	rush
deliver	school bus
direct (v)	take the bus
early	traffic
hard (adv)	truck
mail carrier	unusual
police officer	

READING THE STORY

Optional: *Preview the story by having students talk about the story title and/or illustration. You may choose to introduce new vocabulary beforehand, or have students encounter the new vocabulary within the context of the reading.*

1. Have students read silently, or follow along silently as the story is read aloud by you, by one or more students, or on the audio program.

2. Ask students if they have any questions. Check understanding of vocabulary.

3. Check students' comprehension, using some or all of the following questions:

> Is early Monday morning usually a very busy time in Centerville?
> What do men and women usually do?
> How do they get there?
> What do children usually do?
> How do they get there?
> Is the city usually busy?

> What do trucks do?
> What do mail carriers do?
> What do police officers do?
> Is Monday morning usually quiet in Centerville?

✓ READING *CHECK-UP*

THE SNOWSTORM

1. driving
2. taking
3. going
4. walking
5. take
6. taking
7. ride
8. riding
9. deliver
10. delivering
11. deliver
12. delivering
13. direct
14. directing

READING EXTENSION

Read the following sentences aloud. Have students decide whether they describe a typical Monday morning in Centerville.

> Some children take the school bus.
> There's a lot of traffic.
> Everyone sleeps late.
> Mail carriers go on strike.
> Children play in the parks.
> Police officers sit in their cars.
> Mail carriers direct traffic.
> The streets are quiet.
> The supermarkets are busy.
> Businesses are open.
> The city is noisy.

PRONUNCIATION

> **Reduced *to*:** In conversational English, the vowel sound in the word *to* is reduced to the schwa sound.

Focus on Listening

Practice the sentences in the left column. Say each sentence or play the audio one or more times. Have students listen carefully and repeat.

Focus on Pronunciation

Practice the sentences in the right column. Have students say each sentence and then listen carefully as you say it or play the audio.

If you wish, have students continue practicing the sentences to improve their pronunciation.

JOURNAL

Have students write their journal entries at home or in class. Encourage students to use a dictionary to look up words they would like to use in their descriptions. They can share their written work with other students if appropriate. As a class, in pairs, or in small groups, have students discuss what they have written.

WORKBOOK

Check-Up Test: Page 91

CHAPTER SUMMARY

GRAMMAR

1. Divide the class into pairs or small groups.
2. Have students take turns reading the sentences in the grammar boxes.

KEY VOCABULARY

Have students ask you any questions about the meaning or pronunciation of the vocabulary. If students ask for the pronunciation, repeat after the student until the student is satisfied with his or her pronunciation.

EXPANSION ACTIVITIES

1. **Vocabulary Check**

   Check students' retention of the vocabulary depicted on the opening page of Chapter 12 by doing the following activity:

   a. Have students open their books to page 107 and cover the list of vocabulary words.

   b. Either call out a number and have students tell you the word, or say a word and have students tell you the number.

   Variation: You can also do this activity as a game with competing teams.

2. **Student-Led Dictation**

   a. Tell each student to choose a word or phrase from the Key Vocabulary list on text page 106 and look at it very carefully.

   b. Have students take turns dictating their words to the class. Everybody writes down that student's word.

3. **Beanbag Toss**

   a. Call out a topic from the chapter—for example: *Feelings and Emotions.*

   b. Have students toss a beanbag back and forth. The student to whom the beanbag is tossed must name a word in that category. For example:

      Student 1: sad
      Student 2: happy
      Student 3: embarrassed

   c. Continue until all the words in the category have been named.

1. Board Game

a. On poster boards or on manila file folders, make up game boards with a pathway consisting of separate spaces. You may use any theme or design you wish.

b. Divide the class into groups of 2 to 4 students and give each group a game board, a die, and something to be used as a playing piece.

c. Give each group a pile of cards face down with sentences written on them. Some sentences should be correct, and others should be incorrect. For example:

> Some people are shouting when they're angry.
> People often shiver when they're cold.
> My baby cry when she's tired.
> People often smile when they're sad.
> Today I bite my nails because I'm nervous.
> He always drink milk when he tired.
> I'm shame to hear that.
> I never sleep on the floor, but I'm sleeping on the floor today!
> She never ride her bike to work.
> We go to work on the bus always.

d. Each student in turn rolls the die, moves the playing piece along the game path, and after landing on a space, picks a card, reads the sentence, and says if it is *correct* or *incorrect*. If the sentence is incorrect and the student is able to give the correct version, that student takes an additional turn.

e. The first student to reach the end of the pathway is the winner.

2. Match the Sentences

a. Make a set of split sentence cards such as the following:

A receptionist . . .	answers the phone.
A police officer . . .	directs traffic.

A custodian . . .	cleans offices.
A mail carrier . . .	delivers mail.
Trucks . . .	deliver food to supermarkets.
A secretary . . .	types letters.

b. Distribute a card to each student.

c. Have students memorize the sentence portion on their cards, then walk around the room trying to find their corresponding match.

d. Then have pairs of students say their completed sentences aloud to the class.

3. Class Story

a. Use your own visuals or *Side by Side* Picture Cards 110–121. Have the class look at one visual and develop a story.

b. Ask questions to help students imagine a storyline. For example:

> What's her name?
> What's she doing?
> How does she feel?
> Why does she feel that way?

c. Have students dictate the story to you as you write it on the board. Ask them how to spell various words as they're dictating the story to you. Also, ask the class to point out any grammar errors they find in the story.

4. Describe the Pictures

a. Bring in several pictures of people at work, or ask students to bring in pictures of their own.

b. In pairs, have students select a picture to describe in writing.

c. Have students read their descriptions aloud as the class listens and tries to identify the picture.

WORKBOOK ANSWER KEY AND LISTENING SCRIPTS

WORKBOOK PAGE 83

A. WHAT'S THE WORD?

1. sad	2. tired
3. hot	4. angry
5. sick	6. happy
7. hungry	8. cold
9. nervous	10. scared
11. thirsty	12. embarrassed

WORKBOOK PAGE 84

B. TELL ME WHY

1. They're yawning because they're
   yawn when they're tired
2. She's crying because she's
   cries when she's sad
3. He's shivering because he's
   shivers when he's cold
4. I'm perspiring because I'm
   perspire when I'm hot
5. She's smiling because she's
   smiles when she's happy
6. They're eating because they're
   eat when they're hungry
7. We're shouting because we're
   shout when we're angry
8. He's covering his eyes because he's
   cover his eyes when he's scared

WORKBOOK PAGE 87

E. THAT'S STRANGE!

1. cooks	2. study
3. walks	4. brushes
5. eats	6. dance
7. is sweeping	8. are reading
9. I'm using	10. are sleeping

WORKBOOK PAGE 88

F. WHAT'S THE QUESTION?

1. Why are you blushing?
2. Where do they play tennis?
3. When does she read her e-mail?
4. What kind of food do you like?
5. How many cats do you have?
6. What is/What's he using?
7. What kind of shows does he watch?

8. How often do you call your grandchildren?
9. What do they do every weekend?
10. Why are you smiling?
11. Where is she eating today?
12. How many sweaters are you wearing?

G. WHICH ONE DOESN'T BELONG?

1. we (The others are object pronouns.)
2. noisy (The others are adverbs of frequency.)
3. has (The others are forms of *do*.)
4. yoga (The others are emotions.)
5. Wednesday (The others are WH-question words.)
6. outgoing (The others are verbs.)
7. shy (The others are verbs.)
8. year (The others are times of the day.)

WORKBOOK PAGES 89–90

H.   LISTENING

As you listen to each story, read the sentences and check *yes* or *no*.

Jennifer and Jason

Jennifer and Jason are visiting their grandfather in California. They're sad today. Their grandfather usually takes them to the park, but he isn't taking them to the park today.

Our Boss

Our boss usually smiles at the office, but he isn't smiling today. He's upset because the people in the office aren't working very hard today. It's Friday, and everybody is thinking about the weekend.

On Vacation

When my family and I are on vacation, I always have a good time. I usually play tennis, but when it's cold, I play games on my computer and watch videos. Today is a beautiful day, and I'm swimming at the beach.

Timmy and His Brother

Timmy and his brother are watching a science fiction movie. Timmy is covering his eyes because he's scared. He doesn't like science fiction movies. Timmy's brother isn't scared. He likes science fiction movies.

Answers

1. yes ☐   no ☑
2. yes ☐   no ☑
3. yes ☑   no ☐

4. yes ☑   no ☐
5. yes ☐   no ☑
6. yes ☑   no ☐

7. yes ☑   no ☐
8. yes ☐   no ☑
9. yes ☐   no ☑

10. yes ☐   no ☑
11. yes ☑   no ☐
12. yes ☐   no ☑

I. LOUD AND CLEAR

1. Sally, sorry, sister, sick, hospital
2. What's, scientist, speaking, experiments
3. cousin, Athens is always, busy
4. Sally's husband doesn't, clothes, closet
5. Steven is sweeping, because it's
6. Mrs. Garcia reads, newspaper, Sunday
7. students, school sometimes, zoo, bus
8. son, plays soccer, friends, Tuesday

WORKBOOK PAGE 91

CHECK-UP TEST: Chapters 11-12

A.

1. him
2. them
3. her
4. me
5. us

B.

1. feeding
2. goes
3. baking
4. fixes

5. washes

C.

1. is
2. do
3. Does
4. do
5. Are

D.

1. Where do they work every day?
2. When do you get together?
3. Why is he crying?
4. How many children does she have?
5. What are you drinking?

E.

Listen and choose the correct response.

Ex. What are Peter and Tom doing today?

1. What do mail carriers do every day?
2. Where are you going today?
3. What do you do when you're scared?
4. Do you usually use a typewriter?
5. Where do you usually study?

Answers

1. b
2. a
3. b
4. a
5. b

FEATURE ARTICLE
Traffic: A Global Problem

PREVIEWING THE ARTICLE

1. Have students talk about the title of the article and the accompanying photograph.

2. You may choose to introduce the following new vocabulary beforehand, or have students encounter it within the context of the article:

build	license plate
carpool lane	reduce
certain	road
ending	rush hour
especially	solve
expand	subway
global	system
highway	traffic

READING THE ARTICLE

1. Have students read silently or follow along silently as the article is read aloud by you, by one or more students, or on the audio program.

2. Ask students if they have any questions. Check understanding of vocabulary.

3. Check students' comprehension, using some or all of the following questions:

> When is traffic especially bad?
> What are two ways that cities are trying to solve their traffic problems?
> What are two ways to reduce the number of cars on the road?
> Why is traffic a global problem?

4. As a class, discuss the following questions:

> Does your city have a bus or subway system?
> Does your city have carpool lanes?
> Does your city have traffic problems?
> What time of day is the traffic especially bad in your city?

What are ways to solve your city's traffic problems?

LISTENING *And Now, Here's Today's News!*

Set the scene: "You're listening to the news on the radio from different cities in North America."

LISTENING SCRIPT

Listen to these news reports. Match the news and the city.

A. You're listening to WBOS in Boston. And now, here's Randy Ryan with today's news.
B. Good morning. Well, the people in Boston who usually take the subway to work aren't taking it today. There's a big problem with the subway system in Boston.

A. You're listening to KSAC in Sacramento. And now here's Jessica Chen with the morning news.
B. Good morning. The big news here in Sacramento is the traffic! Sacramento police officers are on strike today, and nobody is directing traffic. There are traffic problems all around the city!

A. This is WCHI in Chicago. And now, here's Mike Maxwell with today's news.
B. Good morning. It's snowing very hard in Chicago right now. As a result, the streets of the city are empty. People aren't walking or driving to work. There aren't any trucks or buses on the street. And mail carriers aren't delivering the mail.

A. You're listening to CTOR in Toronto. And now, here's Mark Mitchell with today's news.
B. It's a quiet Tuesday morning in Toronto. There aren't any bad traffic problems right now, and there aren't any problems with the subway system or the buses.

A. You're listening to WMIA in Miami. And now, here's today's news.
B. Good morning. This is Rita Rodriguez with the news. The children of Miami who usually take school buses to school aren't taking them this morning. The men and women who drive the school buses are on strike. Some children are walking to school today. Many students are staying home.

Answers

1. b
2. d
3. e
4. a
5. c

BUILD YOUR VOCABULARY!
How Do You Get to Work?

walk	take a taxi
drive	ride a bicycle
take the bus	ride a motor scooter
take the train	ride a motorcycle
take the subway	

1. Have students look at the illustrations and identify any words they already know.

2. Present the vocabulary. Say each word and have the class repeat it chorally and individually. Check students' understanding and pronunciation of the words.

EXPANSION ACTIVITIES

1. Clap in Rhythm

Object: Once a clapping rhythm is established, the students must continue naming different ways to get to work.

a. Have students sit in a circle.

b. Establish a steady even beat—one-two-three-four, one-two-three-four—by having students clap their hands to their laps twice and then clap their hands together twice. Repeat throughout the game, maintaining the same rhythm.

c. The object is for each student in turn to name a transportation word each time the hands are clapped together twice. Nothing is said when students clap their hands on their laps.

Note: The beat never stops! If a student misses a beat, he or she can either wait for the next beat or pass to the next student.

2. Drawing Game

a. Write the transportation words from text page 115 on two sets of separate cards.

b. Place the two piles of cards on a table or desk in the front of the room. Also have a pad of paper and pencil next to each team's set of cards.

c. Divide the class into two teams. Have each team sit together in a different part of the room.

d. When you say "Go!", a person from each team comes to the front of his or her team, picks a card from the pile, and draws the type of transportation. The rest of the team then guesses what the type of transportation is.

e. When a team correctly guesses the word, another team member picks a card and draws the item written on that card.

f. Continue until each team has guessed all the words in their pile.

The team that guesses all the words in the shortest time wins the game.

3. Ranking

a. Have students rank these types of transportation by cost—from *very expensive* to *very cheap*, with the first being *very expensive*. For example:

1. take a taxi
2. drive a car
3. ride a motorcycle
4. ride a motor scooter
5. take the train
6. take the subway
7. take the bus
6. ride a bicycle
7. walk

b. As a class, in pairs, or in small groups, have students compare their lists.

(continued)

c. Then have students rank the types of transportation from *very noisy to very quiet*, from *good exercise to no exercise*, and from *very fast to very slow*.

4. Survey

a. Have students conduct a survey by circulating around the room and asking each other, "How do you get to school or work?"

b. Have students report back to the class.

c. For homework, have students draw up the survey results in graph form (such as a bar graph or pie chart.) In class, have groups of students share their graphs.

Variation: Instead of interviewing fellow class members, have students interview friends, family members, or students in another English class.

5. Advantages and Disadvantages

a. Have students draw two columns on a piece of paper. At the top of one column, have them write <u>Good</u>. At the top of the other column, have them write <u>Bad</u>.

b. Dictate one of the following ways to get to work:

    walk
    ride a bike
    take the bus
    drive a car
    take a taxi
    ride a motor scooter

c. As a class, have students brainstorm ways in which that form of transportation is *good* and ways in which it's *bad*. Write students' ideas in the columns and have students copy them on their papers. For example:

drive a car

<u>Good</u>	<u>Bad</u>
fast	traffic
listen to the radio	expensive

d. For homework, have students write a paragraph about how they to get to school or work. In their paragraphs, have them include the advantages and disadvantages of that type of transportation.

AROUND THE WORLD

1. Have students read silently or follow along silently as the text is read aloud by you, by one or more students, or on the audio program. Check understanding of new vocabulary: *roller-blade.*

2. Have students first work in pairs or small groups responding to the question. Then have students tell the class what they talked about. Write any new vocabulary on the board.

   Option: You might want to see if your students can guess the country where people in the photograph are taking the subway (Tokyo, Japan) and where people are riding bicycles (Beijing, China).

EXPANSION ACTIVITIES

1. Tell Me a Story

Have each student choose one of the photographs and write a description. In their descriptions, have them answer the following questions:

    Is it noisy or quiet?
    Are the people/Is the person in a hurry?
    Is there a lot of traffic?
    Is this fun? Why or why not?

2. Be an Observer!

Have students take a tour of their neighborhoods, describe the types of transportation they see, and then report back to class.

FACT FILE *World's Largest Subway Systems*

1. Before reading the Fact File, ask the class: "What cities do you think have very large subway systems?" Write students' ideas on the board. After reading the table, have students check their predictions.

2. Read the table aloud as the class follows along. See if students know the countries where these cities are located:

Moscow, Russia
Tokyo, Japan
Mexico City, Mexico
Seoul, Korea
New York, USA
Paris, France
Osaka, Japan
Hong Kong, China
London, England
Sao Paulo, Brazil

3. Explain that the numbers in the table are in millions. A thousand million is one billion. Therefore, the number of Russian subway riders, 3,160 million, can also be read as 3 billion, 160 million.

4. For additional practice, do either or both of the following:

• Ask students: "Do you know any of these large subways systems? Can you describe them?"

• Ask students: "Why do so many people take subways? What is good about subways? What is bad?"

 GLOBAL EXCHANGE

1. Set the scene: "JeffZ, is writing to his keypal."

2. Have students read silently or follow along silently as the message is read aloud by you, by one or more students, or on the audio program.

3. Ask students if they have any questions. Check understanding of vocabulary.

4. Suggestions for additional practice:

• Have students write a response to JeffZ and share their writing in pairs.

• Have students correspond with a keypal on the Internet and then share their experience with the class.

 WHAT ARE THEY SAYING?

FOCUS

• Unusual Activities
• Contrast: Simple Present and Present Continuous Tenses

Have students talk about the people and the situation and then create role plays based on the scene. Students may refer back to previous lessons as a resource, but they should not simply reuse specific conversations.

Note: You may want to assign this exercise as written homework, having students prepare their role plays, practice them the next day with other students, and then present them to the class.

GRAMMAR

CAN

Can	I he she it we you they	sing?

I He She It We You They	can ――― can't	sing.

Yes,	I he she it we you they	can.

No,	I he she it we you they	can't.

HAVE TO

I We You They	have to	work.
He She It	has to	

FUNCTIONS

INQUIRING ABOUT ABILITY

Can you *speak Hungarian?*
Can *you go to Herbert's party?*

What can you do?

EXPRESSING ABILITY

I can *speak Romanian.*

Of course *he* can.

EXPRESSING INABILITY

No, I can't.

ASKING FOR AND REPORTING INFORMATION

He *fixes* cars every day.
He's a *mechanic.*

What's your name?
     Natalie Kramer.

Tell me, *Natalie,* _____?

INQUIRING ABOUT WANT-DESIRE

What kind of job are you looking for?
     I'm looking for a job as a *secretary.*

EXPRESSING OBLIGATION

I have to *work.*
He has to *go to the doctor.*

EXTENDING AN INVITATION

Can you *go to a movie* with me on *Saturday?*

APOLOGIZING

I'm sorry. I can't.

NEW VOCABULARY

Occupations

baker
chef
construction worker
dancer
mechanic
salesperson
singer
superintendent
truck driver

Skills

build
file (v)
operate equipment
repair *locks*
take inventory
talk to *customers*
use *a cash register / business
software / tools*

Applying for a Driver's License

application
application fee
application form
apply (v)
attach (v)
black and white photograph
driver's license
duplicate
eye examination
fill out (v)
ink
left turn
line
make a *right* turn

Motor Vehicles Department
park
print
right turn
road test
script
start *the car*
submit
take *a test*
U-turn
wait *in line*
written test

Feelings and Emotions

annoyed
depressed

Expressing Ability

can
can't

Expressing Obligation

has to
have to

Leisure Activities

go bowling
go dancing
go shopping
go skating
go skiing
go swimming
skate
ski

Miscellaneous

another
ask for
believe
crowded
do *my* laundry
employment service
finally
find
first
hope
Hungarian
loan (n)
lock
marriage license
passport
pay *a fee*
pick up (v)
reception room
Romanian
then
thing

EXPRESSIONS

believe it or not
have a party
in person
no wonder

VOCABULARY PREVIEW

You may want to introduce these words before beginning the chapter, or you may choose to wait until they first occur in a specific lesson. If you choose to introduce them at this point, here are some suggestions:

1. Have students look at the illustrations on text page 117 and identify the words they already know.

2. Present the vocabulary. Say each word and have the class repeat it chorally and individually. Check students' understanding and pronunciation of the words.

3. Practice the vocabulary as a class, in pairs, or in small groups. Have students cover the word list and look at the pictures. Practice the words in the following ways:

   • Say a word and have students tell the number of the illustration.

   • Give the number of an illustration and have students say the word.

Text Page 118: Can You?

FOCUS

- Can/Can't

CLOSE UP

RULE:	The modal verb *can* describes a person's ability. It does not change form.
EXAMPLES:	I **can** speak Romanian. She **can** drive a taxi. They **can** play soccer.

RULE:	The modal verb *can* functions as an auxiliary or *helping* verb in questions and in negative statements.
EXAMPLES:	**Can** you skate? No, I **can't**.

GETTING READY

1. Introduce *can* and *can't*. Have students look at the right hand box at the top of text page 118, or write on the board:

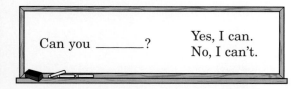

Can you _____?   Yes, I can.
                    No, I can't.

   a. Have students repeat "Yes, I can," chorally and individually.

   b. Have several students answer "Yes, I can" as you ask about their ability to speak their native language:

      A. Can you speak _____?
      B. Yes, I can.

   c. Call on a few pairs of students to ask and answer the same question.

   d. Have students repeat "No, I can't," chorally and individually.

   e. Have several students answer "No, I can't," as you ask about a language they don't know:

      A. Can you speak _____?
      B. No, I can't.

   f. Call on a few pairs of students to ask the same or a similar question and answer "No, I can't."

2. Make sentences using the forms in the box at the top of the page. Have students repeat chorally and individually. For example:

      I can sing. I can't sing.
      He can sing. He can't sing.

INTRODUCING THE MODEL

1. Have students look at the model illustration.

2. Set the scene: "Two diplomats are talking in front of the United Nations Building in New York City."

3. Present the model.

4. Full-Class Repetition.

Pronunciation Note

The pronunciation focus of Chapter 13 is **Can & Can't** (text page 126). You should model this pronunciation at this point and encourage students to incorporate it into their language practice.

5. Ask students if they have any questions. Check understanding of new vocabulary: *can, can't, Hungarian, Romanian.*

6. Group Choral Repetition.

7. Choral Conversation.

8. Call on one or two pairs of students to present the dialog.

   (For additional practice, do Choral Conversation in small groups or by rows.)

SIDE BY SIDE EXERCISES

Examples

1. A. Can Betty drive a bus?
   B. No, she can't. But she can drive a taxi.

2. A. Can Fred cook Italian food?
   B. No, he can't. But he can cook Chinese food.

3. A. Can they ski?
   B. No, they can't. But they can swim.

1. **Exercise 1:** Call on two students to present the dialog. Then do Choral Repetition and Choral Conversation practice.

2. **Exercise 2:** Same as above.

3. **Exercise 3:** Introduce the new word *ski.* Same as above.

4. **Exercises 4–8:** Either Full Class Practice or Pair Practice.

   > **New Vocabulary**
   > 4. skate
   > 5. cash register
   > 8. pictures

5. **Ask Another Student:** Here students talk about themselves. Have pairs of students ask and answer, using any vocabulary they wish.

WORKBOOK

Pages 92–93 Exercise B

EXPANSION ACTIVITIES

1. Can You Hear the Difference?

a. Write on the board:

Positive	Negative
She can drive a truck.	She can't drive a truck.
He can swim.	He can't swim.
They can paint pictures.	They can't paint pictures.
We can play soccer.	We can't play soccer.
I can play the drums.	I can't play the drums.

b. Choose a sentence randomly from one of the two columns and say it to the class. Have the class listen and identify whether the sentence is *positive* or *negative*.

c. Have students continue the activity in pairs. One student pronounces a sentence, and the other identifies it. Then have them reverse roles.

d. Write similar sentences on the board and continue the practice.

2. Chain Game

a. Begin the game by saying:

I can do a lot of things. I can ski.

b. Have each student take a turn in which he or she repeats what the person before said and adds a new activity. For example:

I can do a lot of things. I can ski and I can skate.

I can do a lot of things. I can ski, I can skate, and I can play soccer.

3. Memory Chain

a. Divide the class into groups of 5 or 6 students each.

b. Tell each student to think of something that he or she can do.

c. One group at a time, have Student 1 begin. For example:

I can play tennis.

d. Student 2 repeats what Student 1 said and adds a statement about himself or herself, naming a different ability. For example:

Linda can play tennis, and I can ski.

e. Student 3 continues in the same way. For example:

Linda can play tennis, David can ski, and I can play the piano.

f. Continue until everyone has had a chance to play the *memory chain*.

Variation: Do the same activity, this time having students tell things they can't do. For example:

Student 1: I can't swim.
Student 2: John can't swim, and I can't skate.
Student 3: John can't swim, Susan can't skate, and I can't play the drums.

4. Find the Right Person!

a. Collect some information about students' abilities.

b. Put the information on a handout in the following form:

Find someone who . . .

1. can play the guitar. _____
2. can fix a TV set. _____
3. can speak Chinese. _____
4. can skate. _____
5. can ski. _____
6. can play tennis. _____

c. Have students circulate around the room, asking each other questions to identify the above people. For example:

Can you play the guitar?
Can you fix a TV set?

d. The first student to find all the people, raise his or her hand, and tell the class who they are is the winner of the game.

Text Page 119: Of Course They Can

FOCUS

- Occupations and Related Activities:
    He's a mechanic. He fixes cars every day.
    She's a teacher. She teaches every day.

- Emphatic Short Answers with *can*:
    Of course he can.
    Of course she can.

CLOSE UP

RULE: The singular indefinite article *a/an* is used when describing one's occupation. No article is used in the plural.

EXAMPLES: She's **a** teacher./He's **an** actor.
They're dancers.
They're actresses.

GETTING READY

1. Practice *Of Course _____ can*, using *I, he, she, you, they.*

   a. Ask questions about students' ability to speak their native language(s). Encourage students to answer emphatically: "Of course _____ can!"

   b. Ask the following questions:

      Can I speak _____?
      Can *(David)* speak _____?
      Can *(Maria)* speak _____?
      Can *(Tom and Tina)* speak _____?
      Can we speak _____?

2. Introduce or review the following occupations depicted on text page 117: *actor, actress, baker, chef, dancer, mechanic, secretary, singer, teacher, truck driver.* If you are introducing the vocabulary for the first time, refer to the suggestions for presenting it on Teacher's Guide page 288. (You can also use *Side by Side* Picture Cards 131-140.)

INTRODUCING THE MODEL

1. Have students look at the model illustration.

2. Set the scene: "Two people are talking about Jack."

3. Present the model.

4. Full-Class Repetition.

5. Ask students if they have any questions. Check understanding of new vocabulary: *mechanic.*

6. Group Choral Repetition.

7. Choral Conversation.

8. Call on one or two pairs of students to present the dialog.

   (For additional practice, do Choral Conversation in small groups or by rows.)

SIDE BY SIDE EXERCISES

Examples

> 1. A. Can Michael type?
>   B. Of course he can.
>   He types every day. He's a secretary.
>
> 2. A. Can Barbara teach?
>   B. Of course she can.
>   She teaches every day. She's a teacher.
>
> 7. A. Can Bruce and Helen dance?
>   B. Of course they can.
>   They dance every day. They're dancers.

1. **Exercise 1:** Call on two students to present the dialog. Then do Choral Repetition and Choral Conversation practice.

2. **Exercise 2:** Same as above.

3. **Exercises 3–9:** Either Full Class Practice or Pair Practice.

> ### New Vocabulary
>
> 3. pies, baker   6. singer
> 4. truck driver   7. dancer
> 5. chef

WORKBOOK

Pages 93 Exercise C–95.

EXPANSION ACTIVITIES

1. Miming: What's My Occupation?

a. Write down on cards the occupations from text page 119.

b. Have students take turns picking a card from the pile and pantomiming the skill associated with that occupation.

c. The class must guess what the occupation is.

2. Who Am I?

Make statements about the people on text page 119. Have students respond by telling who you're talking about. For example:

Teacher	Students
I work in a classroom.	Barbara
I have a restaurant.	Stanley
I like music.	Claudia
I work in an office.	Michael
I work in a garage.	Jack
We like the theater.	Arthur, Elizabeth, Katherine

3. Guessing Game

For this activity, write the occupations from text page 119 on word cards or use *Side by Side Picture Cards* 131–140.

a. Give an occupation card to a student.

b. Have other students ask Yes/No questions about that person's skills in order to guess the occupation. For example:

Do you drive a truck every day?	No, I don't.
Do you fix cars?	No, I don't.
Do you type?	Yes, I do.
Are you a secretary?	Yes, I am.

c. Continue the game with other students.

4. Associations

a. Divide the class into pairs or small groups.

b. Call out the name of an occupation and tell students to write down all the words they associate with that occupation. For example:

mechanic:	car, fix, garage
chef:	cook, restaurant, food
baker:	pies, cakes, bakery

c. Have a student from each pair or group come to the board and write their words.

Variation: Do the activity as a game in which you divide the class into teams. The team with the most number of associations is the winner.

(continued)

5. Concentration

a. Write 16 sentences based on the skills and occupations in the exercises on page 119. For example:

I can fix cars.	I'm a mechanic.
I can type.	I'm a secretary.
I can teach.	I'm a teacher.
I can bake pies.	I'm a baker.
I can drive a truck.	I'm a truck driver.
I can cook.	I'm a chef.
I can dance.	I'm a dancer.
I can act.	I'm an actress.

b. Shuffle the cards and place them face down in four rows of four each.

c. Divide the class into two teams. The object of the game is for students to find the matching cards. Both teams should be able to see all the cards, since *concentrating* on their location is an important part of playing the game.

d. A student from Team 1 turns over two cards. If they match, the student picks up the cards, that team gets a point, and the student takes another turn. If the cards don't match, the student turns them face down, and a member of Team 2 takes a turn.

e. The game continues until all the cards have been matched. The team with the most correct matches wins the game.

Variation: This game can also be played in groups or pairs.

6. Match the Conversations

a. Make a set of matching cards based on occupations. For example:

Can you fix cars?	Of course I can. I'm a very good mechanic.
Can you sing?	Of course I can. I'm a very good singer.
Can you cook?	Of course I can. I'm a very good chef.
Can you act?	Of course I can. I'm a very good actor/actress.
Can you drive a truck?	Of course I can. I'm a very good truck driver.
Can you dance?	Of course I can. I'm a very good dancer.
Can you teach?	Of course I can. I'm a very good teacher.
Can you bake pies?	Of course I can. I'm a very good baker.

b. Distribute a card to each student.

c. Have students memorize the sentences on their cards, and then have students walk around the room saying their sentences until they find their match.

d. Then have pairs of students say their matched sentences aloud to the class.

READING *The Ace Employment Service*

FOCUS

* Can

NEW VOCABULARY

build things	hope
business software	lock
construction worker	operate
customers	reception room
employment service	repair
equipment	superintendent
file	take inventory
find	tools

READING THE STORY

Optional: Preview the story by having students talk about the story title and/or illustration. You may choose to introduce new vocabulary beforehand, or have students encounter the new vocabulary within the context of the reading.

1. Have students read silently or follow along silently as the story is read aloud by you, by one or more students, or on the audio program.

2. Ask students if they have any questions. Check understanding of vocabulary.

Culture Note

An employment service, or employment agency, finds jobs for people by matching their skills with the lists of available jobs they have on file.

3. Check students' comprehension, using some or all of the following questions:

> Where are the people sitting?
> Why are they there?
> What kind of job is Natalie looking for?
> What can she do?
> What kind of job is William looking for?
> What can he do?
> What kind of job is Sandra looking for?
> What can she do?
> What kind of job is Nick looking for?
> What can he do?
> What kinds of jobs are Stephanie and
>   Tiffany looking for?
> What can they do?

✓ READING *CHECK-UP*

Q & A

1. Introduce the new word *skills*. Call on a pair of students to present the model.

2. Have students work in pairs to create new dialogs.

3. Call on pairs to present their dialogs to the class.

READING EXTENSION

Read the following list of workplaces aloud. Have students identify which characters from the story want to work in each workplace.

an office	*(Natalie)*
a department store	*(Nick)*
an apartment building	*(William)*
a theater	*(Stephanie and Tiffany)*
a construction site	*(Sandra)*

EXPANSION ACTIVITIES

1. Tic Tac Vocabulary

a. Have students draw a tic tac grid and fill it in with the following words:

secretary	superintendent
mechanic	salesperson
actor	truck driver
chef	baker
construction worker	

b. Say the following incomplete sentences and tell students to cross out the word that completes each sentence:

A person who can type, file, and use business software is a . . .

A person who can paint walls, repair locks, and fix stoves and refrigerators is a . . .

A person who can use tools, operate equipment, and build things is a . . .

A person who can sell things, use a cash register, and take inventory is a . . .

A person who can sing, dance, and act is an . . .

A person who can fix cars and trucks is a . . .

A person who can make wonderful food is a . . .

A person who can drive a truck is a . . .

A person who can make pies and cakes is a . . .

c. The first student to cross out three words in a straight line—either horizontally, vertically, or diagonally—wins the game.

d. To check for accuracy, have the winner call out the words.

2. Concentration

a. Make sentence cards from the above activity, writing the description on one card and the occupation on another.

b. Shuffle the cards and place them face down in three rows of 6 each.

c. Divide the class into two teams. The object of the game is for students to find the matching cards. Both teams should be able to see all the cards, since *concentrating* on their location is an important part of playing the game.

d. A student from Team 1 turns over two cards. If they match, the student picks up the cards, that team gets a point, and the student takes another turn. If the cards don't match, the student turns them face down, and a member of Team 2 takes a turn.

e. The game continues until all the cards have been matched. The team with the most correct matches wins the game.

Variation: This game can also be played in groups or pairs.

 LISTENING

CAN OR CAN'T?

Listen and choose the word you hear.

1. I can speak Spanish.
2. He can't paint.
3. She can type.
4. We can't build things.
5. They can use tools.
6. We can't operate equipment.

Answers

1. a
2. b
3. a
4. b
5. a
6. b

WHAT CAN THEY DO?

Listen and choose what each person can do.

1. He can't file. He can type.
2. They can cook. They can't bake.
3. She can repair locks. She can't repair stoves.
4. I can't drive a truck. I can drive a bus.
5. He can teach French. He can't teach English.
6. We can take inventory. We can't paint.

Answers

1. b
2. a
3. a
4. b
5. a
6. a

 ON YOUR OWN *Your Skills*

1. Have students complete their lists in class or for homework.
2. Divide the class into pairs and have students talk about their skills.
3. After five minutes, have students change partners and talk with someone else.
4. Ask students to share what they learned about each other with the class.

FOCUS

* Have to

CLOSE UP

RULE:	The affirmative form of *have to* + *verb* expresses obligation. The present tense form follows the conjugation of the verb *have*.
EXAMPLES:	I **have to work**. We **have to fix** our car. They **have to do** their homework. He **has to go** to the doctor. She **has to go** to the dentist.

GETTING READY

1. Write *have to* and *has to* on the board. Introduce *have to* by describing typical obligations. For example:

   You *have to* go to school on Monday, but you *don't have to* go to school on Sunday.
   In this class you *have to* speak English.
   You *have to* eat every day.

2. Form sentences using the words in the grammar box. Have students repeat chorally after you. For example:

   I have to work.
   We have to work.
   She has to work.

INTRODUCING THE MODELS

There are two model conversations. Introduce and practice the first model before going on to the second. For each model:

1. Have students look at the model illustration.

2. Set the scene: "Herbert is depressed. He's having a party today, but his friends can't go to his party. They're all busy."

3. Present the model.

4. Full-Class Repetition.

5. Ask students if they have any questions. Check understanding of new vocabulary: *depressed, have a party, has to.*

   ### Pronunciation Note

   In informal speech, *have to* is usually pronounced [hafta], and *has to* is usually pronounced [hasta].

6. Group Choral Repetition.

7. Choral Conversation.

8. Call on one or two pairs of students to present the dialog.

   (For additional practice, do Choral Conversation in small groups or by rows.)

Examples

> 1. A. Can you and Tom go to Herbert's party?
>   B. No, we can't. We have to fix our car.
>
> 2. A. Can Susan go to Herbert's party?
>   B. No, she can't. She has to go to the dentist.

1. **Exercise 1:** Call on two students to present the dialog. Then do Choral Repetition and Choral Conversation practice.

2. **Exercise 2:** Same as above.

3. **Exercises 3–5:** Either Full-Class Practice or Pair Practice.

4. **Exercise 6:** Here students pretend they are Herbert's friends and tell why they can't go to his party.

WORKBOOK

Pages 96–97

EXPANSION ACTIVITIES

1. Who Is It?

Make statements about the people in the exercises. Have students respond by telling who you're talking about. For example:

Teacher	Students
This person is having problems with her teeth.	Susan (Exercise 2)
These people are studying.	the children (Exercise 3)
This person has dirty laundry.	John (Exercise 4)
This person is in the garage.	Tom (Exercise 1)
This person is sick.	Michael (model conversation)

2. Memory Chain

a. Divide the class into groups of 5 or 6 students each.

b. Tell each student to think of reason that he or she can't go to Herbert's party (from Exercise 6).

c. One group at a time, have Student 1 begin. For example:

> I have to wash my car.

d. Student 2 repeats what Student 1 said and adds a statement about himself or herself. For example:

> Robert has to wash his car, and I have to go to the supermarket.

e. Student 3 continues in the same way. For example:

> Robert has to wash his car, Julie has to go to the supermarket, and I have to call my parents.

f. Continue until everyone has had a chance to play the *memory chain*.

3. Role Play: Having a Party

a. Have each student write a simple schedule showing *Monday* through *Friday* and one thing he or she has to do on each day. Students can use the vocabulary on text page 122 or any vocabulary they wish. For example:

Monday	—	wash my car
Tuesday	—	go to the dentist
Wednesday	—	fix my TV
Thursday	—	study English
Friday	—	go to the bank

b. Call on pairs of students to create conversations, using the following framework:

> A. What do you have to do on _____?
> B. On _____ I have to _____.

c. Pretend you're having a party. Create conversations with your students where you *invite* them and they either accept or decline, depending upon their *schedules* from above. For example:

(continued)

You: I'm having a party on Monday. (Gesture to a student) Can you go to my party?

Student: No, I can't. I have to go to the doctor.

You: (gesturing to another student) Can you go to my party?

Student: No, I can't. I have to wash my car.

Keep changing the day of your party to expand the practice.

3. Information Gap Handouts

a. Tell students that your friend John is going to have a very busy week. He has to do a lot of things. Make up a schedule for John's week, but divide the information between two different schedules. For example (see below):

b. Divide the class into pairs. Give each member of the pair a different schedule. Have students share their information and fill in their schedules. For example:

Student A: John has to clean his house on Sunday.

Student B: Okay. [writes the information in Schedule B]. On Monday he has to paint his living room.

c. The pairs continue until each has a filled calendar.

d. Have students look at their partner's schedule to make sure that they have written the information correctly.

Schedule A:

SUN	MON	TUES	WED	THU	FRI	SAT
clean his house		go to the bank		wash his car		visit his cousins

Schedule B:

SUN	MON	TUES	WED	THU	FRI	SAT
	paint his living room		bake pies for the school party		repair his bike	

FOCUS

- Apologizing
- Can/Can't
- Have to

How to Say It!

> **Apologizing:** When refusing an invitation, it is polite to apologize and give a reason for the refusal.

1. Set the scene: "Two friends are talking."
2. Present the conversation.
3. Full-Class Repetition.
4. Ask students if they have any questions. Check understanding of vocabulary.
5. Group Choral Repetition.
6. Choral Conversation.

 INTERACTIONS

1. Brainstorm with the class possible reasons for refusing an invitation. Write their ideas on the board for student reference during the conversation practice.
2. Go over the vocabulary using your own visuals, the illustrations in the book, or *Side by Side* Picture Cards 141-148. Introduce the new expression: go *bowling*.

   Language Note: *Go + verb -ing* (the gerund form of the verb) is common in expressions for recreational activities.

3. Call one or two pairs to present possible conversations.

Examples

> A. Can you go to a soccer game with me on Sunday?
> B. I'm sorry. I can't. I have to visit my grandparents.
> A. Can you have lunch with me on Wednesday?
> B. I'm sorry. I can't. I have to go to the dentist.

4. Divide the class into pairs. Have the pairs create conversations for each of the situations. In their conversations, students can use any day of the week and any reason they wish for refusing the invitation.
5. Call on several pairs to present their conversations to the class.

WORKBOOK

Pages 98–99

EXPANSION ACTIVITIES

1. True Regret?

   a. Have students reread the conversation at the top of text page 123 and imagine how it would sound if the woman really *didn't* want to go out with the man, and how it would sound if she really *did* want to go out with him but couldn't because of her messy apartment.

   b. Have students practice with their partners a few of the conversations they created for the other situations on the page, with the two different dynamics of regret.

   c. Have students present their conversations to the class, and have the class decide whether or not the person who is apologizing is expressing *true regret*.

EXPANSION ACTIVITIES (Continued)

2. Obligation Game

a. Write on the board:

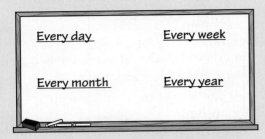

Every day   Every week

Every month   Every year

b. Divide the class into several teams.

c. Tell students to write down all the things they have to do *every day*, *every week*, *every month*, and *every year*.

d. Have students in each group work together to see how many obligations they can think of for each time interval. For example:

> Every day
> I have to go to school.
> I have to go to work.
> I have to wash the dishes.

e. The team with the most obligations listed wins.

3. Category Dictation

a. Have students draw two columns on a piece of paper. At the top of one column, have students write Good Reason. At the top of the other column, have them write Not a Good Reason.

b. Dictate various reasons for refusing an invitation, and have students write them in what they think is the appropriate column. For example:

Good Reason	Not a Good Reason
I have to go to the doctor	I have to wash my hair.
I have to work.	I have to go dancing.

c. Have the class compare which reasons they wrote in each column.

4. Pantomime Role Plays

a. Divide the class into pairs.

b. Write the following situations on index cards, and give one of the situations to each pair. Give Role A to one member of the pair and Role B to the other.

c. Have students practice *pantomiming* the situations and then present them to the class. The class watches each pantomime and guesses what the people are saying.

> **Role A:**
> Invite a friend to go dancing.

> **Role B:**
> Apologize. You can't go because you have to go to the dentist.

> **Role A:**
> Invite a friend to go skating.

> **Role B:**
> Apologize. You can't go because you have to work.

> **Role A:**
> Invite a friend to go skiing.

> **Role B:**
> Apologize. You can't go because you have to go to the doctor.

> **Role A:**
> Invite a friend to go bowling.

> **Role B:**
> Apologize. You can't go because you have to clean your apartment.

> **Role A:**
> Invite a friend to go swimming.

> **Role B:**
> Apologize. You can't go because you have to wash your clothes.

> **Role A:**
> Invite a friend to go to a movie.

> **Role B:**
> Apologize. You can't go because you have to do your homework.

Text Pages 124–125

READING *Applying for a Driver's License*

FOCUS

- Have to

NEW VOCABULARY

annoyed	line
another	make a turn
application	Motor Vehicles
application fee	Department
application form	no wonder
apply	park (v)
ask for	pay
attach	pick up
believe	print
believe it or not	right turn
black and white	road test
crowded	script
driver's license	start
duplicate	submit
eye examination	take a test
fill out	then
finally	thing
first	U-turn
ink	wait
in person	written test
left turn	

READING THE STORY

Optional: *Preview the story by having students talk about the story title and/or illustrations. You may choose to introduce new vocabulary beforehand, or have students encounter the new vocabulary within the context of the reading.*

1. Have students read silently or follow along silently as the story is read aloud by you, by one or more students, or on the audio program.

2. Ask students if they have any questions. Check understanding of vocabulary.

   Culture Note

   The Motor Vehicles Department gives driving tests to people. If they pass, the Motor Vehicles Department gives them licenses.

3. Check students' comprehension, using some or all of the following questions:

   Why is Henry annoyed?
   What does he have to do first?
   Can he ask for the form on the telephone?
   Can he ask for it by mail?
   Where does he have to go?
   How many copies of the form does he have to fill out?
   Can he use a pencil?
   Can he use blue ink?
   Can he write in script?
   What does he have to attach to the application form?
   Can they be old?
   Can they be large?
   Can they be black and white?
   Then how many long lines does he have to wait in? Why?
   What does he have to do during the road test?

✓ READING *CHECK-UP*

WHAT'S THE ANSWER?

1. No, he can't.

2. He has to go to the Motor Vehicles Department.

3. He has to fill out the form in duplicate.

4. He has to attach two photographs.

5. They have to be new, they have to be small, and they have to be color.

6. He has to start the car, make a right turn, a left turn, and a U-turn, and he has to park his car on a crowded city street.

Fix This Sign!

1. Pick up an application form.

2. Fill out the form in duplicate.

3. Pay the application fee.

4. Have an eye examination.

5. Take a written test.

6. Take a road test.

READING EXTENSION

Read the following sentences aloud. Have students say whether they *true* or *false*.

    Henry can get the application form on the Internet.
    Henry has to fill out the form three times.
    Henry has use a black pen to fill out the form.
    Henry can use an old school picture for the application.

Henry has to pay money with the application.
Henry has to wait in three lines at the Motor Vehicles Department.
Henry has to take three tests.
In his road test, Henry has to park on a busy street.
Henry has to do a lot of things to get his license.

 IN YOUR OWN WORDS

1. Introduce the new vocabulary: *passport, marriage license, loan.*

2. Make sure students understand the instructions.

3. Have students do the activity as written homework, using a dictionary for any new words they wish to use.

4. Have students present and discuss what they have written, in pairs or as a class.

PRONUNCIATION

> **Can & Can't:** The /a/ in the word *can* is
> reduced to a schwa sound in positive
> statements. *(She cạn teach. We cạn dance.)*
>
> The /a/ of *can* is pronounced /ae/ in
> negative sentences and in short answers.
> *(I can't swim. Yes, they can. No, he can't.)*

Focus on Listening

Practice the sentences in the left column. Say
each sentence or play the audio one or more times.
Have students listen carefully and repeat.

Focus on Pronunciation

Practice the sentences in the right column.
Have students say each sentence and then listen
carefully as you say it or play the audio.

If you wish, have students continue practicing
the sentences to improve their pronunciation.

 JOURNAL

Have students write their journal entries at
home or in class. Encourage students to use a
dictionary to look up words they would like to
use. Students can share their written work with
other students if appropriate. Have students
discuss what they have written as a class, in
pairs, or in small groups.

 CHAPTER SUMMARY

GRAMMAR

1. Divide the class into pairs or small groups.

2. Have students take turns forming sentences
from the words in the grammar boxes.
Student A says a sentence, and Student B
points to the words from each column that
are in the sentence. Then have students
switch: Student B says a sentence, and
Student A points to the words.

KEY VOCABULARY

Have students ask you any questions about the
meaning or pronunciation of the vocabulary. If
students ask for the pronunciation, repeat after
the student until the student is satisfied with
his or her own pronunciation.

EXPANSION ACTIVITIES

1. **Do You Remember the Words?**

   Check students' retention of the vocabulary
   depicted on the opening page of Chapter 13 by
   doing the following activity:

   a. Have students open their books to page 117
   and cover the list of vocabulary words.

   b. Either call out a number and have students
   tell you the word, or say a word and have
   students tell you the number.

   Variation: You can also do this activity as a game
   with competing teams.

2. **Student-Led Dictation**

   a. Tell each student to choose a word or phrase
   from the Key Vocabulary list on text page 126
   and look at it very carefully.

   b. Have students take turns dictating their
   words to the class. Everybody writes down
   that student's word.

   c. When the dictation is completed, call on
   different students to write each word on
   the board to check the spelling.

3. **Beanbag Toss**

   a. Call out a topic from the chapter—for
   example: *Occupations.*

   (continued)

EXPANSION ACTIVITIES (Continued)

b. Have students toss a beanbag back and forth. The student to whom the beanbag is tossed must name a word in that category. For example:

> Student 1: actor
> Student 2: teacher
> Student 3: secretary

c. Continue until all the words in the category have been named.

END-OF-CHAPTER ACTIVITIES

1. Board Game

a. On poster boards or on manila file folders, make up game boards with a pathway consisting of separate spaces. You may use any theme or design you wish.

b. Divide the class into groups of 2 to 4 students and give each group a game board, a die, and something to be used as a playing piece.

c. Give each group a pile of cards face-down with sentences written on them. Some sentences should be correct, and others should be incorrect. For example:

> We have to speak English in class.
> She can't to go to his party.
> They're mechanic.
> My mother have to go to the doctor.
> Do you can play the piano?
> She's a teacher.
> He cans speak Japanese.
> They can sing beautiful songs because
>   they're singers.
> She can use a computer.
> He has do his homework every night.

d. Each student in turn rolls the die, moves the playing piece along the game path, and after landing on a space, picks a card, reads the sentence, and says if it is *correct* or *incorrect*. If the sentence is incorrect and the student is able to give the correct version, that student takes an additional turn.

e. The first student to reach the end of the pathway is the winner.

2. Sense or Nonsense?

a. Divide the class into four groups.

b. Make four sets of split sentence cards such as the following:

She can speak	Romanian.
He can drive	a bus.
We can bake	an apple pie.
They can fix	TV sets and radios.
She can sing	songs.
They can play	the piano.
You can paint	beautiful pictures.

c. Mix up the cards and distribute sets of cards to each group, keeping the beginning and ending cards in different piles.

d. Have students take turns picking up one card from each pile and reading the sentence to the group. For example:

We can bake	the piano.

e. The group decides if the sentence makes *sense* or is *nonsense*.

f. After all the cards have been picked, have the group lay out all the cards and put together all the sentence combinations that *make sense*.

3. Guess the Occupation!

a. Divide the class into pairs.

b. Give each pair a card with one of the following occupations on it:

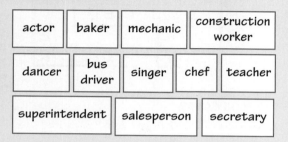

c. Have each pair think of a sentence that describes the skills required in that occupation. For example:

This person can drive buses in the city.
(bus driver)

This person can repair doors and paint walls.
(superintendent)

d. One student from each pair then reads their sentence aloud and the class tries to guess the occupation.

Variation: Do the activity as a game in which each pair scores a point for identifying the correct occupation. The pair with the most points wins the game.

WORKBOOK ANSWER KEY AND LISTENING SCRIPTS

WORKBOOK PAGE 92

A. *CAN* OR *CAN'T*?

1. can't ski, can skate
2. can sing, can't dance
3. can paint, can't paint
4. can't speak, can speak
5. can cook, can't cook
6. can't use, can use
7. can't play, can play
8. can drive, can't drive

WORKBOOK PAGE 93

C. WHAT'S THE QUESTION?

1. Can he cook?
2. Can she ski?
3. Can they swim?
4. Can you drive a bus?
5. Can he skate?
6. Can you play baseball?

D. LISTENING

Listen and circle the word you hear.

1. Our teacher can speak French.
2. I can't play the piano.
3. He can paint houses.
4. My sister can play soccer.
5. They can't sing.
6. Can you drive a bus?
7. I can't read Japanese newspapers.
8. My son Tommy can play the drums.
9. Their children can't swim.
10. Can your husband cook?
11. We can't skate.
12. I can use a cash register.

Answers

1. can	7. can't
2. can't	8. can
3. can	9. can't
4. can	10. can
5. can't	11. can't
6. can	12. can

WORKBOOK PAGE 94

E. PUZZLE

F. *CAN* OR *CAN'T*?

1. can	7. Can, can
2. can't	8. can
3. Can, can	9. can't, can't
4. can't	10. can, can, can
5. can	11. can't, can't
6. can't	

WORKBOOK PAGE 96

H. WHAT ARE THEY SAYING?

1. have to	2. has to
3. has to	4. have to, have to
5. Does, have to, does, has to	6. Do, have to, don't
7. have to	8. have to

WORKBOOK PAGE 97

I. A BUSY FAMILY

1. He has to speak to the superintendent.
2. She has to meet with Danny's teacher.
3. They have to go to the doctor.
4. He has to fix the car.
5. She has to go to the dentist.
6. She has to baby-sit.
7. They have to clean the apartment.
8. They have to plant flowers in the yard.

K. LISTENING

Listen and circle the words you hear.

1. We have to go to the supermarket.
2. My son has to play his violin every day.
3. We can use business software on our computers.
4. Boris has to speak English every day now.
5. I can't cook Italian food.
6. Apartment building superintendents have to repair locks and paint apartments.
7. That actress can't act!
8. Our children have to use a computer to do their homework.
9. Mr. Johnson can operate equipment.

Answers

1. have to	**4.** has to	**7.** can't
2. has to	**5.** can't	**8.** have to
3. can	**6.** have to	**9.** can

WORKBOOK PAGE 98

L. THEY'RE BUSY

1. can't go swimming, have to go to the dentist
2. can't go bowling, has to baby-sit
3. can't go dancing, have to work
4. can't go to a soccer game, has to study
5. can't go to a movie, have to clean the house
6. can't have dinner, have to wash my clothes

M. LISTENING

Listen and choose the correct answer.

1. I'm sorry. I can't go to the movies with you today. I have to go to the dentist.
2. I can't go to the party on Saturday. I have to wash my clothes.
3. I can't have lunch with you, but I can have dinner.
4. We can't go skiing this weekend. We have to paint our kitchen.
5. I'm very busy today. I have to go shopping, and I have to cook dinner for my family.
6. I can't see a play with you on Friday because I have to baby-sit. But I can see a play with you on Saturday.

Answers

1. a	**4.** a
2. b	**5.** b
3. b	**6.** a

GRAMMAR

FUTURE: GOING TO

What	am	I	going to do?
	is	he she it	
	are	we you they	

(I am)	I'm	going to read.
(He is)	He's	
(She is)	She's	
(It is)	It's	
(We are)	We're	
(You are)	You're	
(They are)	They're	

TIME EXPRESSIONS

I'm going to wash my clothes	today. this morning. this afternoon. this evening. tonight.	tomorrow. tomorrow morning. tomorrow afternoon. tomorrow evening. tomorrow night.	right now. right away. immediately. at once.

I'm going to fix my car	this next	week / month / year. Sunday / Monday / Tuesday / . . . / Saturday. January / February / March /. . . / December. spring / summer / fall (autumn) / winter.

It's	eleven o'clock.		11:00
	eleven fifteen.	a quarter after eleven.	11:15
	eleven thirty.	half past eleven.	11:30
	eleven forty-five.	a quarter to twelve.	11:45

WANT TO

I We You They	want to	study.
He She It	wants to	

FUNCTIONS

INQUIRING ABOUT INTENTION

What are you going to do *tomorrow*?

When are you going to *wash your clothes*?

EXPRESSING INTENTION

I'm going to *fix it next Friday*.

I'm going to *wash them this week*.

EXPRESSING WANT-DESIRE

I want to *go swimming*.

I really want to *go swimming*.

ASKING FOR AND REPORTING INFORMATION

What's the forecast?

What's the weather today?

What's the weather forecast for tomorrow?

The radio says it's going to *rain*.

According to the newspaper, it's going to *be sunny*.

What time is it?

What's the time?

Can you tell me the time?

Do you know the time?

It's *7:30*.

What time does the *movie* begin?

It begins at *8:00*.

Tell me, _____?

NEW VOCABULARY

Everyday Activities

begin
cut *your hair*
finish
get
get a haircut
give
go sailing
have a picnic
hurry
iron (v)
leave
meet
shave
take *my children to the zoo*
try
want (to)
win
work *in my garden*

Months of the Year

January
February
March
April
May
June
July
August
September
October
November
December

Telling Time

a quarter after
a quarter to
half past
midnight
noon
o'clock

Seasons

winter
spring
summer
autumn/fall

Time Expressions

at once
evening
future
immediately
next
next month
next week
next year
right away
right now
this afternoon
this evening
this month
this morning
this week
tomorrow
tomorrow afternoon
tomorrow evening
tomorrow morning
tomorrow night
tonight

Travel

pack *a suitcase*
suitcase
take a trip
take a vacation
train

Talking about Money

buy
dollar
money
salary
save

Places Around the World

Alaska

Miscellaneous

according to
become
celebrate
clear
cold (n)
college
computer chat
concerned
doorbell
DVD player
entire
fire (n)
fire (v)
foggy
forecast
fortune
fortune teller
get married
happen
high school
hurt
move
New Year's Eve
plumber
thirty-first
to be late for
used car
wondering

EXPRESSIONS

be in a car accident
fall in love
Happy New Year!
I don't know.
just in case
look forward to
New Year's Eve
Oh, no!
the radio says

Text Page 127: Chapter Opening Page

VOCABULARY PREVIEW

You may want to introduce these words before beginning the chapter, or you may choose to wait until they first occur in a specific lesson. If you choose to introduce them at this point, here are some suggestions:

1. Have students look at the illustrations on text page 127 and identify the words they already know.

2. Present the vocabulary. Say each word and have the class repeat it chorally and individually. Check students' understanding and pronunciation of the words.

3. Practice the vocabulary as a class, in pairs, or in small groups.

   • For telling the time, have students cover the words and look at the clock faces. Say a time and have students point to the correct clock face.

   • Give the name of a season and have students say months that belong to that season.

FOCUS

- Future: Going to

CLOSE UP

RULE:	The future with *going to* is formed with *to be* + *going to* + the base form of the verb.
EXAMPLES:	**I'm going to read.** **She's going to paint.** **They're going to study.**
RULE:	The future with *going to* is used to express a plan for the future.
EXAMPLE:	What's Tony going to do tomorrow? He's going to cook.

GETTING READY

1. Introduce the word *tomorrow*. Use a calendar to indicate *tomorrow*.

2. Introduce *going to*. For example:

   Every day I read the newspaper.
   Tomorrow I'm *going to read* the newspaper.

   I'm wearing my glasses.
   I always wear my glasses.
   Tomorrow I'm *going to wear* my glasses.

3. Form sentences with *going to* and the words in the boxes at the top of text page 128. Have students repeat chorally. (When you read from the box on the right, form contractions.) For example:

   I'm *going to* read.
   He's *going to* read.

INTRODUCING THE MODEL

1. Have students look at the model illustration.

2. Set the scene: "Two people are talking about Fred."

3. Present the model.

4. Full-Class Repetition.

   ### Pronunciation Note

   The pronunciation focus of Chapter 14 is **Going to & Want to** (text page 137). Tell students that this is very common in informal speech. You may wish to model this pronunciation at this point and encourage students to incorporate it into their language practice.

   He's "gonna" fix his car.
   She's "gonna" paint her bathroom.

5. Ask students if they have any questions. Check understanding of new vocabulary: *tomorrow, going to.*

6. Group Choral Repetition.

7. Choral Conversation.

8. Call on one or two pairs of students to present the dialog.

   (For additional practice, do Choral Conversation in small groups or by rows.)

SIDE BY SIDE EXERCISES

Examples

1. A. What's Jenny going to do tomorrow?
   B. She's going to paint her bedroom.

2. A. What are Cathy and Dave going to do tomorrow?
   B. They're going to wash their windows.

Answer Key:

3. He's going to cook.
4. We're going to study.
5. He's going to clean his apartment.
6. She's going to listen to music.

1. **Exercise 1:** Call on two students to present the dialog. Then do Choral Repetition and Choral Conversation practice.

2. **Exercise 2:** Same as above.

3. **Exercises 3–6:** Either Full-Class Practice or Pair Practice.

WORKBOOK

Page 100

EXPANSION ACTIVITIES

1. Finish the Sentence!

Begin a sentence with a verb in the future. Have students repeat what you said and complete the sentence with any appropriate ending. For example:

Teacher	Students
I'm going to wash . . .	I'm going to wash my car. I'm going to wash my windows. I'm going to wash my clothes.
He's going to read . . .	He's going to read a book. He's going to read the newspaper.
She's going to fix . . .	She's going to fix her car. She's going to fix her TV. She's going to fix her bicycle.
We're going to listen to . . .	We're going to listen to music. We're going to listen to the radio. We're going to listen to CDs.
They're going to do . . .	They're going to do their homework. They're going to do their exercises.

Variation: This activity may be done as a class, in pairs or small groups, or as a game with competing teams.

2. Sentence Cues

a. On separate cards, write key words that can be put together to form sentences. Clip together the cards for each sentence. For example:

I	visit	grandparents	tomorrow
My sister	paint	kitchen	tomorrow
Tom	cook	dinner	tomorrow
The mechanic	fix	car	tomorrow
The students	study	English	tomorrow
My husband and I	wash	car	tomorrow

b. Divide the class into small groups and give a clipped set of cards to each group.

c. Have each group write a sentence based on their set of cards.

d. Have one member of each group write that group's sentence on the board and compare everybody's sentences.

3. Memory Chain

a. Divide the class into groups of 5 or 6 students each.

b. Tell students they will answer the question *What are you going to do tomorrow?*

c. One group at a time, have Student 1 begin. For example:

   I'm going to read a book.

d. Student 2 repeats what Student 1 said and adds a statement about himself or herself. For example:

   Susan is going to read a book, and I'm going to clean my bedroom.

e. Student 3 continues in the same way. For example:

   Susan is going to read a book, Dave is going to clean his bedroom, and I'm going to listen to music.

f. Continue until everyone has had a chance to play the *memory chain.*

4. Interview

a. Write the following on the board:

   What are you going to do tomorrow?

b. Have pairs of students interview each other and then report back to the class about their partner's plans for tomorrow.

Text Page 129: They're Going to the Beach

FOCUS

- Future: Going to + Go
- Future Time Expressions

CLOSE UP

RULE: To avoid repetition when combining the *going to* future with the base verb *go*, speakers often omit *to go*.

EXAMPLES: **I'm going to go** to a concert.
I'm going to a concert

I'm going to go swimming.
I'm going swimming.

GETTING READY

1. Model the following conversations and have students repeat after you:

   A. What's John going to do tomorrow?
   B. He's going to go to a concert. (or)
   He's going to a concert.

   A. What's Maria going to do tomorrow?
   B. She's going to go swimming. (or)
   She's going swimming.

   A. What are Bob and Bill going to do tomorrow?
   B. They're going to go to the bank. (or)
   They're going to the bank.

2. Write on the board and point out *going to go = going to*:

   > He's going to go to a concert tomorrow. =
   > He's going to a concert tomorrow.

3. Write cues on word cards and have students answer questions in the future: For example:

   go swimming

   Teacher: What are you going to do tomorrow?

Student: I'm going to go swimming. (or)
I'm going swimming.

   go to the beach

Teacher: What's Betty going to do tomorrow?
Student: She's going to go to the beach. (or)
She's going to the beach.

   go dancing

Teacher: What are Mr. and Mrs. Lane going to do tomorrow?
Student: They're going to go dancing. (or)
They're going dancing.

4. Introduce future time expressions for *today* and *tomorrow*. Read the examples in the boxes at the top of text page 129. Have students repeat chorally.

INTRODUCING THE MODEL

1. Have students look at the model illustration.

2. Set the scene: "Two people are talking about Mr. and Mrs. Brown."

3. Present the model.

4. Full-Class Repetition.

5. Ask students if they have any questions. Check understanding of vocabulary.

6. Group Choral Repetition.

7. Choral Conversation.

8. Call on one or two pairs of students to present the dialog.

   (For additional practice, do Choral Conversation in small groups or by rows.)

9. Practice future time expressions for *today* and *tomorrow*. Replace the words in the box at the top of text page 129 for the expression in the model. For example:

   A. What are Mr. and Mrs. Brown going to do this morning?
   B. They're going (to go) to the beach.

   A. What are Mr. and Mrs. Brown going to do tomorrow afternoon?
   B. They're going (to go) to the beach.

   Do Choral Repetition and Choral Conversation, and call on pairs of students.

SIDE BY SIDE EXERCISES

Examples

1. A. What's Anita going to do this morning?
   B. She's going (to go) to the library.

2. A. What are Steve and Brenda going to do tonight?
   B. They're going (to go) dancing.

Answer Key:

3. He's going (to go) to a concert.
4. We're going (to go) to a baseball game.

1. **Exercise 1:** Call on two students to present the dialog. Then do Choral Repetition and Choral Conversation practice.

2. **Exercise 2:** Same as above.

3. **Exercises 3–4:** Either Full-Class Practice or Pair Practice.

   New Vocabulary
   4. baseball game

4. **What Are YOU Going to Do Tomorrow?** Have pairs of students ask and answer the question, and then call on students to tell about each other's plans.

WORKBOOK

Page 101

EXPANSION ACTIVITIES

1. Beanbag Toss

a. Have students toss a beanbag back and forth. The student to whom the beanbag is tossed tells what he or she is going to do tonight. For example:

   Student 1: I'm going to go to a concert.
   Student 2: I'm going to cook dinner.
   Student 3: I'm going to go bowling.

b. Continue until all students have taken a turn.

2. George's Vacation

a. Put the following on the board:

Sun	Mon	Tue	Wed	Thu	Fri	Sat
go swimming	go shopping	go to the beach	go to a restaurant	go to a concert		

b. Tell a story about George.

   George is going on vacation.
   On Sunday George is going swimming.
   On Monday he's going shopping.
   (Continue with Tuesday, Wednesday, Thursday.)

c. Ask students *What* and *When* questions about George's plans. Students can answer by looking at the schedule on the board. For example:

   A. What's George going to do on Monday?
   B. On Monday he's going to go shopping. (or) He's going shopping.

   A. When is George going to a concert?
   B. He's going to go to a concert on Thursday. (or) He's going to a concert on Thursday.

d. Call on pairs of students to ask and answer questions about George's vacation schedule. Leave Friday and Saturday open. Have students decide what George is going to do.

3. Students' Plans

Have students make up their own schedules similar to the one in Expansion Activity 2 above. In pairs, have students ask one another what their plans are. Encourage them to use all the future time expressions practiced in this lesson. For example:

   A. What are you going to do tomorrow night?
   B. I'm going to a movie. What are YOU going to do tomorrow night?
   A. I'm going to stay home and watch TV.

4. Match the Sentences

a. Make a set of paired sentence cards such as the following:

They're going to the beach.	They're going to go swimming.
They're going to a concert.	They're going to listen to music.
They're going to a health club.	They're going to do exercises.
They're going to a restaurant.	They're going to have dinner.
They're going to the theater.	They're going to see a play.
They're going to the park.	They're going to play soccer.
They're going to the laundromat.	They're going to wash their clothes.
They're going to the bank.	They're going to ask for a loan.

b. Distribute a card to each student.

c. Have students memorize the sentence on their cards, then walk around the room trying to find their corresponding related sentence.

d. Then have pairs of students say their sentences aloud to the class.

5. Concentration

a. Use the sentence cards from the above activity.

b. Shuffle the cards and place them face down in four rows of 4 each.

c. Divide the class into two teams. The object of the game is for students to find the matching cards. Both teams should be able to see all the cards, since *concentrating* on their location is an important part of playing the game.

d. A student from Team 1 turns over two cards. If they match, the student picks up the cards, that team gets a point, and the student takes another turn. If the cards don't match, the student turns them face down, and a member of Team 2 takes a turn.

e. The game continues until all the cards have been matched. The team with the most correct matches wins the game.

Variation: This game can also be played in groups or pairs.

FOCUS

- Time Expressions
- Future: Going to
- Expressing Intention

CLOSE UP

RULE:	The future with *going to* is used to express an intention.
EXAMPLES:	When are you going to wash your clothes? I'm going to wash them this week. When are you going to cut your hair? I'm going to cut it this summer.

RULE:	The months of the year are capitalized.
EXAMPLES:	January, February, March, . . .

GETTING READY

1. Introduce or review the months of the year and seasons depicted on text page 127. If you are introducing the vocabulary for the first time, refer to the suggestions for presenting it on Teacher's Guide page 312.

   a. Have students practice naming the months and seasons.

   b. Ask students about the months of their birthdays or special holidays. For example:

   > When is your birthday?
   > *(It's in March.)*

   c. Ask about typical weather in different seasons. For example:

   > How's the weather in the summer?
   > *(It's usually hot.)*

2. Review object pronouns.

   a. Have students listen as you say each of the sentences in the next column.

   b. Call on students to replace the object (and possessive adjective) with an object pronoun and say the sentence.

Teacher	Students
I'm going to wash *my windows*.	I'm going to wash *them*.
I'm going to clean *my apartment*.	I'm going to clean *it*.
I'm going to visit *my friends*.	I'm going to visit *them*.
I'm going to visit *Maria*.	I'm going to visit *her*.
I'm going to visit *Tom*.	I'm going to visit *him*.
I'm going to visit *Mr. and Mrs. Park*.	I'm going to visit *them*.
I'm going to wash *my car*.	I'm going to wash *it*.

INTRODUCING THE MODELS

There are four model conversations. Introduce and practice each separately. For each model:

1. Have students look at the model illustration.

2. Set the scene:

   1st model: "Two roommates are talking."
   2nd model: "Two tenants and their landlord are talking."
   3rd model: "A mother and son are talking."
   4th model: "A wife and husband are talking."

3. Present the model.

4. Full-Class Repetition.

5. Ask students if they have any questions. Check understanding of new vocabulary.

   1st model: *this week*
   2nd model: *doorbell, next*
   3rd model: *cut, summer*
   4th model: *plumber, right now*

6. Group Choral Repetition.

7. Choral Conversation.

8. Call on one or two pairs of students to present the dialog.

   (For additional practice, do Choral Conversation in small groups or by rows.)

9. Introduce the time expressions at the top of the page. Have students practice the models again, replacing some of the time expressions. For example:

   1st model: A. When are you going to wash your clothes?
   B. I'm going to wash them *next month*.

   2nd model: A. When are you going to fix our doorbell?
   B. I'm going to fix it *this Tuesday*.

   3rd model: A. When are you going to cut your hair?
   B. I'm going to cut it *next winter*.

   4th model: A. When are you going to call the plumber?
   B. I'm going to call him *immediately*.

SIDE BY SIDE EXERCISES

In these exercises, students answer the questions, using any of the time expressions on text page 130.

Examples

> 1. A. When are you going to clean your garage?
>   B. We're going to clean it *(next week)*.
>
> 2. A. When are you going to call your grandmother?
>   B. I'm going to call her *(right now)*.

1. **Exercise 1:** Call on two students to present the dialog. Then do Choral Repetition and Choral Conversation practice.

2. **Exercise 2:** Same as above.

3. **Exercises 3–8:** Either Full-Class Practice or Pair Practice.

> **New Vocabulary**
> 8. iron

4. **Now Ask Another Student:** Have pairs of students create dialogs using any of the time expressions on text page 130. Call on pairs to present their conversations to the class.

WORKBOOK

Pages 102–103 Exercise I

EXPANSION ACTIVITIES

1. Tell Me When

a. Write on the board:

> A. When are you going to _____ ?
> B. I'm going to _____ _____ .

b. Make word cards for a variety of activities. You can also use your own visuals or *Side by Side* Picture Cards. Some possible activities:

go to the beach	write to _____
go to the dentist	call _____
go to Paris	visit _____
plant flowers	play _____
do your laundry	go to a movie
cut your hair	go to the supermarket
do _____ homework	

c. Have a pair of students come to the front of the room. Student A picks a card and asks Student B a question with the phrase on the card. Student B answers using any time expression he or she wishes. For example:

> Student A: When are you going to go to the beach?
> Student B: I'm going to go to the beach next summer.

d. Continue the activity with other pairs. For example:

> Student C: When are you going to do your laundry?
> Student D: I'm going to do it this Sunday.

2. Change the Sentence!

a. Write a sentence on the board, underlining and numbering different portions of the sentence. For example:

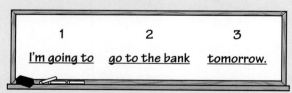

> 1   2   3
> I'm going to go to the bank tomorrow.

b. If possible, have students sit in a circle.

c. Tell them that when you say a number, the first student in the circle makes a change in that part of the sentence. For example:

> Teacher: Two.
> Student 1: I'm going to <u>go swimming</u> tomorrow.

d. The second student keeps the first student's sentence, but changes it based on the next number you say. For example:

> Teacher: Three.
> Student 2: I'm going to go swimming <u>this week.</u>

e. Continue this way with the rest of the students in the circle. For example:

> Teacher: One.
> Student 3: <u>He's going to</u> go swimming this week.

> Teacher: Two.
> Student 4: He's going to <u>see a movie</u> this week.

3. Sense or Nonsense?

a. Divide the class into four groups.

b. Make four sets of split sentence cards with beginnings and ends of sentences. For example:

She's going to wash …	her car.
I'm going to visit …	my grandfather.
He's going to paint …	his living room.
We're going to play …	baseball.
I'm going to iron …	my pants.
She's going to cut …	her hair.
They're going to go to …	the beach.
I'm going to fix …	my car.
They're going to plant …	flowers.
He's going to go …	skating.

c. Mix up the cards and distribute sets of cards to each group, keeping the beginning and ending cards in different piles.

d. Have students take turns picking up one card from each pile and reading the sentence to the group. For example:

| I'm going to iron . . . | my car. |

e. That group decides if the sentence makes *sense* or is *nonsense*.

f. After all the cards have been picked, have the groups lay out all the cards and put together all the sentence combinations that make sense.

4. Scrambled Story: The Smiths Are Going on Vacation

Here is the Smith family's vacation schedule:

> On Sunday the Smiths are going to Acapulco, Mexico.
> On Monday they're going to go swimming.
> On Tuesday they're going to eat in a Mexican restaurant.
> On Wednesday they're going to visit friends in another city.
> On Thursday they're going to write letters to their friends.
> On Friday they're going to go shopping, and then they're going to go dancing.
> On Saturday they're going to go to a concert.

a. Write each sentence on a strip of paper. Then cut the words apart. Mix up the words in each sentence and clip them together.

b. Divide the class into small groups. Give each group one sentence to unscramble.

c. When everyone has put the words in correct order, have one student from each group write that group's sentence on the board in order of the days of the week.

d. Once all the sentences are on the board, call on several pairs of students to ask and answer questions about the Smiths. For example:

> When are they going to eat in a Mexican restaurant?
> What are they going to do on Friday?

5. Information Gap Handouts

a. Tell students that Peter and Pam are going to do a lot this week. Make up a schedule for their week, but divide the information between two different schedules. For example:

Schedule A:

S	M	T	W	T	F	S
	wash and iron the clothes		clean the garage		fix the kitchen window	

Schedule B:

S	M	T	W	T	F	S
wash the dog		fix their bicycles		plant flowers in the garden		visit their friends

b. Divide the class into pairs. Give each member of the pair a different schedule. Have students share their information and fill in their schedules. For example:

> Student A: What are Peter and Pam going to do on Sunday?
> Student B: They're going to wash the dog.
> Student A: Okay. *[writes the information in Schedule A]*
> Student B: What are they going to do on Monday?

c. The pairs continue until each has a filled calendar.

d. Have students look at their partner's schedule to make sure that they have written the information correctly.

READING *Happy New Year!*

FOCUS

- Future: Going to

NEW VOCABULARY

Alaska	high school
begin	looking forward to
buy	money
celebrate	move
college	New Year's Eve
entire	save
finish	take a vacation
get	thirty-first
Happy New Year!	used car

READING THE STORY

Optional: Preview the story by having students talk about the story title and/or illustration. You may choose to introduce new vocabulary beforehand, or have students encounter the new vocabulary within the context of the reading.

1. Have students read silently or follow along silently as the story is read aloud by you, by one or more students, or on the audio program.

2. Ask students if they have any questions. Check understanding of vocabulary.

3. Check students' comprehension, using some or all of the following questions:

   What day is it?
   Why are the Carters happy this New Year's Eve?
   What are Ruth and Larry going to do next year?
   What's Nicole going to do next year?
   What's Jonathan going to do next year?

✔ **READING** *CHECK-UP*

1. Have students look at the illustration in the student book.

2. Set the scene: "Jonathan, from the story, and a friend are communicating with each other on the Internet. This type of Internet dialog is called a *computer chat*."

3. Have students read the Internet exchange. Ask students if they have any questions. Check understanding of vocabulary.

4. Have students complete the computer chat and, in pairs, present it to the class.

Answer Key:

1. What are you going to
2. I'm going to
3. What's she going to
4. She's going to
5. What are they going to do
6. They're going to

READING EXTENSION

Have students tell you whether the following statements are *true* or *false*.

Ruth and Larry are going to Alaska with their children.
Nicole and Jonathan are teenagers.
Nicole is going to finish college this year.
Jonathan is going to buy a used car.
The Carters are looking forward to the new year because it's going to be a good year for all of them.

 LISTENING

Listen and choose the words you hear.

1. A. When are you going to buy a computer?
   B. Tomorrow.

2. A. When are your neighbors going to move?
   B. Next November.

3. A. When are you going to visit me?
   B. Next month.

4. A. When are you going to do your laundry?
   B. This evening.

5. A. When are you going to begin your vacation?
   B. This Sunday.

6. A. When are we going to go to the concert?
   B. This Thursday.

7. A. When are you going to wash the windows?
   B. This afternoon.

8. A. When is she going to get her driver's license?
   B. Next week.

9. A. When is your daughter going to finish college?
   B. Next winter.

10. A. When is the landlord going to fix the kitchen sink?
   B. At once.

Answers

1. a

2. b

3. a

4. a

5. b

6. b

7. a

8. b

9. a

10. b

FOCUS

- Want to
- Future: Going to
- Talking about Plans

CLOSE UP

RULE:	*Want to* + verb expresses a desire.
EXAMPLES:	I **want to** go swimming. I **want to** take my children to the zoo.
RULE:	*Going to* + verb is used to make predictions about the future.
EXAMPLES:	The radio says it**'s going to rain**. According to the newspaper, it**'s going to be sunny**.

GETTING READY

1. Introduce *want to* by telling about something you want to do. For example:

   I *want to* watch TV tonight, but I can't.
   I have to work.

2. Introduce *wants to* by telling what someone else wants to do.

   Joe *wants to* buy a car, but he can't. He doesn't have $15,000.

3. Form sentences with the words in the box at the top of text page 133. Have students repeat chorally and individually. For example:

   I want to study.
   We want to study.

INTRODUCING THE MODEL

1. Have students look at the model illustration.

2. Set the scene: "Two friends are talking after work on Friday afternoon."

3. Present the model.

4. Full-Class Repetition.

   ### Pronunciation Note

   The pronunciation focus of Chapter 14 is **Going to & Want to** (text page 137). Tell students that this is very common in informal speech. You may wish to model this pronunciation at this point and encourage students to incorporate it into their language practice.

   I "wanna" go swimming.
   It's "gonna" rain.

5. Ask students if they have any questions. Check understanding of new vocabulary: *I don't know, want to, forecast, the radio says, according to.*

   ### Culture Note

   Weather forecasts are a regular part of TV and radio news programs in the United States. Daily newspapers also publish weather forecasts.

 326 CHAPTER 14

Language Note

Note going to + verb: going to rain, going to snow; with adjectives: going to be sunny, going to be cloudy, etc.

6. Group Choral Repetition.

7. Choral Conversation.

8. Call on one or two pairs of students to present the dialog.

   (For additional practice, do Choral Conversation in small groups or by rows.)

SIDE BY SIDE EXERCISES

Examples

1. A. What are you going to do tomorrow?
    B. I don't know. I want to have a picnic, but I think the weather is going to be bad.
    A. Really? What's the forecast?
    B. The radio says it's going to rain.
    A. That's strange! According to the newspaper, it's going to be nice.
    B. I hope you're right. I REALLY want to have a picnic.

2. A. What are you going to do tomorrow?
    B. I don't know. I want to go to the beach, but I think the weather is going to be bad.
    A. Really? What's the forecast?
    B. The radio says it's going to be cloudy.
    A. That's strange! According to the newspaper, it's going to be sunny.
    B. I hope you're right. I REALLY want to go to the beach.

1. **Exercise 1:** Introduce the new expression *have a picnic.* Call on two students to present the dialog. Then do Choral Repetition and Choral Conversation practice.

2. **Exercise 2:** Same as above.

3. **Exercises 3–6:** Either Full-Class Practice or Pair Practice.

New Vocabulary

3. sailing, foggy, clear
5. work (in my garden)
6. take (my children to the zoo)

---

4. **Discuss in Class:** As a class, in pairs, or in small groups, have students answer the questions about weather at the bottom of text page 133. Encourage students to listen to the weather forecast on the radio and/or watch it on television and see if they were correct about their predictions.

WORKBOOK

Pages 103 Exercise J–107

1. Beanbag Toss

Have students toss a beanbag back and forth. The student to whom the beanbag is tossed gives a prediction for tomorrow's weather. For example:

Student 1:   It's going to rain.
Student 2:   It's going to be hot.
Student 3:   It's going to be foggy.
    etc.

2. Scrambled Dialog

a. Write each line of the model conversation on a separate card.

b. Distribute the cards to students and have them practice saying their lines, then talk with each other to figure out what the correct order of the lines should be.

c. Have them present the dialog to the class, each student in turn reading his or her line. Have the class decide if it's in the correct order. Then practice the dialog with the class.

3. Let's Talk!

a. For homework, have each student make a list of several things he or she wants to do next year. Encourage students to use dictionaries to find new words to express their real-life goals.

b. In the next class, have students present their ideas conversationally. Call on pairs of students to ask and answer:

A. What do you want to do next year?
B. Next year I want to (learn German, visit my aunt in Mexico, and buy a bicycle).

c. Practice "He/She wants to " _____ ." After a few students have presented their ideas, talk about them:

A. What does (Bob) want to do next year?
B. He wants to _____ .

4. Common Goals

This is an extension of the prior activity.

a. Put the following on the board:

Next year I want to _____ .
Next year he/she wants to _____ .
Next year we both want to _____ .

b. Divide the class into pairs.

c. Have students interview each other about what they want to do next year. The object is for students to find two things that are different and one thing they have in common and then report back to the class. For example:

I want to go to Mexico for vacation.
She wants to get her driver's license.
We both want to learn a lot of English.

5. Be a Weather Forecaster!

a. Bring to class a map of your country or draw one on the board.

b. Have students volunteer to be *weather forecasters* and come to the front of the room and present the weather forecast while pointing to the map.

6. Dialog Builder!

a. Divide the class into pairs.

b. Write a line on the board from a conversation, such as the following:

That's strange! According to the newspaper, it's going to _____ .

c. Have each pair create a conversation incorporating that line. Students can begin and end their conversations any way they wish, but they must include that line in their dialogs.

d. Call on students to present their conversations to the class.

Text Pages 134–135: What Time Is It?

FOCUS

- Time Expressions
- Review of the Present Continuous Tense
- Review of Going to, Have to, Want to

GETTING READY

Practice time expressions using a large clock or clock face with movable hands to display the time.

1. Review the numbers 1–12.

2. Introduce the time expressions for each hour, as you point to the hands of the clock.

  > It's one o'clock.
  > It's two o'clock.
  > It's three o'clock.
  > .
  > .
  > .
  > It's twelve o'clock.
  > It's (twelve o'clock) noon.
  > It's (twelve o'clock) midnight.

  a. Say each new expression one or more times.

  b. Have students repeat chorally and individually.

  c. Practice conversationally. Ask students: "What time is it?" as you point to the clock.

3. Review numbers 1–60.

4. Using the same approach as above, practice the time expressions for the quarter and half hours.

5. Using the same approach, introduce *noon* and *midnight*.

INTRODUCING THE MODEL

1. Have students look at the model illustration.

2. Set the scene: "A wife and husband are talking. They're going to a movie, and she's upset because he isn't ready."

3. Present the model.

4. Full-Class Repetition.

5. Ask students if they have any questions. Check understanding of new vocabulary: *at (8:00), late (for), leave, shave, Please try to hurry! Oh, no!*

6. Group Choral Repetition.

7. Choral Conversation.

8. Call on one or two pairs of students to present the dialog.

   (For additional practice, do Choral Conversation in small groups or by rows.)

SIDE BY SIDE EXERCISES

Examples

1. A. What time does the football game begin?
   B. It begins at 3:00.
   A. At 3:00?! Oh, no! We're going to be late!
   B. Why? What time is it?
   A. It's 2:30! We have to leave RIGHT NOW!
   B. I can't leave now. I'm taking a bath!
   A. Please try to hurry! I don't want to be late for the football game.

2. A. What time does the bus leave?
   B. It leaves at 7:15.
   A. At 7:15?! Oh, no! We're going to be late!
   B. Why? What time is it?
   A. It's 6:45! We have to leave RIGHT NOW!
   B. I can't leave now. I'm packing my suitcase!
   A. Please try to hurry! I don't want to be late for the bus.

1. **Exercise 1:** Introduce the new vocabulary: *football game.* Call on two students to present the dialog. Then do Choral Repetition and Choral Conversation practice.

2. **Exercise 2:** Introduce the new vocabulary: *pack, suitcase.* Same as above.

3. **Exercises 3–4:** Either Full-Class Practice or Pair Practice.

WORKBOOK

Pages 108–111

EXPANSION ACTIVITIES

1. Role Play: I Think We're Going to Be Late!

Have students role-play new situations, using the same conversational framework at the top of text page 135.

a. Make up situation cues like the ones below and write them on cards.

b. Give cards to pairs of students and allow some time for preparation.

c. Have students present their conversations to the class (with books closed).

d. Sample situation cues:

two roommates
a movie
4:15/3:45
one roommate/
    doing homework
	husband and wife a
	party
	8:00/7:45
	one is talking to the
	    boss on the phone

a parent and child
a baseball game
2:00/1:30
parent/taking/bath

2. Pantomime Role Play

a. Make up role-play cards such as the following:

A wife is upset. She and her husband are going to a concert, but her husband is still taking a shower. She doesn't want to be late.

A mother is upset. She and her son are going to a baseball game, but her son is still sleeping. She doesn't want to be late.

A husband is upset. He and his wife are going on a vacation, but his wife is still packing her suitcase. He doesn't want to be late for the plane.

b. Have pairs of students pantomime their role plays. The class watches and guesses the situation and what the two characters are saying.

3. David's Daily Schedule

a. Put the following cues on the board:

David

6:00 get up
6:30 have breakfast
7:00 take a shower
7:15 get dressed
7:30 go to work

b. Tell the class that this is David's morning schedule. Begin by saying "David gets up every day at 6:30." Then ask about the rest of his routine. For example:

What time does he have breakfast?
What does he do at 7:00?
What does he do at 7:15?
When does he go to work?

c. Talk about *tomorrow*. Ask a few questions, and then call on pairs of students to ask and answer questions about David's schedule for tomorrow. For example:

When is he going to get up tomorrow?
What's he going to do at 6:30?

d. Then divide the class into pairs, and have students ask and answer questions about their own daily schedules.

4. What's Playing at the Movies?

Make copies of the movie schedule from the newspaper and hand them out to the class. Ask about the times that different movies are playing.

5. Bus, Train, and Plane Schedules

Bring to class copies of bus, plane, or train schedules. Ask such questions as:

What time does the train for _____ leave?
What time does the bus for _____ leave?
What time does the flight to _____ leave?
What time does Flight _____ leave?

6. Dialog Builder

a. Divide the class into pairs.

b. Write the following line on the board:

We have to leave RIGHT NOW!

c. Have each pair create a conversation incorporating that line. Students can begin and end their conversations any way they wish, but they must include that line in their dialogs.

d. Call on students to present their conversations to the class.

How to Say It!

Asking the Time: There are several ways to ask for the time. The requests for the time in these two examples are direct questions and would normally be used when people are already engaged in conversation. If someone needs to stop a stranger to ask the time, the question would normally be prefaced with "Excuse me" or "Pardon me."

There are two model conversations. Introduce and practice each separately. For each conversation:

1. Set the scene: "Two co-workers are talking."
2. Present the conversation.
3. Full-Class Repetition.
4. Ask students if they have any questions. Check understanding of vocabulary.
5. Group Choral Repetition.
6. Choral Conversation.
7. Draw various clock faces with different times on the board.
8. Have students practice conversations asking for and telling the time.

READING *The Fortune Teller*

FOCUS

- Future: Going to

NEW VOCABULARY

be in a car accident	fortune teller
become	future
cold (n)	get a haircut
concerned	give
dollar	happen
DVD player	hurt
fall in love	just in case
fire (n)	meet
fire (v)	salary
fortune	take a trip
	win

READING THE STORY

Optional: *Preview the story by having students talk about the story title and/or illustrations. You may choose to introduce new vocabulary beforehand or have students encounter the new vocabulary within the context of the reading.*

1. Have students read silently or follow along silently as the story is read aloud by you, by one or more students, or on the audio program.

2. Ask students if they have any questions. Check understanding of vocabulary.

3. Check students' comprehension, using some or all of the following questions:

Who is Walter visiting?
What's he concerned about?
What's Madame Sophia telling him?
According to Madame Sophia, what's going to happen in January? in February? in March? in April? in May? in June? in July? in August? in September? in October? in November? in December?
Does Walter believe any of this?
What's he going to do, just in case?

✓ READING *CHECK-UP*

Q & A

1. Call on a pair of students to present the models.

2. Have students work in pairs to create new dialogs.

3. Call on pairs to present their new dialogs to the class.

READING EXTENSION

1. Write the following on the board.

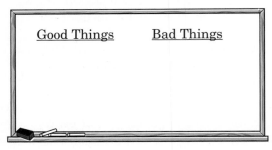

Good Things   Bad Things

2. Tell the students to take out a piece of paper and make a similar chart.

3. Then have students read the text again and complete the chart by writing all the events in Walter's future in the appropriate column.

4. Have the students compare their completed charts.

EXPANSION ACTIVITIES

1. Tic Tac Question Formation

a. Draw a tic tac grid on the board and fill it with question words. For example:

When?	Who?	Where?
What?	Is?	How much?
What kind?	Why?	Are?

b. Divide the class into two teams. Give each team a mark: *X* or *O*.

c. Have each team ask a question about the text that begins with one of the question words and then provide the answer to the question. If the question and answer are correct, the team gets to put its mark in that space. For example:

X Team: When is Walter going to fall in love?
In January.

X	Who?	Where?
What?	Is?	How much?
What kind?	Why?	Are?

d. The first team to mark out three boxes in a straight line—vertically, horizontally, or diagonally—wins.

2. Personal Predictions

a. Have students write predictions about themselves for next year.

b. Collect everyone's predictions, mix them up, read them aloud without saying the person's name, and see if the class can guess whose predictions they are.

PRONUNCIATION

Going to & Want to: In daily English usage, the pronunciation of the verb phrases *going to* and *want to* is reduced to *gonna* and *wanna*.

Focus on Listening

Practice the sentences in the left column. Say each sentence or play the audio one or more times. Have students listen carefully and repeat.

Focus on Pronunciation

Practice the sentences in the right column. Have students say each sentence and then listen carefully as you say it or play the audio.

If you wish, have students continue practicing the sentences to improve their pronunciation.

JOURNAL

Have students write their journal entries at home or in class. Encourage students to use a dictionary to look up words they would like to use. Students can share their written work with other students if appropriate. Have students discuss what they have written as a class, in pairs, or in small groups.

WORKBOOK

Check-Up Test: Pages 112–113

CHAPTER SUMMARY

GRAMMAR

1. Divide the class into pairs or small groups.
2. Have students take turns forming sentences from the words in the grammar boxes. Student A says a sentence, and Student B points to the words from each column that are in the sentence. Then have students switch: Student B says a sentence, and Student A points to the words.

KEY VOCABULARY

Have students ask you any questions about the meaning or pronunciation of the vocabulary. If students ask for the pronunciation, repeat after the student until the student is satisfied with his or her own pronunciation.

EXPANSION ACTIVITIES

1. Do You Remember the Words?

   Check students' retention of the vocabulary depicted on the opening page of Chapter 14 by doing the following activity:

   a. Have students open their books to page 127 and cover the list of vocabulary words.

   b. Tell students to cover the time expressions and look just at the clocks. Point to each clock and have students tell the time.

   c. Have students cover the calendar and see if they can name the months of the year.

   d. Have students cover the list of seasons and see if they can name them while looking just at the illustrations.

   Variation: You can also do this activity as a game with competing teams.

2. Student-Led Dictation

   a. Tell each student to choose a word from the Key Vocabulary list on text page 138 and look at it very carefully.

   b. Have students take turns dictating their words to the class. Everybody writes down that student's word.

   c. When the dictation is completed, call on different students to write each word on the board to check the spelling.

3. Beanbag Toss

   a. Call out a topic from the chapter—for example: *Months of the Year.*

   b. Have students toss a beanbag back and forth. The student to whom the beanbag is tossed must name a word in that category. For example:

   Student 1: January
   Student 2: February
   Student 3: March

   c. Continue until all the words in the category have been named.

END-OF-CHAPTER ACTIVITIES

1. Question Game

a. Write the following sentence on the board:

> Jane is going to move to New York in September because she's going to begin college.

b. Underline different elements of the sentence, and have students create a question based on that portion of the sentence. For example:

> Jane is going to move to New York <u>in September</u> because she's going to begin college.

When is Jane going to move to New York?

> Jane is going to move <u>to New York</u> in September because she's going to begin college.

Where is Jane going to move in September?

> <u>Jane</u> is going to move to New York in September because she's going to begin college.

Who is going to move to New York in September?

> Jane is going to move to New York in September <u>because she's going to begin college</u>.

Why is Jane going to move to New York in September?

c. Continue with other sentences.

2. Board Game

a. On poster boards or on manila file folders, make up game boards with a pathway consisting of separate spaces. You may use any theme or design you wish.

b. Divide the class into groups of 2 to 4 students and give each group a game board, a die, and something to use as a playing piece.

c. Give each group a pile of cards face down with challenges written on them. For example:

> Name three winter months.
> Name three spring months.
> Name three summer months.
> Name three autumn months.
> Name the days of the week.
> Name the four seasons.
> Tell this time in two different ways: 2:15
> Tell this time in two different ways: 10:30
> Tell this time in two different ways: 8:45
> Tell this time in two different ways: 12:00 at night.
> Tell this time in two different ways: 12:00 during the day.

d. Each student in turn rolls the die, moves the playing piece along the game path, and after landing on a space, picks a card, reads the challenge, and answers it. If the answer is correct, that student takes an additional turn.

e. The first student to reach the end of the pathway is the winner.

3. Class Story

a. Find a visual, such as a photograph from a magazine or newspaper, that would be interesting to talk about.

b. Show the visual to the class and ask questions to help students imagine a storyline. For example:

> What's his name?
> What's he doing?
> How does he feel?
> What's going to happen next?

(continued)

c. Have students dictate the story to you as you write it on the board. Ask them how to spell various words as they're dictating the story. Also, ask the class to point out any grammar errors they find in the story.

4. Interview

a. Write the following on the board:

> What are you going to do this weekend?

b. Have pairs of students interview each other and then report back to the class about their partner's weekend plans.

5. Find the Right Person!

a. Collect information about students' plans for the future.

b. Put the information on a handout in the form below:

c. Have students circulate around the room, asking each other questions to identify the correct people.

d. The first student to find all the people, raise his or her hand, and tell the class who they are is the winner of the game.

> Find someone who . . .
>
> 1. is going to move this weekend. _____
> 2. is going to visit her family in Venezuela. _____
> 3. is going to visit Los Angeles this summer. _____
> 4. is going to get a driver's license this year. _____
> 5. is going to get married next June. _____

WORKBOOK ANSWER KEY AND LISTENING SCRIPTS

WORKBOOK PAGE 100

A. WHAT ARE THEY GOING TO DO?

1. He's going to cook.
2. She's going to read.
3. I'm going to study English.
4. They're going to wash their car.
5. We're going to play baseball.
6. He's going to watch TV.

B. WHAT ARE THEY SAYING?

1. What are, going to do
   I'm going to
2. What's, going to do
   He's going to
3. What's, going to do
   She's going to
4. What are, going to do
   They're going to

WORKBOOK PAGE 101

C. WHAT ARE THEY GOING TO DO?

1. going to go
2. going
3. going to go
4. is going to
5. is going to go to
6. are going
7. are going to go to
8. going to, is going to go to

WORKBOOK PAGE 102

E. WHICH WORD DOESN'T BELONG?

1. Monday (The others are months.)
2. September (The others are days of the week.)
3. at once (The others are seasons.)
4. Friday (The others are months.)
5. he (The others are object pronouns.)
6. next week (The others refer to right now.)

F. WHAT'S NEXT?

1. August
2. Wednesday
3. April
4. winter
5. Sunday
6. December

G. MATCH THE SENTENCES

1. c
2. f
3. b
4. a
5. d
6. e

H. LISTENING

Listen and circle the words you hear.

1. I'm going to visit her this year.
2. I'm going to write to my uncle right away.
3. I'm going to call them this Monday.
4. When are you going to cut your hair?
5. I'm going to fix it next Tuesday.
6. We're going to see them this December.
7. They're going to visit us this winter.
8. I'm going to clean it at once.
9. We're going to spend time with them this August.
10. I'm going to wash them immediately.
11. You're going to see us next week.
12. When are you going to call the plumber?

Answers

1. this
2. right away
3. Monday
4. cut
5. Tuesday
6. December
7. winter
8. at once
9. August
10. wash
11. next
12. plumber

WORKBOOK PAGE 103

I. WHAT'S THE QUESTION?

1. are you going to do right now?
2. is she going to baby-sit?
3. are you going next April?
4. are you going to clean it?
5. are they going to do today?
6. are you going to fix the doorbell?
7. is she going to plant flowers?
8. is he going to read his e-mail?
9. are you going to bed now?

J. LISTENING

Listen to the following weather forecasts and circle the correct answers.

Today's Weather Forecast

This is Mike Martinez with today's weather forecast. This afternoon it's going to be cool and cloudy, with temperatures from 50 to 55 degrees Fahrenheit. This evening it's going to be foggy and warm, but it isn't going to rain.

This Weekend's Weather Forecast

This is Barbara Burrows with your weekend weather forecast. Tonight it's going to be clear and warm, with 60 degree temperatures. On Saturday

(continued)

you can swim at the beach. It's going to be sunny and very hot, with temperatures between 90 and 95 degrees Fahrenheit. But take your umbrella with you on Sunday because it's going to be cool, and it's going to rain.

Monday's Weather Forecast

This is Al Alberts with Monday's weather forecast. Monday morning it's going to be cool and nice, but Monday afternoon wear your gloves and your boots because it's going to be very cold and it's going to snow! On Tuesday morning the skiing is going to be wonderful because it's going to be sunny and very warm!

Answers

Today's Weather Forecast

This afternoon:	cool, cloudy
This evening:	foggy, warm

This Weekend's Forecast

Tonight:	clear, warm
Saturday:	sunny, hot
Sunday:	cool, rain

Monday's Weather Forecast

Monday morning:	cool, nice
Monday afternoon:	cold, snow
Tuesday morning:	sunny, warm

WORKBOOK PAGE 104

K. WHAT DOES EVERYBODY WANT TO DO TOMORROW?

1. want to
2. wants to
3. wants to
4. want to
5. want to
6. want to
7. want to

L. BAD WEATHER

1. He wants to go sailing.
   It's going to rain.
2. She wants to take her son to the zoo.
   It's going to be cold.
3. They want to go jogging.
   It's going to snow.
4. He wants to go skiing.
   It's going to be warm.

WORKBOOK PAGE 105

M. YES AND NO

1. They don't want to buy
2. He doesn't want to go
3. I don't want to wash

4. They don't want to play
5. He doesn't want to cook
6. We don't want to study
7. She doesn't want to dance
8. I don't want to work

N. YES AND NO

1. He isn't going to go
2. I'm not going to take
3. We aren't going to go
4. She isn't going to go
5. They aren't going to clean
6. It isn't going to be
7. He isn't going to listen to
8. You aren't going to buy

WORKBOOK PAGE 106

O. WHAT DO THEY WANT TO BE?

1. What does, want to
   She wants to be
2. Where does, want to
   She wants to work
3. What does she want to
   She wants to bake
4. What does, want to
   He wants to be
5. Where does, want to
   He wants to work
6. What does he want to
   He wants to

WORKBOOK PAGE 108

R. WHAT TIME IS IT?

S. WHICH TIMES ARE CORRECT?

1. b	4. a	7. a
2. b	5. b	8. b
3. a	6. b	9. b

T. LISTENING

Listen and write the time you hear.

1. It's seven forty-five.
2. It's six fifteen.
3. It's four thirty.
4. It's nine fifteen.
5. It's midnight.
6. It's five o'clock.

7. It's a quarter to nine.
8. It's a quarter after eight.
9. It's one forty-five.
10. It's noon.
11. It's eleven thirty.
12. It's a quarter to three.

Answers

1. 7:45	7. 8:45
2. 6:15	8. 8:15
3. 4:30	9. 1:45
4. 9:15	10. 12:00
5. 12:00	11. 11:30
6. 5:00	12. 2:45

WORKBOOK PAGE 109

U. ALAN CHANG'S DAY

1. He gets up at 7:15.
2. He eats breakfast at 7:45.
3. He leaves the house at 8:30.
4. He begins work at 9:00.
5. He works at a computer company.
6. He eats lunch in the cafeteria.
7. He leaves work.
8. He eats dinner at 6:00.
9. He watches videos on his new DVD player.

WORKBOOK PAGE 111

X. GrammarSong

1. week	13. December
2. year	14. It's
3. going to	15. after
4. In	16. past
5. summer	17. to
6. fall	18. to wait
7. waiting	19. day
8. I'm going	20. month
9. February	21. right
10. April	22. with
11. July	23. to be
12. September	24. you

WORKBOOK PAGES 112–113

CHECK-UP TEST: Chapters 13-14

A.

1. want to watch TV
   we can't
   have to study
2. wants to play tennis
   she can't
   has to go to the dentist

3. want to go dancing
   I can't
   have to work

B.

1. are	4. do
2. Do	5. does
3. are	6. Is

C.

1. I don't want to teach
2. We aren't going to bed
3. She can't bake
4. He doesn't have to go to
5. They can't speak
6. We don't have to do

D.

1. going to eat
2. she's going to go
3. she's going to have
4. she's going to take the bus

E.

1. What's she going to do tomorrow?
2. Where is he going to play tennis?
3. When are you going to go to the zoo?
4. What are they going to study next year?

F.

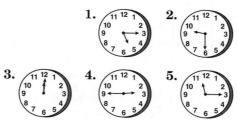

G.

Listen to the story. Fill in the correct times.

Every day at school I study English, science, mathematics, music, and Chinese. English class begins at 8:30. I go to science at 10:15 and mathematics at 11:00. We have lunch at 12:15. We go to music at 12:45, and we have Chinese at 1:30.

Answers

English <u>8:30</u>	Chinese <u>1:30</u>	lunch <u>12:15</u>
mathematics <u>11:00</u>	science <u>10:15</u>	music <u>12:45</u>

 FEATURE ARTICLE *Time Zones*

PREVIEWING THE ARTICLE

1. Have students talk about the title of the article and the accompanying chart.

2. You may choose to introduce the following new vocabulary beforehand, or have students encounter it within the context of the article:

A.M.	New Zealand
ahead	P.M.
behind	time zone
east	west
hour	

READING THE ARTICLE

1. Have students read silently or follow along silently as the article is read aloud by you, by one or more students, or on the audio program.

2. Ask students if they have any questions. Check understanding of vocabulary.

3. Check students' comprehension by having students decide whether the following statements are true or false:

> There are 22 time zones.
> Each time zone is a different hour of the day.
> The time zone that is west of your time zone is an hour ahead.
> The time zone to your east is an hour behind.
> There are four time zones in the United States.
> When it's midnight in London, it's 11:00 A.M. in New Zealand.

 FACT FILE

1. Read the table aloud as the class follows along. Point to each location on the world map as you read the city and country name. Highlight the new vocabulary: *USA; Caracas, Venezuela; Buenos Aires, Argentina; England; Lisbon, Portugal; Spain; Italy; Greece; Istanbul, Turkey; Russia; China; Korea; Japan; Sydney, Australia.*

2. For additional practice do either or both of the following:

   a. Tell students to imagine that they're in New York, and ask:

   > How many hours ahead is Rio de Janeiro?
   > How many hours ahead is Hong Kong?
   > How many hours ahead is Sydney, Australia?
   > How many hours behind is Los Angeles?

   b. Ask students:

   > Which time zone do we live in?
   > What time is it right now?
   > What time is it right now in *(Caracas, Venezuela)*?
   > How about in *(Lisbon, Portugal)*?

   c. Continue naming places around the world and having students determine the time right now.

 BUILD YOUR VOCABULARY!
Occupations

architect	painter
carpenter	pilot
cashier	translator
farmer	waiter
lawyer	waitress

EXPANSION ACTIVITIES

1. Clap in Rhythm

Object: Once a clapping rhythm is established, students must continue naming different occupations.

a. Have students sit in a circle.

b. Establish a steady even beat—one-two-three-four, one-two-three-four—by having students clap their hands to their laps twice and then clap their hands together twice. Repeat throughout the game, maintaining the same rhythm.

c. The object is for each student in turn to name an occupation word each time the hands are clapped together twice. Nothing is said when students clap their hands on their laps.

Note: The beat never stops! If a student misses a beat, he or she can either wait for the next beat or pass to the next student.

2. Miming Game

a. Write down on cards the occupations from text pages 126 and 139.

b. Have students take turns picking a card from the pile and pantomiming the occupation on the card.

c. The class must guess the occupation.

Variation: This can be done as a game with competing teams.

3. Associations

a. Divide the class into pairs or small groups.

b. Call out the name of an occupation and tell students to write down all the words they associate with that occupation. For example:

 cashier: supermarket, store, money
 painter: houses, paint, colors
  pilot: airplanes, travel, uniform

c. Have a student from each pair or group come to the board and write their words.

Variation: Do the activity as a game in which you divide the class into teams. The team with the most number of associations is the winner.

4. Ranking

a. Have students rank these the occupations from *very interesting* to *not interesting*, with the first being *very interesting*.

b. As a class, in pairs, or in small groups, have students compare their lists.

c. Then have students rank the items from *make a lot of money* to *don't' make a lot of money*, and from *work a lot of hours* to *don't work a lot of hours*.

5. Survey

a. Have students conduct a survey by circulating around the room and asking each other, "What do you do?" or, if students are not yet employed, "What occupation do you want to have?"

b. Have students take notes and report back to the class.

c. For homework, have students draw up the survey results in graph form (such as a bar graph or pie chart.) In class, have students share their graphs in small groups before submitting them to you for review.

Variation: Instead of interviewing fellow class members, have students interview friends, family members, or students in another English class.

6. Advantages and Disadvantages

a. Have students draw two columns on a piece of paper. At the top of one column, have students write <u>Good</u>. At the top of the other column, have them write <u>Bad</u>.

b. Dictate the name of an occupation—for example: *farmer.*

c. As a class, have students brainstorm the advantages and disadvantages of that occupation. Write their ideas in columns on the board and have students copy on their papers. For example:

<u>Good</u>	<u>Bad</u>
work outside	work a lot
fun	doesn't make a lot of money

(continued)

d. For homework, have students write a paragraph about any occupation they like. In their paragraphs, have them discuss the advantages and disadvantages of that occupation.

e. Have students discuss their paragraphs with each other.

AROUND THE WORLD *Time and Culture*

1. Have students read silently or follow along silently as the text is read aloud by you, by one or more students, or on the audio program. Check understanding of new vocabulary: *on time, appointment.*

    ### Culture Note

    The expression *on time* represents an important concept in U.S. culture. In the United States people are generally expected to arrive on time (at the invited or appointed time).

2. Have students first work in pairs or small groups, responding to the questions. Then have students tell the class what they talked about. Write any new vocabulary on the board.

LISTENING *Thank You for Calling the Multiplex Cinema!*

Set the scene: "You're listening to a recorded message at the Multiplex Cinema."

LISTENING SCRIPT

Listen and match the theaters and the movies.

Thank you for calling the Multiplex Cinema! The Multiplex Cinema has five theaters with the best movies in town!

Now showing in Theater One: *The Spanish Dancer,* a film from Spain about the life of the famous dancer Carlos Montero. Show times are at one fifteen, three thirty, and seven o'clock.

Now showing in Theater Two: *When Are You Going to Call the Plumber?,* starring Julie Richards and Harry Grant. In this comedy, a husband and wife have a lot of problems in their new house. Show times are at two thirty, four forty-five, and seven fifteen.

Now showing in Theater Three: *The Fortune Teller.* In this film from Brazil, a woman tells people all the things that are going to happen in their lives. Show times are at five o'clock, seven forty-five, and ten fifteen.

Now showing in Theater Four: *The Time Zone Machine,* the exciting new science fiction movie. Professor Stanley Carrington's new machine can send people to different time zones around the world. Show times are at five fifteen, eight o'clock, and ten thirty. There's also a special show at midnight.

Now showing in Theater Five: *Tomorrow Is Right Now.* In this new drama, a truck driver from Australia falls in love with a businesswoman from Paris. Where are they going to live, and what are they going to tell their friends? See it and find out! Show times are at six o'clock, eight thirty, and ten forty-five.

The Multiplex Cinema is on Harrison Avenue, across from the shopping mall. So come and see a movie at the Multiplex Cinema. You're going to have a good time! Thank you, and have a nice day!

Answers

1. c
2. e
3. a
4. d
5. b

EXPANSION ACTIVITY

Describe a Movie!

1. Divide the class into pairs.

2. Have each pair create a description for each of these movie titles:

   The English Lawyer
   The Application
   College Days
   Late for Love
   The Accident

3. Have students share their descriptions with the class.

GLOBAL EXCHANGE

1. Set the scene: "JulieP is writing to her keypal."

2. Have students read silently or follow along silently as the message is read aloud by you, by one or more students, or on the audio program.

3. Ask students if they have any questions. Check understanding of *Sunday school*.

4. Options for additional practice:

   • Have students write a response to JulieP and share their writing in pairs.

   • Have students correspond with a keypal on the Internet and then share their experience with the class.

WHAT ARE THEY SAYING?

FOCUS

• Making Predictions

Have students talk about the people and the situation, and then create role plays based on the scene. Students may refer back to previous lessons as a resource, but they should not simply reuse specific conversations.

Note: You may want to assign this exercise as written homework, having students prepare their role plays, practice them the next day with other students, and then present them to the class.

GRAMMAR

PAST TENSE

I			[t]	I worked.
He				I danced.
She	worked yesterday.		[d]	I cleaned.
It				I played.
We			[ɪd]	I rested.
You				I shouted.
They				

IRREGULAR VERBS

eat – ate
drink – drank
ride – rode
sing – sang
sit – sat

FUNCTIONS

ASKING FOR AND REPORTING INFORMATION

How do you feel today?
  I feel great/fine/okay.
  So-so.
  Not so good.
  I feel terrible.
  I don't feel very well today.

What's the matter?
What seems to be the problem?
  I have *a headache*.
  I have a terrible *headache*.

What did you do yesterday?
  I *worked*.

How *did he get a backache*?

RESPONDING TO INFORMATION

I'm glad to hear that.
I'm sorry to hear that.

GREETING PEOPLE

Hello. This is _____.
  Hello, _____.

CHECKING UNDERSTANDING

A backache?

INDICATING UNDERSTANDING

I see.

INQUIRING ABOUT WANT–DESIRE

Do you want to *make an appointment*?

INQUIRING ABOUT ABILITY

Can you come in *tomorrow at 2 o'clock*?

EXPRESSING GRATITUDE

Thank you very much.

NEW VOCABULARY

Ailments

backache
cough
earache
fever
headache
sore throat
stomachache
toothache

Describing How You Feel

great
not so good
so-so
terrible

Foods

apple pie
cheese
cookies
cracker
dessert
meal
spaghetti

Time Expressions

all afternoon
all day
all evening
all morning
all night
last night
yesterday

Places Around the World

Hawaii

Verbs

arrive
come in
did
dust
enjoy
feel
go home
invite
love
make an appointment
prepare for
rest
serve
show
turn on

Miscellaneous

again
fence
front steps
furniture
glad
guest
inside
seconds

EXPRESSIONS

I'm glad to hear that.
inside and out
What seems to be the problem?
What's the matter?

Text Page 141: Chapter Opening Page

VOCABULARY PREVIEW

You may want to introduce these words before beginning the chapter, or you may choose to wait until they first occur in a specific lesson. If you choose to introduce them at this point, here are some suggestions:

1. Have students look at the illustrations on text page 141 and identify the words they already know.

2. Present the vocabulary. Say each word and have the class repeat it chorally and individually. Check students' understanding and pronunciation of the words.

3. Practice the vocabulary as a class, in pairs, or in small groups. Have students cover the word list and look at the pictures. Practice the words in the following ways:

   - Say a word and have students tell the number of the illustration.
   - Give the number of an illustration and have students say the word.

Text Page 142: How Do You Feel Today?

FOCUS

- Talking About How One Feels
- Describing Common Physical Ailments

GETTING READY

Introduce or review the ailments, using the illustrations in the book, your own visuals, or *Side by Side* Picture Cards 149–157. Point to a visual and say the word. Have students repeat chorally and individually.

INTRODUCING THE MODEL

1. Have students look at the model illustration.
2. Set the scene: "Two co-workers are talking."
3. Present the model.
4. Full-Class Repetition.
5. Ask students if they have any questions. Check understanding of new vocabulary: *feel, not so good, What's the matter? headache.*
6. Group Choral Repetition.
7. Choral Conversation.
8. Call on one or two pairs of students to present the dialog.

   (For additional practice, do Choral Conversation in small groups or by rows.)

SIDE BY SIDE EXERCISES

Examples

1. A. How do you feel today?
   B. Not so good.
   A. What's the matter?
   B. I have a stomachache.
   A. I'm sorry to hear that.

2. A. How do you feel today?
   B. Not so good.
   A. What's the matter?
   B. I have a toothache.
   A. I'm sorry to hear that.

1. **Exercise 1:** Introduce the new word *stomachache.* Call on two students to present the dialog. Then do Choral Repetition and Choral Conversation practice.

2. **Exercise 2:** Introduce the new word *toothache.* Same as above.

3. **Exercises 3–8:** Either Full-Class Practice or Pair Practice.

New Vocabulary

3. backache	6. fever
4. earache	7. cough
5. cold	8. sore throat

WORKBOOK

Pages 114–115

1. Beanbag Toss

Have students toss a beanbag back and forth. The student to whom the beanbag is tossed names an ailment he or she *has*. For example:

Student 1: I have a headache.
Student 2: I have a stomachache.
Student 3: I have a cold.

2. Chain Game

a. Begin the game by saying:

"I feel terrible. I have a headache."

b. Have each student take a turn in which he or she repeats what the person before said and adds a new ailment. For example:

"I feel terrible. I have a headache and a stomachache."

"I feel terrible. I have a headache, a stomachache, and a cold."

3. Telephone: Sam Doesn't Feel Well Today

a. Divide the class into large groups. Have each group sit in a circle.

b. Whisper a short story to one student. For example:

"Sam doesn't feel well today. He has a headache, a sore throat, an earache, and a fever. He's going to visit the doctor."

c. The first student whispers the story to the second student, and so forth around the circle.

d. When the story gets to the last student, that person writes the story down. Is it the same story you started with? The group with the most accurate story at the end wins.

4. Miming

a. Write down on cards the ailments from text page 142 or use *Side by Side* Picture Cards 149–157.

b. Have students take turns picking a card from the pile and pantomiming the ailment on the card.

c. The class must guess what ailment the person has.

Variation: This can be done as a game with competing teams.

5. Picture Story: My Friends Are Sick

Practice talking about how people feel by telling a story and having students ask and answer questions about it.

a. Draw the following nine stick figures on the board and write names under them:

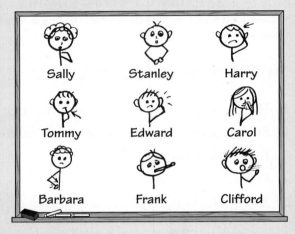

b. Tell this story, pointing to each person as you tell about him or her. "All my friends are sick today. They all feel terrible! What's the matter with them?"

Sally has a *sore throat.*
Stanley has a *stomachache.*
Harry has a *headache.*
Tommy has a *toothache.*
Edward has an *earache.*
Carol has a *cold.*
Barbara has a *backache.*
Frank has a *fever.*
Clifford has a *cough.*

c. Create conversations about the story. First you ask the questions. Then have students ask and answer. For example:

A. How does Sally feel today?
B. Not so good.
A. What's the matter?
B. She has a sore throat.
A. I'm sorry to hear that.

6. Class Story

a. Have students look at one of the illustrations on text page 142.

b. Ask questions about one of the situations to help them imagine a storyline. For example:

> What's this person's name?
> How does he/she feel?
> What's the matter?
> What's going to happen next?

c. Have students dictate the story to you as you write it on the board. As they dictate, ask them how to spell various words. Also, ask the class to point out any grammar errors they find in the story.

How to Say It!

Saying How You Feel: There are many ways to describe how you feel, ranging from very positive (*I feel great!*) to very negative (*I feel terrible*). The phrases on text page 142 are presented in a continuum from positive to negative. When responding to positive news, it's common to say, "I'm glad to hear that!" When responding to negative news it's common to say, "I'm sorry to hear that."

1. Set the scene: "People are talking about how they feel."

2. There are six short conversations. Introduce and practice each before going on to the next.

> A. How do you feel today?
> B. I feel great!
> A. I'm glad to hear that.
>
> A. How do you feel today?
> B. I feel fine.
> A. I'm glad to hear that.
>
> A. How do you feel today?
> B. I feel okay.
> A. I'm glad to hear that.
>
> A. How do you feel today?
> B. So-so.
> A. I'm sorry to hear that.
>
> A. How do you feel today?
> B. Not so good.
> A. I'm sorry to hear that.
>
> A. How do you feel today?
> B. I feel terrible.
> A. I'm sorry to hear that.

3. Full-Class Repetition.

4. Ask students if they have any questions. Check understanding of new vocabulary: *great, so-so, terrible.*

5. Group Choral Repetition.

6. Choral Conversation.

7. Have students circulate around the room practicing conversations with each other.

EXPANSION ACTIVITY

Dialog Builder!

1. Divide the class into pairs.

2. Write the following line on the board:

I'm sorry to hear that.

3. Have each pair create a conversation incorporating that line. Students can begin and end their conversations any way they wish, but they must include that line in their dialogs.

4. Call on students to present their conversations to the class.

5. Repeat the activity with students creating dialogs that incorporate the line *I'm glad to hear that.*

FOCUS

- Past Tense of Regular Verbs
- Pronunciation of *-ed* Endings: [t], [d], [ɪd]

CLOSE UP

RULE:	The word order of a question in the simple past tense is: Question word + auxiliary + subject + base form of the verb. The auxiliary in the simple past tense is *did*.
EXAMPLE:	**What** + **did** + **you** + **do** yesterday?
RULE:	The simple past tense with regular verbs is formed with *-ed*.
EXAMPLES:	I work**ed** yesterday. I play**ed** yesterday I rest**ed** yesterday.
RULE:	When a verb ends in a voiceless consonant sound other than [t], the *ed* ending is pronounced [t].
EXAMPLES:	I worked yesterday. I washed my car yesterday. I fixed my bicycle yesterday.
RULE:	When a verb ends in a voiced sound other than [d], the *ed* ending is pronounced [d].
EXAMPLES:	I cleaned yesterday. I played the piano yesterday. I yawned yesterday.
RULE:	When a verb ends in a [t] or a [d], the *ed* ending is pronounced [ɪd] and forms an additional syllable.
EXAMPLES:	I painted yesterday. I rested yesterday.
SPELLING RULE:	If a verb ends with *y* preceded by a consonant, the *y* changes to *i* when adding *ed*.
EXAMPLES:	cry–cr**ied** study–stud**ied**

SPELLING RULE:	If a verb ends in an *e*, only *d* is added in the simple past tense.

EXAMPLES: type–type**d**
             dance–dance**d**

GETTING READY

1. Introduce the word *yesterday*.

2. Introduce the past tense. Read each pair of sentences at the top of text page 143. Point out that *ed* is added to indicate past tense.

3. Introduce the three different pronunciations of the past tense as they are shown in the three boxes at the top of text page 143.

   a. Begin with the final [t] sound. Say the present and past form of the verb. Then say the verbs again and have students repeat after you chorally and individually.

   b. Practice the verbs with the final [d] sound in the same way, then the verbs with the final [ɪd] sound.

4. Listening practice with books closed:

   a. Write on the board:

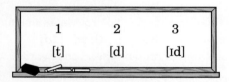

   b. Have students listen as you say several of the verbs on the page in the past tense form. For each verb have students say

   "one" if they hear a final [t] sound.
   "two" if they hear a final [d] sound.
   "three" if they hear a final [ɪd] sound.

INTRODUCING THE MODEL

1. Set the scene: "Two friends are talking."

2. Present the model.

3. Full-Class Repetition.

4. Ask students if they have any questions.

5. Group Choral Repetition.

6. Choral Conversation.

7. Call on one or two pairs to present the dialog.

   (For additional practice, do Choral Conversation in small groups or by rows.)

SIDE BY SIDE EXERCISES

The exercises are presented in three groups: verbs with final [t], [d], and [ɪd] sounds.

Examples

> 1. A. What did you do yesterday?
>   B. I cooked.
>
> 2. A. What did you do yesterday?
>   B. I washed my car.

1. **Exercise 1:** Call on two students to present the dialog. Then do Choral Repetition and Choral Conversation practice.

2. **Exercise 2:** Same as above.

3. **Exercises 3–20:** Either Full Class Practice or Pair Practice.

> **New Vocabulary**
> 18. rest

WORKBOOK

Pages 116–117

EXPANSION ACTIVITIES

1. Practice with Visuals

Use your own visuals for the verbs on text page 143 or the following *Side by Side* Picture Cards:

Picture Card: Verb
- 37: cook
- 38: study
- 40: watch TV
- 42: play the piano
- 43: play the guitar
- 44: play cards
- 45: play baseball
- 49: listen to music
- 50: plant
- 53: fix __ sink
- 54: fix __ car
- 55: fix __ TV
- 56: fix __ bicycle
- 57: clean __ apartment
- 58: clean __ yard
- 61: paint

Picture Card: Verb
- 63: wash __ clothes
- 64: wash __ windows
- 65: wash __ car
- 66: brush __ teeth
- 67: wash __ hair
- 89: bake
- 90: dance
- 122: cry
- 123: smile
- 124: shout
- 127: shiver
- 128: blush
- 129: yawn
- 158: work
- 159: type
- 160: shave
- 161: wait for the bus

a. Hold up a visual and ask, "What did you do yesterday?"

b. Have students answer, using the past of the verb shown in the visual.

Note: Vary the type of verb you show, so students practice the contrasts between the three different past tense pronunciations.

2. Can You Hear the Difference?

a. Write on the board:

Yesterday	Every Day
I fixed my car.	I fix my car.
I cleaned my house.	I clean my house.
I smiled.	I smile.
I waited for the bus.	I wait for the bus.
I studied English.	I study English.
I baked.	I bake.
I talked on the phone.	I talk on the phone.
I planted flowers.	I plant flowers.

b. Choose any sentence from one of the two columns and say it to the class. Have the class listen and identify whether the sentence is about *yesterday* or *every day*.

c. Have students continue the activity in pairs. One student says a sentence, and the other identifies the time. Then have students reverse roles.

d. Write other similar sentences on the board and continue the practice.

3. Category Dictation

a. Have students draw three columns on a piece of paper. Have students write /d/ at the top of the first column, /t/ at the top of the second column, and /Id/ at the top of the third.

b. Dictate various verbs from the text in the past tense, and have students write them in the appropriate column. For example:

/t/	/d/	/Id/
cooked	played	waited
typed	studied	painted

4. Pronunciation Stories: Pete, Ted, and David

Tell the following stories to provide additional practice with the final [t], [d], and [Id] pronunciations of regular past tense verbs.

a. *A Story about Pete – [t]*

1) Write on the board:

```
              Pete
cooked  fixed  talked  washed
```

2) Say: "This is my friend Pete. Yesterday Pete cooked breakfast, he fixed his bicycle, he talked to his sister on the telephone, and he washed his car."

3) Have students tell you what *Pete* did. For example:

   A. What did Pete do yesterday?
   B. He cooked breakfast.

4) Have students pretend to be *Pete*. Have them tell you everything they did:

A. Pete, what did you do yesterday?
B. I cooked breakfast, I fixed my bicycle, I talked to my sister on the telephone, and I washed my car.

b. A Story about Ted – [d]

1) Write on the board:

Ted

cleaned listened played studied

2) Say: "This is my cousin, Ted. Yesterday, Ted cleaned his apartment, he listened to the radio, he played cards, and he studied English."

3) Have students practice talking about *Ted* the same way they did for *Pete*.

c. A Story about David – [Id]

1) Write on the board:

David

planted painted rested waited

2) Say: "This is my neighbor, David. Yesterday David planted flowers, he painted his living room, and then he rested and waited for a telephone call."

3) Have students practice talking about *David* the same way they did for *Pete* and *Ted*.

5. Find the Right Person!

a. Have students write a statement about what they did yesterday, using one of the verbs on text page 143.

b. Put the information on a handout in the following form:

Find someone who . . .
1. cleaned the house.   _____
2. watched a movie on TV.   _____
3. talked to his grandmother. _____
4. fixed her bicycle.   _____
5. worked in the garden.   _____

c. Have students circulate around the room, asking each other "What did you do yesterday?" to identify the above people.

d. The first student to find all the people, raise his or her hand, and tell the class who they are is the winner of the game.

6. Information Gap Handouts

a. Tell students that Charlie and Linda are tired. They moved last week. Make up a calendar for their past week, but divide the information between two different calendars. For example:

Calendar A:

Sun	Mon	Tue	Wed	Thu	Fri	Sat
	cleaned their kitchen		moved to their new house		vacuumed all the rugs	

Calendar B:

Sun	Mon	Tue	Wed	Thu	Fri	Sat
called their landlord		packed their clothes		painted their new kitchen		visited their new neighbors

b. Divide the class into pairs. Give each member of the pair a different calendar. Have students share their information and fill in their calendars. For example:

Student A: What did Charlie and Linda do on Sunday?
Student B: They called their landlord.
Student A: Okay. [*writes the information in Schedule A*].
Student B: What did they do on Monday?

c. The pairs continue until each has a complete calendar.

d. Have students look at their partner's calendar to make sure that they have written the information correctly.

Text Pages 144–145: What's the Matter?

FOCUS

- Past Tense of Regular Verbs
- Introduction of Irregular Verbs:

  drink–drank   sing–sang
  eat–ate   sit–sat
  ride–rode

CLOSE UP

RULE:	Verbs in the simple past tense have the same form with all persons.
EXAMPLES:	I talked. We talked. He talked. You talked. She talked. They talked. It talked.

RULE:	Many verbs have irregular past tense forms.
EXAMPLES:	drink – drank sing – sang eat – ate sit – sat ride – rode

GETTING READY

1. Read all the forms in the right-hand box at the top of text page 144. Have students repeat chorally. For example:

   I worked yesterday.
   We worked yesterday.
   You worked yesterday.

2. Continue the practice with other regular verbs.

INTRODUCING THE MODEL

1. Have students look at the model illustration.

2. Set the scene: "Two people are talking about David."

3. Present the model.

4. Full-Class Repetition.

5. Ask students if they have any questions. Check understanding of new vocabulary: *all day, How did he get it?*

6. Group Choral Repetition.

7. Choral Conversation.

8. Call on one or two pairs of students to present the dialog.

   (For additional practice, do Choral Conversation in small groups or by rows.)

9. Introduce the expressions *all morning, all afternoon, all evening, all night*. Have pairs of students practice the model again, using these expressions in place of *all day*.

SIDE BY SIDE EXERCISES 1–9

Examples

1. A. How does Brian feel?
   B. Not so good.
   A. What's the matter?
   B. He has a sore throat.
   A. A sore throat? How did he get it?
   B. He talked on the telephone all day (morning/afternoon/evening/night).

2. A. How does Linda feel?
   B. Not so good.
   A. What's the matter?
   B. She has a backache.
   A. A backache? How did she get it?
   B. She danced all day (morning/afternoon/evening/night).

1. **Exercise 1:** Call on two students to present the dialog. Then do Choral Repetition and Choral Conversation practice.

2. **Exercise 2:** Same as above.

3. **Exercises 3–9:** Either Full Class Practice or Pair Practice.

> **Key Words for Exercises 3–9:**
>
> 3. headache – studied English
> 4. earache – listened to music
> 5. cold – waited for the bus
> 6. sore throat – shouted
> 7. headache – her baby cried
> 8. earache – my dog barked
> 9. backache – planted flowers

INTRODUCTION OF IRREGULAR VERBS

Introduce the irregular verbs at the top of text page 145:

1. Write the following on the board:

eat – ate

2. Model the following and have students repeat chorally and individually:

   Every day I eat. Yesterday I ate.

3. Continue in the same way with the verbs *sing, drink, sit,* and *ride*.

4. Erase the verbs on the board and give

students additional practice, using word cards or *Side by Side* Picture Cards.

a. Write the base form of the verbs on cards or use the following *Side by Side* Picture Cards: 39 *(eat)*, 46 *(drink)*, 48 *(sing)*, 88 *(ride)*, 162 *(sit)*.

b. Hold up a word card or Picture Card and ask, "What did you do yesterday?" Students answer: "I ate," "I drank," "I sang," etc.

SIDE BY SIDE EXERCISES 10–15

10. A. How does Daniel feel?
    B. Not so good.
    A. What's the matter?
    B. He has a toothache.
    A. A toothache? How did he get it?
    B. He ate candy all day (morning/afternoon/evening/night).

11. A. How does Jennifer feel?
    B. Not so good.
    A. What's the matter?
    B. She has a sore throat.
    A. A sore throat? How did she get it?
    B. She sang all day (morning/afternoon/evening/night).

1. **Exercise 10:** Introduce the new word *candy*. Call on two students to present the dialog. Then do Choral Repetition and Choral Conversation practice.

2. **Exercise 11:** Same as above.

3. **Exercises 12–15:** Either Full-Class Practice or Pair Practice.

> **New Vocabulary**
>
> 12. soda   14. cookies
>
> **Key Words for Exercises 10–15:**
>
> 10. toothache–ate candy
> 11. sore throat–sang
> 12. toothache–drank soda
> 13. backache–sat
> 14. stomachache–ate cookies
> 15. backache–rode his bicycle

WORKBOOK

Pages 118–121

EXPANSION ACTIVITIES

1. Role Play: How Do You Feel?

a. Divide the class into pairs.

b. Have each pair write an original dialog based on the conversations on text pages 144–145. The dialogs should all begin: "How do you feel?"

c. Call on pairs to present their role plays to the class.

2. Pantomime the Problem

a. Make up word cards or use *Side by Side* Picture Cards for the following ailments: *backache, headache, sore throat, cold, earache, stomachache, toothache.*

b. Have a student come to the front of the room, pick up a card or visual, and pantomime the ailment. The class must guess the ailment. For example: "You have a backache."

c. The student must then pantomime a reason why he or she has that ailment, and the class guesses what the reason for the ailment is. For example: "You planted flowers all day."

d. Continue with other students and other ailments.

3. Present, Past, and Future

a. Write the following conversation framework on the board:

> A. Do you _____ very often?
> B. Yes. I _____ yesterday, and I'm going to _____ tomorrow.

b. Model the following conversation:

> A. Do you study English very often?
> B. Yes. I studied English yesterday, and I'm going to study English tomorrow.

c. Have pairs of students create conversations based on this model. As cues for their conversations, either write regular and irregular base forms of verbs on word cards or use the *Side by Side* Picture Cards that were suggested in Expansion Activity 1 for text page 143 and in the *Introduction of Irregular Verbs* in this lesson.

4. Student Stories: A Sick Family

a. Divide the class into pairs or small groups.

b. Have students write a story about a family, in which all the members of the family feel terrible because of what they did yesterday.

c. Have students share their sad stories with the class.

5. Sense or Nonsense?

a. Divide the class into four groups.

b. Make four sets of split sentence cards with beginnings and ends of sentences. For example:

She ate	candy all day.
He sang	Italian songs all night.
They planted	flowers in the garden all day.
We played	tic tac toe all afternoon.
They drank	soda all night.
I cleaned	my apartment all day.
She sat	in a chair all day.
She waited for	the bus all morning.
She studied	English all night.
They baked	pies all morning.

c. Mix up the cards and distribute sets of cards to each group, keeping the beginning and ending cards in different piles.

d. Have students take turns picking up one card from each pile and reading the sentence to the group. For example:

| I cleaned | pies all morning. |

e. That group decides if the sentence makes sense or is nonsense.

f. After all the cards have been picked, have the groups lay out all the cards and put together all the sentence combinations that make sense.

ROLE PLAY *Do You Want to Make an Appointment?*

In this activity, students use the skeletal model to create their own conversations, using any vocabulary they wish.

1. Introduce the new words and expressions: *doctor's office, come in, make an appointment, That's fine, What seems to be the problem?*

2. Have students write their conversations at home for homework and then present them in class the next day.

Example

> A. Doctor's office.
> B. Hello. This is Elsa Montero.
> A. Hello, Mrs. Montero. How are you?
> B. Not so good.
> A. I'm sorry to hear that. What seems to be the problem?
> B. I ate candy all day yesterday, and now I have a terrible stomachache.
> A. I see. Do you want to make an appointment?
> B. Yes, please.
> A. Can you come in tomorrow at three o'clock?
> B. At three o'clock? Yes. That's fine. Thank you.

EXPANSION ACTIVITIES

1. Scrambled Dialog

   a. Divide the class into three groups.

   b. Make three sets of the role-play dialog, filling in the blanks with different information, and writing each line on a separate card.

   c. Give each group one set of the cards, and have the group members reorder the conversation.

2. Unusual Activities

   This activity is designed to contrast the simple present and simple past tenses.

   a. Put this conversational model on the board:

   > A. What did _____ do yesterday?
   > B. _____ all day.
   > A. Does __ usually _____ all day?
   > B. No. But _____ all day yesterday!

   b. Use your own visuals or *Side by Side* Picture Cards of everyday and leisure activities to provide cues for pairs of students to create conversations based on the model. For example:

   (visual: a man sitting in the park)

   > A. What did Bill do yesterday?
   > B. He sat in the park all day.
   > A. Does he usually sit in the park all day?
   > B. No. But he sat in the park all day yesterday!

READING *The Wilsons' Party*

FOCUS

- Past Tense: Regular and Irregular Verbs

NEW VOCABULARY

again	inside
apple pie	inside and out
arrive	invite
cheese	last night
cracker	love (v)
dessert	meal
dust (v)	prepare (for)
enjoy	seconds
fence	serve
front steps	show (v)
furniture	spaghetti
go home	steps
guest	turn on
Hawaii	

READING THE STORY

Optional: Preview the story by having students talk about the story title and/or illustrations. You may choose to introduce new vocabulary beforehand, or have students encounter the new vocabulary within the context of the reading.

1. Have students read silently or follow along silently as the story is read aloud by you, by one or more students, or on the audio program.

2. Ask students if they have any questions. Check understanding of vocabulary.

3. Check students' comprehension, using some or all of the following questions:

> What did Margaret Wilson do in the morning?
> What did Bob do?

What did Mrs. Wilson do?
What did Mr. Wilson do?
What did Margaret do in the afternoon?
What did Bob do?
What did Mr. and Mrs. Wilson do?
What did the guests do after they arrived at the Wilsons' party?
What did they talk about?
What did the Wilsons do at 9:00?
Tell about the meal.
What did everybody do after dinner?
What did Bob do?
What did Margaret do?
What did Mr. and Mrs. Wilson do?
What did everybody do after that?

✓ READING *CHECK-UP*

WHAT'S THE ANSWER?

1. Margaret cleaned the yard, and Bob painted the fence.

2. Mr. Wilson cooked spaghetti for dinner, and Mrs. Wilson baked apple pies for dessert.

3. They arrived at about 7:30.

4. They sat in the living room.

5. They ate cheese and crackers and drank lemonade.

6. She sang.

7. They showed a video of their trip to Hawaii.

READING EXTENSION

1. **True or False?**

Have students tell you whether the following statements are *true* or *false*.

The Wilsons' party was during the day.
The whole Wilson family worked outside in the morning.
The Wilson children cooked dinner and baked pies.
The house looked beautiful at 12:00 noon.
The Wilsons invited a lot of people to the party.
The Wilsons went to Hawaii after dinner.
The Wilson children danced at the party.
The guests stayed at the party for a long time.

2. What's the Order?

a. Dictate these sentences.

> The guests arrived.
> Everyone ate cheese and crackers in the living room.
> The Wilsons cleaned the inside of the house.
> Everyone ate spaghetti.
> Everyone stayed up late.
> Then everyone ate dessert.
> The guests sat in the living room and listened to the children.
> The house looked great.
> Everyone sat at the dining room table.
> The Wilsons worked outside in the yard.
> Everyone turned on the music and danced.

b. Have students work in pairs to put the sentences into the correct order.

c. Call on students to read their reordered sentences to the rest of the class.

EXPANSION ACTIVITY

Tic Tac Question Formation

1. Draw a tic tac grid on the board and fill it with the following question words:

When?	Who?	Where?
What?	When?	Who?
How?	Why?	What?

2. Divide the class into two teams. Give each team a mark: *X* or *O*.

3. Have each team ask a question about the text that begins with one of the question words and then provide the answer to the question. If the question and answer are correct, the team gets to put its mark in that space. For example:

> X Team: When did they finish all their work?
> At 6:00.

X	Who?	Where?
What?	When?	Who?
How?	Why?	What?

4. The first team to mark out three boxes in a straight line—vertically, horizontally, or diagonally—wins.

 LISTENING

Listen and choose the word you hear.

1. We plant flowers in our garden in the spring.
2. I worked at the office all day.
3. They studied English all morning.
4. Mr. and Mrs. Jones sit in their living room all day.
5. They drank lemonade all summer.
6. I waited for the bus all morning.
7. They finish their work at five o'clock.
8. We invited our friends to the party.
9. I eat cheese and crackers.
10. She cleaned her apartment all afternoon.
11. We wash our clothes at the laundromat.
12. He watched TV all evening.

Answers

1. a	**7.** a
2. b	**8.** b
3. b	**9.** a
4. a	**10.** b
5. b	**11.** a
6. b	**12.** b

IN YOUR OWN WORDS

1. Make sure students understand the instructions.

2. Have students do the activity as written homework, using a dictionary for any new words they wish to use.

3. Have students present and discuss what they have written, in pairs or as a class.

PRONUNCIATION

> **Past Tense Endings:** The pronunciation of the *ed* ending of regular past tense verbs depends on the final consonant sound of the base verb. See the *Close Up* notes for text page 143. Remind students that the /t/ and /d/ sound endings do not form an extra syllable, but just add a consonant sound.

Divide the class into pairs or small groups and have students say each verb and put it in the correct column. Then do the activity together as a class.

Focus on Listening

Practice the sentences in the left column. Say each sentence or play the audio one or more times. Have students listen carefully and repeat.

Focus on Pronunciation

Practice the sentences in the right column. Have students say each sentence and then listen carefully as you say it or play the audio.

If you wish, have students continue practicing the sentences to improve their pronunciation.

 JOURNAL

Have students write their journal entries at home or in class. Encourage students to use a dictionary to look up words they would like to use. Students can share their written work with other students if appropriate. Have students discuss what they have written as a class, in pairs, or in small groups.

 CHAPTER SUMMARY

GRAMMAR

1. Divide the class into pairs or small groups.
2. Have students take turns forming sentences from the words in the grammar boxes. Student A says a sentence, and Student B points to the words from each column that are in the sentence. Then have students switch: Student B says a sentence, and Student A points to the words.

KEY VOCABULARY

Have students ask you any questions about the meaning or pronunciation of the vocabulary. If students ask for the pronunciation, repeat after the student until the student is satisfied with his or her own pronunciation.

EXPANSION ACTIVITIES

1. **Do You Remember the Words?**

   Check students' retention of the vocabulary depicted on the opening page of Chapter 15 by doing the following activity:

   a. Have students open their books to page 141 and cover the list of vocabulary words.

   b. Either call out a number and have students tell you the word, or say a word and have students tell you the number.

   Variation: You can also do this activity as a game with competing teams.

   (continued)

EXPANSION ACTIVITIES (Continued)

2. Student-Led Dictation

a. Tell each student to choose a word or phrase from the Key Vocabulary list on text page 148 and look at it very carefully.

b. Have students take turns dictating their words to the class. Everybody writes down that student's word.

c. When the dictation is completed, call on different students to write each word on the board to check the spelling.

3. Beanbag Toss

a. Call out a topic from the chapter—for example: *Ailments*.

b. Have students toss a beanbag back and forth. The student to whom the beanbag is tossed must name a word in that category. For example:

   Student 1: headache
   Student 2: toothache
   Student 3: cough

c. Continue until all the words have been named.

END-OF-CHAPTER ACTIVITIES

1. Question Game

a. Write the following sentences on the board:

> Linda feels terrible today. She has a backache because she worked in the garden all day yesterday.

b. Underline different elements of a sentence, and have students create a question based on that portion of the sentence. For example:

> Linda feels <u>terrible</u> today. She has a backache because she worked in the garden all day yesterday.

How does Linda feel today?

> Linda feels terrible today. <u>She has a backache</u> because she worked in the garden all day yesterday.

What's the matter with Linda?

> Linda feels terrible today. She has a backache <u>because she worked in the garden all day yesterday</u>.

How did Linda get a backache?

> Linda feels terrible today. She has a backache because she worked in the garden <u>all day yesterday</u>.

When did Linda work in the garden?

c. Continue with other sentences.

2. Board Game

a. On poster boards or on manila file folders, make up game boards with a pathway consisting of separate spaces. You may use any theme or design you wish.

b. Divide the class into groups of 2 to 4 students and give each group a game board, a die, and something to use as a playing piece.

c. Give each group a pile of cards face down with questions written on them. For example:

> What is the past tense of *sit*?
> What is the past tense of *ride*?
> What is the past tense of *drink*?
> What is the past tense of *sing*?
> What is the past tense of *eat*?
> How do you pronounce the past tense of *wash*?
> How do you pronounce the past tense of *play*?
> How do you pronounce the past tense of *wait*?
> How do you pronounce the past tense of *fix*?
> How do you pronounce the past tense of *shave*?
> How do you pronounce the past tense of *shout*?

d. Each student in turn rolls the die, moves the playing piece along the game path, and after landing on a space, picks a card, reads the question, and answers it. If the answer is correct, that student takes an additional turn.

e. The first student to reach the end of the pathway is the winner.

3. Miming

a. Write down on cards the following verbs:

dust	invite	serve	turn on
rest	fix	study	yawn
play	listen	clean	drink
cook	eat	paint	shout
plant	wait	cry	sing
smile	shave	brush	type
ride	sit	watch	wash

b. Have students take turns picking a card from the pile and pantomiming an action with that verb.

c. The class must guess what the person is doing and then pronounce the verb in the past tense.

Variation: This can be done as a game with competing teams.

4. Common Activities

a. Put the following on the board:

> Yesterday I _____.
> Yesterday he/she _____.
> Yesterday we both _____.

b. Divide the class into pairs.

c. Have students interview each other about what they did yesterday. The object is for students to find two activities that are different and one that they have in common and then report back to the class. For example:

> Yesterday I rode my bicycle.
> Yesterday Rita washed her car.
> Yesterday we both watched the news on TV.

WORKBOOK ANSWER KEY AND LISTENING SCRIPTS

WORKBOOK PAGE 114

A. WHAT'S THE MATTER?

1. has a cold
2. has a cough
3. have an earache
4. has a stomachache
5. have a sore throat
6. has a headache
7. has a backache
8. have a fever
9. has a toothache

B. LISTENING

Listen to the story. Put the number under the correct picture.

Everybody in my family is sick today.

My parents are sick.
1. My father he has a stomachache.
2. My mother has a backache.

My brother and my sister are sick, too.
3. My sister Alice has an earache.
4. My brother David has a toothache.

My grandparents are also sick.
5. My grandmother has a cold.
6. My grandfather has a sore throat.

7. Even my dog is sick! He has a fever!

Yes, everybody in my family is sick today . . .
everybody except me! How do I feel today?
8. I feel fine!

Answers

5	1	8	3
4	7	2	6

WORKBOOK PAGE 116

D. WHAT DID YOU DO YESTERDAY?

1. cooked
2. cleaned
3. painted
4. shaved
5. typed
6. rested
7. danced
8. shouted
9. studied
10. baked
11. smiled
12. cried

WORKBOOK PAGE 117

E. WHAT'S THE WORD?

1. work
2. played
3. brush
4. planted
5. cook
6. studied
7. painted
8. watch
9. waited

F. LISTENING

Listen and circle the correct answer.

Example 1: I study
Example 2: I played cards.

1. I planted flowers.
2. I shave.
3. I cried.
4. I typed.
5. I work.
6. I shouted.
7. I clean.
8. I studied.
9. I fixed my car.
10. I paint.
11. I smile.
12. I cooked.

Answers

1. yesterday
2. every day
3. yesterday
4. yesterday
5. every day
6. yesterday
7. every day
8. yesterday
9. yesterday
10. every day
11. every day
12. yesterday

WORKBOOK PAGE 118

G. WHAT DID EVERYBODY DO?

1. He cleaned
2. She typed
3. They sang
4. We skated
5. She drank
6. He ate
7. They cried
8. They barked
9. He sat
10. She rode

H. PUZZLE

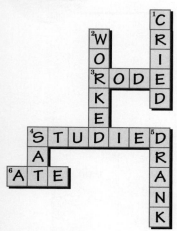

I. PETER'S DAY AT HOME

1. He cooked dinner.
2. He baked a cake.
3. He washed the car.
4. He planted flowers
5. He painted the kitchen.
6. He fixed the sink.
7. He rested.

K. MY GRANDFATHER'S BIRTHDAY PARTY

1.	listened	7.	laughed
2.	danced	8.	smiled
3.	sang	9.	cried
4.	played	10.	talked
5.	sat	11.	drank
6.	looked	12.	ate

L. MATCHING

1.	e	5.	b
2.	c	6.	a
3.	g	7.	d
4.	f		

GRAMMAR

PAST TENSE:
YES/NO QUESTIONS

Did	I he she it we you they	work?

SHORT ANSWERS

Yes,	I he she it we you they	did.

No,	I he she it we you they	didn't.

PAST TENSE:
WH-QUESTIONS

What did	I he she it we you they	do?

TIME EXPRESSIONS

Did you study English	yesterday? yesterday morning? yesterday afternoon? yesterday evening? last night?

FUNCTIONS

ASKING FOR AND REPORTING INFORMATION

Did you *go to the bank this afternoon?*
   Yes, I did.
   No, I didn't.

I had a *stomachache this morning.*
I met *an old friend on the way to class.*

EXPRESSING OBLIGATION

I had to *go to the doctor.*

FORGETTING

I forgot *my English book.*

APOLOGIZING

I'm sorry *I'm late.*

INDICATING UNDERSTANDING

I see.

NEW VOCABULARY

Time Expressions

an hour early
minute
yesterday afternoon
yesterday evening
yesterday morning

Verbs

didn't
get angry
go back home
make
miss
steal

Miscellaneous

backpack
even though
excuse (n)
half a mile
mile
morning exercises
on the way
quick
repair shop
supervisor
thief

EXPRESSIONS

have a good day

VOCABULARY PREVIEW

These are the irregular verb forms that are introduced in Chapter 16. You may want to introduce these past tense forms before beginning the chapter, or you may choose to wait until they first occur in a specific lesson. If you choose to introduce them at this point, here are some suggestions:

1. Write the phrases with their present tense verb forms on the board:

```
 1. get up
 2. take a shower
 3. have breakfast
 4. read the newspaper
 5. do exercises
 6. eat lunch
 7. drive to the supermarket
 8. buy groceries
 9. make dinner
10. write a letter
11. see a movie
12. go to sleep
```

2. Have students look at the illustrations on text page 149. Say each phrase on the board and have the class repeat after you. Check students' understanding and pronunciation of the words.

3. One phrase at a time, erase the present tense form of the verb and replace it with the past tense form. Say the phrase with the past tense form and have students repeat it chorally and individually. Check students' understanding and pronunciation of the verb forms.

4. After students have practiced saying the past tense forms, erase the phrases on the board and have students look again at the illustrations on text page 149.

5. Practice the vocabulary as a class, in pairs, or in small groups. Have students cover the word list and look at the pictures. Practice the words in the following ways:

- Say a phrase and have students tell the number of the illustration.

- Give the number of an illustration and have students say the phrase.

Text Page 150: I Brushed My Teeth

FOCUS

- Yes/No Questions with the Past Tense of Regular Verbs
- Time Expressions

CLOSE UP

RULE:	The past tense describes completed states, actions, and situations in the past. It doesn't matter how recently the action occurred, as long as it has finished by the time of speaking.

EXAMPLES:	Did they study English yesterday morning?
	   Yes, they did.
	
	Did you listen to the news tonight?
	   Yes, I did.

RULE:	The word order of a Yes/No question in the past tense is: Auxiliary verb *(Did)* + subject + base verb + complement.
EXAMPLE:	**Did + you + brush + your hair?**
RULE:	Short answers to Yes/No questions include the subject and the auxiliary verb. The auxiliary verb for the simple past tense is *did*.

EXAMPLES:	Did he wash his windows yesterday morning?
	   Yes, he **did**.
	   No, he **didn't**.

GETTING READY

1. Read the sample past tense sentences in the boxes at the top of text page 150. Have students repeat each one chorally.

2. Write the framework below on the board and practice it, using each of the persons *(I, he, she, we, you, they)*:

   _____ cooked.   Yes, _____ did.
   Did _____ cook? No, _____ didn't.

a. Read each sentence using a pronoun. For example:

   He cooked.
   Did he cook?
   Yes, he did.
   No, he didn't.

b. Have students repeat each line chorally.

INTRODUCING THE MODEL

1. Have students look at the model illustration.

2. Set the scene: "A mother is talking to her son."

3. Present the model.

4. Full-Class Repetition.

   ### Pronunciation Note

   The pronunciation focus of Chapter 16 is the informal pronunciation of *Did you* (text page 156). You may wish to model this pronunciation at this point *(Did you brush your hair this morning? Did you listen to the news this morning?)* and encourage students to incorporate it into their language practice.

5. Ask students if they have any questions. Check understanding of new vocabulary: *brush*.

6. Group Choral Repetition.

7. Choral Conversation.

8. Call on one or two pairs of students to present the dialog.

   (For additional practice, do Choral Conversation in small groups or by rows.)

9. Introduce the time expressions above the model. Have pairs of students practice the model again, using these time expressions in place of *this morning*.

SIDE BY SIDE EXERCISES

Examples

1. A. Did he wash his windows yesterday morning?
   B. No, he didn't. He washed his car.
2. A. Did she paint her kitchen this afternoon?
   B. No, she didn't. She painted her bedroom.

Answers to Exercises 3–6:

3. No, they didn't. They studied Chinese.
4. No, we didn't. We played basketball.
5. No, he didn't. He baked a cake.
6. No, I didn't. I listened to music.

1. **Exercise 1:** Call on two students to present the dialog. Then do Choral Repetition and Choral Conversation practice.

2. **Exercise 2:** Same as above.

3. **Exercises 3–6:** Either Full-Class or Pair Practice.

WORKBOOK

Pages 122–123

EXPANSION ACTIVITIES

1. Yes, I Did/No, I Didn't

a. Use your own visuals or *Side by Side* Picture Cards, or write the following verbs on the board:

study	paint
wash	brush
play	visit
listen to	work
watch	dance
call	ski
plant	skate

b. Have students ask each other Yes/No questions about *yesterday*, using the verbs on the visuals or on the board. For example:

Student 1: Did you study English yesterday?
Student 2: Yes, I did.

Student 3: Did you play cards yesterday?
Student 4: No, I didn't.

2. Find the Right Person!

a. From the prior activity, write down information about what students did yesterday.

b. Put the information on a handout in the following form:

Find someone who . . .

1. listened to the news on the radio. _____
2. watched a football game on TV. _____
3. visited his grandfather. _____
4. played soccer. _____
5. washed the dishes. _____

c. Have students circulate around the room, asking each other Yes/No questions to identify the above people. For example:

Student 1: Did you listen to the news on the radio yesterday?
Student 2: No, I didn't. Did you watch the football game on TV?
Student 1: Yes, I did.

d. The first student to find all the people, raise his or her hand, and tell the class who they are is the winner of the game.

3. Dictation

Dictate the following sentences to the class. Tell students to listen carefully to the endings of the words before they write them.

1. She worked.
2. Did he work?
3. They didn't work.
4. Did you study?
5. He studied.
6. They didn't study.

4. Find Your Match!

a. Make the following set of matching cards:

Did you brush your teeth?	No, I didn't. I brushed my hair.
Did you play the piano?	No, I didn't. I played the guitar.
Did you visit your uncle?	No, I didn't. I visited my cousin.
Did you call the mechanic?	No, I didn't. I called the plumber.
Did you wash your windows?	No, I didn't. I washed my car.
Did you paint your bedroom?	No, I didn't. I painted my kitchen.
Did you study English?	No, I didn't. I studied Spanish.
Did you watch the news?	No, I didn't. I watched a game show.

b. Distribute a card to each student.

c. Have students memorize the sentences on their cards, and then have students walk around the room saying their sentences until they find their match.

d. Then have pairs of students say their matched sentences aloud to the class.

(continued)

5. **Tim and Jim: Opposite Friends**

   a. Begin by saying "I have two friends, Tim and Jim. They're very different. I'm going to tell YOU about Tim, and you're going to tell ME about Jim".

   b. As an example, write these two sentences on the board and read them:

   > Tim worked yesterday.
   > Jim didn't work yesterday.

   c. Have students listen as you read each statement about *Tim*. Then ask a student, "What about Jim?" (Students will need to change the verb to the negative form and make a statement about Jim.)

Teacher:	Tim shaved yesterday morning.
Student:	Jim didn't shave yesterday morning.
Teacher:	Tim cleaned his apartment.
Student:	Jim didn't clean his apartment.

Teacher:	Tim called his grandmother yesterday.
Student:	Jim didn't call his grandmother yesterday.
Teacher:	Tim used his computer yesterday.
Student:	Jim didn't use his computer yesterday.
Teacher:	Tim painted his apartment yesterday.
Student:	Jim didn't paint his apartment yesterday.
Teacher:	Tim cooked dinner last night.
Student:	Jim didn't cook dinner last night.
Teacher:	Tim listened to music last night.
Student:	Jim didn't listen to music last night.

   d. Divide the class into pairs or small groups and ask, "What did *Jim* do yesterday?" Have students make up answers, using any vocabulary they wish, and then share their answers with the class.

Text Page 151: We Went to the Supermarket

FOCUS

- Past Tense Irregular Verbs
- Yes/No Questions with Irregular Verbs
- Time Expressions

CLOSE UP

RULE:	Some verbs have irregular past tense forms.

EXAMPLES:		
	buy	– bought
	do	– did
	drive	– drove
	eat	– ate
	forget	– forgot
	get	– got
	go	– went
	have	– had
	make	– made
	meet	– met
	read	– read
	see	– saw
	steal	– stole
	take	– took
	write	– wrote

GETTING READY

1. Introduce the past tense of *go*: *went*.

2. Read the sample sentences in the boxes at the top of text page 151. Have students repeat chorally.

3. Introduce the irregular past tense forms that are included in the exercises on this page.

a. Write on the board:

take	took
have	had
get	got
make	made
buy	bought
do	did
write	wrote
read	read

b. Say present tense forms and have students say the past tense forms chorally and individually.

INTRODUCING THE MODEL

1. Have students look at the model illustration.

2. Set the scene: "Friends are talking."

3. Present the model.

4. Full-Class Repetition.

5. Ask students if they have any questions. Check understanding of new vocabulary: *went*.

6. Group Choral Repetition.

7. Choral Conversation.

8. Call on one or two pairs of students to present the dialog.

   (For additional practice, do Choral Conversation in small groups or by rows.)

9. Practice the model with other pronouns. Put on the board:

Sally   Bob   Mr. and Mrs. Jones

Call on pairs of students to practice the model again, using these names. For example:

   A. Did Sally go to the bank this afternoon?
   B. No, she didn't. She went to the supermarket.

SIDE BY SIDE EXERCISES

Examples

1. A. Did you take the subway this morning?
   B. No, I didn't. I took the bus.

2. A. Did he have a headache last night?
   B. No, he didn't. He had a backache.

Answers to Exercises 3–8:

3. No, she didn't. She got up at 7:00.
4. No, they didn't. They made breakfast.
5. No, he didn't. He bought a bicycle.
6. No, they didn't. They did their exercises.
7. No, he didn't. He wrote to his grandmother.
8. No, I didn't. I read a book.

1. **Exercise 1:** Call on two students to present the dialog. Then do Choral Repetition and Choral Conversation practice.

2. **Exercise 2:** Same as above.

3. **Exercises 3–8:** Either Full Class Practice or Pair Practice.

   ### Language Note

   Exercise 8: The present and past forms of the verb *read* are spelled the same, but are pronounced differently:

   present tense: [rid]
   past tense: [red]

WORKBOOK

Pages 124–125

EXPANSION ACTIVITIES

1. What's the Verb?

a. Write the following verbs on the board:

go	take	have
get	make	buy
read	write	do
eat	sing	sit
ride	drink	

b. Call out a verb and have students tell you the past form of that verb.

Variation: You can do this activity as a game with competing teams.

2. Tic Tac Verbs

a. Have students draw a tic tac grid on a piece of paper and fill it in with any of the following verbs:

go	take	have
get	make	buy
read	write	do
eat	sing	sit
ride	drink	

b. Call out the past tense of any of these verbs. Tell students to cross out on their grid the present tense form of the verb for which you gave the past form.

c. The first person to cross out three verbs in a straight line—either vertically, horizontally, or diagonally—wins the game.

d. Have the winner call out the words to check the accuracy.

3. Tim and Jim: Opposite Friends

a. Begin by saying "I have two friends, Tim and Jim. They're very different. I'm going to tell YOU about Tim, and you're going to tell ME about Jim."

b. As an example, write these two sentences on the board and read them:

> Tim didn't get up at 7:00 yesterday.
> Jim got up at 7:00 yesterday.

c. Have students listen as you read each statement about *Tim*. Then ask a student, "What about Jim?" (Students will need to change the verb from the negative to the affirmative and make a statement about Jim.)

Teacher:	Tim didn't take a shower yesterday.
Student:	Jim took a shower yesterday.
Teacher:	Tim didn't have breakfast yesterday.
Student:	Jim had breakfast yesterday.
Teacher:	Tim didn't eat lunch at a restaurant.
Student:	Jim ate lunch at a restaurant.
Teacher:	Tim didn't go to the supermarket yesterday.
Student:	Jim went to the supermarket yesterday.
Teacher:	Tim didn't buy food yesterday.
Student:	Jim bought food yesterday.
Teacher:	Tim didn't write to his friend yesterday.
Student:	Jim wrote to his friend yesterday.
Teacher:	Tim didn't make dinner yesterday.
Student:	Jim made dinner yesterday.
Teacher:	Tim didn't read a book last night.
Student:	Jim read a book last night
Teacher:	Tim didn't do his exercises yesterday.
Student:	Jim did his exercises yesterday.
Teacher:	Tim didn't have a good day yesterday.
Student:	Jim had a good day yesterday.

d. Divide the class into pairs or small groups and ask, "What did Jim do yesterday?" Have students make up answers, using any vocabulary they wish, and then share their answers with the class.

4. Chain Game

a. Begin the game by saying:

> "I had a busy day today. I went to the bank."

b. Have each student take a turn in which he or she repeats what the person before said and adds a new activity. For example:

> "I had a busy day today. I went to the bank, and I read a book."

> "I had a busy day today. I went to the bank, I read a book, and I wrote to my friend."

5. Grammar Chain

a. Start the chain game:

> Teacher: I went skiing yesterday.
> (to Student A) Did you go skiing yesterday?

b. Student A must answer, "No, I didn't," make a new statement using the verb *go*, and ask Student B, who then continues the chain. For example:

> Student A: No, I didn't. I went skating.
> (to Student B) Did you go skating yesterday?
> Student B: No, I didn't. I went bowling.
> (to Student C) Did you go bowling yesterday?

6. Scrambled Story: Peter's Terrible Day!

Here is the story *Peter's Terrible Day*.

> Peter went to a party last night.
> He got up very late this morning.
> He missed the train.
> He had to walk to work.
> He arrived at work at 10 o'clock.
> His boss shouted at him.
> Peter had a headache all afternoon.

(continued)

EXPANSION ACTIVITIES (Continued)

a. Write each sentence on a strip of paper. Then cut the words apart. Mix up the words in each sentence and clip them together.

b. Divide the class into small groups. Give each group one sentence to unscramble.

c. When everyone has put the words in correct order, have one student from each group write that group's sentence on the board.

d. Once all the sentences are on the board, have students decide what the correct order should be in order to tell the story *Peter's Terrible Day.*

Variation: Instead of having students write the sentences on the board, have one student from each group come to the front of the room and say the sentence aloud. The class should then decide what the correct order is and have the students line up accordingly and retell the story.

Text Page 152

TALK ABOUT IT! *What Did They Do Yesterday?*

FOCUS

> • Past Tense: Yes/No Questions
> • Past Tense: Short Answers
> • Time Expressions

INTRODUCING THE PEOPLE

1. Call on individual students to read about each person.

2. Ask students if they have any questions. Check understanding of vocabulary.

3. Check students' comprehension, using some or all of the following questions:

   What did Betty do yesterday morning?
   What did Betty do yesterday afternoon?
   When did Betty listen to music?

   When did Bob read the newspaper?
   Where did Bob go yesterday afternoon?
   What did Bob do last night?

   Where did Nick and Nancy go yesterday morning?
   What did Nick and Nancy buy yesterday afternoon?
   What did Nick and Nancy do last night?

   When did Jennifer do her exercises?
   What did Jennifer do yesterday afternoon?
   What did Jennifer do last night?

CONVERSATION PRACTICE

1. There are two conversational models for talking about the characters. Call on a few pairs of students to present each model.

2. Have pairs of students ask and answer questions about the people on the page. This can be done as either Full-Class Practice or Pair Practice. You can also assign it as written homework.

3. Call on pairs to present some of their conversations to the class.

Examples

> A. Did Bob read the newspaper yesterday morning?
> B. Yes, he did.
>
> A. Did Nick and Nancy buy a new car yesterday afternoon?
> B. Yes, they did.
>
> A. Did Jennifer do her exercises yesterday afternoon?
> B. No, she didn't. She did her exercises yesterday morning.
>
> A. Did Nick and Nancy go to the supermarket last night?
> B. No, they didn't. They went to the supermarket yesterday morning.

How About You?

Have students answer the questions, in pairs or as a class. If you do it as pair practice, call on students to report to the class about their conversation partner.

WORKBOOK

Page 126

EXPANSION ACTIVITIES

1. True or False?

a. Have students open their books to text page 152 and look only at the illustrations.

b. Make statements about the characters on text page 152, and have students tell you *true* or *false*. If the statement is false, have students correct it. For example:

> Teacher: Nick and Nancy cleaned their apartment last night.
> Student: True.
>
> Teacher: Betty fixed her bicycle yesterday morning.
> Student: False. Betty didn't fix her bicycle yesterday morning. She fixed her car.

Variation: You can call on students to make true or false statements about the characters in the illustrations and have other students respond.

2. Guess Who!

a. Have students look at the illustrations on text page 152.

b. Make a statement about a character, and have students identify who you're talking about. For example:

> Teacher: He wrote letters last night.
> Student: Bob.
>
> Teacher: She planted flowers yesterday.
> Student: Jennifer.
>
> Teacher: She went to the supermarket yesterday morning.
> Student: Nancy.

3. Memory Game

a. Have students open their books to text page 152 and look at it for one minute.

b. Tell students to close their books and see how much they can remember about the people. Make statements about the characters on text page 152, and have students tell you *true* or *false* based on what they remember.

Variation: You can do the activity as a game with competing teams.

4. Tic Tac Question Formation

a. Draw a tic tac grid on the board and fill it with the following question words:

When?	Who?	Did he?
What?	Did she?	When?
Did they?	What?	When?

b. Divide the class into two teams. Give each team a mark: *X* or *O*.

c. Have each team ask a question that begins with one of the question words and then provide the answer to the question. If the question and answer are correct, the team puts its mark in that space. For example:

> X Team: When did Nick and Nancy buy a new car?
> They bought a new car yesterday afternoon.

X?	Who?	Did he?
What?	Did she?	When?
Did they?	What?	When?

d. The first team to mark out three boxes in a straight line—vertically, horizontally, or diagonally—wins.

5. Question the Answers

a. Dictate answers such as these to the class:

> He wrote letters.
> They bought a new car.
> She did her exercises.

b. Have students write questions for which these answers would be correct. For example:

> Answer: He wrote letters.
> Question: What did Bob do last night?
>
> Answer: They bought a new car.
> Question: What did Nick and Nancy do yesterday afternoon?
>
> Answer: She did her exercises.
> Question: What did Jennifer do yesterday morning?

c. Have students compare their questions with each other.

Variation: Write the answers on cards. Divide the class into groups and give each group a set of cards.

How to Say It!

> **Giving an Excuse:** When arriving late, it is polite to apologize and give a reason for the tardiness.

1. Set the scene: "An employee and his supervisor are talking."

2. Present the conversation.

3. Full-Class Repetition.

4. Ask students if they have any questions. Check understanding of the word *miss*.

> ### Culture Note
>
> The notion of time is an important concept in U.S. culture. In the United States, people are generally expected to arrive on time at the invited or appointed hour. When people are late, they commonly offer an excuse, giving the reason why they are late.

5. Group Choral Repetition.

6. Choral Conversation.

7. Call on one or two pairs to present the dialog.

 INTERACTIONS

1. Read each excuse, using one of the suggestions in parentheses to complete the sentence. Have students repeat.

2. Ask students if they have any questions. Check understanding of new vocabulary:

miss	go back home
forget–forgot	thief
backpack	steal–stole

3. Call on students to say each excuse, using different vocabulary. For example:

I missed the bus.
I missed the train.
I missed the subway.

4. Divide the class into pairs. Have students practice conversations based on the skeletal model on text page 153. Then call on pairs to present their conversations to the class.

Examples

> A. I'm sorry I'm late. I missed the train.
> B. I see.
>
> A. I'm sorry I'm late. I had a backache.
> B. I see.
>
> A. I'm sorry I'm late. I forgot my backpack and had to go back home and get it.
> B. I see.

 THINK ABOUT IT! *Good Excuses & Bad Excuses*

1. Read the excuses aloud as the class follows along.

2. Ask students if they have any questions. Check understanding of new vocabulary: *meet–met, on the way*.

3. As a class, in pairs, or in small groups, have students discuss good and bad excuses.

4. If you do the activity as pair or group practice, call on students to share their thoughts with the class.

WORKBOOK

Pages 127–128

EXPANSION ACTIVITIES

1. Category Dictation

   a. Have students draw two columns on a piece of paper. At the top of one column, have students write <u>Good Excuses</u>, and at the top of the other column, have them write <u>Bad Excuses</u>.

   b. Dictate various reasons for being late, and have students write them in the appropriate column.

2. Continue the Conversation

   a. Divide the class into pairs.

   b. Have each pair begin a conversation using the skeletal dialog on page 153 and then continue it any way they wish.

   c. Call on pairs to present their conversations to the class.

READING *Late for Work*

FOCUS

- Past Tense

NEW VOCABULARY

an hour early	morning exercises
even though	on time
got (get) angry	quick
half a mile	repair shop
however	rush out of the house
mile	supervisor
minute	

READING THE STORY

Optional: *Preview the story by having students talk about the story title and/or illustrations. You may choose to introduce new vocabulary beforehand, or have students encounter the new vocabulary within the context of the reading.*

1. Have students read silently or follow along silently as the story is read aloud by you, by one or more students, or on the audio program.

2. Ask students if they have any questions. Check understanding of vocabulary.

3. Check students' comprehension. Dictate the following sentences. Have students work in pairs to put the sentences in order. Call on students to read the correct sequence to the class.

> He left his car.
> Victor got up at 6:30.
> He left his home at 7:00.
> He drove to the repair shop.
> He got on the train.

He walked to the train station.
He had a small breakfast.
He arrived 45 minutes late.
He waited for a train.
He took a quick shower.
He got off the train and walked to his office.
He did his exercises for five minutes.

✓ READING *CHECK-UP*

WHAT'S THE ANSWER?

1. No, he didn't.
2. He got up at 6:30.
3. No, he didn't.
4. He left for work at 7:00.
5. Yes, he did.
6. He walked.
7. No, he didn't.
8. Yes, she did.
9. She shouted at him for five minutes.

WHICH IS CORRECT?

1. got up
2. didn't do
3. took
4. didn't leave
5. took
6. didn't get

READING EXTENSION

Have students answer the following questions:

> Why didn't Victor take a long shower?
> Why didn't Victor have a big breakfast?
> What time did he arrive at work this morning?
> How long did he take to get to work?
> Why did his supervisor get angry?

 **LISTENING**

Listen and put a check next to all the things these people did today.

Carla got up early this morning. She took a shower, she had breakfast, and she took the subway to work. She didn't have lunch today. She left work at five thirty, and she met her mother at six o'clock. They had dinner at a restaurant. Then they saw a movie.

Brian had a busy day today. This morning he fixed his car. Then he cleaned his yard. This afternoon he planted flowers, and then he washed his windows. This evening he read the newspaper, and he wrote to his brother. Then he took a bath.

Answers

Carla's Day	*Brian's Day*
✔ got up early	✔ fixed his car
____ got up late	____ fixed his bicycle
____ took a bath	____ cleaned his garage
✔ took a shower	✔ cleaned his yard
✔ had breakfast	____ painted his bedroom
____ had lunch	✔ planted flowers
✔ took the subway	✔ washed his windows
____ took the bus	____ watched TV
____ met her brother	✔ read the newspaper
✔ met her mother	____ read a magazine
✔ had dinner	____ rode his bicycle
____ made dinner	✔ wrote to his brother
✔ saw a movie	____ took a shower
____ saw a play	✔ took a bath

 COMPLETE THE STORY

Have students complete the story with the correct forms of the verbs. This exercise may be assigned as homework.

Answers

1. got
2. went
3. took
4. ate
5. saw
6. bought
7. made
8. sat

EXPANSION ACTIVITY

What's the Order?

Dictate the following sentences. Have students work in pairs to put the sentences in order. Call on students to read the correct sequence to the class.

> She bought groceries at the supermarket.
> She went jogging in the park.
> Shirley and her parents sat in the living room and talked.
> Shirley got up.
> She made a big dinner for her parents.
> She took a long shower.
> She saw a movie.
> She ate a big breakfast.

Variation: Do the activity as a game. The first pair to put the sentences in the correct order is the winning team.

How About You?

Have students answer the questions in pairs or as a class. If you do it as a pair activity, call on students to report about the other person's day off.

PRONUNCIATION

> ***Did you:*** The end sound /d/ of the verb *did* and the beginning vowel sound /y/ of the word *you*, blend to make a /j/ sound when spoken rapidly (*did you—dɪju*).

Focus on Listening

Practice the sentences in the left column. Say each sentence or play the audio one or more times. Have students listen carefully and repeat.

Focus on Pronunciation

Practice the sentences in the right column. Have students say each sentence and then listen carefully as you say it or play the audio.

If you wish, have students continue practicing the sentences to improve their pronunciation.

JOURNAL

Have students write their journal entries at home or in class. Encourage students to use a dictionary to look up words they would like to use. Students can share their written work with other students if appropriate. Have students discuss what they have written as a class, in pairs, or in small groups.

CHAPTER SUMMARY

GRAMMAR

1. Divide the class into pairs or small groups.
2. Have students take turns forming sentences from the words in the grammar boxes. Student A says a sentence, and Student B points to the words from each column that

are in the sentence. Then have students switch: Student B says a sentence, and Student A points to the words.

KEY VOCABULARY

Have students ask you any questions about the meaning or pronunciation of the vocabulary. If students ask for the pronunciation, repeat after the student until the student is satisfied with his or her own pronunciation.

EXPANSION ACTIVITIES

1. Do You Remember the Verbs?

   Check students' retention of the vocabulary depicted on the opening page of Chapter 16 by doing the following activity:

   a. Have students open their books to page 149 and cover the list of verb phrases.

   b. Either call out a number and have students tell you the phrase, or say a phrase and have students tell you the number.

   Variation: You can also do this activity as a game with competing teams.

2. Student-Led Dictation

   a. Tell each student to choose a verb from the Key Vocabulary list on text page 156 and look at it very carefully.

   b. Have students take turns dictating their words to the class. Everybody writes down that student's word.

   c. When the dictation is completed, call on different students to write each word on the board to check the spelling.

END-OF-CHAPTER ACTIVITIES

1. **Question Game**

   a. Write the following sentence on the board:

   > Victor got to work at 10:00 because he had to take his car to the repair shop.

   b. Underline different elements of the sentence, and have students create a question based on that portion of the sentence. For example:

   > <u>Victor</u> got to work at 10:00 because he had to take his car to the auto repair shop.

   Who got to work at 10:00?

   > Victor got to work <u>at 10:00</u> because he had to take his car to the auto repair shop.

   When did Victor get to work?

   > Victor got to work at 10:00 <u>because he had to take his car to</u> the auto repair shop.

   Why did Victor get to work at 10:00?

   > Victor got to work at 10:00 because he had to take his car <u>to the auto repair shop.</u>

   Where did Victor have to take his car?

   c. Continue with other sentences.

2. **Board Game**

   a. On poster boards or on manila file folders, make up game boards with a pathway consisting of separate spaces. You may use any theme or design you wish.

   b. Divide the class into groups of 2 to 4 students and give each group a game board, a die, and something to use as a playing piece.

   c. Give each group a pile of cards face-down with questions written on them. For example:

   > What's the past tense of *buy*?
   > What's the past tense of *do*?
   > What's the past tense of *drive*?
   > What's the past tense of *eat*?
   > What's the past tense of *forget*?
   > What's the past tense of *get*?
   > What's the past tense of *go*?
   > What's the past tense of *have*?
   > What's the past tense of *meet*?
   > What's the past tense of *make*?
   > What's the past tense of *read*?
   > What's the past tense of *see*?
   > What's the past tense of *steal*?
   > What's the past tense of *take*?
   > What's the past tense of *write*?

   d. Each student in turn rolls the die, moves the playing piece along the game path, and after landing on a space, picks a card, reads the question, and answers it. If the answer is correct, that student takes an additional turn.

   e. The first student to reach the end of the pathway is the winner.

3. **Miming: What Did I Do Yesterday?**

   a. Write down on cards the following verbs:

buy	drive	eat	meet
read	see	steal	write
take	sing	ride	drink
sit	forget		

   b. Have students take turns picking a card from the pile and pantomiming the action on the card.

   c. The class must guess what the person *did* yesterday. For example:

   (continued)

You bought something.
You drove.
You met a friend.
You read a book.
You saw a movie.

Variation: This can be done as a game with competing teams.

4. In Common

   a. Put the following on the board:

   Last weekend I _____.
   Last weekend she/he _____.
   Last weekend we both _____.

   b. Divide the class into pairs.

   c. Have students interview each other about what they did last weekend. The object is for students to find two activities that are different and one activity that they have in common and then report back to the class. For example:

   Last weekend I saw the new Tom Harris movie.
   Last weekend she went to a new Brazilian restaurant.
   Last weekend we both studied English.

5. Information Gap Handouts

   a. Tell students that Betty and Bob had a wonderful long weekend in New York. Make up a calendar for their weekend vacation, but divide the information between two different calendars. For example:

   Calendar A:

	Friday	Saturday	Sunday
morning		did exercises in the hotel health club	
afternoon	walked in Central Park		wrote letters to friends
evening		ate dinner at a very nice restaurant	

   Calendar B:

	Friday	Saturday	Sunday
morning	visited a museum		went to church
afternoon		bought a painting	
evening	saw a play		took the train home

   b. Divide the class into pairs. Give each member of the pair a different calendar. Have students share their information and fill in their calendars. For example:

   Student A: What did Betty and Bob do Friday morning?
   Student B: They visited a museum.
   Student A: Okay. [*writes the information in Schedule A*].
   Student B: What did they do Friday afternoon?

   c. The pairs continue until each has a complete calendar.

   d. Have students look at their partner's calendar to make sure that they have written the information correctly.

WORKBOOK ANSWER KEY AND LISTENING SCRIPTS

WORKBOOK PAGE 122

A. CORRECT THE SENTENCE

1. She didn't brush her teeth.
   She brushed her hair.
2. He didn't play the violin.
   He played the piano.
3. They didn't listen to the news.
   They listened to music.
4. She didn't wait for the train.
   She waited for the bus.
5. He didn't fix his fence.
   He fixed his bicycle.
6. They didn't clean their attic.
   They cleaned their yard.
7. He didn't bake a pie.
   He baked a cake.
8. She didn't call her grandmother.
   She called her grandfather.

WORKBOOK PAGE 123

B. ALAN AND HIS SISTER

1. rested
2. work
3. study
4. listened
5. watched
6. talked
7. played
8. listen
9. watch
10. play
11. studied
12. cleaned
13. cooked

C. YES AND NO

1. Yes, he did.
2. No, she didn't.
3. Yes, she did.
4. No, he didn't.
5. Yes, he did.
6. Did Ellen clean
7. Did Alan talk
8. Did Alan cook
9. Did Ellen listen
10. Did Ellen watch
11. Did Alan study

WORKBOOK PAGE 124

D. WHAT DID THEY DO?

1. bought
2. had
3. wrote
4. did
5. took
6. got
7. went
8. read
9. made

E. THEY DIDN'T DO WHAT THEY USUALLY DO

1. didn't write, wrote
2. didn't have, had
3. didn't eat, ate
4. didn't get, got
5. didn't go, went
6. didn't drink, drank
7. didn't make, made
8. didn't take, took
9. didn't buy, bought
10. didn't sit, sat

WORKBOOK PAGE 126

G. WHAT'S THE ANSWER?

1. he did
2. I didn't
3. she did
4. they didn't
5. we did
6. he didn't
7. you did
8. I didn't

H. WHAT'S THE QUESTION?

1. Did she buy
2. Did he have
3. Did you take
4. Did they go
5. Did you sit
6. Did I make

I. LISTENING

Listen and choose the correct response.

1. When did you write to your girlfriend?
2. When does your neighbor wash his car?
3. Who did your parents visit?
4. Where does Irene do yoga?
5. When did your son go to sleep?
6. When do you clean your apartment?
7. Where did you take your grandchildren?
8. What did you make for dinner?
9. When does Carla read her e-mail?
10. When did you get up today?

Answers

1. b
2. a
3. b
4. b
5. a
6. a
7. b
8. b
9. a
10. b

J. I'M SORRY I'M LATE!

1. missed		2. had	
3. forgot		4. met	
5. got up		6. stole	
7. had to		8. went	

K. MATCHING

1. d		7. j	
2. f		8. l	
3. b		9. g	
4. e		10. k	
5. c		11. i	
6. a		12. h	

Teacher's Notes

GRAMMAR

TO BE: PAST TENSE

I He She It	was	
We You They	were	happy.

I He She It	wasn't	
We You They	weren't	tired.

Was	I he she it	
Were	we you they	late?

Yes,	I he she it	was.
	we you they	were.

No,	I he she it	wasn't.
	we you they	weren't.

FUNCTIONS

ASKING FOR AND REPORTING INFORMATION

How about you?

Were you *at the ballgame last night*?
  No, I wasn't. I was *at the movies*.

Did you *sleep well last night*?
  Yes, I did.
  No, I didn't.

Where were you born?
Where did you grow up?
Where did you go to school?
What did you study?
When did you move?
Where?
What did you look like?
What did you do *with your friends*?

Were you *tall*?
Did you have *curly hair*?

INQUIRING ABOUT LIKES/DISLIKES

Did you like *school*?

Who was your favorite *teacher*?
What was your favorite *subject*?

DESCRIBING

We were always *sad*.
Now we're *happy*.

MAKING A RECOMMENDATION

Can you recommend _____?
  Yes. I recommend _____.
Thanks for the recommendation.

NEW VOCABULARY

Adjectives

comfortable
cute
dull
enormous
full
healthy
shiny
tiny
uncomfortable

Verbs

communicate
grow up
recommend
was
wasn't
were
weren't

Personal Hygiene

shampoo
soap
toothpaste

Countries

Peru
United States

Miscellaneous

advertising
armchair
assembly line
back home
ballgame
before
born
business school

commercials
dimple
dog food
elementary school
factory
floor wax
freckles
hero
hobby
paint (n)
recommendation
spare time
still
subject
village
vitamins
window cleaner
word
(six) years old

Text Page 157: Chapter Opening Page

VOCABULARY PREVIEW

You may want to introduce these words before beginning the chapter, or you may choose to wait until they first occur in a specific lesson. If you choose to introduce them at this point, here are some suggestions:

1. Have students look at the illustrations on text page 157 and identify the words they already know.

2. Present the vocabulary. Say each word and have the class repeat it chorally and individually. Check students' understanding and pronunciation of the words.

3. Practice the vocabulary as a class, in pairs, or in small groups. Have students cover the word list and look at the pictures. Practice the words in the following ways:

   - Say a word and have students tell the number of the illustration.
   - Give the number of an illustration and have students say the word.

Text Page 158: PRESTO Commercials

FOCUS

- Introduction of the Past Forms of *To Be*

CLOSE UP

RULE: The verb *to be* in the past tense is irregular.

EXAMPLES:
I **was** sad.   We **were** sad.
My wife **was** sad.   My children **were** sad.
My husband **was** sad.

GETTING READY

Introduce *was* and *were*. Form sentences using the words in the box at the top of text page 158. Say each sentence and have students repeat chorally and individually.

INTRODUCTION THE MODEL

1. Have students look at the model illustration.
2. Set the scene: "This is a TV commercial for PRESTO Vitamins."
3. Present the model.
4. Full-Class Repetition.
5. Ask students if they have any questions. Check understanding of new vocabulary: *before, vitamins, How about you?*

   ### Culture Note

   The following exercises are versions of TV commercials for household products. These types of commercials are common on U.S. television. They often include claims that using the advertised product will improve the viewer's appearance, health, or happiness.

6. Call on one or two students to present the commercial

   (For additional practice, do Choral Repetition in small groups or by rows.)

SIDE BY SIDE EXERCISES

Examples

1. Before our family bought PRESTO Ice Cream, we were always sad.
   I was sad.
   My husband was sad.
   My children were sad, too.
   Now we're happy because WE bought PRESTO Ice Cream. How about you?

2. Before our family bought PRESTO Bread, we were always hungry.
   I was hungry.
   My wife was hungry.
   My children were hungry, too.
   Now we're full because WE bought PRESTO Bread. How about you?

1. **Exercise 1:** Introduce the new word *ice cream*. Call on one or two students to present the commercial. Then do Choral Repetition and Choral Conversation practice.

2. **Exercise 2:** Introduce the new words *bread, full*. Same as above.

3. **Exercises 3–5:** Either Full-Class Practice or Pair Practice.

Page 129

> **New Vocabulary**
>
> 3. soap
> 4. cereal, healthy
> 5. skim milk

4. **Exercise 6:** Have students use the model as a guide to create a new commercial for another PRESTO product, using vocabulary of their choice. Encourage students to use dictionaries to find new words they want to use. This exercise can be done orally in class or for written homework. If you assign it for homework, do one example in class to make sure students understand what's expected. Have students act out their commercials in class the next day.

EXPANSION ACTIVITIES

1. Where Were You?

a. Begin by telling this story:

"Yesterday I really wanted to see you. I called you on the phone, but you weren't there. I went to your house, but you weren't there. *Where were you?*"

b. Use *Side by Side* Picture Cards, your own visuals, or word cards for places around town. Hold up different visuals as you ask students the questions below. Students answer according to the visuals. For example:

Where were you?
I was at the bank.
I was at the movies.

Where were you and (any name)?
We were at the supermarket.
We were at a concert.

Where was (male's name)?
He was in the park.
He was at Stanley's International Restaurant.

Where was (female's name)?
She was at the train station.
She was at the zoo.

2. Can You Hear the Difference?

a. Write on the board:

Today	Yesterday
He's tired.	He was tired.
We're late.	We were late.
She's hungry.	She was hungry.
They're sick.	They were sick.
It's heavy.	It was heavy.

b. Choose a sentence at random from one of the two columns and say it to the class. Have the class listen and identify whether the sentence refers to *today* or *yesterday*.

c. Have students continue the activity in pairs. One student pronounces a sentence, and the other identifies the time. Then have them reverse roles.

d. Write similar sentences on the board and continue the practice.

3. Opposite Match Game

a. Make a set of opposite sentence cards such as the following:

We were tired.	Now we're energetic.
We were sad.	Now we're happy.
We were hungry.	Now we're full.
We were dirty.	Now we're clean.
We were sick.	Now we're healthy.
We were heavy.	Now we're thin.

b. Distribute a card to each student.

c. Have students memorize the sentence on their cards, then walk around the room trying to find their corresponding *opposite* match.

d. Then have pairs of students say their matched sentences aloud to the class.

4. Mystery Word

a. Divide the class into pairs.

b. Give each pair a card with one of the following *mystery words* written on it:

sad	dirty	full	healthy
hungry	sick	happy	heavy
thin	tired	energetic	

c. Have each pair create a sentence in which that word is in final position. For example:

I went to the doctor because I was _____. (sick)
I drank some lemonade because I was _____. (thirsty)

(continued)

EXPANSION ACTIVITIES (Continued)

d. One student from each pair then reads aloud the sentence with the final word missing. The other pairs of students try to guess the missing word.

Variation: Do the activity as a game in which each pair scores a point for identifying the correct mystery word. The pair with the most points wins the game.

Text Page 159: Before I Bought PRESTO Shampoo

FOCUS

- Contrast: Present and Past Forms of *To Be*

INTRODUCING THE MODEL

1. Have students look at the model illustration.
2. Set the scene: "A woman is talking about PRESTO Shampoo."
3. Present the model.
4. Full-Class Repetition.
5. Ask students if they have any questions. Check understanding of new vocabulary: *shampoo*.
6. Call on one or two students to tell about PRESTO Shampoo.

   (For additional practice, do Choral Repetition in small groups or by rows.)

SIDE BY SIDE EXERCISES

Examples

1. Before we bought PRESTO Toothpaste, our teeth were yellow. Now they're white.
2. Before we bought PRESTO Paint, our house was ugly. Now it's beautiful.

1. **Exercise 1:** Introduce the new word *toothpaste*. Call on a student to tell about PRESTO Toothpaste. Then do Choral Repetition.
2. **Exercise 2:** Introduce the new word *paint*. Call on a student to tell about PRESTO Paint. Then do Choral Repetition.
3. **Exercises 3–6:**

   ### New Vocabulary
   3. armchair comfortable, uncomfortable
   4. dog food, tiny, enormous
   5. window cleaner
   6. floor wax, dull, shiny

Introduce the new vocabulary one exercise at a time. Call on one or two students to do each exercise. (For more practice, do Choral Repetition.)

WORKBOOK

Page 130

EXPANSION ACTIVITIES

1. Tic Tac Vocabulary

a. Have students draw a tic tac grid on their papers and then fill in their grids with the following adjectives:

tired	heavy	hungry
tiny	dirty	beautiful
sick	comfortable	dull

b. Tell students that you're going to say the *opposites* of the words in their grids. So when they hear a word, they should look for the *opposite* of that word and cross it out.

c. The first person to cross out three opposites in a straight line—either vertically horizontally, or diagonally—wins the game.

d. Have the winner call out the words to check the accuracy.

2. Concentration: Opposites

a. Write the following adjectives on cards:

sad	happy
dirty	clean
heavy	thin
hungry	full
sick	healthy
tiny	enormous
dull	shiny
comfortable	uncomfortable
tired	energetic
ugly	beautiful

b. Shuffle the cards and place them face down in five rows of 4 each.

c. Divide the class into two teams. The object of the game is for students to find the matching cards. Both teams should be able to see all the cards, since *concentrating* on their location is an important part of playing the game.

d. A student from Team 1 turns over two cards. If they match, the student picks up the cards, that team gets a point, and the student takes another turn. If the cards don't match, the student turns them face down, and a member of Team 2 takes a turn.

e. The game continues until all the cards have been matched. The team with the most correct matches wins the game.

Variation: This game can also be played in groups and pairs.

3. Miming

a. Write down on cards the following adjectives:

hungry	thin	heavy	full
sick	shiny	tired	heavy
comfortable	energetic	uncomfortable	

b. Have students take turns picking a card from the pile and pantomiming the adjective on the card.

c. The class must guess the adjective.

Variation: This can be done as a game with competing teams.

4. Category Dictation

a. Have students draw two columns on a piece of paper. At the top of one column, have students write <u>Now</u>, and at the top of the other column, have them write <u>Before</u>.

b. Dictate sentences such as the following and have students write them in the appropriate column. For example:

<u>Now</u>	<u>Before</u>
I'm tired.	I was tired.
He's sick.	He was sick.
It's clean.	It was clean.
She's comfortable.	She was comfortable.
It's dull.	It was dull.
We're sad.	We were sad
You're happy.	You were happy.

5. More PRESTO Commercials

a. Bring real objects to class and provide key words on the board, such as:

   a PRESTO watch (late/on time)
   a pair of PRESTO shoes (uncomfortable/
      comfortable) (tired/energetic)
   a PRESTO exercise video (thin/heavy)
   a PRESTO coat (cold/warm)
   a PRESTO fan (hot/cool)

b. Give the *products* to students and allow a short time for preparation. Encourage students to expand their commercials and say as much as possible about the *products*.

How to Say It!

Making a Recommendation: People often ask salespeople in stores for their recommendations on items they wish to buy. In this situation, a customer is asking a pharmacist in a drug store to recommend a specific personal care product. It is appropriate to express thanks when given a recommendation.

1. Set the scene: "A customer is talking to a pharmacist in a drug store."

2. Present the conversation.

3. Full-Class Repetition.

4. Ask students if they have any questions. Check understanding of new vocabulary: *recommend, recommendation.*

5. Group Choral Repetition.

6. Choral Conversation.

7. Call on one or two pairs to present the dialog.

8. Have students practice conversations about various products and then present their conversations to the class. Help students with any new vocabulary words they might need in their conversations.

Text Page 160: Were You at the Ballgame Last Night?

FOCUS

- Past Negative Forms of *To Be*

CLOSE UP

RULE:	In informal English, the word *not* usually contracts with *was* and *were*.
EXAMPLES:	Were you at the ballgame? No, I (was not) **wasn't**.
	Was I a quiet baby? No, you (were not) **weren't**.

GETTING READY

Introduce *wasn't* and *weren't*. Form sentences with the words in the grammar box at the top of text page 160. Say each sentence and have students repeat chorally and individually. For example:

I wasn't at home.
He wasn't tired.
They weren't hungry.

INTRODUCING THE MODEL

1. Have students look at the model illustration.
2. Set the scene: "Two friends are talking."
3. Present the model.
4. Full-Class Repetition.

   ### Pronunciation Note

   A pronunciation focus of Chapter 17 is the **Intonation of Yes/No Questions** (text page 164). You should model this intonation at this point and encourage students to incorporate it into their language practice.

   Were you at the ballgame last night?

5. Ask students if they have any questions. Check understanding of new vocabulary: *ballgame*.
6. Group Choral Repetition.
7. Choral Conversation.
8. Call on one or two pairs of students to present the dialog.

   (For additional practice, do Choral Conversation in small groups or by rows.)

SIDE BY SIDE EXERCISES

Examples

1. A. Was Albert happy yesterday?
   B. No, he wasn't. He was sad.

2. A. Were they at home this morning?
   B. No, they weren't. They were at school.

Answers to Exercises 3–9:

3. No, it wasn't. It was hot.
4. No, he wasn't. He was an actor.
5. No, you weren't. You were a noisy baby.
6. No, we weren't. We were at the beach.
7. No, she wasn't. She was late.
8. No, they weren't. They were on time.
9. No, it wasn't. It was bad.

1. **Exercise 1:** Call on two students to present the dialog. Then do Choral Repetition and Choral Conversation practice.

2. **Exercise 2:** Same as above.

3. **Exercises 3–9:** Either Full-Class Practice or Pair Practice.

WORKBOOK

Page 131

EXPANSION ACTIVITIES

1. Sentences Alive!

a. Make up several sentences based on this lesson. For example:

> They were at home this morning.
> She was on time for her plane.
> Your children were late for the school bus.
> You were at the ballgame last night.

b. Write the words to each of these sentences on separate cards.

c. One sentence at a time, distribute the cards randomly to students in the class.

d. Have students decide on the correct word order of the sentence and then come to the front of the room, and make the sentence *come alive* by standing in order while holding up their cards and saying the sentence aloud one word at a time.

e. Have the same students rearrange themselves to make a question and then say it aloud one word at a time.

f. Repeat with other sentences and other students.

2. Grammar Chain

a. Write on the board:

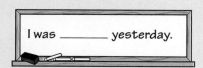

> I was _____ yesterday.

b. Start the chain game.

> Teacher: I was at home yesterday.
> *(to Student A)* Were you at home yesterday?

c. Student A answers, "No, I wasn't," makes a new statement, and asks Student B, who then continues the chain. For example:

> Student A: No, I wasn't. I was at the beach. *(to Student B)* Were you at the beach?
> Student B: No, I wasn't. I was at the ballgame. *(to Student C)* Were you at the ballgame?
> etc.

3. Match the Sentences

a. Make a set of paired sentence cards such as the following:

It wasn't cold.	It was hot.
They weren't at the movies.	They were at the beach.
She wasn't on time.	She was late.
It wasn't noisy.	It was quiet.
They weren't tired.	They were energetic.
He wasn't a teacher.	He was a student.
She wasn't a lawyer.	She was a doctor.

b. Distribute a card to each student.

c. Have students memorize the sentence on their cards, then walk around the room trying to find their corresponding match.

d. Then have pairs of students say their matched sentences aloud to the class.

(continued)

EXPANSION ACTIVITIES (Continued)

4. Do You Remember?

a. Find a picture from a magazine and show it to the class for one minute. The picture should depict a scene that lends itself to being described with several adjectives.

b. Put the picture away, then make several false statements about the picture using *was* and *were*. Students must correct the statements based on what they remember from the picture.

Teacher: The boy in the picture was happy.
Student: No, he wasn't. He was sad.

Teacher: The flowers were yellow.
Student: No, they weren't. They were red.

c. Then have students look at the picture to see if they were right.

Variation: This activity can be done as a game with competing teams.

Text Page 161: Did You Sleep Well Last Night?

FOCUS

- Contrast: Simple Past Tense and Past of *To Be*

INTRODUCING THE MODELS

There are two model conversations. Introduce and practice each model before going on to the next. For each model:

1. Have students look at the model illustration.
2. Set the scene: "Two people are talking."
3. Present the model.
4. Full-Class Repetition.
5. Ask students if they have any questions. Check understanding of vocabulary.
6. Group Choral Repetition.
7. Choral Conversation.
8. Call on one or two pairs of students to present the dialog.

   (For additional practice, do Choral Conversation in small groups or by rows.)

SIDE BY SIDE EXERCISES

Examples

1. A. Did Frank have a big breakfast today?
   B. Yes, he did. He was hungry.
2. A. Did Thelma have a big breakfast today?
   B. No, she didn't. She wasn't hungry.

1. **Exercise 1:** Call on two students to present the dialog. Then do Choral Repetition and Choral Conversation Practice.
2. **Exercise 2:** Same as above.
3. **Exercises 3–8:** Either Full-Class Practice or Pair Practice.

WORKBOOK

Pages 132–133

EXPANSION ACTIVITIES

1. Guided Conversation Match Game

a. Make a set of cards with Speaker A's and Speaker B's lines from the following conversations:

Did you sleep well last night?	Yes, I did. I was tired.
Did Roger sleep well last night?	No, he didn't. He wasn't tired.
Did Frank have a big breakfast today?	Yes, he did. He was hungry.
Did Thelma have a big breakfast today?	No, she didn't. She wasn't hungry.
Did Mr. Chen go to the doctor yesterday?	Yes, he did. He was sick.
Did Mrs. Chen go to the doctor yesterday?	No, she didn't. She wasn't sick.
Did Billy finish his milk?	Yes, he did. He was thirsty.
Did Katie finish her milk?	No, she didn't. She wasn't thirsty.
Did Sonia miss the train?	Yes, she did. She was late.
Did Stuart miss the train?	No, he didn't. He wasn't late.

b. Distribute the cards to students.

c. Have students memorize the sentences on their cards and then walk around the room, saying their sentences until they find their match.

d. Then have pairs of students say their matched sentences aloud to the class.

2. Guess Who!

a. Have students look at the illustrations on text page 161.

b. Describe a character and have students identify who it is. For example:

    Teacher: He had a big breakfast.
    Student: Frank.

    Teacher: She didn't go to the doctor.
    Student: Mrs. Chen.

    Teacher: She missed the train.
    Student: Sonia.

3. Question the Answers!

a. Dictate answers such as the following to the class:

    Yes, she did. She was tired.
    Yes, he did. He was late.
    No, he didn't. He wasn't thirsty.
    Yes, she did. She was sick.

b. Have students write questions for which these answers would be correct. For example:

Answers	Questions
Yes, she did. She was tired.	Did Betty sleep well last night?
Yes, he did. He was late.	Did John miss the train?
No, I didn't. I wasn't thirsty.	Did you finish your milk?
Yes, she did. She was sick.	Did your sister go to the doctor?

c. Have students compare their questions.

4. Find the Right Person!

a. Find out what students did last weekend.

b. Put the information on a handout in the following form:

> Find someone who . . .
>
> 1. saw the new Tim Cruiser movie. _____
> 2. was sick in bed. _____
> 3. visited her grandparents. _____
> 4. made spaghetti for dinner. _____
> 5. was home all weekend. _____

c. Have students circulate around the room, asking each other Yes/No questions to identify the above people.

d. The first student to find all the people, raise his or her hand, and tell the class who they are is the winner of the game.

READING *Maria Gomez*

FOCUS

- Past Tense of *To Be*

NEW VOCABULARY

advertising	grew up (grow up)
assembly line	Peru
back home	six years old
born	still
business school	United States
communicate	village
elementary school	word
factory	

READING THE STORY

Optional: Preview the story by having students talk about the story title and/or illustrations. You may choose to introduce new vocabulary beforehand, or have students encounter the new vocabulary within the context of the reading.

1. Have students read silently or follow along silently as the story is read aloud by you, by one or more students, or on the audio program.

2. Ask students if they have any questions. Check understanding of vocabulary.

3. Check students' comprehension, using some or all of the following questions:

   Where was Maria Gomez born?
   Where did she grow up?
   When did she begin school?
   Did she go to high school?
   Why not?
   When did she go to work?
   Where did she work?

When did Maria's family move to the United States?
Where did the family move first?
Where did they go after Los Angeles?
Was Maria happy?
Why not?
When did she study English?
Does Maria speak English now?
What does she study now?
What does she want to do?
Does she still miss her friends back home?
How does she communicate with them?
How does she feel about her future?

✔ READING *CHECK-UP*

WHAT'S THE ANSWER?

1. She was born in Peru.

2. No, she didn't.

3. She began school when she was six years old.

4. Her family moved to the United States.

5. She missed her friends back in Peru.

6. She's a secretary.

7. She wants to work for an advertising company and write commercials.

8. She communicates with them over the Internet.

WHAT'S THE ORDER?

 4 Maria's family moved to the United States.

 9 Maria studies advertising now.

 1 Maria grew up in a small village.

 6 Maria's family moved to San Francisco.

 3 Maria worked in a shoe factory.

 7 Maria began to study English at night.

 2 Maria went to elementary school.

 5 Maria's family lived in Los Angeles.

 8 Maria got a job as a secretary.

Have students tell you whether the following statements are *true* or *false*. If they're false, have students correct them.

When Maria Gomez was a child, she lived in a big city.
  (*False. She lived in a small village.*)

In Peru, she went to school for twelve years.
  (*False. She went to school for seven years.*)

She worked for four years in Peru.
  (*True.*)

Maria's family moved to the Los Angeles when Maria was seventeen.
  (*True.*)

Maria's family stayed in Los Angeles.
  (*False. They moved to San Francisco.*)

Maria studied at night.
  (*True.*)

Maria works for an advertising company.
  (*False. She wants to work for an advertising company.*)

Maria's old friends are still in Peru.
  (*True.*)

EXPANSION ACTIVITY

Tic Tac Question Formation

1. Draw a tic tac grid on the board and fill it with the following question words.

When?	Who?	Where?
What?	Was?	Did?
How?	Why?	Is?

2. Divide the class into two teams. Give each team a mark: *X* or *O*.

3. Have each team ask a question about the text that begins with one of the question words and then provide the answer to the question. If the question and answer are correct, the team gets to put its mark in that space. For example:

  X Team: When did Maria move to the United States?
  When she was seventeen years old.

X	Who?	Where?
What?	Was?	Did?
How?	Why?	Is?

4. The first team to mark out three boxes in a straight line—vertically, horizontally, or diagonally—wins.

Text Page 163

 LISTENING

Listen and choose the correct answer.

1. Before we bought Captain Crispy Cereal, we were always sick. Now we're always healthy.

2. We bought new chairs for our living room because our old chairs were very uncomfortable. We love our new chairs. They're VERY comfortable.

3. My daughter Lucy didn't finish her milk this morning. She wasn't very thirsty.

4. Fred was very upset this morning. He was late for the bus, and he didn't get to work on time.

5. Hmm. Where are Peter and Mary? They were at work yesterday, but they aren't here today.

6. Our kitchen floor was very dull. Our neighbors recommended Sparkle Floor Wax, and now our kitchen floor isn't dull any more. It's shiny!

Answers

1. a
2. b
3. b
4. b
5. a
6. a

 Autobiography

Have students do the activity as written homework, using a dictionary for any new words they wish to use. Then have students present and discuss what they have written, in pairs or as a class.

 ON YOUR OWN *Do You Remember Your Childhood?*

1. Go over the questions. Introduce the following new vocabulary:

1. cute dimples freckles	4. spare time hobby
3. subject	5. hero

2. For homework, have students write the answers to the questions.

3. In the next class, have students share their childhood remembrances as a class, in pairs, or in small groups. Encourage students to tell about themselves without referring to their written homework.

If you choose to do the activity as pair practice, have students report to the class about the other member of the pair.

Variation: If you do the activity in small groups, have members of each group report to the class about someone in that group. The class has to guess who the *mystery person* is.

WORKBOOK

Pages 134–135

PRONUNCIATION

> **Intonation of Yes/No Questions and WH-Questions:** The intonation of Yes/No questions starts low and rises sharply on the last stressed syllable. In contrast, the intonation of WH-questions starts a little higher and then descends until the final stressed syllable, where it rises sharply.

Focus on Listening

Practice the sentences in the left column. Say each sentence or play the audio one or more times. Have students listen carefully and repeat.

Focus on Pronunciation

Practice the sentences in the right column. Have students say each sentence and then listen carefully as you say it or play the audio.

If you wish, have students continue practicing the sentences to improve their pronunciation.

JOURNAL

Have students write their journal entries at home or in class. Encourage students to use a dictionary to look up words they would like to use. Students can share their written work with other students if appropriate. Have students discuss what they have written as a class, in pairs, or in small groups.

CHAPTER SUMMARY

GRAMMAR

1. Divide the class into pairs or small groups.

2. Have students take turns forming sentences from the words in the grammar boxes. Student A says a sentence, and Student B points to the words from each column that are in the sentence. Then have students switch: Student B says a sentence, and Student A points to the words.

KEY VOCABULARY

Have students ask you any questions about the meaning or pronunciation of the vocabulary. If students ask for the pronunciation, repeat after the student until the student is satisfied with his or her own pronunciation.

WORKBOOK

Check Up Test: Pages 136–137

EXPANSION ACTIVITIES

1. Do You Remember the Words?

Check students' retention of the vocabulary depicted on the opening page of Chapter 17 by doing the following activity:

a. Have students open their books to page 157 and cover the list of vocabulary words.

b. Either call out a number and have students tell you the word, or say a word and have students tell you the number.

Variation: You can also do this activity as a game with competing teams.

2. Student-Led Dictation

a. Tell each student to choose a word from the Key Vocabulary list on text page 164 and look at it very carefully.

b. Have students take turns dictating their words to the class. Everybody writes down that student's word.

c. When the dictation is completed, call on different students to write each word on the board to check the spelling.

3. Letter Game

a. Divide the class into two teams.

b. Say, "I'm thinking of an adjective that starts with *d*."

c. The first person to raise his or her hand and guess correctly [*dull*] wins a point for his or her team.

d. Continue with other letters of the alphabet and other adjectives.

The team that gets the most correct answers wins the game.

END-OF-CHAPTER ACTIVITIES

1. Question Game

a. Write the following sentence on the board:

> Anna stayed home yesterday because she was very sick.

b. Underline different elements of the sentence, and have students create a question based on that portion of the sentence. For example:

> <u>Anna</u> stayed home yesterday because she was very sick.

Who stayed home yesterday?

> Anna stayed home <u>yesterday</u> because she was very sick.

When did Anna stay home?

> Anna stayed home yesterday <u>because she was very sick.</u>

Why did Anna stay home?

c. Continue with other sentences.

2. Board Game

a. On poster boards or on manila file folders, make up game boards with a pathway consisting of separate spaces. You may use any theme or design you wish.

b. Divide the class into groups of 2 to 4 students and give each group a game board, a die, and something to use as a playing piece.

c. Give each group a pile of cards face-down with questions written on them. For example:

What's the opposite of *beautiful*?
What's the opposite of *clean*?
What's the opposite of *comfortable*?
What's the opposite of *dull*?
What's the opposite of *energetic*?
What's the opposite of *enormous*?
What's the opposite of *late*?
What's the opposite of *poor*?
What's the opposite of *sad*?
What's the opposite of *sick*?
What's the opposite of *thin*?
What's the opposite of *quiet*?
What's the opposite of *hungry*?

(continued)

d. Each student in turn rolls the die, moves the playing piece along the game path, and after landing on a space, picks a card, reads the question, and answers it. If the student is correct, that student takes an additional turn.

e. The first student to reach the end of the pathway is the winner.

3. Information Gap Handouts

a. Tell students that Mr. and Mrs. Chen had a busy day yesterday. Write out their activities, but divide the information between two different charts. For example:

Chart A:

	Place	Activity
morning		bought presents for their children
afternoon	health club	
evening		ate a big dinner

Chart B:

	Place	Activity
morning	the mall	
afternoon		went swimming
evening	Stanley's Restaurant	

b. Divide the class into pairs. Give each member of the pair a different chart. Have students share their information and fill in their charts. For example:

Student A: Where were Mr. and Mrs. Chen yesterday morning?
Student B: They were at the mall.
Student A: I see. [writes the information in Chart A].
Student B: What did they do at the mall?

c. The pairs continue until each has a complete chart.

d. Have students look at their partner's chart to make sure that they have written the information correctly.

4. Who Am I?

a. Divide the class into groups of three or four.

b. One student in each group thinks of a famous person in history, identifies the person's nationality, and then *becomes* that person.

c. The other students in the group try to guess who the person is by asking Yes/No questions. For example:

[thinking of Leonardo Da Vinci]

Student 1: I'm a famous Italian person.

Student 2: Were you a famous politician?
Student 1: No, I wasn't.

Student 3: Were you an artist?
Student 1: Yes, I was.

Student 4: Did you paint pictures?
Student 1: Yes, I did.

Student 2: Did you paint a picture on a ceiling?
Student 1: No, I didn't.

Student 3: Did you paint a very famous picture of a woman?
Student 1: Yes, I did.

Student 4: Are you Leonardo Da Vinci?
Student 1: Yes, I am.

d. Have the remaining students in each group take turns thinking of someone famous for the others to guess.

WORKBOOK ANSWER KEY AND LISTENING SCRIPTS

WORKBOOK PAGE 129

A. A TERRIBLE DAY AND A WONDERFUL DAY!

1. were	11. was
2. were	12. were
3. was	13. were
4. was	14. was
5. were	15. were
6. was	16. was
7. was	17. was
8. were	18. were
9. was	19. were
10. were	20. was

B. LISTENING

Listen and circle the word you hear.

1. My husband is thin.
2. She was very hungry.
3. They were tired today.
4. He was very energetic at school today.
5. My wife is at the clinic.
6. Their clothes were clean.
7. My children are very sick today.
8. My parents are home tonight.
9. He was very full this morning.
10. The Lopez family is on vacation.
11. Their neighbors are very noisy.
12. These clothes were dirty.

Answers

1. is	7. are
2. was	8. are
3. were	9. was
4. was	10. is
5. is	11. are
6. were	12. were

WORKBOOK PAGE 130

C. BEFORE AND AFTER

1. was, I'm healthy
2. was, he's happy
3. were, we're full
4. was, she's, comfortable
5. were, you're thin
6. was, it's shiny
7. were, they're clean
8. was, was, I'm tall
9. were, they're enormous

WORKBOOK PAGE 131

D. WHAT'S THE WORD?

1. Were, wasn't, was
2. Were, weren't, were
3. Was, wasn't, was
4. Were, weren't were
5. Were, weren't, were
6. Was, wasn't, was

E. LISTENING

Listen and circle the word you hear.

1. I wasn't busy yesterday.
2. We were at the movies last night.
3. They weren't home today.
4. Tom was on time for his plane.
5. It wasn't cold yesterday.
6. They weren't at the baseball game.
7. My friends were late for the party.
8. The doctor was in her office at noon.

Answers

1. wasn't
2. were
3. weren't
4. was
5. wasn't
6. weren't
7. were
8. was

WORKBOOK PAGE 132

F. WHAT'S THE WORD?

1. did	
2. didn't	18. Did
3. was	19. didn't
4. wasn't	20. was
5. weren't	21. wasn't
6. were	22. didn't
7. weren't	23. were
8. wasn't	24. Did
9. Were	25. didn't
10. was	26. was
11. was	27. Did
12. Did	28. didn't
13. didn't	29. Were
14. didn't	30. didn't
15. was	31. was
16. was	32. were
17. was	33. didn't

H. WHAT ARE THEY SAYING?

1. did	12. freckles
2. were	13. were
3. Were	14. did
4. wasn't	15. sports
5. was	16. basketball
6. short	17. did
7. did	18. were
8. didn't	19. subjects
9. curly	20. Did
10. Did	21. hobby
11. didn't	22. did

I. LISTENING

Listen and choose the correct response.

1. Where were you born?
2. Where did you grow up?
3. What was your favorite subject in school?
4. When did you move here?
5. What did you look like when you were young?
6. Did you have freckles?
7. What do you do in your spare time?
8. Did you have a favorite hero?

Answers

1. b		5. a	
2. b		6. b	
3. a		7. a	
4. b		8. b	

CHECK-UP TEST: Chapters 15–17

A.

1. wasn't, was
2. were, was, wasn't
3. were, weren't, were

B.

1. was, I'm full
2. were, they're enormous
3. were, were, we're heavy
4. was, I'm tired

C.

1. didn't drive, drove
2. didn't arrive, arrived
3. didn't shave, shaved
4. didn't go, went
5. didn't read, read

D.

1. Did he meet
2. Did she ride
3. Did you have
4. Did they make
5. Did you see

E.

1. brushed
2. did
3. sat
4. ate
5. went
6. walked
7. bought
8. took
9. didn't take
10. didn't drive

F.

Listen and circle the word you hear.

Ex. Is Jane rich or poor?

1. It was a nice day today.
2. My friends were thirsty at lunch.
3. Who is your favorite hero?
4. Were Mr. and Mrs. Parker at home last weekend?
5. My new couch is uncomfortable.
6. My cousins were late for their plane.
7. Before I met Howard, I was very sad.
8. Your children are very cute.

Answers

1. was		5. is	
2. were		6. were	
3. is		7. was	
4. were		8. are	

FEATURE ARTICLE
Advertisements

PREVIEWING THE ARTICLE

1. Have students talk about the title of the article and the accompanying photographs.

2. You may choose to introduce the following new vocabulary beforehand, or have students encounter it within the context of the article:

ads	on top of
advertisements	products
advertisers	public
airplane	sign
billboard	sky
carry	spend
everywhere	

READING THE ARTICLE

1. Have students read silently, or follow along silently as the article is read aloud by you, by one or more students, or on the audio program.

2. Ask students if they have any questions. Check understanding of vocabulary.

3. a. Write the following on the board:

> Advertisements You   Advertisements You
> See at Home   See on the Way to Work

b. Have students read the article again and categorize the locations of the advertisements according to the categories on the board.

> Advertisements You   Advertisements You
> See at Home   See on the Way to Work
>   mail   buses
>   television   taxis

4. Divide the class into small groups. Have students brainstorm all the places they see advertisements and then tell their ideas to the class.

FACT FILE *Countries Where Advertisers Spend the Most Money*

1. Before reading the Fact File, ask students, "In which countries do you think advertisers spend the most money?" Have students name ten countries.

2. Read the table aloud as the class follows along. Ask students, "Is this list different from your list? How is your list different?"

3. For additional practice, show the class a world map. Have students locate each country from the Fact File on the map. Ask, "Are these big countries? Why do you think advertisers spend a lot of money in these countries?"

LISTENING *And Now a Word from Our Sponsors!*

Set the scene: "You're watching TV and you hear these advertisements." Introduce these new words: *sponsor, lozenges, dog's fur.*

LISTENING SCRIPT

Listen and match the products.

ANNOUNCER: And now a word from our sponsors.

WOMAN: I had a problem with my teeth. They were very yellow, and I was upset. I went to my dentist, and she recommended Dazzle. So I went to the store and I bought some. Now I brush my teeth with Dazzle every day. My teeth aren't yellow any more. They're white. They're VERY white! Thank you, Dazzle!

ANNOUNCER: Are YOUR teeth yellow? Try Dazzle today!

TED: Bob! This kitchen floor is beautiful!
BOB: Thanks, Ted.
TED: Is it new?
BOB: Oh, no! This is my old kitchen floor.
TED: But it's so shiny!
BOB: That's right, Ted. It IS shiny, because I bought Shiny-Time!
TED: Shiny-Time?
BOB: Yes. Shiny-Time!
ANNOUNCER: That's right, Ted. YOU can have a shiny kitchen floor, too. Use Shiny-Time . . . every time!

WOMAN: Alan? What's the matter?
MAN: I don't know. I jog all the time, but today I'm really tired. Tell me, Julie, you're NEVER tired. You're always energetic. How do you do it?
WOMAN: Energy Plus!
MAN: Energy Plus?
WOMAN: Yes, Alan, Energy Plus! Before I bought Energy Plus, I was always tired like you. But now I'm energetic all the time!
ANNOUNCER: Tired? Try Energy Plus today! You can find it in supermarkets and drug stores everywhere.

PRESIDENT: Thank you. Thank you very much.
ASSISTANT: That was excellent, Mr. President.
PRESIDENT: Thank you, Ron. You know, I have a terrible sore throat.
ASSISTANT: I can hear that, Mr. President. Here. Try one of these.
PRESIDENT: What are they?
ASSISTANT: Lucky Lemon Drops.
PRESIDENT : Lucky Lemon Drops?
ASSISTANT: Yes, Mr. President. They're really good for a sore throat.
PRESIDENT: Thanks, Ron.
ANNOUNCER: Lucky Lemon Drops. They're good for the president! They're good for you!

WOMAN: My dog's fur was dull. It was VERY dull, and my dog was very sad. Then I bought K-9 Shine! Yes, K-9 Shine. I washed my dog with K-9 Shine, and now his fur is shiny! It's very shiny, and my dog is very happy! Try K-9 Shine today! YOUR dog's fur can be shiny, too!

Answers

1. d

2. a

3. e

4. c

5. b

BUILD YOUR VOCABULARY!
Opposites

dark	– light	high	– low
fancy	– plain	long	– short
fast	– slow	neat	– messy
good	– bad	open	– closed
heavy	– light	wet	– dry

1. Have students look at the illustrations and identify any words they already know.

2. Present the vocabulary. Say each word and have the class repeat it chorally and individually. Check students' understanding and pronunciation of the words.

3. Say a word, and have students identify its opposite.

EXPANSION ACTIVITIES

1. Tic Tac Vocabulary

a. Have students draw a tic tac grid on their papers and then fill in their grids with the following adjectives:

plain	short
fast	neat
bad	dry
heavy	open
low	short

b. Tell students that you're going to say the *opposites* of the words in their grids. So when they hear a word, they should look for the opposite of that word and cross it out.

c. The first person to cross out three opposites in a straight line—either vertically horizontally, or diagonally—wins the game.

d. Have the winner call out the words to check the accuracy.

2. Opposites Concentration

a. Write the following adjectives on cards:

dark	light
fancy	plain
fast	slow
good	bad
heavy	light
high	low
long	short
neat	messy
open	closed
wet	dry

b. Shuffle the cards and place them face down in five rows of 4 each.

c. Divide the class into two teams. The object of the game is for students to find the matching cards. Both teams should be able to see all the cards, since *concentrating* on their location is an important part of playing the game.

d. A student from Team 1 turns over two cards. If they match, the student picks up the cards, that team gets a point, and the student takes another turn. If the cards don't match, the student turns them face down, and a member of Team 2 takes a turn.

e. The game continues until all the cards have been matched. The team with the most correct matches wins the game.

Variation: This game can also be played in groups and pairs.

3. Associations

a. Divide the class into pairs or small groups.

b. Call out the an adjective and tell students to write down all the words they associate with that adjective. For example:

> fancy: clothes, car, house
> neat: room, desk, closet
> long: hair, time, visit

c. Have a student from each pair or group come to the board and write their words.

Variation: Do the activity as a game, in which you divide the class into teams. The team with the most number of associations is the winner.

4. True or False Memory Game

a. Find an advertisement from a magazine and show it to the class for one minute.

b. Put the advertisement away, and then make several statements about it using adjectives from this lesson. The statements may be true or false.

c. Students have to decide if each statement is true or false. If the statement is false, have students correct it. For example:

> Teacher: The kitchen in the advertisement was neat.
> Student: True.
>
> Teacher: The door in the kitchen was closed.
> Student: False. It was open.

d. Then have students look at the picture to see if they were right.

AROUND THE WORLD
Shopping

1. Have students read silently or follow along silently as the text is read aloud by you, by one or more students, or on the audio program. Check understanding of new vocabulary: *outdoor, market, order, catalog, home shopping channel, yard sale.*

   ### *Culture Note*

   When people wish to sell things they no longer want or need, they might have a *yard sale*. They display everything they wish to sell in their garage, in their driveway, or in their *yard*. They advertise the sale in the newspaper or on signs they put around their neighborhood. Many people like to shop at yard sales because they might find something they want at a low cost. Everybody loves a bargain!

2. Have students first work in pairs or small groups responding to the question. Then have students tell the class what they talked about. Write any new vocabulary on the board.

EXPANSION ACTIVITIES

1. Ranking

a. Have students rank the ways to shop from *expensive to cheap*, with the first being *most expensive*. For example:

   1. store
   2. catalog
   3. Internet
   4. home shopping channel on TV
   5. outdoor market
   6. yard sale

b. As a class, in pairs, or in small groups, have students compare their lists.

c. Then have students rank the items form *easy to difficult*, from *takes a long time to takes little time*, and from *fun to not fun*.

2. Shopping Survey

a. Have the class brainstorm different items people buy and write their ideas on the board. For example:

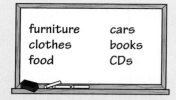

furniture	cars
clothes	books
food	CDs

b. Have each student choose a different type of product and then conduct a survey of students in the class to see how they shop for that product. For example:

   When you want to buy furniture, how do you shop?

   By catalog?　　　　Over the Internet?
   In the store?　　　At yard sales?

c. Have students conduct their surveys by circulating around the room asking each other their questions.

d. For homework, have students draw up the survey results in graph form (for example, a bar graph or pie chart.) In class, have students share their graphs and report their results.

Variation: Instead of interviewing other class members, have students interview friends, family members, or students in another English class.

3. Advantages and Disadvantages

a. Have students draw two columns on a piece of paper. At the top of one column, have them write <u>Good</u>, and at the top of the other column, have them write <u>Bad</u>.

b. Say one of the ways to shop and have students brainstorm ways in which it is good and ways in which it is bad. Write their ideas in the columns and have students copy the list on their papers. For example:

Yard Sales	
<u>Good</u>	<u>Bad</u>
Things are cheap. You have a good time.	They aren't new. Sometimes you don't find what you want.

c. For homework, have students write a paragraph about how they like to shop. In their paragraphs, have them tell about the advantages and disadvantages.

GLOBAL EXCHANGE

1. Set the scene: "TedG is writing to his keypal."

2. Have students read silently or follow along silently as the message is read aloud by you, by one or more students, or on the audio program.

3. Ask students if they have any questions. Check understanding of vocabulary.

4. Options for additional practice:

   - Have students write a response to TedG and share their writing in pairs.

   - Have students correspond with a keypal on the Internet and then share their experience with the class.

WHAT ARE THEY SAYING?

- Advertising

Have students talk about the people and the situation, and then create role plays based on the scene. Students may refer back to previous lessons as a resource, but they should not simply reuse specific conversations.

Note: You may want to assign this exercise as written homework, having students prepare their role plays, practice them the next day with other students, and then present them to the class.

SIDE BY SIDE PICTURE CARDS

Numerical List

1. pen	56. fix ___ bicycle	109. train station	164. bananas
2. book	57. clean ___ apartment	110. sad	165. bread
3. pencil	58. clean ___ yard	111. happy	166. cake
4. notebook	59. feed ___ cat	112. angry	167. carrots
5. bookshelf	60. feed ___ dog	113. nervous	168. cheese
6. globe	61. paint	114. thirsty	169. chicken
7. map	62. do ___ exercises	115. hungry	170. eggs
8. board	63. wash ___ clothes	116. hot	171. fish
9. wall	64. wash ___ windows	117. cold	172. grapes
10. clock	65. wash ___ car	118. sick	173. ketchup
11. bulletin board	66. brush ___ teeth	119. embarrassed	174. lemons
12. computer	67. wash ___ hair	120. tired	175. lettuce
13. table	68. tall – short	121. scared	176. mayonnaise
14. chair	69. young – old	122. cry	177. meat
15. ruler	70. heavy/fat – thin	123. smile	178. mustard
16. desk	71. new – old	124. shout	179. onions
17. dictionary	72. married – single	125. bite ___ nails	180. oranges
18. living room	73. handsome – ugly	126. perspire	181. pears
19. dining room	74. beautiful/pretty –	127. shiver	182. pepper
20. kitchen	ugly	128. blush	183. potatoes
21. bedroom	75. large/big –	129. yawn	184. salt
22. bathroom	small/little	130. cover ___ eyes	185. soy sauce
23. attic	76. noisy – quiet	131. mechanic	186. tomatoes
24. yard	77. expensive – cheap	132. secretary	187. butter
25. garage	78. easy – difficult	133. teacher	188. coffee
26. basement	79. rich – poor	134. baker	189. cookies
27. restaurant	80. sunny	135. truck driver	190. flour
28. bank	81. cloudy	136. chef	191. ice cream
29. supermarket	82. raining	137. singer	192. milk
30. library	83. snowing	138. dancer	193. orange juice
31. park	84. hot	139. actor	194. rice
32. movie theater	85. warm	140. actress	195. soda
33. post office	86. cool	141. have lunch	196. sugar
34. zoo	87. cold	142. have dinner	197. tea
35. hospital	88. ride ___ bicycle	143. go swimming	198. yogurt
36. read	89. bake	144. go shopping	199. airport
37. cook	90. dance	145. go dancing	200. baseball stadium
38. study	91. school	146. go skating	201. concert hall
39. eat	92. hotel	147. go skiing	202. courthouse
40. watch TV	93. gas station	148. go bowling	203. flower shop
41. sleep	94. bus station	149. headache	204. hardware store
42. play the piano	95. clinic	150. stomachache	205. ice cream shop
43. play the guitar	96. fire station	151. toothache	206. motel
44. play cards	97. bakery	152. backache	207. museum
45. play baseball	98. video store	153. earache	208. parking garage
46. drink	99. barber shop	154. cold	209. pet shop
47. teach	100. laundromat	155. fever	210. playground
48. sing	101. drug store	156. cough	211. shoe store
49. listen to music	102. church	157. sore throat	212. toy store
50. plant	103. department store	158. work	213. university
51. listen to the radio	104. police station	159. type	214. high school
52. swim	105. hair salon	160. shave	
53. fix ___ sink	106. book store	161. wait for the bus	
54. fix ___ car	107. health club	162. sit	
55. fix ___ TV	108. cafeteria	163. apples	

Alphabetical List

actor 139
actress 140
airport 199
angry 112
apples 163
attic 23

backache 152
bake 89
baker 134
bakery 97
bananas 164
bank 28
barber shop 99
baseball stadium 200
basement 26
bathroom 22
beautiful 74
bedroom 21
big 75
bite ___ nails 125
blush 128
board 8
book 2
book store 106
bookshelf 5
bread 165
brush ___ teeth 66
bulletin board 11
bus station 94
butter 187

cafeteria 108
cake 166
carrots 167
chair 14
cheap 77
cheese 168
chef 136
chicken 169
church 102
clean ___ apartment 57
clean ___ yard 58
clinic 95
clock 10
cloudy 81
coffee 188
cold 117
cold 154
cold 87
computer 12
concert hall 201
cook 37
cookies 189
cool 86
cough 156
courthouse 202
cover ___ eyes 130
cry 122

dance 90
dancer 138

department store 103
desk 16
dictionary 17
difficult 78
dining room 19
do ___ exercises 62
drink 46
drug store 101

earache 153
easy 78
eat 39
eggs 170
embarrassed 119
expensive 77

fat 70
feed ___ cat 59
feed ___ dog 60
fever 155
fire station 96
fish 171
fix ___ bicycle 56
fix ___ car 54
fix ___ sink 53
fix ___ TV 55
flour 190
flower shop 203

garage 25
gas station 93
globe 6
go bowling 148
go dancing 145
go shopping 144
go skating 146
go skiing 147
go swimming 143
grapes 172

hair salon 105
handsome 73
happy 111
hardware store 204
have dinner 142
have lunch 141
headache 149
health club 107
heavy 70
high school 214
hospital 35
hot 116
hot 84
hotel 92
hungry 115

ice cream 191
ice cream shop 205

ketchup 173
kitchen 20

large 75

laundromat 100
lemons 174
lettuce 175
library 30
listen to music 49
listen to the radio 51
little 75
living room 18

map 7
married 72
mayonnaise 176
meat 177
mechanic 131
milk 192
motel 206
movie theater 32
museum 207
mustard 178

nervous 113
new 71
noisy 76
notebook 4

old 69, 71
onions 179
orange juice 193
oranges 180

paint 61
park 31
parking garage 208
pears 181
pen 1
pencil 3
pepper 182
perspire 126
pet shop 209
plant 50
play baseball 45
play cards 44
play the guitar 43
play the piano 42
playground 210
police station 104
poor 79
post office 33
potatoes 183
pretty 74

quiet 76

raining 82
read 36
restaurant 27
rice 194
rich 79
ride ___ bicycle 88
ruler 15

sad 110
salt 184

scared 121
school 91
secretary 132
shave 160
shiver 127
shoe store 211
short 68
shout 124
sick 118
sing 48
singer 137
single 72
sit 162
sleep 41
small 75
smile 123
snowing 83
soda 195
sore throat 157
soy sauce 185
stomachache 150
study 38
sugar 196
sunny 80
supermarket 29
swim 52

table 13
tall 68
tea 197
teach 47
teacher 133
thin 70
thirsty 114
tired 120
tomatoes 186
toothache 151
toy store 212
train station 109
truck driver 135
type 159

ugly 73, 74
university 213

video store 98

wait for the bus 161
wall 9
warm 85
wash ___ car 65
wash ___ clothes 63
wash ___ hair 67
wash ___ windows 64
watch TV 40
work 158

yard 24
yawn 129
yogurt 198
young 69

zoo 34

Categories

Adjectives
angry 112
beautiful 74
big 75
cheap 77
cold 117
difficult 78
easy 78
embarrassed 119
expensive 77
fat 70
handsome 73
happy 111
heavy 70
hot 116
hungry 115
large 75
little 75
married 72
nervous 113
new 71
noisy 76
old 69, 71
poor 79
pretty 74
quiet 76
rich 79
sad 110
scared 121
short 68
sick 118
single 72
small 75
tall 68
thin 70
thirsty 114
tired 120
ugly 73, 74
young 69

Ailments
backache 152
cold 154
cough 156
earache 153
fever 155
headache 149
sore throat 157
stomachache 150
toothache 151

Classroom
board 8
book 2
bookshelf 5
bulletin board 11
chair 14
clock 10
computer 12
desk 16
dictionary 17
globe 6
map 7
notebook 4
pen 1
pencil 3
ruler 15
table 13
wall 9

Community
airport 199
bakery 97
bank 28
barber shop 99
baseball stadium 200
book store 106
bus station 94
cafeteria 108
church 102
clinic 95
concert hall 201
courthouse 202
department store 103
drug store 101
fire station 96
flower shop 203
gas station 93
hair salon 105
hardware store 204
health club 107
high school 214
hospital 35
hotel 92
ice cream shop 205
laundromat 100
library 30
motel 206
movie theater 32
museum 207
park 31
parking garage 208
pet shop 209
playground 210
police station 104
post office 33
restaurant 27
school 91
shoe store 211
supermarket 29
toy store 212
train station 109
university 213
video store 98
zoo 34

Foods
apples 163
bananas 164
bread 165
butter 187
cake 166
carrots 167
cheese 168
chicken 169
coffee 188
cookies 189
eggs 170
fish 171
flour 190
grapes 172
ice cream 191
ketchup 173
lemons 174
lettuce 175
mayonnaise 176
meat 177
milk 192
mustard 178
onions 179
orange juice 193
oranges 180
pears 181
pepper 182
potatoes 183
rice 194
salt 184
soda 195
soy sauce 185
sugar 196
tea 197
tomatoes 186
yogurt 198

Home
attic 23
basement 26
bathroom 22
bedroom 21
dining room 19
garage 25
kitchen 20
living room 18
yard 24

Occupations
actor 139
actress 140
baker 134
chef 136
dancer 138
mechanic 131
secretary 132
singer 137
teacher 133
truck driver 135

Verbs
bake 89
bite ___ nails 125
blush 128
brush ___ teeth 66
clean ___ apartment 57
clean ___ yard 58
cook 37
cover ___ eyes 130
cry 122
dance 90
do ___ exercises 62
drink 46
eat 39
feed ___ cat 59
feed ___ dog 60
fix ___ bicycle 56
fix ___ car 54
fix ___ sink 53
fix ___ TV 55
go bowling 148
go dancing 145
go shopping 144
go skating 146
go skiing 147
go swimming 143
have dinner 142
have lunch 141
listen to music 49
listen to the radio 51
paint 61
perspire 126
plant 50
play baseball 45
play cards 44
play the guitar 43
play the piano 42
read 36
ride ___ bicycle 88
shave 160
shiver 127
shout 124
sing 48
sit 162
sleep 41
smile 123
study 38
swim 52
teach 47
type 159
wait for the bus 161
wash ___ car 65
wash ___ clothes 63
wash ___ hair 67
wash ___ windows 64
watch TV 40
work 158
yawn 129

Weather
cloudy 81
cold 87
cool 86
hot 84
raining 82
snowing 83
sunny 80
warm 85

GLOSSARY

The number after each word indicates the page where the word first appears in the text.
(adj) = adjective, (adv) = adverb, (n) = noun, (v) = verb.

a 3
a few 42
a little 83
a lot of 49
a quarter after 134
a quarter to 134
about 38
absent 15
according to 133
across from 56
act 48
active 90
activity 90
actor 3
actress 3
ad 165
address 1
adventure movie 95
advertisement 165
advertiser 165
advertising 162
afraid 83
after 101
afternoon 92
again 147
ahead 139
air conditioner 59
airplane 165
airport 63
aisle 77
Alaska 132
all 15
all afternoon 144
all day 64
all evening 144
all morning 144
all night 64
all the time 100
almost 63
alone 92
also 25
always 83
am 11
A.M. 56
American 4
and 11
angry 49
animal 100
annoyed 124
another 54
answer (v) 112

any 62
apartment 4
apartment building 47
apartment number 1
apple pie 146
application 124
application fee 124
application form 124
apply 124
appointment 145
Arabic 81
architect 139
are 2
aren't 38
Argentina 139
argument 49
armchair 159
around the corner from 56
arrive 146
as 104
ask 91
ask for 124
assembly line 162
at 15
at once 130
Athens 13
athlete 3
athletic 90
Atlanta 54
attach 124
attention 77
attic 10
aunt 45
Australia 139
author 95
autumn 127
avenue 57

baby 102
baby-sit 87
back and forth 109
backache 141
backpack 153
bad 112
bake 47
baker 117
bakery 55
ballgame 160
band 50
bank 7

barber shop 55
bark (v) 49
baseball 21
baseball game 129
basement 10
basketball 25
bathrobe 77
bathroom 7
bathtub 110
be 42
beach 23
beautiful 22
because 63
become 137
bed 15
bedroom 7
before 158
begin 132
behind 139
believe 124
belt 67
bench 48
Bengali 97
Berlin 80
between 56
bicycle 30
big 35
bike 90
billboard 165
biography 95
bird 22
birthday 48
birthday party 48
bite (v) 108
black and white 124
blond 102
blouse 67
blush 108
board 8
book 7
bookshelf 8
book store 55
boot 68
bored 42
born 162
borrow 97
boss 38
Boston 82
both 103
bowling 123
boy 77

boyfriend 100
bracelet 68
Brazilian 81
bread 158
breakfast 20
briefcase 68
British Columbia 41
broken 62
Brooklyn 4
brother 39
brother-in-law 54
brush (v) 150
brush their teeth 27
Buenos Aires 139
Buffalo 82
build 115
building 53
bus 82
bus station 55
bus stop 59
business 113
business school 162
business software 120
busy 29
but 42
buy 132
by 111

cafe 98
cafeteria 21
Cairo 81
cake 47
calculator 53
call (v) 41
can (v) 71
Canadian 81
candy 145
can't 118
car 12
car accident 137
Caracas 139
cards 20
carpenter 139
carpet 111
carpool lane 115
carry 165
cartoon 95
cashier 139
cash register 118
cat 29
catalog 166

future **136**

game **48**
game show **95**
garage **10**
garden **92**
gas station **56**
German **80**
get **132**
get a haircut **137**
get angry **154**
get dressed **72**
get married **136**
get together **104**
get up **97**
gift **75**
girlfriend **101**
give **136**
glad **142**
glasses **68**
global **115**
globe **8**
glove **68**
go **89**
go *dancing* **87**
go home **147**
go out **103**
goes **90**
going to **128**
golf **95**
good **42**
grandchildren **45**
granddaughter **45**
grandfather **45**
grandmother **45**
grandparents **45**
grandson **45**
great **142**
Greece **139**
Greek **13**
groceries **155**
grocery store **83**
grow **97**
grow up **162**
guest **146**
guitar **20**

hair **29**
hair salon **55**
half a mile **154**
half past **127**
hand **53**
handsome **35**
happen **136**
happy **22**
hard (adv) **113**
has to **122**
hat **68**
have **42**

have a picnic **133**
have dinner **46**
have to **122**
Hawaii **147**
he **12**
headache **141**
health club **31**
healthy **157**
hear **41**
heavy **35**
Hello. **3**
help **70**
her **28**
here **41**
hero **163**
Hi. **3**
high **165**
high school **132**
highway **115**
hiking **98**
him **100**
Hindi **97**
his **28**
Hmm. **73**
hobby **163**
hockey **95**
hole **62**
holiday **75**
Hollywood **104**
home **10**
homework **28**
Hong Kong **81**
Honolulu **54**
hope (v) **120**
hospital **14**
hot **40**
hotel **42**
hour **139**
house **37**
houseboat **78**
how **13**
how many **60**
how often **100**
however **64**
hungry **107**
hurry **134**
hurt **136**
husband **45**
hut **78**

I **11**
ice cream **158**
I'd **51**
I'm **2**
immediately **130**
important **92**
in **11**
in front of **46**
inexpensive **75**

ink **124**
inside **146**
interesting **13**
international **88**
Internet **25**
introduce **51**
invite **146**
iron (v) **131**
is **2**
isn't **38**
Istanbul **139**
it **12**
Italian **13**
Italy **139**

jacket **67**
jacuzzi **59**
Japan **139**
Japanese **13**
jeans **67**
job **112**
jog **87**
journalist **103**

karate **90**
keypal **25**
kind (n) **88**
kitchen **7**
know **133**
Korea **139**
Korean **13**

laboratory **104**
lamp **111**
landlord **62**
language **80**
large **35**
largest **116**
last name **4**
last night **146**
late **49**
late (for) **134**
laugh **50**
laundromat **31**
lawyer **139**
leather **75**
leave **134**
left **124**
left turn **124**
lemonade **22**
lesson **90**
letter **112**
library **7**
license number **4**
license plate **115**
life **83**
light **165**
like **89**
line **124**

Lisbon **139**
list **9**
listen to **17**
little **35**
live (v) **64**
living room **7**
loan (n) **125**
lock **120**
London **82**
long **103**
look **42**
look for **25**
look like **103**
Los Angeles **54**
lost and found **74**
loud **35**
love (v) **146**
low **165**
lucky **77**
lunch **20**

Madrid **80**
magazine **101**
mail **112**
mail carrier **113**
mailbox **62**
make **104**
make a *right* turn **124**
make an appointment **145**
make noise **49**
mall **3**
man **49**
Mandarin Chinese **97**
many **13**
map **8**
market **166**
marriage license **125**
married **35**
mathematics **21**
matter **142**
may **70**
me **15**
meal **146**
meaning **77**
mechanic **117**
meet **3**
member **53**
men **63**
messy **165**
Mexican **13**
Mexico City **2**
Miami **41**
mice **62**
midnight **134**
mile **154**
milk **21**
million **97**
minute **154**

school bus **113**
science fiction movie **95**
scientist **104**
script **124**
seconds **146**
secretary **112**
see **87**
seem **145**
sell **79**
sentimental **50**
Seoul **13**
serve **146**
shampoo **159**
Shanghai **13**
shave **134**
she **12**
shine **22**
shiny **157**
shirt **67**
shiver **108**
shoe **67**
shop (n) **69**
shop (v) **63**
shopper **77**
shopping mall **63**
short **35**
shorts **77**
short story **95**
shout **108**
show (v) **147**
shower **97**
shy **94**
sick **107**
sidewalk **64**
sign **165**
sing **17**
singer **117**
single **35**
sink **28**
sister **39**
sister-in-law **54**
sit **42**
skate (v) **118**
skateboard **47**
ski (v) **118**
skill **121**
skim milk **158**
skirt **67**
sky **165**
sleep **17**
slipper **77**
slow **165**
small **35**
smile **108**
sneaker **77**
snow (v) **40**
so **43**
soap **158**

soccer **25**
soccer game **123**
social security number **4**
social security office **15**
sock **67**
soda **145**
sofa **47**
solve **115**
some **63**
something **72**
sometimes **101**
son **45**
song **80**
son-in-law **54**
soon **43**
sore throat **141**
sorry **41**
sort (v) **112**
So-so. **142**
spaghetti **146**
Spain **139**
Spanish **80**
spare time **163**
speak **79**
special **50**
spell **5**
spend **165**
sponsors **165**
sport **90**
sports jacket **72**
spring **127**
staff **112**
stand **47**
start **124**
stay home **92**
steal **153**
steps **146**
still **162**
stocking **68**
stomach **42**
stomachache **141**
store **63**
stove **59**
straight **102**
strange **110**
street **2**
strike (n) **112**
striped **70**
student **13**
study **17**
subject **163**
submit **124**
suburb **83**
suburban **78**
subway **115**
suit **67**
suitcase **135**
summer **127**

sun **22**
Sunday school **140**
sunglasses **3**
sunny **40**
superintendent **59**
supermarket **7**
supervisor **154**
sure **74**
sweater **67**
sweat pants **77**
sweep **111**
swim **17**
Sydney **139**
system **115**

table **8**
Tahiti **41**
take a bath **97**
take a shower **97**
take a test **124**
take a trip **136**
take a vacation **132**
take *her* photograph **50**
take inventory **120**
take the bus **113**
take the subway **115**
talk **50**
tall **35**
Tampa **82**
taxi **82**
teach **17**
teacher **15**
team **95**
technology **97**
tee shirt **77**
teenager **49**
teeth **30**
telephone **83**
telephone book **12**
telephone number **1**
television **104**
tell **25**
tell me **25**
tenant **62**
tennis **25**
terrible **41**
Thai **89**
thank you **57**
thanks **13**
that **73**
the **3**
their **28**
them **100**
then **124**
there **64**
there are **60**
therefore **139**
there's (there is) **57**

these **71**
they **11**
thief **153**
thin **35**
thing **120**
think **73**
thirsty **107**
thirty-first **132**
this **40**
this afternoon **129**
this evening **129**
this month **130**
this morning **72**
this week **130**
this year **70**
those **73**
throat **142**
tic tac toe **25**
tie (n) **67**
time **83**
time zone **139**
tiny **157**
tired **49**
today **15**
together **42**
Tokyo **13**
tomorrow **128**
tomorrow afternoon **129**
tomorrow evening **129**
tomorrow morning **129**
tomorrow night **129**
tonight **129**
too **3**
tool **120**
tooth **69**
toothache **141**
toothpaste **159**
Toronto **54**
town **63**
traditional **77**
traffic **113**
trailer **78**
train (n) **115**
train station **55**
translator **139**
travel **104**
trip (n) **136**
trouble **75**
truck **113**
truck driver **117**
trumpet **25**
try **134**
Turkey **139**
turn on **147**
TV **18**
TV antenna **102**
TV show **80**
TV star **95**

type **112**
typewriter **111**

U turn **124**
ugly **35**
umbrella **68**
uncle **45**
uncomfortable **157**
unfortunately **104**
United States **162**
unusual **113**
upset **63**
urban **78**
us **100**
USA **139**
use **53**
used car **132**
usually **83**

vacation **40**
vacuum (v) **49**
Vancouver **82**
Venezuela **139**
very **13**
video **92**
video store **55**
Vietnamese **89**
village **162**
vinyl **75**
violin **25**
visit (v) **79**
vitamins **158**
volleyball **90**

wait **124**
waiter **139**
waitress **139**
walk (v) **109**
wall **8**
wallet **77**
want (to) **133**
warm **40**
was **158**
wash **27**
washing machine **60**
Washington, D.C. **47**
wasn't **160**
watch (n) **68**
watch (v) **32**
watch TV **17**
we **11**
wear **50**
weather **40**

wedding **47**
wedding cake **50**
wedding day **50**
wedding gown **50**
week **92**
weekend **83**
well **84**
were **158**
weren't **160**
West **139**
western **95**
wet **165**
what **2**
what kind of **88**
what time **134**
when **83**
where **2**
white **50**
White House **47**
who **46**
why **89**
why not **89**
wife **45**
win **137**
window **30**
window cleaner **159**
winter **127**
with **22**
woman **49**
women **63**
wonder **136**
wonderful **50**
wool **75**
word **162**
work (n) **72**
work (v) **79**
world **104**
write **42**
written test **124**

yard **10**
yard sale **166**
yawn **108**
year **70**
yes **13**
yesterday **143**
yesterday afternoon **150**
yesterday evening **150**
yesterday morning **150**
you **2**
young **35**
your **2**

zoo **14**

Expressions

an hour early **154**
as a result **112**
back home **162**
be in a car accident **137**
believe it or not **124**
Can I help you? **71**
Can you tell me the time? **135**
Dear *Mother*, **42**
Do you know the time? **135**
Excuse me. **57**
fall in love **136**
for a few days **42**
for example **77**
get to know each other **50**
go back home **153**
go to bed **97**
Happy New Year! **132**
have a bad day **112**
have a difficult time **72**
have a good time **41**
have a lot of trouble **75**
have a party **122**
have a terrible time **41**
have a wonderful time **50**
have an argument **49**
have problems (with) **42**
Hello. **3**
Hi. **3**
Hi, *Jack*. **41**
Hmm. **84**
How are you? **13**
I'd like to introduce **51**
I don't know. **133**
I don't think so. **73**
I guess I made a mistake. **73**
I'm glad to hear that. **142**
I'm sorry to hear that. **41**
in fact **42**
in bed **15**
in person **125**
inside and out **146**
It's a beautiful day! **22**

It's snowing very hard. **113**
just in case **137**
life back in "the old country" **83**
look forward to **132**
Love, *Ethel*. **43**
May I help you? **70**
Nice to meet you. **3**
Nice to meet you, too. **3**
no wonder **124**
Not so good. **142**
Oh. **73**
Oh, good. **59**
Oh, I see. **59**
Oh, no! **134**
Oh, really? **103**
on strike **112**
on the other hand **97**
on time **140**
on vacation **41**
over there **69**
Please try to hurry! **134**
"rain cats and dogs" **42**
Really? **133**
rush out of the house **154**
See you soon. **43**
six years old **162**
So, **43**
spend time **92**
Tell me, . . . **60**
tell me about **38**
Thank you. **57**
Thanks. **13**
That's okay. **70**
That's right. **60**
That's strange! **110**
That's too bad! **111**
"the good old days" **50**
the radio says **133**
to tell the truth **42**
Well, . . . **84**
What a shame! **15**
What a *terrible night!* **49**
What seems to be the problem? **145**
What time is it? **135**
What's the matter? **142**
What's the time? **135**
You're right. **73**
You're welcome. **57**

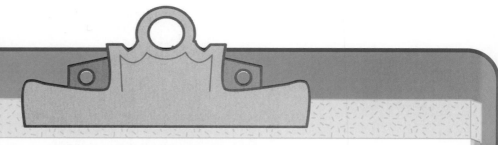

Teacher's Notes

Teacher's Notes

Teacher's Notes

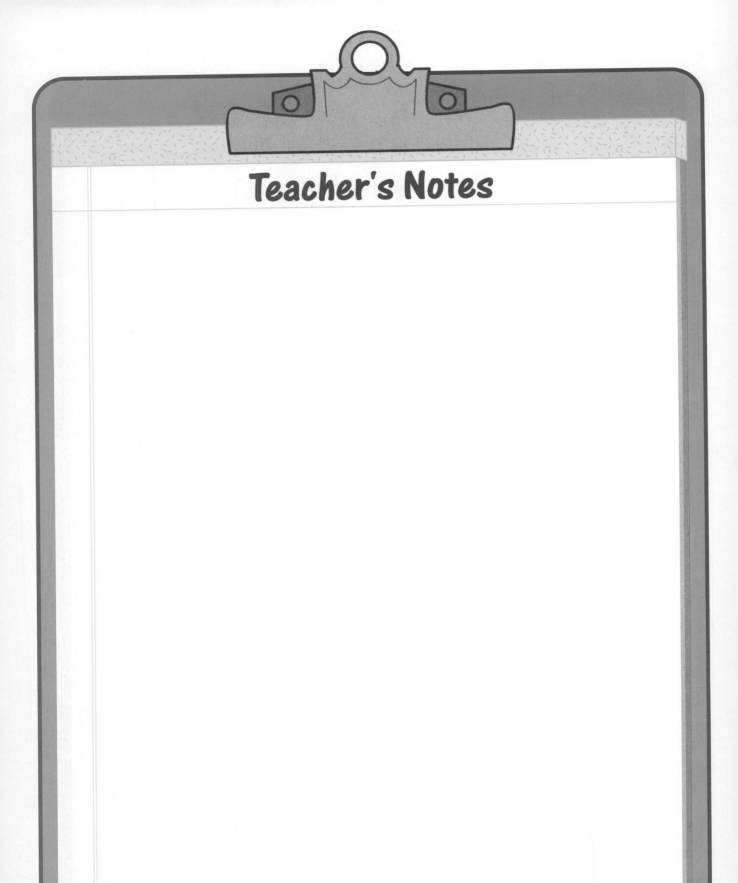

Teacher's Notes

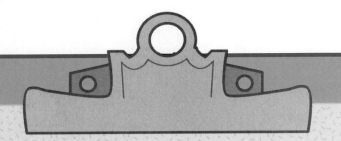

Teacher's Notes

Teacher's Notes